A.S.A. MONOGRAPHS

General Editor: MICHAEL BANTON

7

History and
Social Anthropology

A.S.A. MONOGRAPHS

Published under the auspices of the Association of Social
Anthropologists of the Commonwealth

General Editor: Michael Banton

HISTORY AND
SOCIAL ANTHROPOLOGY

Edited by I. M. Lewis

TAVISTOCK PUBLICATIONS

London · New York · Sydney · Toronto · Wellington

First published in 1968
by Tavistock Publications Limited
11 New Fetter Lane, London, E.C.4
Second impression 1970
SBN 422 71860 2
First published as a Social Science Paperback in 1970
SBN 422 73660 0

This book has been set in Modern Series 7
and was printed by T. & A. Constable Ltd.
Edinburgh
© Association of Social Anthropologists of the Commonwealth,
1968

This volume brings together papers presented at the annual conference of the Association of Social Anthropologists of the Commonwealth on the theme 'History and Anthropology', which was held at Edinburgh University at Easter 1966. The Association wishes to record its gratitude to the University of Edinburgh, and particularly to the Department of Social Anthropology, for its hospitality on that occasion.

Distributed in the U.S.A. by
Barnes & Noble, Inc.

Contents

Contents

Contents

Contents

NOTE ON ORTHOGRAPHY

In this volume foreign titles are normally indicated by italics, and printed with an initial capital letter when accompanied by a proper name. This usage which is here applied alike to Nigerian, Roman, and Albanian titles departs from the preferred style of some of the contributors but has the merits of simplicity and consistency; it also conforms to the general 'house style' of the publishers.

I. M. Lewis

Introduction

The presentation of a collection of essays ranging in content from pre-Christian Rome to post-colonial Benin may strike the orthodox historian as unhistorical in the extreme; particularly since it is very far from being our intention to suggest that any significant historical connexions exist between the diverse milieux represented in this volume. Yet our object here is very far from being anti-historical. These essays were written and discussed at a conference of social anthropologists in order to explore in what respects the two subjects might draw strength from each other to their mutual advantage. And it is only fair to add, since this occasion was mainly a gathering of professional anthropologists to which a few historians had been invited as guests, that we looked at this question primarily from the viewpoint of our own discipline. This bias should be borne in mind, for it is that from which I start in the following remarks on the two disciplines.

Although it must inevitably approach the past through the present, history, as every schoolboy knows, ultimately regards the present as the product of the past. Historians consequently explore the relations between events in the realm of ideas, values, and action over time, within a dynamic which is somehow always pointing forward and directed towards becoming and fulfilment. Their concern is with the interconnexions of people's actions and aspirations through time, and, to a greater or lesser degree according to their specific interests, with the ordering, of these in terms of some pattern, or theme, of meaningful and persuasive fittingness (I am speaking of analytical history, and not of purely descriptive or chronological work). Here, the apparent inevitability which ultimately makes a 'good' historian's analysis so convincing, at least until new evidence is forthcoming, or new historical interests and problems arise, derives from his fortunate position in enjoying all the advantages of hindsight. However things begin, provided he stops short of current events, he generally knows how they have ended. It consequently often merely remains to speculate how, had other factors entered the picture, events might have turned out differently. Or so it may seem. Yet, in fact, as any historian worth his salt would be the first to point out, the real situation is far from being as cut and dried as this. Since events are part of a never-ending stream and always pointing forwards, subsequent developments immediately suggest new interpretations of the past. The flow never stops, and novel circumstances give new significance to what went before; events which within a particular time sequence seemed of little moment acquire added meaning and importance and new light is also thrown on their causes. Indeed, for E. H. Carr (1964, p. 123), it is only through the ever-widening horizons of the future that an approach may be made to 'ultimate objectivity' in historical studies.

Despite this constant process of retrospective reinterpretation, however, it remains true, I think, to say that beyond the general philosophical positions assumed by particular historians, history has little or no theory. Of course, such differences in philosophical outlook as between say Spengler and Toynbee on the one hand, and the Marxists, or sociological historians (Fustel de Coulanges, Bloch, or, in some respects, Namier) on the other, lead to wide divergences in orientation, to contrasting formulations of the problems to be explained, and even to opposed standards of what constitutes legitimate explanation. Other than this, history remains essentially a way of looking at data, and of asking and answering the question 'Why?' in relation to specific occurrences. It seems generally less concerned to establish and test generalizations about the properties of social institutions than to trace trains of events over time in terms of chains of cause and effect.

Social anthropology is likewise first and foremost a way of collecting and looking at the same sort of data, although their geographical and chronological placement have traditionally differed considerably from those which until recently have held the attention of most orthodox historians. The historian's dialogue, however, is primarily with documents. He cannot directly interrogate his subjects, but can only deal with such artifacts as, by choice or hazard, they have bequeathed to posterity. The social anthropologist in contrast derives most of his primary data from direct personal observation and inquiry, studying social life as and where it is lived, partly at least through the medium of a particular culture. His basic concern is with the interconnexions of events, with the structure of ideas, values, and social relations, but from the perspective of the present rather than the past. For him, although the past may be one source of the imperatives which control the shape and content of men's actions in society, its role in determining how men behave now is secondary to the interconnexions between their *current* beliefs, actions, and institutional arrangements.[1] Current custom replaces the past as the repository of the springs of social behaviour. The past as the subjects of study themselves see it, however it actually was, becomes explicable at least in large measure as a mirror of the present. The past so viewed is the product of the present and may be treated to a considerable extent as myth.[2] In this extreme view, which is not devoid of explanatory power, history is virtually relegated to the status of Malinowski's 'mythological charter'.

Although the monographic studies of anthropologists which present particular societies as neatly integrated, nicely balanced systems, are often just as particularistic as many historians' work, that generalizing, comparative, trend which is by no means entirely absent in orthodox historical writing is here brought into sharper focus and correspondingly developed more fully. While not on the grand systematic scale of the physical sciences, theory is also more in evidence, and is as much a product of the special institutional characteristics of tribal societies as of their smallness in size, or of the intensive nature of the studies to which they are subjected. Theory here relates to the distinctive properties of institutional complexes such as a diversity of types of kinship groups, age-grades, types of kingship, etc. But it goes beyond this to reach what at the lowest evaluation can be characterized as 'insights' into the nature and consequences of conflict and competition, the relations between secular and mystical power, the implications of different types of authority, of marginality, or the social concomitants of the division between the sexes, to name merely a few of the areas in which theoretical developments are currently proceeding.

Thus if, like the historian, the social anthropologist is prepared to study all departments of social life and is in this sense the opposite of a specialist, he is nevertheless usually more concerned to reach generalizations about the distinctive properties of institutions (cf. Forde, 1965a, p. 15). Moreover, whether he likes it or not, he finds himself working within a profession where his own particularistic findings are open to comparative scrutiny and seized upon to advance or negate the theories of others of his colleagues concerning such disparate topics as the stability of marriage or the social nexus of witchcraft accusations. More pervasively and explicitly than history, social anthropology is problem-oriented, and dedicated to the elaboration of theory. Mere ethnographic 'reporting' consequently, has a more derogatory connotation than descriptive writing in history.

HISTORY IN SOCIAL ANTHROPOLOGY

Nevertheless, the most significant differences between history and social anthropology, as the latter has developed under the influence of Malinowski and Radcliffe-Brown, lie in the two subjects' conflicting evaluations of the importance of antecedent events. Within anthropology this distinction has its own history. When Radcliffe-Brown was formulating his conceptions of the nature of society and of the social anthropologist's task in elucidating the 'social function' of institutions, the historical approach within anthropology was represented by two main branches. Social evolutionists tended to 'explain' institutions in terms of a line of progress through immutable stages from earlier forms; the 'Jacob's ladder approach' as Gellner (1962) has dubbed it. The diffusionists, on the other hand, sought in any particular setting the origins of institutions in terms of the effects of external contacts and connexions. Ideas and customs had legs and travelled widely, spanning continents and oceans in the wake of postulated trade networks and migrations.

Both these approaches, the evolutionary and the diffusionist, increasingly refined and sophisticated, and reinforced by a growing interest in ecology, continued to develop in an unbroken tradition in America, where local ethnographic data drawn from the dead or decaying cultures of Indian societies encouraged their persistence. This naturally promoted the strengthening of the links between prehistory, archaeology, and anthropology as these subjects were studied and taught in American universities and widened the gulf between them and sociology.

In England, inspired by the works of Weber and Durkheim and his associates, it was the sociological tradition rather than the historical which received most forceful advocacy. Here, re-acting against the methods of the evolutionists and diffusionists with their often, but by no means always, spurious historicity, or 'conjectural history' as he stigmatized it, Radcliffe-Brown turned to assert the relative irrelevance of the past for the present which he considered was to be understood in terms of its own contemporary structure, the organismic interdependence of the parts as elements of a greater whole, each part inexorably 'functioning' to maintain the integrity of the whole. This im-mediately gave societies so conceived, and social structures, a timelessness which set them outside history, generating what M. G. Smith has appropriately termed the 'fallacy of the ethno-graphic present' (Smith, 1962, p. 77). And it was easy, at least in general terms, to justify this stance by an appeal to the imputed lack of real historical data available for many of the more remote and exotic tribal peoples studied by anthro-pologists. This assessment often, of course, coincided with such societies' own view of their past, and their lack of a true sense of history.[3] And it had the effect, I think, of further entrenching anthropological concern in societies of this type, and even of reinforcing the subject's public image as the quest of the exotic.

Radcliffe-Brown's weighty presentation of the subject re-ceived further support from the fact that Evans-Pritchard con-sidered it necessary to attack the extreme structural approach precisely for its neglect of history (Evans-Pritchard, 1950, 1961). And since he wrote as though propounding a novel and controversial point of view, this could only further serve to establish, at least for those who were outside the discipline, that British social anthropology had turned its back on history. Others, and not least historians, in this country, must therefore be forgiven if they have come to regard social anthropology and history as opposed disciplines. This, of course, has not facilitated mutual understanding when historians have begun to enter fields customarily monopolized by anthropologists, although it may have emboldened some of the former to claim that they were doing something which had not been done before.

In fact, whatever our leading exponents may have said or implied, the majority of monographs based on field research in the structural-functional tradition have included some excursions into history, however unsophisticated or unsystematic these may seem to the orthodox historian. This may well have often arisen, as Southwold suggests (p. 136), as a product of the acculturation which the anthropologist himself undergoes in the course of his fieldwork. But whether this is the cause or not, there can be no question that anthropologists have long been trying to write some history, even if they have not often taken full account of its implications. Indeed, as Schapera (1962) among others has recently stressed, the number of essentially and explicitly historical anthropological studies is considerably larger than is often supposed. This tradition which runs from such works as Wilson's *Constitution of Ngonde* (1939) through Evans-Pritchard's *Sanusi of Cyrenaica* (1949) and Barnes' *Politics in a Changing Society* (1954) to the more elaborate recent studies of Smith (1960), Goody (1967), and Vansina (1965) is thus by no means a fringe activity, but an integral part of the mainstream of British social anthropology. The tradition of historical studies in the field of social change produced by what, significantly, used to be called 'culture contact' between tribal and Western societies spans a similar period of time. Recent works here, such as those of Southall (1961), Bailey (1960), and Lloyd (1966), are less novel in subject-matter than in their style of analysis and methodology.

Appearances based on the strictures of Radcliffe-Brown, or on the counter-arguments of Evans-Pritchard, are therefore somewhat deceptive, especially when associated with such wider issues as the metaphysical status of anthropology whether as a science or as one of the humanities. Little purpose would be served by re-opening that turgid debate here; for our purpose it is sufficient to record that today the position is paradoxically different. On the one hand, we find those historians and others who are now turning to employ their professional skills in the old African and Asian stamping-grounds of anthropologists increasingly looking to our subject for guidance and elucidation as they wrestle with what for them are very unfamiliar institutions. Here social anthropology seems to be viewed as a complementary source of data, and also as an additional expertise which, once mastered, can be harnessed as an ancillary research tool.

On the other hand, others both within the discipline (e.g. Worsley, 1965; Goody, 1966) and outside it (Hooker, 1963) tell us more or less explicitly that anthropology is an epiphenomenon of colonialism, and as such old hat, and doomed to extinction in the new circumstances of liberated Africa and Asia. (This roughly coincides with the opinion held until recently by many African nationalists, but now apparently declining in popularity: that anthropologists are tribalists and consequently opposed to nationalism and modernity.) Thus, according to some anthropologists who seem to confound the discipline's traditional subject-matter with its essence, the choice today is between continuing to study dead and decaying tribal cultures and thus becoming a special province of history, or marching forward to confront the new under the more acceptable label of 'sociology'. This conclusion is of course far from novel: Maitland suggested the first part, and Spencer the second, many years ago.

THE RELEVANCE OF PAST EVENTS

Although traditional tribal studies are indeed on the wane, and with them the ultimately stultifying mystique of *status quo* maintenance according to which the only significant function of institutions lies in the contribution they make to the perpetuation of the established order, there is little evidence that the discipline itself is yet *in extremis*. But if therefore to remain alive social anthropology need not become a branch of history, there is nevertheless a great deal to be said in favour of an increasing involvement with history. It is not merely that, even from the pooling of resources and techniques in the narrow field of ethno-history, historians may in the end take over from anthropology something more than the facts and 'know-how' which constitute their immediate objective. They may fertilize their own discipline in the direction urged by Evans-Pritchard (1961, p. 20), who, in effect, argues that the trouble with so much history is not that it is historical, but that it does not sufficiently apply to the study of any particular period the structural approach of social anthropology. And it is heartening to find E. H. Carr (1964, p. 66) making much the same point from the other side of the fence when he writes: 'the more sociological history becomes, and the more historical sociology becomes, the better for both'.

In the present volume, the papers by Ardener and Morton-Williams indicate the special contributions that anthropologists may be expected to make in historical studies within their own special fields of expertise. Cregeen's paper, on the other hand, shows how an orthodox historian can utilize this anthropological approach to bring new elucidation to an important field of history. The advantages of increasing understanding between the two disciplines are, however, by no means one-sided. If anthropology has something to offer, so has history. Indeed, whether in the anthropological study of tribal or of non-tribal societies, history's contribution is as I shall now argue vital, and this for a number of different reasons.

The most obvious, but not the least significant, of these arises from the fact that whether he likes it or not, even the most extreme structuralist anthropologist is forced in practice to dip into the past. The phenomena which he studies in the course of his eighteen to twenty-four months' field trip are set in a time dimension; and it becomes impossible to treat the waxing and waning of families, of other domestic groups, or of lineages, except within a developmental framework which, if essentially repetitive, is still a sequence of forms and stages over time. The advantages of even this limited historical approach are very great, since it becomes possible to correlate such changes with variations in patterns of property interest, or in the structure of authority, as Middleton has so elegantly shown in relation to the mystical powers attributed to elders among the Lugbara (Middleton, 1960).

The need to look at institutions over time is even more obvious when it comes to establishing patterns of succession to office. Rules of succession to office may be elucidated by direct questioning, but these may be so ambiguous or latitudinarian that they tell little; or there may be grounds for suspecting that in practice they are not strictly followed. Here numbers of instances must be studied to elicit what the practice really is, and the more unique the office under consideration, the more the investigator is driven to history to elucidate sequences. The range of candidates and the criteria for selection among them in appointments to a major dynasty, for example, may be susceptible to exploration only by recourse to what happened in the past. In the present volume this is well illustrated in Southwold's study of fraternal succession in Buganda.

In the same sort of way, in a most stimulating recent paper, J. Argyle (1966) has used historical evidence to elucidate the real circumstances surrounding the assumption of chiefly office by 'lost and found' successors among the Soli of Zambia, and has thus been able to demonstrate that this theme is a convenient rationalization for dynastic usurpation. This, as he persuasively argues, throws a surprising degree of new light on a host of returning 'rightful' candidates for office well known in the 'myths' of classical antiquity and ranging from those of Oedipus to Cyrus the Elder. These figures now seem all to have usurped power, this being the central theme that the attendant myths celebrate.

More generally, historical data are not merely relevant, but are quite decisive in evaluating a given society's own view of its past. Peoples' views of time, and their own ethnocentric 'history' are very much part of the picture which even the most particularistic anthropologist seeks to delineate. Here the elucidation, in so far as this is possible, of what actually happened in the past is obviously crucial. Some traditions plainly relating events that could not have occurred and including grotesque situations and actions that are travesties of approved customary behaviour are easily identified as myths and can be treated as such. Yet even accounts which are cast in the style and idiom of myth may state important historical truths, as, for example, when Somali relate how the ancestors of certain of their clans came across the sea from Arabia sailing on prayer-mats. And the status of tales which smack directly of history may be even more difficult to elucidate, and yet of great importance to the understanding of contemporary structure. To know, for instance, that the Bedouin tribes of Cyrenaica derive from Arab immigrants who settled in Cyrenaica in the eleventh century, is not merely a piece of historical padding for the anthropologist, but provides essential information for evaluating the function of genealogies in their society (Peters, 1960).

Here, of course, because of the very lack of sound historical information in most circumstances, such anthropologists as Cunnison (1951) and Bohannan (1952) have with their charter interpretation of genealogies perhaps contributed as much to history as they have taken from it. For they have provided ample evidence of the telescoping and manipulation of oral genealogies, and shown the dangers of reading genealogies or king-lists at their face value. But even in the same social system different portions of genealogies may convey different messages: some recording actual events historically, and others validating the existing situation (see Lewis, 1962). Thus the two approaches are mutually sustaining, and the anthropologist certainly needs historical data to elucidate many aspects of the structural processes in which he is interested.

More generally, and ultimately more importantly, I believe, the enlargement of the time depth through which social structure is studied gives the social anthropologist an added and invaluable perspective into the working both of particular institutions, and of particular societies. Here it is not merely as Collingwood puts it that the past is encapsulated in the present, but rather that the structure of the present is not fully revealed without reference to its development over time. As Firth, contemplating the changes which had taken place in Tikopia thirty years after his first study of the island, put it: 'the study of a situation over time may be necessary in order to allow the relative movement and weighting of factors to be perceived clearly' (Firth, 1959, p. 146). And Evans-Pritchard (1961, p. 11) has approvingly quoted Lévi-Strauss to much the same effect. Historians would take this as axiomatic. Certainly flat, single-dimensional analyses in the ethnographic present are likely to distort fundamentally the perspectives of interpretation. Thus, for example, Krige (Krige & Krige, 1945) in her original study of the Lovedu of the Transvaal laid great weight on the equivalence of marriage payments and the fertility of wives, and found that customarily when a man divorced he was repaid his bridewealth but his children went with his estranged spouse. In a subsequent study, over twenty years later, she has found however that the practice in this respect has changed: divorcing husbands now keep the children and also claim back their marriage payments, and this is described as 'Lovedu custom' as though it had always been so (Krige, 1964). Such circumstances clearly require some reconsideration of the relationship between marriage payments and the rights they confer in relation to women and their fertility.

Again, by examining the changing function over time of lineages among the Arab border villages of Israel, Cohen (1965) has enlarged our understanding of lineage organization and of the interplay between endogamy and lineage solidarity in a direction which is not obvious from the comparative study of other synchronic cases. Equally significantly, many highly stratified and apparently rigidly ascribed political systems (such, for example, as that of the Amharas of Ethiopia) appear very different when viewed in historical persepctive. It is only when examined over time that the real degree of possible status achievement and of social mobility in such systems becomes apparent. Indeed, it is impossible to begin to assess and compare the extent of achieved and ascribed status in social systems unless they are studied historically.

Similarly, as I have argued elsewhere (Lewis, 1966), several recent studies of spirit-possession which include the dimension of time enable us to see how the spirit catchment-area changes with circumstances in a dynamic fashion which is obscured in synchronic studies. And the analysis of such peripheral spirit-possession cults, as of Cargo cults and other spontaneous new religious movements, when set in an appropriately wide developmental framework which traces different relations between cults and social structure over time, greatly enhances our understanding of the social functions of religion in general. Such work emphasizes the multiplicity of functions which a given institution may exercise in various temporal and spatial settings, and increases our comprehension of the essential properties of institutions, particularly of their flexibility and viability.

In this volume this is brought out very clearly in Cregeen's study of the changing significance of Scottish clanship, which, even when it had become by the eighteenth century little more than a sentimental bond expressed in competitive auction-bidding, could still in times of insecurity be reasserted as a socio-political force of consequence. Hence the historical approach may be seen as the most tightly controlled type of comparative analysis, serving to reveal the multiplicity of functions which, within a continuous temporal setting, may be served by what appears formally (and culturally) as the same institution. As Evans-Pritchard rightly insists, therefore, and it is here that his strictures are most compelling, history affords the social anthropologist a much neglected laboratory for testing the validity of structural assumptions and social mechanisms. It is in this respect that social anthropologists have been remarkably negligent and unperceptive in their use of historical material, even when, as we have seen, they have often tried to write history. In this context Barnes's study, *Marriage in a Changing Society* (1951), is particularly interesting, because although he does not explicitly set out to do so, he is in effect using historical data to examine the validity of Gluckman's theory of the correlation between patrilineal descent, high marriage payments, and stable marriage by contrasting the circumstances of traditional Ngoni society with those of its less patrilineal modern equivalent. And although the correlation which these data validate applies in fact only to certain kinds of patriliny (see Lewis, 1963), this modest monograph is nevertheless a model of the kind of study I am advocating, since it applies historical methods as anthropologists should to test their theories.[4]

PAST, PRESENT, AND FUTURE: CONSERVATISM AND CONFLICT IN SOCIAL STRUCTURES

Further developments are just as important here as the train of past events. Thus by the same token, looking forwards rather than backwards, quite apart from its intrinsic interest as a phase (with structure) in time, what is studied by social anthropologists under the name 'social change' offers special opportunities for an enhanced understanding of the working of institutions and for examining the value of particular structural analyses. If the external variables are known, and a society has the structure attributed to it at a particular point in time, it should be possible to make valid predictions of the ways in which it will respond to change; and even of how it may itself generate change. At least it should be possible to see new situations as in some meaningful fashion related to the past. If this is not the case, it is hard to see how much credence can be attached to the previous analysis. Again, since the study is diachronic, we should be able to sift out superficial relationships and correlations from deep attachments between institutional complexes persisting over time. To shrug off deficiencies in the predictive power of the original structural model in terms of its being only an 'heuristic' device is scarcely satisfactory. Thus as the papers by Bradbury, Lloyd, and Whitaker in this volume show particularly well, modern social conditions involving traditional tribal organizations do indeed provide the laboratory conditions forecast by Malinowski for those who are interested in the empirical study of society.

Such unique opportunities as these conditions offer have until recently remained almost as unexploited as those afforded by history. This is partly perhaps because, despite the negative lessons of historians in this respect, many of those anthropologists who work in this field have either been primarily concerned to discover 'laws' or principles of social and cultural change itself; or they have been mainly interested in treating the new circumstances produced by change as an enclosed, self-contained field to which Radcliffe-Brown's model of self-maintaining structure could again be applied (cf. Mitchell, 1966). Yet to understand social change properly, both historically and in its modern setting, and to exploit its theoretical implications, we need to look at institutions less in terms of their contributions to social solidarity at a particular point in time, than in terms of the extent to which they cater for the personal and property security needs of the individual occupants of status positions and of social categories. We thus need to prize apart the notions of function and structure and to see the latter not as the inevitable product of the former, but rather as a partially independent patterned reticulation of social positions and roles; as in fact a framework of possibilities and potentialities as well as of regularities.

This structural framework itself is supported by, or embedded in a set of values and ideals of conduct, not all of which are completely mutually compatible or perfectly integrated. The notion that there exists only one single system of moral evaluation in even the simplest of tribal societies is surely naïve in the extreme. After all, even at the level of such ideal folk-wisdom as is encapsulated in proverbs, is there not for every dictum approving one line of conduct an exact opposite? It is considerations of this elementary kind which make the study of symbolism so fraught with difficulty, and which entitle us to be sceptical of those highly simplistic exercises in analysis which purport to find a single, invariant meaning in a given symbol. In reality, as Lloyd reminds us, all societies are sufficiently complex for some lack of adjustment to exist between their constituent parts: individuals accordingly face role expectations which are at least to some extent discordant or even incompatible, and have to choose between possible alternatives. Many roles are themselves poorly defined, or have wide margins of latitude.

Consequently, to understand how a given structure works, or rather how it is worked, it seems more profitable to pose our questions in terms of the extent to which the individual's commitment to a given pattern, or set of social relations and obligations serves his interests in a fashion which, in the circumstances, he regards as most advantageous. This approach should enable us to take account of the question of the maximization of interests, and to locate the issue of individual choice, which cannot ultimately be escaped (cf. Emmet, 1960), where it belongs, rather than burying it in such curious conceptual ensembles as, for example, 'optative kindship groups' as Firth (1960) sometimes advocates.[5] A similar confusion between the exercise of choice within the idiom of a particular system of behaviour, and its free play explicitly and independently of it, seems to underlie much of the current controversy surrounding the terms 'prescriptive' and 'preferential' alliance applied to certain marriage systems (cf. Homans & Schneider, 1955; Needham, 1962).

Thus the functional approach I am advocating here, which owes more to Malinowski than to Radcliffe-Brown, seems to resolve the conflict between time-centred historical inquiry and timeless structural analysis and not only greatly facilitates the analysis of social change, but should also enable us to deal more satisfactorily with those societies or groups which for want of a better term are despairingly labelled 'loosely structured' or 'optative'. This way of looking at the data in relation to the commitment of the individual according to his various statuses and positions is perhaps most easily amenable to objectification in those traditional systems where injuries and homicide are regularly compounded by the payment of concrete indemnities. I have shown elsewhere (Lewis, 1963) how valuable this approach can be in interpreting the differences between patrilineal systems where marriage involves the jural identification of a wife with her husband and his kin, resulting in a high degree of marital stability, and those other patrilineal societies where the wife remains still partly legally in the care of her own natal kin (cf. Fortes, 1959). But even where such objective means of assessing jural commitment are not readily available traditionally, the increasing participation of all tribal societies in market-economy and modern political conditions provides a new range of circumstances in which some empirical test of involvement can be applied whether in terms of the individual's financial arrangements or in his voting behaviour.

This approach stresses the flexibility of institutions and values, their potential dissensus (as Hopkins puts it) as much as their consensus and fixity. This has the great merit of enabling us to understand change not simply as the product of external factors (e.g. diffusion), but also of internal forces, and permits us to dispense with Gluckman's somewhat lame conclusion that we must accept that real societies are too complex to be represented other than by static models (Gluckman, 1963, pp. 38-39). This is one of the theoretical issues raised later in this book by Morton-Williams (p. 5), when he discusses how internal and external pressures towards institutional change may be distinguished, and one part of a social system treated as being in a static state while other parts or sectors undergo change.

In the present volume, moreover, the papers by Bradbury, Lloyd, and Hopkins particularly seem to suggest that the greatest potential for internal change occurs in relations between positions and statuses whose traditional roles are intrinsically distinct and contradictory. Thus, for example, in the context discussed by Lloyd the conflict among the homologous Yoruba descent groups seems less biased towards overall structural change than towards cohesive equilibrium. But the conflict between the intrinsically *dissimilar* roles of the king and the chiefs, though often lapsing into an equilibrium stalemate, can in fact swing away from this mean in the direction of radical change either towards an increased consolidation of the king's position, or its diminution. The circumstances analysed by Bradbury in the changing character of the conflict between the roles of Oba and Iyase in Benin are very similar. Such change ultimately involves, of course, as Hopkins points out, increasing structural differentiation: the elasticity of roles can only be stretched so far; eventually widening arcs of role latitude lead to the development of entirely new roles, and new roles harden into new statuses and positions.

Hence although, as we have seen, several of the papers in this book illustrate how 'traditional' factionalism provides a fertile soil for the acceptance of new ideas, thus eventually promoting overall social change, the play between factions which group round essentially unlike roles or positions seems to contain a greater potential for internal change. Or, to put the matter somewhat differently, it appears likely that, other things being equal, traditional systems which consist of a homologous array of units and roles will show more continuity in change than will structures which have a more differentiated pattern of roles. Of course, as Lloyd himself emphasizes with reference to Gluckman's useful distinction between rebellions and revolutions, not all competition for political power leads to an innovating revolution. Rebellions do frequently redress the balance of power and reinforce the pre-existing structure in the manner stressed by Gluckman. Yet the potential for changes of the more radical kind is always present; and rebellions more readily shade into revolutions than any stark dichotomy between these two types of insurrection would suggest.

Thus the great value of history for anthropology is that by its very nature and on account of the factual material which it reveals it becomes impossible to sustain any longer the old view of institutions as existing only to maintain the identity of particular structures. Function has meaning and utility less in its *status quo* maintenance aspects than in referring to the actual engagement and interests of people in different roles and positions. The retention of this modified concept of 'function' is, I believe, all the more important for it promotes an approach to the working of institutions which, having its roots in an observ-

Introduction

able field of empirical behaviour, complements the new structuralism of Lévi-Strauss. The latter almost completely discards the notion of function, but paradoxically lapses into a new timelessness, as Mary Douglas (1967, p. 67) among others has recently observed.

NOTES

1. Historians writing on a particular period, of course, also do this. But with the exception of Namier and others with a similar approach, it is I think generally true to say that they tend to emphasize the uniqueness and particularity of their subject-matter, and in their interpretation of events place greater stress on such cultural artifacts as 'the spirit of the age' than on institutional imperatives.

2. E. H. Carr, in his Trevelyan Lectures, seems to come very close to defining history similarly. 'History', he records, 'is an unending dialogue between the present and the past', and 'the past is intelligible to us only in the light of the present'; or again, 'History acquires meaning and objectivity only when it establishes a coherent relation between past and future' (Carr, 1964, pp. 30, 55, 130). On this view, presumably, the history of other times and places, becomes the mythology from which future historians distil 'true' history. But since every historian tends to be a true child of his age (as Carr is at pains to point out) why should future historians be any more objective than their predecessors? The answer, which is tied to Carr's view of history as purposive and progressive, lies in the assumption that each new generation of historians not only knows more about the past but is also more self-aware, and consequently able to make due allowance for the distorting influences which inhere in their own circumstances and times. This seems an optimistic view.

3. It might be noted here that the lack of a historical sense in such tribal communities, and the structural anthropologist's disregard for such historical data as might be discovered, are fully endorsed by traditionalist historical opinion. According to this ethnocentric view, for a people's actions to be historically significant, at least one of two qualifications must be met, and preferably both. Those concerned should have a true sense of history, they should be historically conscious, and they should participate in one or another of the mainstreams of world history. Thus even for such a sociologically enlightened historian as E. H. Carr: 'History begins when men begin to think of the passage of time in terms not of natural processes – the cycle of the seasons, the human life-span – but of a series of specific events in which men are consciously involved and which they can consciously influence'. And again, referring to what he regards as a revolution in the conception of history: 'It is only today that it has become possible to imagine a whole world consisting of peoples who have in the fullest sense entered into history and become the concern, no longer of the colonial administrator or of the anthropologist, but of the historian' (Carr, 1964, pp. 134, 149).

4. More directly perhaps, this is precisely what Gough (1952) has done so elegantly in smaller compass, but with wider implications, in her examination of the way in which the matrilineal Nayar marriage and kinship system has responded to economic and political changes over a long period of time. This, and other studies of less esoteric matrilineal systems increasingly involved in

I. M. Lewis

cash economies, demonstrate beyond doubt that the attendant tensions between a person's maternal uncle and his father postulated by anthropologists
are not ethnocentric fictions but realities which in appropriate circumstances
become explicit and institutionally significant.

5. The necessity of allowing room in analysis for the free play of choice and
personal aggrandizement is fully realized by those social anthropologists who
are currently exploring the characteristics of leadership in traditionally un-
centralized tribal societies, whether in New Guinea or Africa, in terms of the
convenient, if homely, notion of 'Big Men' (cf. Forde, 1965b; Jones, 1963; and
Brown, 1963).

REFERENCES

ARGYLE, J. 1966. Oedipus in Central Africa. UCL Seminar Paper
(MS.).

BAILEY, F. G. 1960. *Tribe, Caste and Nation*, Manchester: Manchester
University Press.

BARNES, J. 1951. *Marriage in a Changing Society*, Rhodes-Livingstone Paper No. 20, Oxford: Oxford University Press.

—— 1954. *Politics in a Changing Society*, Manchester: Manchester
University Press.

BOHANNAN, L. 1952. A Genealogical Charter. *Africa* 22: 301-315.

BRAIMAH, J. A. & GOODY, J. R. 1967. *Salaga: The Struggle for Power*.
London: Longmans.

BROWN, P. 1963. From anarchy to satrapy. *Amer. Anthropol.* 65: 1-15.

CARR, E. H. 1964. *What is History?* Harmondsworth: Penguin Books.

COHEN, A. 1965. *Arab Border Villages in Israel*. Manchester: Manchester University Press.

CUNNISON, I. 1951. *History on the Luapula*. Rhodes-Livingstone
Institute Paper No. 21. Oxford: Oxford University Press.

DOUGLAS, M. 1967. The Meaning of Myth, with special reference to
'La Geste d'Asdiwal'. In Leach, E. (ed.), *The Structural Study
of Myth and Totemism*, pp. 49-70. London: Tavistock.

EMMET, D. 1960. How far can Structural Studies take account of
Individuals? *JRAI* 90: 191-200.

EVANS-PRITCHARD, E. E. 1949. *The Sanusi of Cyrenaica*. Oxford:
Oxford University Press.

—— 1950. Social Anthropology: Past and Present. The Marrett
Lecture. *Man*, 198.

—— 1961. *Anthropology and History*. Manchester: Manchester University Press.

FIRTH, R. 1959. Problem and assumption in an anthropological
study of religion. *JRAI* 89: 129-148.

—— 1960. Bilateral Descent Groups. In Schapera, I. (ed.), *Studies
in Kinship and Marriage*. RAI Paper No. 16, pp. 22-37.

FORDE, D. 1965a. Social Anthropology in African Studies. *African Affairs*, Spring, 15-24.

—— 1965b. Justice and Judgment among the Southern Ibo. In Kuper, H. & Kuper, L., *African Law: Adaptation and Development*, pp. 79-99. Berkeley: University of California Press.

FORTES, M. 1959. Descent, Filiation and Affinity: A Rejoinder to Dr. Leach, Part II. *Man* lix: 206-212.

GELLNER, E. 1962. Concepts and Society. *Transactions Fifth World Congress of Sociology*. Washington.

GLUCKMAN, M. 1963. *Order and Rebellion in Tribal Africa*. London: Cohen & West; New York: Free Press.

GOODY, J. 1966. The Prospects for Social Anthropology. *New Society*, 13 October, pp. 574-576.

GOUGH, K. 1952. Changing Kinship Usages in the Setting of Political and Economic Change among the Nayars of Malabar. *JRAI* 82: 71-87.

HOMANS, G. & SCHNEIDER, D. 1955. *Marriage, Authority and Final Causes*. Glencoe, Illinois: Free Press.

HOOKER, J. R. 1963. The Anthropologists' Frontier: The last Phase of African Exploitation. *Journal of Modern African Studies* 1 (4): 455-459.

JONES, G. I. 1963. *The Trading States of the Oil Rivers*. London: Oxford University Press.

KRIGE, E. J. & KRIGE, J. D. 1945. *The Realm of a Rain Queen*. London: Oxford University Press.

—— 1964. Property, Cross-Cousin Marriage and the Family Cycle among the Lobedu. In Gray, R. F. & Gulliver, P. H. (eds). *The Family Estate in Africa*, pp. 155-196. London: Routledge and Kegan Paul.

LEWIS, I. M. 1962. Historical Aspects of Genealogies in Northern Somali Social Structure. *Journal of African History* 3: 35-48.

—— 1963. *Marriage and the Family in Northern Somaliland*. East African Studies No. 15. Kampala.

—— 1966. Spirit Possession and Deprivation Cults. *Man* (NS) I: 307-329.

LLOYD, P. (ed.) 1966. *The New Elites of Tropical Africa*. London: Oxford University Press.

MIDDLETON, J. 1960. *Lugbara Religion*. London: Oxford University Press.

MITCHELL, J. C. 1966. Theoretical Orientations in Urban Studies. In Banton, M. (ed.), *The Social Anthropology of Complex Societies*, pp. 37-68. London: Tavistock Publications.

NEEDHAM, R. 1962. *Structure and Sentiment*. Chicago: Chicago University Press.

PETERS, E. 1960. The Proliferation of Segments in the Lineage of the Bedouin of Cyrenaica. *JRAI* **90**: 29-53.

SCHAPERA, I. 1962. Should Anthropologists be Historians? *JRAI* **92**: 143-156.

SMITH, M.G. 1960. *Government in Zazzau*. London: Oxford University Press.

—— 1962. History and Social Anthropology. *JRAI* **92**: 73-85.

SOUTHALL, A. (ed.) 1961. *Social Change in Modern Africa*. London: Oxford University Press.

VANSINA, J. 1965. *Oral Tradition: a study in historical methodology*. London: Routledge & Kegan Paul.

WILSON, G. 1939. *The Constitution of Ngonde*. Rhodes-Livingstone Institute Paper No. 3. Oxford: Oxford University Press.

WORSLEY, P. 1966. The End of Anthropology? *Proceedings Sixth World Conference of Sociology*.

Peter Morton-Williams

The Fulani Penetration into Nupe and Yoruba in the Nineteenth Century

'This science, then, like all other sciences, whether based on authority or reasoning, appears to be independent and has its own subject, viz. human society, and its own problems, viz. the social phenomena and the transformations that succeed each other in the nature of society.'

IBN KHALDUN (1375)

'I have learnt that the art of history is the finest of fruits, and the most remote.'

AHMAD IBN ABIBAKR of Ilorin (1912)

INTRODUCTION: HISTORY AND STRUCTURAL CHANGE

The Fulani, following their seizure of power in the Hausa states in the early nineteenth century, gained control of the whole of Nupe and of a large tract of Yoruba territory. Both the means by which quite small numbers of Fulani achieved such striking successes and also their motives for doing so are interesting questions, and the first especially calls for an anthropological approach.

The paramount king of the Oyo Yoruba, the *alafin*, at the beginning of the century ruled an empire that included many subject Yoruba kingdoms in a territory of more than 10,000 square miles. He, like his predecessors from c. 1747, exacted heavy tribute from the powerful Fon kingdom of Dahomey, limited its external expansion, and even on occasion interfered with the fiscal rights of the king of Dahomey. The *alafin*'s capital, Oyo (now referred to as Old Oyo to distinguish it from the present town of Oyo), lay more than two hundred miles from the Atlantic ports; but, from 1670 if not earlier, the Oyo army of mounted archers had commanded the trade routes to the coast, enabling the rulers of Oyo to enrich themselves from the slave trade and to foster an elaborate and luxurious cultural life in the Yoruba towns. Immediately north of Oyo, which was

1

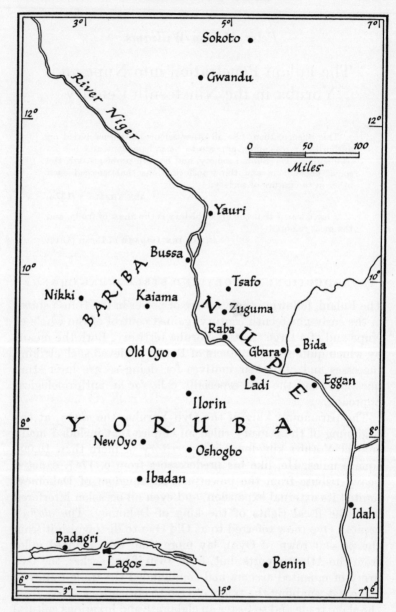

itself in the extreme north of the area inhabited by the Yoruba-speaking peoples, and to the west of the Niger, were the Bariba (or Borgu) territories, comprising the three kingdoms of Nikki, Kaiama, and, on the Niger, Bussa. Their kings were allied to Oyo by marriage, and, although warlike, they were on peaceful terms with the *alafin*, though there are indications that the *alafin* had exerted some kind of pressure on the king of Bussa, perhaps in connexion with trade routes up the Niger above the Bussa rapids.

East of Oyo, straddling the Niger though mainly to the north of the river, was Nupe. Nupe, like Oyo, was flourishing – in the late 1780s its king, *Etsu Nupe* Jia, had increased its territories to their greatest extent and (1789-1790) defeated an Oyo army sent to halt him. Hostilities between Oyo and Nupe seem to have been brief; and these kingdoms, too, had long been linked by dynastic marriages. Trade routes important to the economies of all these kingdoms crossed their territories, continuing to Gonja, Ashanti, Hausa, Bornu, and further afield.

By 1830 there had been a dramatic collapse in the power of the *alafin* (though he still commanded the route from the central Niger to the sea at Badagri); and the kingdom of Nupe had split in two. The failure of these states was contemporary with the emergence of the Fulani as a military power in the region. We have many oral traditions and occasional first-hand travellers' accounts of events in this period of disaster and in the sixty years of turmoil that followed; but they have been on the whole subjected to those two unsatisfactory kinds of historiography for which E. H. Carr has provided depreciatory labels. Attempts to account for the collapse of the kingdoms of Oyo and Nupe, on the one hand, rest on the interpretation of history as the consequence of the activities of a few individuals – the 'great deeds, ignoble ambitions and rivalries' kind of explanation – applied to the roles of the Yoruba and Nupe leaders. On the other hand, the Fulani activities are explained in terms of 'vast impersonal forces' – the onward sweep of Usman Dan Fodio's Islamic Reform Movement and the ensuing Jihad. The source material is rich enough to demand something better, the introduction of sociological analysis.

The question of how it is to be done, of how social anthropology can be used in historical analysis, needs some discussion.

The sociological tradition in social anthropology has developed a coherent, systematic set of concepts for synchronic analysis (we can ignore epistemological debate about the concepts); but in dealing with historical questions, it is more difficult to avoid a suspicion of eclecticism – of picking rather casually upon procedures that do not systematically relate structural analysis to historical process. One of the most difficult problems is that of how individual freedom of action within the social structure results in social change. The social structure is not, of course, merely an organized system of relationships; to members of a society, or at least to those who contribute to change and are therefore, historically speaking, significant, it is a system of opportunities for the exercise of the will. That is a convenient way of restating that the social structure is a moral order.

That property of structure permits social anthropologists to join forces with the historians. What separates them is an anthropological formulation of social structure and structural processes that is functionally independent of the dimension of time as the historian conceives it, structural theory employing a notion of generalized time that, like the scientist's time, has different properties. 'Sociological' time, the time dimension of, say, the office of kingship, or the perpetual lineage, or other corporations, and of the generalized domestic cycle, has the properties of 'before' and 'after', which are all that are needed to understand the continuation of structural form, because individual people are seen only as (social) 'persons', stereotyped by their roles (Radcliffe-Brown, 1940, pp. 3-5; Evans-Pritchard, 1940, p. 262). The historian is apt to give us a succession of 'time present' in a context of retrospect and anticipation, so that historical time has the properties of past, present, and future. The contrast arises because the historian's 'time present' is by no means the same as the 'ethnographic present', as Radcliffe-Brown showed when, having made the questionable assumption that societies are structured systems which perpetuate themselves unchanged except to adapt to extraneous pressures, he asserted that, in making a synchronic structural analysis, one is 'abstracting as far as possible from any changes that the structural system may be undergoing' (Radcliffe-Brown & Forde, 1950, p. 3). The historian is concerned at least as much with the problem of changes originating in the society itself, for

4

instance with acts of will intended to modify 'the actually
existing network of relations', as with acts of God and contact
with other structures. It is merely begging the question to
propose a series of synchronic studies of a changing social
structure at a succession of dates in the hope that the result
will be a diachronic study illustrating laws of change. This
technique in de Saussure's hands elucidated regularities in
linguistic change, but it has never been shown to be satisfactory
in the wider field of human society, and there are theoretical
grounds why that should be so. A notable attempt of the sort
has indeed been made. The results of the Fulani conquest of
Zazzau have been brilliantly analysed by M. G. Smith (1960);
but his book comes off as a *tour de force* in historical anthropology because he does in fact allow himself to move from the
Saussurian method.

Smith moves away by the easiest and only legitimate route –
through the door in the wall dividing social anthropologists
from historians. The key is the realization that institutions have
a different history from the societies that contain them. A
flexible and fertile interplay of methods of analysis then becomes possible. For instance, institutions can be handled from
two aspects: they can be regarded as structural forms and as
situations of choice and opportunity. It is legitimate, also, to
describe institutions (patterns of association) from the aspect
of structural form while describing the relationships between
them in historical terms, which is where opportunity and choice
are evident. Further, it is legitimate, as well as necessary, to
deal with one institution as a constant form while discussing its
relationship to another institution that is changing and is described therefore from the aspects of both form and history.
That, anthropologists will recall, is what Fred Eggan did in his
Social Organization of the Western Pueblos. In those ways it is
possible to trace both the means by which individuals force
change upon an institution, and also the subsequent change in
relations between that institution and others not undergoing
internal change, without too many variables obscuring the
picture – in the short run, there are some constants. The constants give 'the present' its quality of duration, and history its
'periods'. In some periods in English history, for instance, one
can treat the Church as structurally a constant, while the State

C
5

changes, with consequent changes in the political relations between the two institutions. Thoroughgoing structural analysis of institutions and their interrelations can show what the alternatives were (the field of opportunity) as well as showing in detail what changes did take place.

The historical question of the relations between the Yoruba and Nupe and the Fulani in the nineteenth century need much fuller analysis than is possible in this short paper; but it may at least show that a beginning has been made and that there is enough material to carry it further. It has proved necessary to forgo discussion of important technical problems, those of validating the raw materials of any historical research in West Africa: king-lists, oral traditions of many sorts, travellers' records, etc., and assert as facts what are only too often inferences, and perhaps vulnerable ones.

THE FULANI

In the late eighteenth century there were two main categories of Fulani well established in the territories of the Hausa kingdoms, which lay between Songhai in the west and Bornu in the east. There were the nomadic pastoralists, or Cow Fulani, who were, it seems, still predominantly pagan; and the settled or Town Fulani, who were Muslim. The most prominent of the Town Fulani were the Islamic scholars (*'ulama'*), who obtained posts at the courts of the Muslim Hausa kings as imams, scribes in chancery, and tutors to the royal sons. Some may have achieved legal offices, as Islamic judges, but the evidence is not conclusive.

The western Sudan has experienced many Islamic reform movements since the Almoravids broke the kingdom of Ghana in the eleventh century. Those in the eighteenth and nineteenth centuries were led by Town Fulani. The motives and circumstances of the Fulani resurgence have become the subject of intensive research only recently, and interpretations must be regarded as speculative for the present. Several scholarly Fulani travelled widely, visiting learned colleagues throughout the western Sudan, as well as halting in Egypt on the Pilgrimage; and factors both in and beyond Africa need consideration. The former may include a tradition of Fulani statehood preserved

6

in Arabic histories; for, as Barth remarked on reading the *Tarīkh al-Sūdān*, the Fulani had been powerful in the late fifteenth century not only in their western homelands, but also in Gurma, to the south of Songhai (Barth, 1857, vol. iv, pp. 596-599). The opportunity to re-emerge arose first in the Futa Toro, an area remote from the ferocious wars of the *Arma* during the seventeenth century in central Songhai, and one where survivors from the massacres of scholars in Timbuktu and Jenne could have taken refuge. Here, the Almamy proclaimed his jihad in 1725. Further east, the Fulani intellectuals were enjoying the patronage of the Hausa kings; but it has been argued that they were becoming an increasingly discontented class, regarding themselves as the most cultivated of the community, yet debarred from high rank and effective participation in the government of the kingdoms where they lived and where the forefathers of some of them had been settled for generations. It has also been suggested that concern about the political decline of Islam in the Near East following the Russian attacks on the Ottoman Empire in the eighteenth century motivated some of the attempts at reform and proselytizing in the western Sudan, among them that of the *Shehu* (Shaykh) Usman Dan Fodio.

Dan Fodio (born A.H. 1168, A.D. 1754), who was for many years at the court of the Hausa king of Gobir, began reformist activities as early as c. 1775, according to his brother 'Abdullāh's *Tazyīn al-waraqāt*. That date is shortly after the final defeat of the Turks by the Russians and the loss of the Black Sea (1774); but I have seen no reference to any such distant events in the few writings of Dan Fodio and his kinsmen that I have read. The suggestion that Napoleon's invasion of Egypt (1798-1799) was another event alarming to the pious Fulani needs substantiating too; it happened two years *after* Dan Fodio had experienced his call to fight for reform, and he had attracted a numerous and ardent following (*jamā'a*) still earlier.

Once he had decided upon war, Dan Fodio concentrated on the local scene, the focus of his grievances being Hausa kings' neglect and contravention of the Shari'a. The kings tolerated pagan legal institutions and practices – thus debarring learned Muslims from juridical offices. They levied uncanonical taxes – thus the reformers could remind traders that their tolls and

7

market dues were unjustly high, and preach to the nomad Fulani that they were paying unjustly levied cattle tax (*jangali*). And they enslaved Muslim subjects. To Muslims at large, Usman Dan Fodio preached and wrote and distributed a huge amount of propaganda, saying that, according to the learned interpreters of the law, when a ruler had become apostate, his kingdom had to be judged as wholly lapsed into idolatry, and it was the duty of believers to rise and re-establish pure Islam. (See, e.g., M. Hiskett's (1960) translation of, and comments on, Usman Dan Fodio's *Kitāb al-farq*.)

It was an opportune time for revolt. The western Hausa states had been tributary to Songhai and the eastern to Bornu, but the power of both Songhai and Bornu had ended, and none of the Hausa kings was strong enough to dominate the others. Dan Fodio after a last quarrel with the king of Gobir, evaded arrest, fled, and proclaimed a *jihad* against all the Hausa kings: thus closely and deliberately patterning his actions on the Prophet's. He now styled himself Shaykh 'Uthmān (colloquially, Shehu Usman), and as the appeal was to Islam and not to Fulani tribalism, he attracted some support from Hausa, as well as from the enthusiastic Pastoral Fulani, now converting to Islam. He appointed deputies and gave them banners (*tuta* in Hausa) to show their commissions.

The *jihad* began against Gobir, the first great Fulani victory being won in the battle of Kwotto, 21 June 1804. It was soon carried into the other Hausa kingdoms; and its military objectives were substantially achieved by 1809. It is true that Gobir was not itself a Fulani state (although part of its territory had been seized for the new state of Sokoto), and some Hausa rulers driven from their capitals had set up new capitals in rump territories and continued to fight off the Fulani – the Sarkin Katsina at Maradi, the Sarkin Daura at Zango, and the Sarkin Zazzau at Abuja. Nevertheless a huge territory had been won; and in the fifth year of the Fulani *hijra*, 1808 or 1809, Dan Fodio divided it into two zones, one under the suzerainty of his son Muhammad Bello ruling at Sokoto, and the other under his brother 'Abdullāh at Gwandu (Hiskett, 1963, p. 16). He himself retired to live quietly at Sifawa, near Sokoto, until 1815, when he removed to Sokoto and died there in 1817.

Neither Nupe nor Yoruba had been attacked by the armies of

the *jihad* during the years 1804-1809. They were pagan kingdoms (*bilād al-kufr*) unlike the Hausa kingdoms – a difference Dan Fodio still recognized in his *Tanbīh al-ikhwān*, as late as 1809-1810. There is no certain evidence that Dan Fodio had planned to subjugate them. It should indeed be added that it is hard to say how much he had foreseen even of the pattern of the *jihad* in Hausa. The very legalistic bent of the ideas put forward in his writings leads him to describe a model of society that contrasts strikingly with the structures that actually emerged from the war. The interplay between the ambitions and rivalries of the conquerors, the need to reward followers with office, the convenience of adapting administrative institutions in the conquered states, and the economics of politics, administration, and war, combined to produce structures of the sort M. G. Smith describes for Fulani Zazzau. It is furthermore clear that the horizons of Dan Fodio's associates were not limited by the Muslim Hausa states. It was a period of missionary activity as well as Islamic reform. Documentary sources – including Arabic MSS. of the late nineteenth century – agree with oral tradition in recording that two colleagues (some sources say kinsmen) of Shaykh Usman went as missionaries, one to Yoruba and the other to Nupe, during his lifetime. The sources are agreed that they played the roles of missionaries for some years before taking leading parts in warfare. The circumstances of their progression from missionaries working in isolation to founders of Fulani emirates will now be discussed.

YORUBA

The vast empire of the Oyo Yoruba at the beginning of the nineteenth century comprised three regions. The region known as the 'Metropolitan Provinces' was the oldest part of the empire. The Oyo kings had never built up a unitary state even in this region, but continued the previous pattern of government with some central controls. Each large town was ruled by a king, chosen by the local kingmakers from that town's royal lineage. He ruled as vassal of the *alafin* of Oyo, and the relationship was sanctioned by the tradition that the crown had been given to the first of the dynasty by an earlier *alafin*, and also by the *alafin*'s gift of other items of regalia to each succeeding king.

A few vassals were not tied directly to the *alafin*, but to one or other of the Councillors of State, the *oyo mesi*. In no case could vassal and lord communicate except through an intermediary, called the *baba kekere* ('little father') of the vassal. Whether the lord was the *alafin* or one of the *oyo mesi*, the *baba kekere* was invariably one of the *alafin*'s high-ranking slaves, of the *ilari* order of slavery, appointed by the *alafin* and responsible to him. Each vassal paid tribute to his lord and renewed allegiance at the *alafin*'s annual *bere* festival. Vassals had to raise contingents for the External Army of Oyo, which was led by the premier vassal, the *onikoyi* (king of Ikoyi, a town near Oyo). In the course of the far-ranging campaigns of the eighteenth century, the practice had become established of placing both the External and Internal armies under the command of an appointee of the *alafin*'s, a commander whose title was *are ona kakanfo*. Some traditions assert he was one of the *ilari* slaves, as the element *are* in his title would imply.

Beyond the Metropolitan Provinces, to the south-south-west, lay a second region of dependencies, the area occupied now by Egba, Egbado, and other, smaller, cultural units of the Yoruba peoples. There is evidence that the Egba and Egbado had moved southwards to colonize the region in the eighteenth century. In the second half of the century the old trade route, which had been through Dahomey to the coast at Ouidah, was superseded by a better-defended one passing through the newly colonized Egbado territories, and reaching the coast at Badagri and Porto Novo. Those territories were organized as a chain of very small dependent kingdoms, probably none with a population of more than 10,000 and most with fewer than 5,000 inhabitants, which were ruled by dynasties founded by sons of the *alafin* of Oyo. In the period 1825-1829 (when Clapperton and the Landers used the route), though perhaps for not more than a decade before, these rulers were under the jurisdiction of an overlord stationed in a town along the route; he was one of the *alafin*'s high-ranking slaves and generally of non-Yoruba origin.

The third region, Dahomey, had frequently tried to assert independence earlier in the eighteenth century and had been repeatedly devastated by the Oyo cavalry until it accepted its position as tributary. Late in the century, we have accounts of

Oyo emissaries accompanying the Dahomey army in wars on the coast, and of the *alafin* limiting its campaigns.

It can be seen, then, that as the eighteenth century progressed, the territory controlled by Oyo was increased, and measures were elaborated to give the *alafin* firmer control. In assuring Oyo safe access to its port, the *alafin* had set up an executive system that involved a marked increase in administrative staff and a larger military establishment, and the officials were all recruited from the staff of the palace in Oyo. The strength of the kingship had grown. But government within Oyo, and especially policy-making, rested on an uneasy structural opposition between the *alafin* and his Council of State, hereditary office-holders who controlled ward-sectors in Oyo and some territory in the neighbourhood. They were also the kingmakers. They raised and commanded the citizen army of Oyo. They were the *alafin's* political advisers, and their pressures in questions of policy were backed by ritual sanctions and ultimately by the right in certain circumstances to demand the king's suicide. But in strengthening the palace organization, the *alafin* had come to dominate the Council and direct the policies of the kingdom.

When an *alafin* died early in the nineteenth century after a long reign, it is probable that the *oyo mesi* sought to regain their political power by appointing a weak successor they could hope to dominate. There were precedents in Oyo and other kingdoms for choosing as the successor of a strong king a man whose disposition was judged to be more amenable to pressure from his councillors; but the growth in the executive role of the king rendered this crude device hazardous.

The choice on this occasion had dire consequences. Four sources of conflict emerged during the reign of the new *alafin*, Awole Arogangan (1810?-1816?), and lasted to dominate the politics of the next twenty years, ending with the evacuation of Oyo and the depopulation of the surrounding area. They were (i) the Fulani penetration, (ii) an ambitious rival to the king, (iii) the mistrust of the Council of State, and (iv) fears of the rulers in the Metropolitan Provinces that their support of the *alafin* would only result in their greater subordination to Oyo. The most important results of the interplay of these factors were, first, that the *alafin* could never command at the same

11

time the thoroughgoing allegiance of the Oyo town army and of the provincial forces; and, second, that the *alafin*'s enemies were often aided in battle by disgruntled provincial rulers.

The Fulani missionary commissioned by Dan Fodio had already appeared in Oyo. This was al-Sālih, called by the Yoruba Mallam Alimi (they turned the descriptive term *'ālim* into a name). Traditions say he preached the futility of offering sacrifices to the Yoruba gods and taught the practical benefits to be gained by worshipping God. He came, then, to appeal to pagans and not to reform the practices of Yoruba Muslims. Yet there were already some Yoruba Muslims, though not it seems of any great learning; the Faith had probably been propagated by traders. (The Yoruba term for Muslim is *imale* – person of Mali – and the first contact may have been either with merchants from old Mali, or with the Mande colony round Bussa, which was perhaps part of the migration referred to in the Kano Chronicle in the time of Sarkin Kano Yaji, A.D. 1349-1385.) The *alafin*'s advisers were evidently alarmed by the arrival of Alimi, which suggests that the *jihad* had already begun, and, on the advice of the Court diviners, he was driven out of Oyo. He was, however, able to travel in the *alafin*'s dominions for three or four years, and was then to take advantage of an invitation to settle in Ilorin, a town held by a rebellious army commander. Ilorin was to become the Fulani stronghold against the Yoruba. According to a late nineteenth-century Hausa manuscript translated by A. Mischlich (1903, p. 105), this was some time after Dan Fodio had settled at Sifawa, i.e. after 1810 and after the end of the main *jihad*.

The rebellious commander was Afonja, who is believed on the authority of Crowther and of Johnson to have been a member of the ruling house of Oyo and an unsuccessful candidate for the throne. After Awole had been chosen and installed *alafin*, Afonja is said to have intrigued to supplant him. The question of the structural position of men of the royal lineage poses itself. Recently in Oyo, within the last century, succession has alternated between two lines, so that son does not immediately succeed father, though only sons of kings are eligible to succeed. Unfortunately, it is uncertain that the same convention prevailed in the early nineteenth century; but there can be no doubt that there were many royal sons eligible for the succession.

Only the acknowledged first-born son of a king could never himself become king. The eldest son of each reigning *alafin* was appointed to the office of *aremo*, 'Head of the sons of kings', at his father's enthronement; but was debarred from succeeding him: instead, he had to commit suicide at his father's death. Johnson interprets this rule as a means of discouraging the *aremo* from trying to poison his father in the hope of gaining the throne; the interpretation convinces only if it is evident that the *aremo* was powerful enough to coerce the *oyo mesi* into electing him to it. The *aremo* did, it appear, enjoy much power, as Johnson himself reports: he was the only one of the king's sons permitted to live in Oyo, where he kept his own large court near the *alafin*'s; he had his share of state revenues; control over certain religious cult activities; and he alone in Oyo, besides the *alafin*, had the prerogative of the death sentence. The vesting of such power in this office, with its concomitant of death with the *alafin*, must be seen as an effective curb on the ambitions of the rest of the numerous royal sons.

Remembering that some of the royal sons had recently been installed as vassal kings in the small towns along the new trade road to the coast, a development which enabled them to take part in government and to share in the growing prosperity of Oyo, but nevertheless kept them out of the capital, Awole's handling of the problem set by the ambition of Afonja becomes comprehensible. Awole let himself be persuaded into giving Afonja the office of *are ona kakanfo*, thus breaking the rule that it should not go to a man of the royal lineage. It was a political misjudgement which proved not only fatal to the *alafin* himself but also breached the northern and eastern frontiers of Oyo. Afonja insisted on stationing himself not on a frontier, as was proper, but in Ilorin, 35 miles south-south-east of Oyo, where he could threaten the capital and intrigue for the throne. He built his personal following into an army large enough to threaten the *alafin*, partly by coercing neighbouring villagers into moving into his town and arming them, but principally, and fatally both for himself and Oyo, by attracting runaway slaves from the Metropolitan Provinces and by making Ilorin attractive to Yoruba Muslims, and to Hausa and Fulani from the north.

The *alafin* himself meanwhile had become locked in a struggle

13

for power with the Council of State, creating a situation in which the ancient vassal kingdoms of the Metropolitan Provinces allied themselves to the king's opponents. Misjudging his position again, the *alafin* sent Afonja at the head of an army on an expedition he had seen was bound to fail. He had hoped that Afonja, defeated, would follow convention and commit suicide; instead, the army mutinied and the king's own contingent was massacred. The Council now insisted upon the king's suicide.

The next *alafin*, too, failed to subdue Afonja, whose plans to conquer Oyo and seize the throne ended only when he attempted too late to reassert his command over his undisciplined and rapacious troops. He was not helped in the attempt to regain control either by Alimi, who had been joined by his war-like sons and had emerged as an alternative ruler, or by the leader of the free Yoruba Muslims, who had flocked to Ilorin (apparently because the *alafin* had outlawed the Faith – cf. Lander's journal of his first visit to Oyo). He died fighting outside the doors of his burning house, and Alimi became ruler of Ilorin. The attempts of successive *alafin* to drive the Fulani out failed, and instead the Fulani army entered Oyo and compelled the then *alafin* to pay tribute.

Alimi died, it is thought, about 1830, and was succeeded by his eldest son, 'Abd al-Salām. The reigning Emir of Ilorin believes that he was the first of the Fulani of Ilorin to possess a ruler's *tuta*, al-Sālih's having been a missionary's. His reign was marked by continuing war with Oyo. The last king to reign at Old Oyo, *Alafin* Oluewu, called in Bariba allies (why the Bariba allied themselves with the Oyo is an interesting question, but one that cannot be discussed here). By this time (c. 1836) much of the populace of Oyo and the northern Yoruba towns had fled southwards to the southern limits of the Metropolitan Provinces. Among them was another ambitious rival to the *alafin*, a member of another branch of the royal lineage and son of an earlier *alafin*. He had already made himself ruler of a town in the south, Ago Oja, and was perhaps pretending to be *alafin*. His name was Atiba. He had intrigued with the Yoruba vassals of the *alafin* and with the Fulani in Ilorin (who had been reinforced from Gwandu), and there combined factors ensured that the *alafin* and his Bariba allies were defeated. *Alafin*

Oluewu and the Bariba king were slain. Atiba then compelled the proper officials to install him *alafin* with traditional ritual, and he gave the name Oyo to Ago Oja, reigning there from c. 1838 to 1859. Although military power lay in the hands of independent Yoruba warriors who had made good in the wars, and Atiba himself commanded negligible forces, the Yoruba were now able to combine against further Fulani thrusts southwards. The Yoruba had acquired firearms and had learnt infantry warfare, and they inflicted a decisive defeat on the Fulani cavalry in terrain unfavourable to horses near Oshogbo c. 1839-1840 (Schön & Crowther, 1842, p. 317 ff.), and eventually established a frontier containing them some twenty to thirty miles from Ilorin. Much of their northern territory and part of its population had thus been conceded to Fulani sovereignty, and the centre of Yoruba power had swung to the growing towns in the south.

NUPE

Events in Nupe during the first third of the nineteenth century are very uncertain. The account Nadel attempts in *A Black Byzantium* (1942) contains too many inconsistencies to be satisfactory; but although the source material is more plentiful than the references in his bibliography indicate, it has not yet proved possible to develop a sound chronicle. After the successful reign of *Etsu* Jia in the late eighteenth century, rival claims for the kingship led to war and eventually to the splitting of the kingdom. There are traditions that the pattern of succession in Nupe had been that of primogeniture, as in Benin; but if this was in fact the rule, it seems to have been broken once earlier in the century. Jia's successor is given, in the earliest recorded king-list, Baikie's (1867, p. 105), as his son Samaza, but in others as Jimada. In any event, Jia's successor was driven out by his uterine kinsman Maazu. Unfortunately, there is no useful information about the status of the uterine kin of Nupe kings. All we know is that Maazu's son, Majia, fought in vain to keep the throne, retreated northwards to Yauri, and carved out a tiny kingdom for himself.

The Fulani already had a missionary among the Nupe, Mallam Dendo, also called Danyo and Manko. Dendo is said, in the account in Mischlich, to have asked Dan Fodio for an army when the *jihad* began in the north, and to have been ordered to wait for a more suitable time.

Dendo aided Majia against Jimada, who was eventually killed in battle by another Fulani leader, Maliki, at Ragada, to be succeeded as *etsu Nupe* by his son Idrisa. Dendo settled at, or built himself, a small town, Raba, on the Niger at a convenient crossing for traffic to Ilorin and Yoruba. It seems that Majia, also calling himself *etsu Nupe*, installed himself either at Tsafo (north of Raba) or at Zuguma, and reigned over western Nupe, including the Kusopa district; while *Etsu* Idrisa, after a period of refuge in Ilorin, established himself first at Jengi and later at Gbara, reigning over the eastern part of Nupe. The next series of events is hard to unravel. At some stage, Majia had quarrelled with Dendo, who retreated to Ilorin; Majia then attacked Ilorin, in alliance with a Yoruba force, but was defeated, and Dendo with Idrisa's help forced him back on Zuguma (cf. Johnson, 1921, p. 201 f.; Nadel, 1942, p. 78 f.). Idrisa may then have tried to assert his supremacy or independence; but Dendo, back in Raba, continued to play off the one *etsu* against the other, gradually establishing his paramountcy over both. The struggle between Idrisa and Majia was going on fiercely in January 1826, when Clapperton was in Oyo. In 1826 or 1827 Fulani reinforcements had enabled Majia to drive Idrisa from Gbara, to find refuge in the extreme south-east of Nupe, at Eggan, where he apparently was in 1830 when the Landers heard that some 800 of his soldiers had deserted and retreated into Bariba territory at Wawa near Bussa. It was rumoured that the Fulani were, in July 1830, intriguing with Idrisa against Majia. On 11 October, Richard Lander wrote 'The Falatahs are now in the possession of the whole of Nouffie, Ederesa having relinquished his claim, as he has been deserted by the greater part of his troops, who rejoined the army of Mallam Dendo. Both the Magia and Ederesa have little or no authority. The Falatah Prince (Dendo) has sent his messengers, both by land and water, to collect the taxes and tribute throughout the country of Nouffie, which was last year paid to Ederesa.' And on 12 October, he added that the Fulani of Raba, 'to restore their reputation' after an unsuccessful venture in the north, towards Yauri, were preparing an attack on Oyo. A little later he wrote that Majia was in touch with Dendo concerning a plot to delay the Landers, and continued: 'The imbecility of the Magia, and his want of power, are strikingly apparent; he exercises a nominal authority only over his people, Mallam Dendo being evidently the ruling monarch of the whole kingdom of Nouffie'.

Dendo was now aged and almost blind, and attempted to secure the succession by proclaiming (October 1830) his second (or third?) son, Usman Zaki, his successor as *Sarkin Fulanin Nupe*. On 27 September 1833 Dendo died. At this time, *Etsu* Idrisa was in Eggan, 'sick and in pain' (Oldfield) and paying a half-yearly tribute of 60,000 cowries to the Fulani, while Majia, for the moment on good terms with the Fulani, was in Raba.

Usman Zaki seems to have intended to rule from Raba as overlord of the two Nupes, each under its *etsu*. Idrisa was allowed to return to Gbara, and both he and Majia (at Zuguma) paid tribute to Usman Zaki. Usman Zaki's rule, though, was rendered precarious by the ambition of another of Dendo's sons, his half-brother Masaba (Mahama Saba, Dasaba), who in October 1841 was in Eggan, and conspiring with the chief of Eggan and with both Majia and Idrisa to overthrow Usman Zaki. Majia died about this time, but his son and successor *Etsu* Sado (Tsado, Mashado) joined the others in a revolt, and in 1845-1846 they succeeded in ousting Usman Zaki, who took refuge in Sokoto, and Raba was destroyed. Masaba, at Ladi, is said to have proved himself no less exacting and oppressive than Usman Zaki. His own army chief, 'Umar Bahaushe, a Bornuese, who had distinguished himself in the fight against Usman Zaki, rebelled, apparently with much popular support, drove Masaba from Ladi, which was burnt, and made himself a new capital at Bida. Masaba retreated to the south-west, eventually taking refuge in Ilorin, where the American missionary Bowen saw him make his submission to the Emir Shita in 1855 – although, when the rebellion against him began in 1852, Masaba had been planning to seize Ilorin. Masaba and Usman Zaki joined forces and with the aid of contingents from Sokoto and Gwandu, overcame 'Umar Bahaushe early in 1857, and ruled jointly from Bida. Descendants of the rival *etsuzi Nupe* ceased to play any significant part in events from this period, though Majia's line continued in Tsafo and Jimada's in Bida.

FULANI RULE

Both Nupe and Yoruba were assigned to Gwandu when Usman Dan Fodio divided the empire. Gwandu itself was to acknowledge that Sokoto was the senior partner. Combined Sokoto and Gwandu forces helped Ilorin in the victory over the Oyo and Bariba armies that saved it for the Fulani, and other joint expeditions helped Dendo, and later Usman Zaki, to dominate Nupe. The Fulani rulers of Ilorin and Nupe paid tribute to Gwandu, but, living in the extreme south of the lands conquered by the Fulani, appear to have been free to do as they wished.

In Ilorin, two sons of *'ālim* al-Sālih founded dynastic houses and debarred his other four sons and their descendants from succession (the two are believed to have had a Yoruba mother, the other four a Fulani). There seems to have been little dynastic rivalry, at least until c. 1891, but there were difficulties for the rulers. Al-Sālih succeeded in playing upon a growing jealousy between Afonja and Solagberu, the two leading Yoruba, until Afonja was slain and his following broken. Al-Sālih's son, the Emir 'Abd al-Salām, then broke Solagberu. It cannot, however, be assumed that the Fulani found it easy to consolidate their position as rulers in the town, though their problems are not known in detail. Its population was very mixed and the numbers of Fulani were probably small. Besides pagan Yoruba, Muslim Yoruba, and Fulani, there were many Hausa, of various origins. The then *alafin* spoke bitterly of Ilorin to Clapperton as a town of rebellious Hausa slaves; and it may be supposed that the wars in the north following Dan Fodio's rising had resulted in the sale of many captives to the Yoruba. Other Hausa had arrived as refugees – a section of the Ilorin Hausa are today known as the Gobirawa; they seem to be descendants of a group who had fled southwards from Gobir after the early battles with the Fulani and had then been attempting to seize some territory for their own between Yoruba and Nupe, before joining forces with Afonja. There is a tradition that the Gobirawa had hoped to gain control of Ilorin on the death of Alimi. One element that was absent from the population, it is worth remarking, was that of the Pastoral Fulani, who are generally supposed to have elsewhere joined

18

Dan Fodio's movement. Their presence in the savannahs of
the northern Yoruba area was observed in the 1820s and later;
but they took no part in the wars, and it was recorded by the
missionary Bowen (1858, p. xiv), that the Yoruba, who called
them *alabawo*, 'The Hide Wearers', did not regard them as
being of the same stock as their Fulani enemies.

Under the rule of 'Abd al-Salām, the town was divided into
four wards: the Yoruba ward of Afonja's descendants; a ward
of Muslim Yoruba (Oke Suna, Hill of the Faithful), which was
governed by descendants of Solagberu; a Hausa ward, headed
by the Hausa war leader (titled *balogun gambari*); and the
Fulani ward, the emir's. Each of the four ward-heads was
leader of a section of the army – the Fulani section led by a
slave appointed by the emir. In the nineteenth century, the
pattern of government failed to conform in several important
respects to Dan Fodio's design based on the Maliki School of
Islamic Law. Though Fulani was the court language into the
middle of the century, Yoruba was the language of the town;
and Yoruba culture and institutions had so much influence
that descriptions left by visitors to Ilorin, Bowen in 1855,
Campbell in 1860, and Milum in 1879, show that the emirs of
Ilorin were conducting themselves like the traditional secluded
monarchs of the Yoruba. The unending hostility of the Oyo
Yoruba kept Ilorin on a war footing, and it was only by playing
upon the rivalries of the four war leaders that the emirs were
able to maintain their political position, until late in the century
one of the war leaders, the *balogun gambari*, became pre-
eminent and was then able to dictate policy and render the
emir's position insecure.

In Nupe, Usman Zaki died in January 1859, soon after the
defeat of 'Umar Bahaushe's rebellion, and Masaba reigned
many years, until 1873. The succession went as planned to a
nephew, the grandson of Dendo, and Nupe was not again
vexed by dynastic wars. During the struggle for ascendancy,
both the Fulani rulers, Usman Zaki and Masaba, had compromised their Muslim orthodoxy by sacrifices to one, at least,
of the local deities, Ketsa, the spirit of a rock island in the
Niger, as Crowther reported, adding that their offerings were
'perhaps from policy to keep the people quiet' (Crowther &
Taylor, 1859, p. 216). Nadel has shown that there have been

19

other accommodations to Nupe cults; but in the capital they were very much subordinated to the observances of the Islamic state. The constitution developed (along the lines described by Nadel) so securely that when Bida fell to the Niger Company's expeditionary force in 1897, it had what Major Burdon regarded as 'the ideal Fulani constitution', that is a system of rule by aristocratic Fulani apt for the British scheme of Indirect Rule.

A development common to Ilorin and Nupe was the seizure of land by the conquerors, who re-allocated it as fiefs attached to offices of state, both fief and office being the reward of military success or personal service. Later in Ilorin, tenure of important offices generally became vested in certain lineages in every ward of the town; this seems to have been a reversion to the Yoruba system. It was accepted, perhaps, as an integrative device, because the Fulani could neither destroy the lineage organization of the Yoruba wards nor establish themselves as an exclusive aristocracy as they had done in the conquered Hausa states. In the end, both Hausa and Fulani have come to have lineages in structure very like those of the Yoruba. In Nupe, where in contrast the power of the indigenous rulers and office-holders had been eliminated, the development of political clientage and granting of privilege conform to the practice in the more northerly Fulani states.

In both Yoruba and Nupe the Fulani gained their successes through exploiting dynastic rivalries. The fall of Oyo shows clearly the structural opposition between king and Council of State failing as an organizational device when either party could align itself with forces newly on the scene.

The motives that led the Fulani into Nupe and Yoruba are still undecided. Dan Fodio may have encouraged missionaries to go there as part of a plan to extend Islam into the powerful kingdoms bordering the Hausa states. An economic interest may be suspected in Dendo's choice of Raba, on the Niger, as his centre of operations. *'Alim* al-Sālih went to Ilorin because Afonja was there; but Ilorin was near enough to the trade routes that had formerly passed through Old Oyo to capture much of the traffic, so that, by mid-century, it had grown into a large and renowned market centre.

This venture of an anthropologist into history justifies itself, it is hoped, by indicating that a history of institutions can be attempted when little is known about the lives of individuals; and, further, that the little that may be known about them requires interpretation as a drama within an institutional structure which often appears to set its own limits on the changes they can bring about.

ACKNOWLEDGEMENTS

I owe the stimulus to work on the Fulani, as well as most of such understanding as I have of the work of Dan Fodio, to Mr Thomas Hodgkin, when he was Director of the Institute of African Studies, University of Ghana. I am very grateful to Dr B. G. Martin, lately my colleague at the same Institute, for many useful discussions, but especially for the translation of Ahmad Ibn Abībakr's Manuscript History of Ilorin, which was acquired on a visit to Ilorin from the Institute by al-Haj Usman Boyo and myself. My thanks go also to Professor Daryll Forde and Dr Ioan Lewis for helpful comments.

REFERENCES

AJAYI, J. F. A. & SMITH, R. 1964. *Yoruba Warfare in the Nineteenth Century.* London: Cambridge University Press.

ALLEN, W. & THOMSON, T. R. H. 1848. *A Narrative of the Expedition sent by Her Majesty's Government to the River Niger in 1841 . . .* (2 vols.). London.

ARNETT, E. J. 1920. *Gazetteer of Sokoto Province.* London.

— 1922. *The Rise of the Sokoto Fulani* (Transl. of Muhammad Bello, Infāq al-maysūr). Kano.

BAIKIE, W. B. 1856. *Narrative of an Exploring Voyage up the Rivers Kwo'ra and Bi'nue . . . in 1854.* London.

— 1862. Dr Baikie R.N. to Lord J. Russell. *Parl. Paps.* 61.

— 1867. Notes of a Journey from Bida in Nupe, to Kano in Hausa . . . in 1862. *JRGS* **37**.

BAIKIE, W. B. & MAY, D. J. 1857-1858. Extracts of Reports from the Niger Expedition . . . *Proc. RGS* **2**.

BARTH, H. 1854. Extracts from a Letter from Dr Barth to Dr Beke . . . 1853. *JRGS* **24**.

— 1857. *Travels and Discoveries in North and Central Africa . . .* London.

— 1860. A General Historical Description of the State of Human Society in Northern Central Africa. *JRGS* **30**.

BECROFT, J. (otherwise BEECROFT) 1841. On Benin and the Upper Course of the River Quorra, or Niger ... *JRGS* **11.**

BOWEN, T. J. 1857. *Central Africa: Adventures and Missionary Labours.* Charleston and London.

—— 1858. Grammar and Dictionary of the Yoruba Language. *Smithsonian Contribs.* **10**: 4.

BURDON, J. A. 1904. The Fulani Emirates of Northern Nigeria. *Geog. J.* **24.**

—— (ed.) 1909. *Northern Nigeria. Historical Notes on Certain Emirates and Tribes.* London.

CAMPBELL, R. 1861. *A Pilgrimage to my Motherland ... in 1859-60.* London.

CARTER, G. T. 1893-1894. Report in Parl. Paps. C7227. London.

CLAPPERTON, H. 1829. *Journal of a second expedition into the interior of Africa* ... London.

CLARKE, J. 1849. *Specimens of the dialects ... and notes of countries and customs in Africa.* London.

CROWTHER, S. A. 1843. *Vocabulary of the Yoruba language.* London.

—— 1852. *A grammar of the Yoruba language.* London.

—— 1855. *Journal of an expedition up the Niger ... in 1854.* London.

—— 1872. *Bishop Crowther's report on the overland journey from Lokoja to Bida ... 1871 ... 1872.* London.

CROWTHER, S. A. & TAYLOR, J. C. 1859. *The Gospel on the Banks of the Niger ... 1857-59.* London.

DALZEL, A. 1793. *The history of Dahomey.* London.

DUPIGNY, E. G. M. 1920. *Gazetteer of Nupe Province.* London.

DUPUIS, R. 1824. *A residence in Ashantee.* London.

EGGAN, F. 1950. *Social Organization of the Western Pueblos.* Chicago: University of Chicago Press.

ELPHINSTONE, K. V. 1921. *Gazetteer of Ilorin Province.* London.

EVANS-PRITCHARD, E. E. *The Nuer.* Oxford: Clarendon Press.

FERRYMAN, A. F. M. 1892. *Up the Niger.* London.

—— 1900. *British West Africa.* London.

—— 1902. *British Nigeria.* London.

GOLDIE, G. T. 1897. *Report on the Niger-Sudan campaign, 1897.* London.

HERMON-HODGE, H. B. 1929. *Gazetteer of Ilorin Province.* London.

HISKETT, M. 1960. Kitāb al-farq: a work on the Hausa kingdoms attributed to Uthman dan Fodıo. *Bull. SOAS* **23**.

—— 1963. *Tazyīn al-waraqāt by ʿAbdullāh Ibn Muhammad first Emir of Gwandu.* Ibadan.

HODGKIN, T. L. 1962. Islam and national movements in West Africa. *J. Afr. Hist.* **3**.

HUTCHINSON, T. J. 1855. *Narrative of the Niger, Tschadda, and Binuë exploration* . . . London.

JOHNSON, S. 1921. *The history of the Yorubas*. Lagos.

LAIRD, MCG. & OLDFIELD, A. K. R. 1837. *Narrative of an expedition into the interior of Africa*. London.

LANDER, R. L. 1830. *Records of Captain Clapperton's last expedition to Africa* . . . (2 vols.). London.

LANDER, R. L. & LANDER, J. 1832. *Journal of an expedition to determine the course and termination of the Niger* (3 vols.). London.

M'QUEEN, J. 1840. *A geographical survey of Africa* . . . London.

MARTIN, B. G. 1965. A new Arabic history of Ilorin. *Research Bull.*, Centre of Arabic Studies, University of Ibadan. Ibadan.

MAY, D. J. 1857-1858. Reports from the Niger expedition. *Proc. RGS* **2**.

—— 1860. Journey in the Yoruba and Nupe countries . . . in 1858. *JRGS* **30**.

MERCIER, P. 1950. Histoire et légende: la bataille d'Illorin. *Notes Africaines IFAN* **47**.

MILUM, J. 1881. Notes of a journey from Lagos up the River Niger to Bida . . . and Ilorin . . . 1879-80. *Proc. RGS* **3**.

MISCHLICH, A. 1903. Beitrage zur Geschichte der Haussastaten. *Mitteil. des Seminars für Orientalische Sprachen zu Berlin* **6**: 3.

MONTEIL, C. 1895. *De Saint-Louis à Tripoli par le Lac Tchad*. Paris.

MORTON-WILLIAMS, P. 1965. The Oyo Yoruba and the Atlantic trade, 1670-1830. *J. Hist. Soc. Nigeria* **3**, 1.

—— 1967. The Yoruba kingdom of Oyo in the nineteenth century. In D. Forde & P. Kaberry (eds.), *West African kingdoms in the nineteenth century*. London: Oxford University Press.

NADEL, S. F. 1942. *A black Byzantium*. London: Oxford University Press.

PALMER, H. R. 1915-1916. An early Fulani conception of Islam. (Transl. of U. dan Fodio. Tanbih al-ikhwan). *J. Afr. Soc.* **14**.

—— 1928. *Sudanese memoirs* (3 vols.). Lagos.

RADCLIFFE-BROWN, A. R. 1940. On social structure. *JRAI* **70**.

—— 1950. Intro. to Radcliffe-Brown, A. R. & Forde, D. (eds.), *African systems of kinship and marriage*. London: Oxford University Press.

ROHLFS, G. 1875. *Quer durch Afrika* (2 vols.). Leipzig.

SCHÖN, J. F. & CROWTHER, S. A. 1842. *Journals of the . . . expedition up the Niger in 1841*. London.

SIMPSON, W. H. 1871. *Report of the Niger expedition, 1871*. F.O. 84-1351. London.

SMITH, M. G. 1960. *Government in Zazzau.* London: Oxford University Press.

TOUTÉE (Comm.) 1897. *Dahome, Niger, Touareg. Recit de voyage.* Paris.

VANDELEUR, C. F. S. 1897. Nupe and Ilorin. *Geog. J.* **10**.

—— 1898. *Campaigning on the Upper Nile and Niger.* London.

VIARD, E. 1886. (3rd edn.) *Au Bas-Niger.* Paris.

P. C. Lloyd

Conflict Theory and Yoruba Kingdoms

Kingship has existed among the Yoruba of Western Nigeria for many centuries, perhaps for a millennium. Several of the kingdoms extant today had been founded before the first Portuguese visits to the Guinea Coast. For many of these there is little evidence, available today, of any sudden or radical changes in political structure. The kingdom of Oyo, however, did grow into a mighty empire controlling the trade route from the Habe kingdoms of the savana to the coast; and a far more complex political structure developed. But the empire collapsed in the early nineteenth century through civil wars and Fulani attacks. The people of the destroyed towns fled southwards to settle in existing small towns along the forest margins, vastly expanding their size and creating new problems – the government of settlements of fifty or a hundred or more thousand people.

Several authors (Bascom, 1942, 1944; Forde, 1951; Lloyd, 1954, 1955, 1960, 1962, 1965; Morton-Williams, 1960) have already provided outlines of the political structure of some of these Yoruba kingdoms but their accounts have tended to lack analyses of the dynamic processes which produce structural changes. In an earlier paper (Lloyd, 1965), I presented models illustrating three types of African kingdom distinguished by the methods of recruitment to political office and other related variables. For each model I predicted a dominant pattern of conflict in the political process. One of these models was based upon the structure of certain northern Yoruba kingdoms. In this paper I hope to examine this model further to demonstrate the spheres in which conflict exists and the type and direction of change which the resolution of these conflicts is likely to produce.

EQUILIBRIUM MODELS

Although some excellent monographs have appeared in recent years describing the political structure of African kingdoms, these have tended not to stress the possibility of radical change.

A rather static picture has emphasized the functional inter-relationships within the total social structure. Thus Maquet (1961), in his study of the Tutsi dominance in the kingdom of Ruanda, gives no inkling of the depth of Hutu hostility to this system – yet within a decade the latter were in power, the former fleeing to escape massacre. In his book on Zaria, Smith (1960) analyses the changes in the roles of Fulani office-holders consequent upon British colonial rule, but the stress is upon continuity and adaptation in these roles, not upon the opposition to Fulani rule by the *talakawa* – the commoner peasants. For many years the concept of 'conflict' in African kingdoms has been associated with Gluckman. Yet his use of the term is limited to 'the relation between discrepancies that sets in train processes which produce alterations in the personnel of social positions, but not in the pattern of positions' (1965, p. 109). Such conflicts lead to rebellions – the replacement of one king or chief by another more likely to uphold the established norms; they do not lead to revolutions – caused in Gluckman's words by 'contradictions' or 'those relations between discrepant principles and processes in the social structure which must inevitably lead to radical change in the pattern' (1965, p. 109). Cycles of rebellion have indeed been a common phenomenon in African kingdoms; radical structural changes in political systems have perhaps been rare. But the existing literature is largely silent on the processes which occasion revolutions. On the other hand, a study of the processes which lead to radical change will, I believe, be equally illuminating for lesser changes.

The bias in existing studies of African kingdoms seems to be entailed by the use of structural models, with their parts integrated and existing in a state of equilibrium. Thus, if one establishes a model to demonstrate the relationships between the king, the chiefs – his advisory council, and the mass of the people, one stresses the complementarity of role expectations. From these expectations derive the norms and ultimately the values of the society. A consensus among all members of the society is tacitly presumed. Values inherent in the political structure are in accord with those of other subsystems in the society.

As Leach (1954, p. 4) notes, 'conceptual models of society are necessarily models of equilibrium systems, real societies can never be in equilibrium'. Yet many anthropologists have described societies themselves as being in such a state of equilibrium and concentrated their attention upon the processes which lead to repetitious or almost static states. Some would use an organic analogy – the human body acts to rectify any deviation of blood temperature from its normal level. For others a twenty-year cycle of rebellions is cited as an example of equilibrium. Images of the see-saw, of a balance of power, are equally common. In all these approaches interest is focused upon the process of socialization of political values, upon the methods of social control of behaviour deviating from the norms, and upon the attempt of the society to restore a *status quo ante* or to effect a minimal change.

The use of mathematical models frees one from the restraints imposed by biological analogies. The change in value of one of a set of variables does not necessarily lead to a restoration of the original value but to alterations in many or all of the variables as a new equilibrium is established. But such a model does not tell us why one of the values was initially changed nor does it always indicate the probable direction of change.

Those who use equilibrium models to illustrate social processes do not, of course, deny the reality of social change. But the concepts used limit their discussion of this phenomenon. For in the structural model in a state of equilibrium there are no internal processes leading to change. Change must therefore be ascribed either to external factors or to complexities which differentiate real societies from their models (cf. Gluckman, 1963, pp. 38-39).

Factors of change may be external only to the particular structure in question – thus in Smelser's (1959) account of the Lancashire cotton industry, technological changes led to changed patterns of family relationships. The factors may, on the other hand, be external to the whole society – the imposition of colonial rule upon African political systems is a well-quoted example. In each case the introduction of new techniques or of new actors necessitates an adjustment of roles in the original structure. Deviant behaviour by individuals is sometimes unchecked by forces of social control and leads to changed norms and values. But Parsons (1964) holds that such deviance is a personality factor and outside the structure concerned.

27

P. C. Lloyd

In reality, however, all societies are so complex that some lack of adjustment exists between their constituent parts; individuals face incompatible role expectations and have to make a choice between them. Other roles are poorly defined or have wide margins of tolerance. The rigid 'structural functionalist' would stress here the adjustments made by the individual to satisfy the expectations of others. On the other hand, one might, with Leach (1954, p. 8) stress the opportunity open to the individual to pursue his own interests at the expense of his fellows. As Leach adds, 'it is precisely these inconsistencies [between models and reality] which can provide us with an understanding of the processes of social change' (1954, p. 8).

In using a structural model, one may modify the relationships between the actors but one cannot change the actors themselves – by abolishing some statuses or introducing new ones: new individuals may fill pre-existing statuses. One is thus led into differentiating between change within a structure or system and change of structure. Conceptually the distinction may be useful. In practice one runs into difficulties in applying it, for instance, to change within African kingdoms. The distinction between a rebellion and a revolution becomes very blurred.

Weber (1947) stresses that a revolt against a traditional authority is directed against the person and not the system and that the claims of the rebels are that the ruler has failed to observe the traditional limits of his authority. In this context the ruler is castigated as the 'bad king' by his opponents. This approach is followed by Gluckman (1963, p. 11 ff.) and others. The rebellion is led, usually, by rivals eligible for office though the masses are mobilized in support. We are not led to consider the goals of the ruler or to consider the struggle as one between rival interest groups. Suppose the king were not merely a tyrant or an incompetent, but sought to extend the royal power at the expense of that of his chiefs. The rival candidate for the throne would presumably promise to maintain the traditional distribution of power – though the issue may well be less clearly stated. If the rival wins, the 'rebellion' has been successful. But if the king wins, and in his victory reorganizes the political structure, do we call it a revolution? Colloquially, we are apt to speak of rebellions as the failures of the mass to overthrow existing power-holders, of revolutions as their successes. The

28

distinction is in the result, not in the process, though the out-come may well reflect the degree to which the revolting groups formulated their aims and organized themselves. Thus, both in Weber's and in colloquial usage of the term rebellion, attention can be distracted away from the goals and interests of the contesting factions.

The structural model has indeed proved useful – in analysing the civil wars in many African kingdoms, in stressing the 'social functions of conflict' when the norms of kingship are overtly expressed in contests for the throne, and in describing repeti-tive processes such as the break-up of old villages and the establishment of new ones (Turner, 1957). Its weakness lies in its failure to describe processes of change which are internal to the structure. Again, as van den Berghe (1963) has noted, not all adjustment of roles leads to equilibrium – an intensification of the disequilibrium is an equally possible result. Conflict theory attempts to remedy these deficiencies. Its protagonists in fact, see it *par excellence* as the theory of social change, the equili-brium model being appropriate only to the static aspects of society.

CONFLICT THEORY

Conflict theory as outlined today derives from two prime sources: first, from Marxist sociology, still largely ignored in the U.S.A. but recently developed in Western Europe by writers such as Dahrendorf (1959) and Rex (1961); second, from the exploitation of game theory to sociological ends. The current popularity of themes of 'conflict resolution' has provided an added impetus, though the use of the term conflict here differs from that cited above.

In exploring conflict theory one encounters a number of terminological problems. Conflict is used colloquially and in sociological literature to refer both to fighting and tension and to incompatibility. The two usages are related – incompatibility of aims leads to fighting. Fighting is bad, and conflict too be-comes a value-laden term; conflict *ought* to be resolved. Incom-patibility is a more neutral word; it is in this sense that I use the term conflict – as in fact it is used by most sociologists – in role conflict, conflict of interests, for example.

Yet even in this sense conflict embraces concepts which

sociologists have distinguished. It may be contrasted with competition. In competition, the rivals may be seeking an identical end (such as a given piece of land, a titled office), employing the same means (or abiding by the same social rules) to achieve this end. In conflict, the ends are different and the means too may differ (for instance, one faction seeks power through a parliamentary system, the other through a military dictatorship). In competition, though not in conflict, institutionalized means exist to resolve the contest.

Others contrast conflict with contradiction. Gluckman's usage of these two terms has already been cited. Firth (1964, p. 25) argues that 'conflict is observable empirically in behavioural opposition between persons or groups, whereas contradiction may be an inference referring either to a logical opposition, or to an ideological opposition between the parties. In this sense conflict, which may be based on misconception or temporary lack of adjustment by the parties, may be resolved, whereas contradiction cannot be resolved so long as the relevant conditions remain the same.'

To return to our structural model of king, chief, and masses. Many would describe the contests to occupy the statuses of king or chief as competition; though Gluckman would here use conflict. Both Gluckman and Firth would, I surmise, use contradiction for incompatibilities in the goals or values of rival groups in a society. Marx, however, wrote of conflict between such groups – e.g. class conflict – and contradictions between different subsystems in society – the new mode of production and the existing social relationships. Those who are developing conflict theory along Marxist lines would, I expect, adhere to this usage.

In this terminological confusion one may separate the distinct but closely related concepts: the *conflict* of goals and interests between persons; the *competition* for a given status within the social structure; the *incompatibility* of roles – seen either as inconsistencies in the mutual expectations of two actors or as the dilemma of the individual in experiencing the inconsistent expectations of others; the tensions produced by any of the foregoing in interpersonal behaviour; the *contradictions* between different parts of the social structure. It is the conflict of goals and interests (or, perhaps more accurately, the conflict relationship existing between persons or groups having different goals and interests) that provides the basis for the following discussion of change within the political structure of Yoruba kingdoms.

Conflict theory, as I would use the term, is far more than a recognition of role incompatibility (or 'conflict') in society. Unlike the equilibrium model which postulates a consensus of values and role expectations, conflict theory holds that individual interests and goals are inherently incompatible. In any society, material benefits (or 'scarce resources') are not equally distributed – and a man seeks to gain a greater share, necessarily at the expense of his fellows. It follows that all relationships between persons involve an element of power – the degree to which one can force another person to fulfil the role that one expects of him rather than the role that he might wish to play. One's success in this – one's power (itself a 'scarce resource') – generally determines one's ability to achieve one's own goals. (One might speak of a *competition* for power between individuals or groups in a society, as for instance between the African king, his chief, and the mass of the people; but this usage, implying a lack of consensus about the proper distribution of power, differs from that cited above – a *competition* for office in which the role of the office-holder is not disputed.) The values of the individual are developed in accord with his interests; but the more powerful (or ruling) members of society will endeavour to gain acceptance for their own values among the weaker, thus reinforcing their superiority. A contradiction between an individuals' interests, seen objectively, and his values is thus a common phenomenon. The attitudes of weaker individuals range from complete acceptance of the values of the more powerful to their complete rejection.

In the context of this conflict in social relationships, actions are seen as moves in the continual process of bargaining by which each individual or group seeks to maximize its own rewards while minimizing its chances of loss. In game-theory parlance this is a non-zero-sum game: the gains of one party do not necessarily equal the losses of the other. In fact, positions may be reached in which each party feels that it has the most that can be expected in the circumstances and bargaining ceases – or, in other terms, the tension in the behaviour of the parties is reduced, even though the conflict remains latent.

31

The bargaining process does not necessarily imply an institutionalized method of resolving conflict. At one extreme such methods might be highly developed with all inconsistencies of interests calmly discussed in gentlemanly committees. At the other extreme lies the threat or use of force.

In theory one may project into the future the moves of each player in the bargaining game. In the case, however, of the situations with which most sociologists deal, this is a practical impossibility. The variables are too many and often unpredictable. It is easier to use these methods in applying hindsight to past events.

The range of possible ends to the game is infinite; one is not obliged to dichotomize, as with equilibrium models, between changes within and changes of the structure. Bargaining may result equally in a restoration of the *status quo ante* or in radical changes. Thus conflict theory can, I would contend, illuminate those rebellions in African kingdoms which have hitherto been described in terms of the equilibrium model.

Equilibrium models and conflict theory seem mutually opposed; the one stressing integration and consensus, the other conflict and incompatibilities. But social science frequently operates with sets of opposed generalizations. The two approaches are complementary. Yet social anthropologists writing of political structure have tended to work within the framework of one or the other. Thus Gluckman, notwithstanding his emphasis on conflict (as he defines it), is basically working with structural models in states of equilibrium. Leach does not specifically adopt a conflict theory as set out here but ascribes social change to the inconsistencies in social structures. He does, however, argue that structural change embraces not only 'changes in the positions of individuals with regard to an ideal system of status relationships but changes in the ideal system itself: changes, that is, in the power structure' (1954, pp. 9-10). 'Every individual of a society, each in his own interest, endeavours to exploit the situation as he perceives it and in so doing the collectivity of individuals alters the structure of the society itself' (p. 8).

It is claimed that conflict theory can explain radical changes in social structure which are beyond the scope of the equilibrium model. But where the changes consist of minor adjustments to the structure, why should one prefer one approach to the other? How different will the resulting explanation be? In adopting a novel approach, one asks fresh questions and seeks new data. In applying conflict theory to the study of processes of change in African kingdoms, one stresses the divergent interests of king and chief, rather than the consensus on the nature of kingship. Whose interests do the chiefs represent? Too many of the existing monographs omit to tell us how the chiefs are selected for office. External factors of change continue to be important, but one sees the individual exploiting them to his own ends rather than trying to accommodate them to traditional norms and values. Conflict theory stresses force and coercion in the maintenance of stability rather than ideological consensus. Fresh questions provide new answers – not necessarily more correct than earlier ones but conveying broader insight.

In the next part of this paper, I provide a model of the political structure of Yoruba kingdoms stressing the conflict in social relationships and outlining the type of change that these conflicts seem likely to produce.

CONFLICT IN YORUBA KINGDOMS

The Yoruba towns of the pattern with which I am concerned here are densely peopled settlements of tens of thousands of inhabitants; this and allied characteristics often result in their being termed 'urban' in spite of the fact that the majority of their inhabitants are farmers. Structurally the town is composed of a number of patrilineal descent groups, each possessing its own compound. These descent groups are of heterogeneous origin – their legends tell of the migration of their founders from other Yoruba kingdoms. As will be described more fully below, the descent groups are highly corporate, rights to both town and farming land and to political office being vested in them. Government of the town rests with a council of chiefs, each of whom is selected by, and from among, the members of one of the descent groups of the town; the council is responsible to a sacred king or *oba*. The council of chiefs discusses all the public affairs of the town – the resolution of conflicts between individuals and descent groups, the organizing of public activities, the defence of the community. Decisions are ordained by the *oba*. The same chiefs carry out administrative duties within their own descent groups – the collection of tribute, the organization of labour for public work or for war. I propose to analyse the political process in such towns in terms, first, of the conflict between the descent groups and the role of the *oba* in mediating the conflict, and, second, of the conflict between the council of chiefs on the one hand and the sacred king on the other.

Ideally these conflicts should be illustrated by events in one particular kingdom over a number of years. Unfortunately this is not possible. In conducting fieldwork ten years ago these problems were not uppermost in my mind. Even had they been so, the information required – for instance the discussions between the chiefs and the *oba* held within the palace – would not usually be accessible to the resident anthropologist. Furthermore, I am at the moment, more interested in the political processes which operated within these kingdoms in the precolonial period – an era for which the collection of relevant data is even more difficult.

I propose therefore to work with a simply structured model of a Yoruba kingdom based upon that of Ado-Ekiti which I have described elsewhere (Lloyd, 1960, 1962). The various situations of conflict which I describe as operating in my model, have in fact been observed by me in various Yoruba towns in the ethnographic present or have been described as occurring in the past. The analysis of the political process is, however, presented largely in hypothetical terms; descriptive ethnographic data I have reduced to a minimum since these have already been provided elsewhere. Throughout I write in the present tense, though certain situations which I describe are not appropriate either to the colonial or to the post-colonial periods.

The Yoruba town
The Yoruba town is one of Africa's ethnographic anomalies. Its origin probably lies in a period, about a millennium ago, about which we know almost nothing. We may however postulate certain necessary pre-conditions for town-dwelling: first, a sufficiently fertile environment which enables men to sustain their families from such a small area of land, so that 20,000 people

may dwell together in a town and yet be able to walk to their farms – such can be achieved with population densities of 150 or more persons per square mile; second, the aggregation of descent groups of heterogeneous origin poses certain problems of government which the Yoruba seem to have solved with their sacred kingship; kingship is thus a probable prerequisite for town-dwelling on this scale.

Once established, these towns give certain advantages to their inhabitants. With tribal methods of warfare (as described by Ajayi and Smith, 1964) the defence of a community is safeguarded more by its size than by any other factor. The size of the market created by the town permits craft specialization; the aggregation of tribute by *oba* and chiefs creates an affluence which supports specialist workers in luxury crafts and in professions. The more complex patterns of exchange thus engendered result in an increase in the number of traders and of wealth gained through trade. In consequence, town dwelling is held to be prestigious by the Yoruba, who differentiate both between the inhabitant of the flourishing town and the farmer in his hamlet, and between themselves and those neighbouring ethnic groups resident in dispersed settlements. There are thus powerful reasons why the Yoruba should endeavour to preserve the substantial size of their communities, for size is seen as being directly related to safety, affluence, and prestige. Yet the unity of these towns is, in Durkheim's terms, segmental or of the 'mechanical' type and is, in consequence, very fragile.

By African pre-colonial standards the Yoruba were a wealthy people. All the farming was carried out by men, leaving the women free to engage in trade and crafts. The men, furthermore, produced a surplus which supported both affluent chiefs and specialist craftsmen and professionals. But the wide range of individual wealth did not lead to social stratification of the type associated with contemporary industrial society. Rich traders and chiefs lived in the compounds of their own descent groups and acted as members of these groups; they did not form separate associations the corporate activities of which were overwhelmingly incompatible with descent group membership. Thus, save for the specialist descent groups of weavers or blacksmiths, found in the larger towns, each descent group in the Yoruba town consisted of a majority of farmers, perhaps a few male craftsmen and traders, women who were engaged in petty trade and their own crafts, and the titled chief. In these circumstances the members of a descent group might migrate from one town to another with relative ease; the accepting town could, land being available, absorb the newcomers; the rejected town would continue to function in the same manner though on a slightly smaller scale. Since town size is such an important consideration, one may appreciate the efforts made both to prevent the emigration of dissident groups and to attract immigrants from neighbouring kingdoms.

The structure of the descent groups

The structure of the descent groups in the Yoruba town is largely a function of their corporate rights. For ease of description, however, I shall first outline this structure.

The adult male members of the descent group together with their wives and children live in the group's compound – an elaborate series of linked courtyards, each surrounded by an open verandah off which lead the individual sleeping-rooms. Many compounds number a thousand inhabitants. The status of the descent group in the town is defined in its legends which tell of the migration of the founder to the town, of his acceptance by the reigning *oba*, and of the grant to him of land and titled office to be held by his descendants in perpetuity. The individual character of each descent group is demonstrated by its worship of a deity peculiar to its members (and perhaps associated with the founder's original home), by attributes shared by all members – facial or body marks, peculiar appellations, by domestic customs peculiar to the compound, by rites performed by members of the group at the installation or burial of an *oba*. These rights and duties, together with the right of elders to tell the history of their own group, and explain its status, are all most jealously guarded. In stressing the attributes and in performing the duties, descent-group members ensure the recognition of their group as a full and independent constituent of the town; were attributes and duties to be ignored, the group would die out, its surviving members being absorbed by rival groups, its name passing into oblivion.

Within the descent group authority is ascribed by age. In fact, the Yoruba kinship terms for siblings (and collaterals) differentiate by age and not by sex. The oldest living male thus presides over meetings of each descent group; the elected titled chief takes precedence only in affairs involving other groups. Women on their marriage retain most of their rights and duties as members of their descent groups; alienation from the group is slight and is probably an important factor in the high divorce rate among the Yoruba.

Descent groups tend to be segmented into from two to five divisions; the founders of each segment are usually described in the greatly foreshortened genealogies as the sons of the founder of the whole group by his several wives. The town and farm land held by the group is not often apportioned strictly between segments so that each has a territorially defined area. (Land shortage or the alienation of land by modern commercial methods does, however, sometimes lead to a partition equally between segments.) The segmentation of the group is seen most clearly in the selection of the titled chief. All members of the descent group are eligible for the title. To ensure that the honour is not monopolized by any one segment, it is ruled that a son can never directly succeed his own father and that the title, furthermore, should be held by a member of each segment in turn. In the contest for the office, vacated by the death of the previous holder, one can frequently detect a readjustment of segments – the larger ones splitting into two, while smaller ones amalgamate – so that the size of each is equivalent. This process illustrates vividly the egalitarian character of the Yoruba descent group in which, within limits imposed by sex and age, all members have equal rights to the group's land and titled office.

This last statement should be modified inasmuch as many descent groups contain segments whose members trace descent from a female member of the group – perhaps a sister or daughter of the founder. The existence of such a segment often becomes apparent (to the fieldworker) at the time of a succession dispute when its members are seen to be regarded as either ineligible or weak candidates for the chieftaincy title. However, ultimate absorption of such segments into the descent groups seems probable through a slow readjustment of genealogies by which the female links disappear from memory. This process demonstrates furthermore the manner in which a more powerful

E   37

and prestigious descent group can draw members away from a weaker group.

Conflict between descent groups

The individual descent groups comprising the Yoruba town continually rival one another for two forms of scarce resources – land and political power. Negatively, every group fears that failure in this contest will lead, through the inability of the members of the group to attract wives and through the defection of members to their mothers' groups, to the diminution of the group's size, to its further weakness in bargaining, and ultimately to its extinction.[1]

Let us briefly examine this rivalry for scarce resources.

Interests in land

Almost all land in the Yoruba town and surrounding farming area is allocated to one or other of the constituent descent groups; a certain proportion is held to be public land (Lloyd, 1962). Over its own area the members of the descent group corporately exercise such rights to use and to alienate the land as amount to ownership. Individual members of the group have a general right to as much land as they can cultivate, and a specific right to undisturbed use of that land allocated to them; each member participates in the management of the whole area.

However, descent groups expand in numbers at uneven rates through the unequal incidence of disease, the attraction of strangers and maternally related persons, and the success of members in acquiring wives. With the relatively high density of population that exists, individual descent groups frequently grow short of land. Their members have no claim on the land of any other than their own group save in the less favourable status of customary tenants whereby they may gain only a permanent right to use a specific area. It is therefore usual that the members of descent groups short of land spill over on to the unused land of territorially adjacent groups. This gives rise to a boundary dispute in which the senior members of each group, acting on behalf of the group, endeavour to prove that rights tantamount to ownership have been earlier exercised by members of their own group over the disputed land. They may claim too that it is common knowledge that certain landmarks constituted the boundary between the two groups.

The dispute between the two groups eventually comes before the council of chiefs for adjudication. The chiefs' task in such an instance is to elucidate certain disputed facts. The result of their deliberations depends to a large extent on the skill of the parties in formally presenting their case and in the informal influence which they may exert over the adjudicating chiefs. The judgement of the chiefs might grant the land to the trespassing group, confirm their occupation of it but as customary tenants, or order that the trespassers quit the disputed land.

Political power

The council of chiefs sits daily in the palace of the *oba* in a legislative, administrative, and judicial capacity. (In the past the *oba* did not sit with the chiefs, but remained in the inner courtyard of his palace, here to be informed of decisions reached by the chiefs.) Issues tend to be dealt with as they arise; neither the composition of the council nor its time or place of meeting is affected by the nature of the issue for discussion. In a small town each descent group is represented on the chiefs' council by one of its own members selected to hold titled office. In theory each descent group in the town is of equal status – each holds identical rights to land and office, though some groups have greater prestige (resulting in part from their larger areas of land, etc.) than others. But the chieftaincy titles are graded and ranked. This ranking determines, on most occasions, the order of seating in the council. It also determines the order of speaking – the most junior chiefs speak first and the most senior, acting as chairman, sums up the discussion and gives a decision which he interprets as being the sense of the meeting.

In such a situation it is important for a descent group to be represented by a man who can speak with sufficient ability in defence of the interests of his co-members to convince the other chiefs. The need to have an able chief is often incompatible with the rotation of the title through the segments and leads to segments holding the title out of turn and to confusion as to the correct order when the title next becomes vacant.

The ranking of the chiefs furthermore gives advantages to

the descent groups holding the most senior titles, for these chiefs are much better able to manipulate the course of discussion and the ultimate decisions than are the junior chiefs. Hence every descent group aspires to advance the rank of its own title. This is, of course, much easier to wish for than to achieve. When the chiefs sit daily in order of seniority, it is impossible to make a sudden claim that the ranking should be different. Yet the ranking is not immutable. It is believed to have been created by the past *obas*, who gave the chieftaincy titles to their original holders; and hence the *oba* may change the ranking. For the reasons elaborated below, such an action by the *oba* would be impossible save in the event of a serious split, amounting to civil war, occurring among the chiefs. Thus a rebellion in which the chiefs are aligned with and against the *oba* provides the principal opportunity for enhancing the political power of one's descent group through a re-ranking of the chieftaincy titles.[2]

Individual rights

A man holds land as a member of a descent group; his interests in all the public affairs of his community are represented through the titled chief of his group. Almost all of his actions involving members of other descent groups are considered to be the affair of his own group. Proposed marriages are discussed at a descent-group meeting, which is concerned not only to maintain the rules of exogamy but also to assess the general suitability of the match; the bridewealth paid by the fiancé is distributed widely among the members of the girl's descent group. Again, a debtor is responsible for his own debts; but in default the creditor sends his agent to distrain upon the goods of any member of the debtor's compound. Cases of homicide are referred directly to the *oba* and chiefs within whose council lies the power to punish the offender; the descent group of the killed man has no right to seek redress or compensation. However, in most other disputes involving the members of two descent groups the issue will first be discussed within the descent groups, then the heads of the groups will attempt an arbitration, and only if this fails will the matter be brought before the chiefs in council, the chiefs and elders of the groups concerned acting as spokesmen and witnesses for their own members.[3]

As Gough writes of the Ashanti, it is in such societies that the descent group achieves the 'height of collective legal responsibility and its strongest structure of authority' (Schneider & Gough, 1961, p. 506). The importance of being well represented in the council of chiefs is even further emphasized.

Thus one finds that a large number of interests held by the individual are represented through his descent group. In many cases, such as interests relating to land, these become the corporate interest of the whole group. Second, disputes which initially involve only one member of a descent group become the concern of the whole group. A trivial incident can thus affect the relationships between all members of the several groups involved, creating considerable bitterness between them. Conversely, the tension created serves to intensify the cohesion within each descent group.

In emphasizing the status of the individual within his own descent group, one must not overlook those relationships with members of other groups which may serve to ameliorate tensions. Maternal and affinal relationships cut across descent-group divisions. Yet in the Yoruba context it does not appear that a man who is a member of one descent group which is party to a dispute, and maternally or affinally related to the other, acts as a mediator; in fact his role tends to be a negative rather than a positive one. Again, members of an age-set do not mediate in disputes involving their respective descent groups. (An individual may, however, seek the support of other members of his age-set in his dispute with the elders of his own descent group.) Inasmuch as the descent groups are exogamous and as marriages tend to be between persons of the same town and as age-grouping is always organized within the town, relationships deriving from these associations do enhance the cohesion of the town. However, they do not materially affect our general proposition that, in the type of Yoruba town under discussion, most of an individual's interests are represented through his descent group and that conflicts are resolved through the mediation of the elders of the groups involved and ultimately in the council of chiefs.

The resolution of conflict
Politics in the Yoruba town consists in large measure of the settlement of conflicts between descent groups. As indicated

41

above, these are resolved in the council of chiefs meeting within the palace.

In discussion of the merits of each case, chiefs will tend to align themselves with those parties whose interests seem similar to those of their own descent groups. But there will be links between descent groups of an historical character; other alliances may occur between descent groups produced by fission of one from the other, between groups tracing an origin in the same kingdom or town, or between groups claiming a type of patron-client relationship (the founder of the client group having lodged perhaps with the patron group upon his arrival in the town and been supported by the latter in his request for land and independent status). Lastly, chiefs may have old scores to settle against one or other of the disputants; in a council where the issues discussed are so varied and so numerous, the degree of bargaining is intense. In the final decision, descent groups represented by chiefs of dominant personality or high-ranking chiefs have undoubted advantages; again, the latter groups always tend to be among the largest in the town and their very size lends weight to their claims.

Descent groups are occasionally portrayed as static units in society. Yet not only are they continually growing or declining in size through natural factors, but, as a result of continual conflicts, the more powerful ones are aggrandizing themselves at the expense of the weaker. But as the segments of the larger groups come to equal in size many of the smaller groups, their members seek the attributes of independent status – a chieftaincy title, for instance – and secede from their parent group. This process of fission among the larger groups, accompanied by the extinction of smaller ones, tends, over the decades, to preserve the structure of the town as an amalgam of descent groups.

In these attempts to resolve conflicts, the traditional practice of the Yoruba chiefs is to achieve unanimity in their discussions; the most senior chief sums up the arguments presented and announces a decision in which all members of the council can acquiesce. This search for unanimity, rather than a reliance upon a majority vote, seems, perhaps, to be somewhat unnecessary. In each dispute the chiefs are aligned in different factions; one descent group is not in the minority camp on many successive occasions. Nor in the Yoruba town does one find the descent groups segregated into permanent rival blocks. Why, in these circumstances should the losing party to a dispute so fear its minority status? The answer seems to lie in the fact that a conflict over one issue involves all other relationships between members of contesting groups. The losing group fears that its defeat (suggesting perhaps that its members subscribe to different values from other people) will lead to further exploitation by rival groups and victimization by the chiefs. The majority faction are equally anxious lest the minority descent groups, in a state of pique, emigrate from the town, thus severely weakening it. Since, as we have already seen, the unity of the town is fragile, this is a serious threat. The only force by which the chiefs can compel obedience to their decisions lies in the policiary army provided by the age-grades; members of descent groups dissatisfied with a decision would probably refuse to obey the chiefs' demand for punitive action, taking up arms instead in support of their own groups and thus precipitating a civil war. Thus it is no accident that a large part of the time in the hearing of any dispute is taken up with the attempt to gain the support of the losing party for the decision of the chiefs.[4]

A dispute ends with the losing party and its followers and supporters begging for forgiveness from the victor or from the council of chiefs. Once sought, the forgiveness must be granted, for refusal would denote a desire to perpetuate the dispute and thus constitute a reprehensive act.[5] A man, on the other hand, who cannot seek forgiveness no longer merits the support of the members of his society.[6]

A unanimous decision of the chiefs in fact only masks the conflict between descent groups. Furthermore, it places individual chiefs in invidious positions since they are expected by the council of chiefs to uphold decisions which run counter to the interests of their own descent groups. The incompatibility of roles expected of each chief by his fellow chiefs in the council and by the member of his descent group is most difficult to resolve. If the chief quits the council his descent group loses its representation and is in a worse position than before; for the descent-group members to remove their chief is, since these men are expected to hold office for life, an aspersion on the unity of the group which would bring it into disrepute in the town.

The problem in such a political system seems to lie in finding a method whereby the chiefs (representing the mass of the people) make the decisions but where the responsibility for these decisions does not lie with them as individuals. Two methods are practised by the Yoruba – the *ogboni* association and sacred kingship; they are not mutually exclusive and are, in fact, found in conjunction in many Yoruba kingdoms (though not in those of Ekiti which have only sacred kingship).

In the *ogboni* association the most senior chiefs, the *iwarefa*, do not directly represent their descent groups; they have risen through the hierarchy of grades by reason of their personality and wealth. Nevertheless, in aspiring to higher grades men are supported by their kin; no single descent group, however, would be allowed to monopolize the senior offices. In this situation, the role incompatibility experienced by the chiefs, as outlined above, is muted. More important is that meetings of the *ogboni* are secret and highly ritualized. The *ogboni* is associated with the earth cult (Morton-Williams, 1960). The holders of *iwarefa* titles are known only to *ogboni* members, and acts of the *iwarefa* are not divulged to non-members. Thus, to cite an extreme example, a man can condemn to death a member of his own descent group, secure in the knowledge that loyalty to the *ogboni* transcends that to his descent group and that members of the group will either be ignorant of his role in the decision or will not dare challenge him for it. The *ogboni* association thus provides the chief with an extra-descent-group status which protects and enhances the authority of his decisions.

The second method of solving the problem lies in sacred kingship. By the rituals of his succession the king is consecrated; he is all-wise and can do no wrong. His curse is more powerful than that of any other man. The decisions of the council of chiefs are ordained by him in his own name. He thus stands at the apex of the legislative, administrative, and judicial systems. Yet it is as a mediator that the Yoruba conceive their king: 'without the *oba* there could be no town' – for the conflicts between the descent groups would never be mediated; continuing tension would result in descent groups leaving the town, perhaps settling on their farmland. Settlements would become dispersed and the town cease to exist.

Yet having invested their sacred king with so much power,

the chiefs fear that he will override their own political rights. Thus derives the conflict[7] between the *oba* and the council of chiefs which we must now consider.

The conflict between the oba and the chiefs
The sacred king. The members of the royal lineage trace their descent, patrilineally, from the first ruler of the dynasty, described as the founder of the town. The royal lineage is not powerful. Its members are debarred from holding offices in the governing council of chiefs; the royal descent group holds its own land but has no rights over any vast areas of unused land within the frontiers of the kingdom. The rapid increase in size of the group resulting from the large royal harem is balanced by losses occasioned by the exile of losing contestants for the throne and their posting to subordinate settlements in the kingdom, by the absorption of members into matrilaterally related descent groups, and by the fission of segments descended from early kings to become independent descent groups no longer considered royal.

To be eligible for the throne a man should be born to a reigning ruler by a free-born wife. The title rotates between the segments of the royal lineage. Eligible candidates are notified to the council of chiefs, which, after consulting the *ifa* oracle, makes the choice and sets in train the accession ceremonies.

There is almost invariably a contest for the throne between candidates of two or more segments of the royal lineage and of lesser segments within the major ones.[8] One may wonder why such conflicts involve so many members of the royal lineage who will derive so little from the success of their own candidate. In fact, membership of a segment of the royal lineage through which the kingship rotates does confer prestige, if not political power. Should a segment fail to secure the election of one of its own eligible members before death overtakes them, their right to the throne becomes defunct; and while their prestige wanes they do not gain the political power associated with commoner descent groups. The rival candidates for the throne are variously supported by the members of the council of chiefs, who see in the contest only another aspect of their own rivalry. Each hopes that his support for the successful candidate will be rewarded by later favours. These two aspects of the contest for the throne

must be distinguished. Canvassing by the supporters of the
rival candidates is surreptitious; no appeal is made to the mass
of the people, who believe that the choice properly lies with
their chiefs. The candidates do not present themselves as pro-
ponents of different interpretations of the *oba*'s role – the
'traditional' norms of kingship are stressed. Nor are arguments
canvassed about the relative ability or probity of the rivals.
However, the *ifa* oracle does predict in terms of the success
and prosperity of the reign of each candidate should he be
selected to accede. The contest is fought largely in terms either
of the eligibility of the candidates – (e.g. their birth to a reigning *oba* by a free-born wife) or of the rotation of the title between the segments (a certain segment perhaps being described
as a branch of another segment and not one of the major
divisions of the royal lineage). To support its claims, each party
produces its version of the genealogy of the royal lineage; to a
large extent the decision of the council of chiefs rests on their
interpretation of this factual evidence.[9]

The most important of the installation ceremonies is the
eating of the excised heart of the predecessor. The new ruler
not only acquires all the accumulated spiritual power of his
predecessors but also gains strength to withstand, and to use
to his own advantage, the magical powers immanent in the
royal regalia. The sacred king resides in the palace, hidden from
public gaze save on three ceremonial occasions during the year.
Various taboos – for instance he must not be seen eating –
differentiate the king from other men.

The king stands above the conflicts between descent groups.
The town's legends relate that the indigenes of the area (often
described as a single descent group or a band of hunters) invited
the royal migrant to rule over them – he gained the throne not
through conquest but by virtue of his royal descent. Installation
ceremonies demonstrate the reluctance of the chosen candidate
to assume office (rather belying the contest for office just ended).
The sons of *oba*s were not allowed to live in the palace but were
sent to the farm; even today they tend to be among the less
conspicuous members of the town and are not therefore identified with the major disputes in the community. The new ruler
is divorced from contact with his kin; they may not visit him
frequently. All the wealth of the throne passes to succeeding

rulers, never to the issue or kin of a king. Paralleling this alienation from the royal lineage is the emphasis placed on the relationship between the king and each of the other descent groups of his town. Members of each descent group have specific parts to play in the accession and burial ceremonies of the *oba*. Elders of descent groups tell with pride of marriages of their own daughters with kings of the distant past – especially when such daughters bore later rulers; most other marriages of such antiquity are long forgotten. The bonds which link each descent group to the king seem much stronger than those between descent groups.

The wealth of the *oba* symbolizes the prosperity of the town. Of all gifts, tribute, or war booty received by the chiefs, half is given to the *oba* so that his wealth approximates, in theory, to the sum of that of his chiefs. Furthermore, the wealth of the *oba* passes intact to his successor in office, while that of chiefs is distributed according to the normal rules of inheritance among their kin. The income of the *oba* is consumed in maintaining his family and the palace retinue, in providing sacrifices, in generosity to the poor and needy, in gifts to visitors and favoured individuals. An astute *oba* can both create an impression of munificence and increase the capital wealth of his office.

The *oba* is the ritual head of the town. He receives, on behalf of his people, the blessings of such deities as hill spirits, later communicating these, at other ceremonies, to his people. At the worship of the deities of individual descent groups he will, where the role of the deity is considered to involve the whole town, contribute certain sacrifices.

The role of the oba. Much as they may, as individuals, stand in awe of the kingship, the council of chiefs see in the reigning ruler a man selected by themselves. (In addition the *oba* had been trained in the art of government by his chiefs during a three-month period of seclusion forming part of the accession ceremonies.) They believe that decision-making rests with them and that their findings, being communicated to the king, will be announced by him as his own. The effectiveness of this arrangement rests on maximizing the spiritual power of the king – stressing his infallibility and the terrible nature of the royal curse. To counter this, the power of the *oba* to act by force is limited. He has no control over the army, recruited from among all adult men, save through his chiefs. His establishment of palace servants is small – though not negligible. He cannot easily seek support from his own royal descent group.

The respective powers of the council of chiefs and of the *oba* are thus complementary. But while the chiefs are unable to acquire any of the mystic aura of the kingship, a reigning *oba* may seek a much more active role in the decision-making process. To some extent the image held by the *oba* of his own role in the political process will be that transmitted throughout the society by the chiefs. A senile *oba* may well be content to rest within the palace making little effort to influence his chiefs. But most Yoruba kings seem to have been men of a more dominant personality – this would seem to be the inference from the contests for succession. The chiefs too, while anxious to choose a candidate who, as king, will accept their decisions, are in general not keen to select a nonentity – they rely on their ruler being able to coerce them towards agreement in their most divisive conflicts. Again, one of the most favourable predictions given by the *ifa* oracle is that the cited candidate will, if selected, enjoy a long reign; the new ruler may thus be considerably younger than his chiefs.

The aspirations of the *oba* may be satisfied with the exercise of considerable personal influence over his chiefs – but this depends on his possession of a personal charisma in addition to the power inherent in his office. Effective control of the affairs of the town may, to the incumbent ruler, seem to lie through greater control over appointments to titled office and over the finances of the town. If he is to oppose the council of chiefs and to rule independently of them he must needs build up a body of supporters and an administrative cadre responsible to him.

The initial goals of the new ruler may have been relatively limited in scope. But many rulers discovered that events external to the political process within their own kingdoms, obliged them to redefine their roles. Changing technology – the introduction of the horse or of firearms, the expansion of foreign trade – and success or defeat in war, render existing roles obsolescent. New problems face the *oba* and chiefs – the administration of conquered territory, the reorganization of the army. The actions of both *oba* and chiefs will depend on their perception of the situation, on the evaluation of the new opportunities open to them. Although *oba*, chiefs, and people will all share in a prosperity won for their town, the *oba* is perhaps in a better position to advocate a more forward-looking policy, for he is not impeded by the need to win the agreement of men of equal rank. To this extent he will be stealing the initiative from his chiefs, and, perhaps, pursuing policies contrary to their own.

The role expected of their *oba* by the chiefs is an idealized one – a role impossible to a human occupant of the position. Yet their expectations constitute a yardstick by which to measure his activities. Every move to increase the power of the throne will be countered by the council of chiefs. Some subtlety on the part of the *oba* is necessary for success, since he cannot directly proclaim as his goal the strengthening of the royal power. In the following paragraphs I shall outline, first, the possible strategies open to the ambitious *oba* and their chances of success; and, second, the tactics by which *oba* and chiefs pursue their conflicts of interest.[10]

The strategy of the oba. The *oba* is secluded in his palace, isolated from personal friends and followers, dependent on his chiefs for an income, and lacks control of an armed force. Any increase in power depends on overcoming these deficiencies. Yet, short of revolutionary circumstances, the opportunities of the *oba* seem very limited.

Any attempt of the *oba* to increase the power of the royal lineage and to enlist their support would be at once resisted by the chiefs. No ambiguity seems to exist about the weak status of the royal lineage. The rotation of the kingship between the segments of the royal lineage prevents the accumulation of power in any one of them and ensures a rivalry between them that inhibits common action. The rule that a king's eldest son may never reign forestalls somewhat the hope of an *oba* that his policies may one day be continued by the son most closely associated with him in office.

The *oba* is unlikely to win the personal support of immigrants to his town. Individual men will lodge with friends in the compounds of the town, and their descendants will probably be absorbed into these descent groups. Large groups of kinsmen will perhaps constitute separate descent groups, one day to win a title enabling a member to sit on the council of chiefs. Only a very massive influx of migrants is likely to disturb the structure of the town.

Military success increases the number of domestic slaves held by the individual warriors who captured them, by the chiefs, and by the *oba*. Of those held by the *oba* many are needed to farm to supply the needs of the palace residents and to perform menial tasks; but the remainder may be organized as messengers or as a personal cadre of advisers. A series of successful wars enables the *oba* to build up a palace retinue far larger than that held by any of his chiefs; furthermore, this retinue passes intact to his successor – whereas that of the chiefs is distributed on their death among their kin.

Traders almost always live in the compounds of their own descent group and their loyalties are to these groups. They do not form a special class from whom the *oba* can seek support. Yet increased trading activity can yield new forms of income – tolls at frontiers and markets, monopolies of certain commodities – which need not be controlled by the chiefs. So an *oba* may increase his wealth without a commensurate increase in that of his chiefs; this he cannot achieve through the normal taxation of the masses which is collected by the chiefs.

Thus under normal circumstances there seem to be few means by which the *oba* can increase his power. He may gain temporary advantages through the tactical exploitation of dissension among his chiefs; this method becomes of even greater importance, of course, in the manipulation of new situations and opportunities.

The tactical struggle. The council of chiefs endeavours to limit the extension of the power of their *oba*. If the council is united and if the *oba* has, as yet, little or no force at his command, it is in a strong position to coerce the *oba* into submission. Against a recalcitrant *oba* the chiefs can impose the sanctions of non-cooperation and dismissal. They may boycott the palace, thus cutting the *oba* off from income in gifts and tribute usually channelled though the chiefs. Government creaks to a standstill – but few issues are so urgent that they cannot be left for several weeks. The chiefs may boycott the major religious ceremonies of the town; the failure to perform these will, it is believed, harm the town; but the purpose of the action is to mobilize public opinion against the *oba*. If he continues to oppose his chiefs they will demand that he die, thus vacating the throne for a new incumbent whom the chiefs will select as more tractable. In contrast, the *oba* has no similar sanctions to employ against his chiefs. He cannot dismiss them all from office. He may refuse to perform rituals, but only at the risk of the most severe sanctions being employed against him. If he refuses to take his own life upon request, the chiefs and people will, with force, destroy his palace and kill him. He has no like means of retaliation.

But, as the first part of this paper has shown, the chiefs (and their descent groups) are continually in conflict with one another. The skilful *oba* manipulates these conflicts to his own ends. Considerable astuteness is necessary as the 'good *oba*' is one who settles disputes – the 'bad *oba*' is unable to resolve them; the amount of dissension in the town is an index of the *oba*'s success in fulfilling the role expected by his chiefs and people.

The *oba* must first have a good intelligence service. Unable to leave the palace himself, he relies on his palace retinue to provide him with the gossip of the town, and an assessment of the loyalties and allegiances within the council of chiefs. His messengers can be equally active in fermenting intrigue. To those chiefs who support his privately held opinions, he can promise reward – support in a land dispute or a favourable judicial decision, the expectation of a more highly ranked chieftaincy title. Similarly, those who oppose him may, if the majority of the chiefs concur, be punished – a chief may be banned from the palace for a period (and hence from effective participation in the council of chiefs); or the *oba* may delay in installing a chief selected by the descent group, claiming that the selection did not follow the traditional procedures.

If the *oba* has the support of a majority among his chiefs, the minority will quickly come to terms with him. The reasons have been given earlier. The minority fears that it will be further victimized and may consider emigration though this will involve some hardship; the majority seek to avoid the latter course and the loss which it will cause the town to suffer.

51

Even when the *oba* is assured of the support of only a minority among his chiefs, his position is far from hopeless, for the majority is unlikely to be strongly united. Within the latter faction fears will be expressed that the ring-leaders will claim all the benefits of a successful revolt for their own descent groups; the lesser conspirators may suddenly change sides, seduced by the *oba* with promises of greater rewards should they support him than if they successfully oppose him. The chiefs need to be experts in the art of 'brinkmanship'. A successful struggle against an *oba* results in his death, his replacement by a successor committed to upholding the traditional norms, the maintenance of the *status quo ante* save for the punishment of those (few) chiefs who remained loyal to the *oba* until the end. It is the unsuccessful attempts at dethronement which allow the *oba* most freedom in redistributing rewards to those who were most loyal to him.

In the context of the Yoruba political system analysed in this model, it is difficult for the chiefs to see each issue as one involving a conflict for power between the *oba* and themselves; instead of pursuing common goals, they each seek to further the interests of their own descent groups. For his part, the *oba* may obscure the fact that a majority of the chiefs are opposed to him, by portraying the current dispute as one between two groups of rival chiefs which he is endeavouring to mediate.[11] In thus rising above the conflict, the *oba* can seek the approval of the mass of the people, and thus counter the opposition which his chiefs may be fomenting within their own descent groups.

Thus even when the *oba* has no control of force independent of his chiefs and when his personal supporters are few in number, the extent to which he can influence policy and judicial decision through manipulating the conflicts between his chiefs remains considerable. The ultimate sanction to be applied against him – that of deposition – is rarely used by the chiefs. Not only is it difficult for them to achieve sufficient unity to make such a demand, but a division between the chiefs would probably be opened wider as they supported rival candidates for the throne and the long interregnum threatened to paralyse political and ritual activity in the town. In the second place, the consecration of the king is his defence; by virtue of the rituals performed his rule is wise, his decisions are good. It is no mean task for the chiefs to overcome such popular assumptions.[12]

In the series of tactical moves discussed above, the *oba* probably has a further advantage. To the extent that the chiefs accuse him of deviating from the role which they expect, they will apply the recognized sanctions and their probable moves are known in advance by the *oba*. While the *oba* is endeavouring to reinterpret his role and to take advantage of the changing environment, his own moves will not follow oft-recurrent patterns; the chiefs will be taken unawares and their initial responses will thus tend to be confused and lacking in coordination.

CONFLICT AND SOCIAL CHANGE

In this paper I have approached the political process of one type of Yoruba kingdom from a particular point of view – that of stressing conflicts of interest between individuals and groups. In the Yoruba example, I have described two different patterns of conflict – that between the descent groups and that between the council of chiefs and the sacred king. Is it possible to indicate the types of change wrought in the social and political structure by these conflicts? We cannot indicate specific changes for these depend too heavily on a particular series of historical events, on factors impinging on the kingdoms from without, on the roles played by key individuals. But in very general terms, it is possible, I believe, to indicate the effect of the conflicts on structural developments.

The conflict between descent groups
The rival descent groups each have interests of identical character – land, political power, etc. In contesting for the 'scarce resources' allocated by the community, they are emphasizing their membership of it. In stressing the same values in support of their own claims, they proclaim their own support for these values and in addition reiterate their importance to the benefit of non-participants in the contest. It is not difficult to predict in advance the moves made by each of the rival descent groups; the ultimate arbitration procedure by the council of chiefs is understood and accepted by all. In these circumstances one may stress the function of conflict in maintaining the cohesion of the community.

In very many disputes the ultimate arbitration restores the *status quo ante* – the trespassers are ordered, for example, to quit the land. In these situations one could perhaps use the image of the see-saw and refer to the restoration of equilibrium. In some situations, however, the more powerful descent groups succeed in aggrandizing themselves at the expense of the weaker. Yet, as they grow, they become more liable to internal division, with their constituent segments becoming independent descent groups. Thus the structural pattern of the society remains constant, though the membership of the units is continually changing. Again, to the extent that each party to a dispute stressed slightly different values in supporting its claims, those values of the successful party will tend to rank above those of the losers, and the total pattern of values held in the society may slowly alter.

Short of substantial external factors, however, the conflict between descent groups seems unlikely to produce major structural changes in the society. In fact, the recurrent disputes tend to intensify cohesion within the descent groups and maintain the social boundaries between them, reducing the force of cross-cutting relationships and thus perpetuating the system we have described – one in which there is a continual conflict of interest between the descent groups, punctuated by a never-ending series of disputes, the settlement of which does not remove the underlying conflict.

The conflict between oba *and chiefs*

The conflict between *oba* and chiefs has the character of the non-zero-sum game – the range of possible outcomes is extremely wide. One can but crudely outline some of the directions of change which seem probable.

At one end of the scale is the situation where the attempts by the *oba* to exceed his powers (as defined by the chiefs) are successfully resisted by the council of chiefs. Here again we have the 'see-saw' restoration of equilibrium. Other disputes between *oba* and chiefs may result in a compromise which leaves the *oba* in a stronger position than before – strength here being indicated by the greater control possessed by the *oba* over the appointment of his chiefs or over the finances of the kingdom: he may institute, for instance, a new grade of chiefs appointed by himself and not by the descent groups; he may develop the palace slaves into cadres, usurping the administrative roles of the chiefs.[13] A less substantial victory for the *oba* may, however, result only in a re-ranking of chiefs (or reallocation of titles between rival descent groups), thus maintaining the existing political structure and, ultimately, the conflicts inherent in it. Each victory of the *oba* over his chiefs strengthens his position in succeeding disputes with them; ultimately this leads to a weakening of the political representation of the descent group and the preservation of individual rights being more effectively achieved through systems of patronage than through the descent group. Conversely, however, an intensification of the conflict with the *oba* promotes the cohesion of the descent group, since, on the one hand, lesser issues are dropped in favour of the more important struggle, and, on the other hand, the rivalry between the groups intensifies as each seeks to turn the pattern of events to its own advantage.

In these contests the chiefs continually reiterate the traditional role of the *oba* as conceived by them. The *oba* endeavours to reinterpret these roles in the light of his own goals. His isolation from his people and the infallibility credited to him enable him to adopt, if he so wishes, a far more flexible position than can his chiefs. Or, in other words, he is better placed to exploit a changing environment to his own advantage than are his chiefs. It could be argued further that technological changes in the society render the material substructure of society incompatible with the pattern of social relationships – i.e. that contradictions exist in the social system. The king finds that the role expected by his chiefs is quite unrealistic and endeavours to reinterpret it. The chiefs, with interests in maintaining the existing political structure, have to cope with technological changes that are dysfunctional to it.

These patterns of change are illustrated in what little we know of this history of Yoruba kingdoms over past centuries. Most of the kingdoms have remained small in size and the relationship between *oba* and chiefs has tended to conform to the model outlined above. In some kingdoms which suddenly grew large with an influx of immigrants in the early nineteenth century, the problems of governing the larger communities have been met by a variety of forms of federation; in these, the traditional patterns of relationship between *oba* and chief have again been maintained. In Ijebu and Ondo, however, we see a political structure markedly different from that described in the model used above; each kingdom has associations of chiefs who are appointed and promoted, ultimately, by the *oba*. This pattern resembles that of Benin (and of my second model in the earlier paper (1965)); it may derive from Benin, for these two kingdoms have had close links with Benin and their ruling dynasties may have originated in the latter kingdom.[14]

Oyo, alone among Yoruba kingdoms, developed into a great empire. Aided by the possession of the horse (and thus of an armed cavalry), it dominated the trade route from the River Niger to the coast. Its imperial expansion seems to have taken place in the seventeenth and early eighteenth centuries. During the same period, perhaps, the palace slaves (*ilari*) were developed into a cadre which administered conquered territories. However, the process of building up the power of the king seems to have become stuck halfway. The political strength of the descent groups and of the council of chiefs does not seem to have much weakened. It is significant that the new cadres organized within the palace were of slaves, and that free-born Oyo were not detached from loyalty to their descent groups. The specialized armed cavalry force, the *eso*, seems to have remained largely under the control of the chiefs. The history of this period tells of frequent deposition of rulers with a succession of strong kings and dominant senior chiefs. It would seem to be the intensity of this conflict, which produced clear victories for neither side, that led, at the end of the eighteenth century, to the civil wars that (abetted by Fulani intervention) resulted in the collapse of the empire. The history of Oyo would thus seem an admirable example with which to assess the manner in which conflict within the political system leads to its changes; whether, from the oral evidence still available, the appropriate data could be salvaged is, however, problematical.

CONCLUSIONS

In presenting this model of a Yoruba kingdom, I have tried to demonstrate the manner in which the study of conflicts of interest may provide explanations of the process of change in the political structure. This approach focuses attention upon factors that have been ignored or understressed in recent literature on African political systems. Here the emphasis has been on the integration of kingdoms, on their stability. This bias is in a sense justified by the way in which in some kingdoms even repeated rebellions do not lead to any radical changes in political structure. The use of equilibrium models seems adequate to describe the processes taking place. Yet the analogies of the human body or of the see-saw are misleading; the *status quo ante* can never be fully restored; for at the very least, each series of events creates new precedents which will influence future events.

The discussion of the conflict between descent groups parallels in many respects that of 'segmentary opposition' – the balanced opposition of segments within a lineage. But here again the emphasis is shifted. Instead of stressing the balance between segments and the processes which maintain it, the 'conflict' approach examines the rivalry of the groups, the potentiality for their aggrandizement or extinction, the role of the mediator in the conflict.

The introduction of a mediator raises the issue of the distribution of power between him and the heads of the descent groups. The mediator may seek to extend his power at the expense of the descent-group leaders. Where the mediator is a sacred king the potentiality for severe conflict is considerable. I would suspect that in most African kingdoms the distinction of power has been an important issue in rebellions or civil wars. This issue must, however, be clearly distinguished from another – the rivalry or competition for office which does not question the degree of power attributed to the office. This factor too is probably an element in most rebellions. In the Yoruba kingdoms it seems to be a minor factor. In other kingdoms in which political power is wielded by a closed aristocracy – the third model in my earlier paper (Lloyd, 1965) and exemplified by the Hausa-Fulani emirates – competition between the rival royal houses, the segments of the ruling descent group, seems to be the dominant factor. (One might perhaps argue that the issue here is the distribution of power between the segments. But this relationship more closely resembles the rivalry between Yoruba descent groups; it is clearly different from the relationship between the ruler, the ruled, and their representatives.) It is most necessary that we should distinguish between competition for office and the conflicts arising over the distribution of power between offices. Each may lead to tension and to fighting. In the actual events the issues may be obscured; the most effective charges against a ruler are cruelty or tyranny; rival royal houses offer to provide a more acceptable substitute; few men remain to argue the case of the deposed king. In situations of change, African kingdoms have not produced theorists who neatly analyse the processes taking place. Equilibrium models as used by social anthropologists tend to emphasize competition for office at the expense of a study of the distribution of power within the structure. Conflict theory tends, to an equally exaggerated degree, to stress the latter.

NOTES

1. In one Ekiti town an informant claimed membership of a certain descent group, describing where the compound and farmland of this group once lay; the members of the group currently exercising rights over the land asserted that the name cited by the first informant as that of a descent group and compound referred in fact only to a geographical locality and not to any social group.

2. In Oyo, the title of *bashorun*, the most senior of the chiefs, has been held by four descent groups in recent centuries (Johnson, 1921, pp. 70-72). In other kingdoms too, the oral histories tell of titles lapsing after a civil war and later being bestowed on other groups.

3. In customary courts today, the bench of chiefs will usually ask the parties to a divorce suit or land dispute if they have referred the matter to their chiefs and elders; if they have not done so the court will adjourn the case for arbitration to be attempted.

4. In cases heard today in the customary courts, the chiefs sitting on the bench will, as soon as the facts of the issue are clear to them, put a series of rhetorical questions about the relevant norms of behaviour to the wrongdoer so that he convicts himself with his own words.

5. In the recent dispute in the Action Group between Chief O. Awolowo and Chief S. L. Akintola, it was alleged, in the town gossip, that the latter had begged forgiveness for his various acts of opposition by prostrating himself in the party meeting before Awolowo. The latter had not accepted this gesture and the rumour thus reflected more discredit upon Awolowo than upon his political rival.

6. The origin legends of many descent groups relate that their founder had contested for the throne in his town but had lost to a junior brother. When, on the grounds of his seniority, he had refused to prostrate himself in allegiance to the new ruler, he had been obliged to emigrate.

7. It would seem likely that any society simply structured of strongly corporate groups with similar interests, needs an institutionalized mediator

between groups. But the two solutions found by the Yoruba are not the only possible ones. In fact, other societies stress rather different qualities in their mediator; in some, he is essentially a stranger to the community, thus standing apart from local disputes; in others, his ritual status is stressed though his priesthood brings little material reward. The Yoruba *oba*, however, is seen as the founder of his town; priestly duties are delegated to representatives of the cults; the material rewards of his office are considerable.

8. Each segment puts forward one candidate behind whom it stands in united support: it naturally chooses a man most likely to impress the council of chiefs with his claims. Division within the segment is often the result of a failure to agree on a single candidate – the split then follows genealogical lines.

9. When two or more candidates each suffer from some degree of ineligibility, the final selection will be determined, in part, by the ranking in order of importance of the legal principles involved.

10. In this paper I postulate only such changes in the external environment as are of insufficient magnitude to lead to radical changes in the relationship between *oba* and chiefs. I do this in order to concentrate attention upon the internal processes in the Yoruba town. The political structure of many of the smaller kingdoms has, in fact, undergone little apparent change in the last two centuries. In a later paper I shall analyse the changes which have taken place in certain kingdoms as a result of massive migrations, trading prosperity, and aggressive wars.

11. For inasmuch as ego is faced with conflicting role expectations by two alters, in close relationship with one another, he can demand that they collaborate in devising a role for him which will satisfy both of them.

12. I know of two Yoruba kingdoms in which several *oba*s have been deposed – Shaki and Ikere. In each the present dynasty of rulers traces descent from an immigrant prince or warrior who was given the secular duties of kingship by the incumbent *oba*. The title of the former rulers continues to be held by a member of the descent group; the duties of this title-holder are concerned mainly with the major rituals of the town. The separation of the secular and sacred power thus seems to weaken the position of the *oba*.

13. Cf. the changes wrought in the kingdom of Buganda (Southwold, 1961).

14. In Benin itself, the offices of the *uzama* chiefs, lacking political power in the day-to-day government of the kingdom but retaining a role in the installation of the king, suggest that a political structure of the Yoruba type outlined here existed in the early period of the kingdoms, to be replaced by one in which the king occupied an autocratic position, ruling through associations of palace officials. Such relics of an earlier structure do not seem to be evident in Ijebu or Ondo.

REFERENCES

AJAYI, J. F. ADE & SMITH, R. S. 1964. *Yoruba Warfare in the Nineteenth Century.* London: Cambridge University Press for Institute of African Studies, Ibadan.

BASCOM, W. R. 1942. The Principle of Seniority in the Social Structure of the Yoruba. *Amer. Anthropol.* **44**: 37-46.

—— 1944. The Sociological Role of the Yoruba Cult Group. *Mem. Amer. Anthropol. Assoc.* **63**.

VAN DEN BERGHE, P. L. 1963. Dialectic and Functionalism. *Amer. sociol. Rev.* **28**: 695-705.

COSER, L. 1956. *The Functions of Social Conflict.* Glencoe, Ill.: Free Press; London: Routledge & Kegan Paul.

DAHRENDORF, R. 1959. *Class and Class Conflict in Industrial Society.* London: Routledge & Kegan Paul.

FIRTH, R. 1964. *Essays on Social Organisation and Values.* London: The Athlone Press.

FORDE, DARYLL. 1951. The Yoruba-speaking Peoples of South-western Nigeria. *Ethnographic Survey of Africa, Western Africa, Part IV.* London: International African Institute.

GLUCKMAN, M. 1955. *Custom and Conflict in Africa.* Oxford: Blackwell.

— 1963. *Order and Rebellion in Tribal Africa.* London: Cohen & West.

— 1965. *Politics, Law and Ritual in Tribal Society.* Oxford: Blackwell.

JOHNSON, S. 1921. *The History of the Yorubas.* Lagos: C.M.S. Press.

LEACH, E. R. 1954. *Political Systems of Highland Burma.* London: Bell.

LLOYD, P. C. 1954. The Traditional Political System of the Yoruba. *Southwestern Journal of Anthropology* **10**: 366-384.

— 1955. The Yoruba Lineage. *Africa* **25**: 235-251.

— 1960. Sacred Kingship and Government among the Yoruba. *Africa* **30**: 221-237.

— 1962. *Yoruba Land Law.* London: Oxford University Press for Nigerian Institute of Social and Economic Research, Ibadan.

— 1965. The Political Structure of African Kingdoms. In M. Banton (ed.), *Political Systems and the Distribution of Power.* London: Tavistock Publications.

MAQUET, J. J. 1961. *The Premise of Inequality in Ruanda.* London: Oxford University Press for International African Institute.

MORTON-WILLIAMS, P. 1960. The Yoruba Ogboni Cult in Oyo. *Africa* **30**: 362-374.

PARSONS, T. 1964. A Functional Theory of Change. In Etzioni, A. & Etzioni, E. (eds.), *Social Change,* pp. 83-97. New York: Basic Books.

REX, J. 1961. *Key Problems in Sociological Theory.* London: Routledge & Kegan Paul.

SCHNEIDER, D. M. & GOUGH, K. (eds.) 1961. *Matrilineal Kinship.* Berkeley: University of California Press.

SMELSER, N. 1959. *Social Change in the Industrial Revolution.* London: Routledge & Kegan Paul.

SMITH, M. G. 1960. *Government in Zazzau*. London: Oxford University Press for International African Institute.

SOUTHWOLD, M. 1961. *Bureaucracy and Chieftainship in Buganda*. East African Studies No. 14. East African Institute of Social Research, Kampala, Uganda.

TURNER, V. W. 1957. *Schism and Continuity in an African Society*. Manchester: Manchester University Press.

WEBER, M. 1947. *The Theory of Social and Economic Organisation* (trans. A. R. Henderson and Talcott Parsons), pp. 313-314. London: William Hodge.

Keith Hopkins

Structural Differentiation in Rome
(200-31 B.C.)

The Genesis of an Historical Bureaucratic Society

SOCIAL CHANGE AND SPECIALIZATION

This paper has two purposes: first to analyse major changes in the social structure of Roman society during the later Roman Republic (200-31 B.C.). In this period, rapid expansion through conquest brought about a tremendous influx of wealth and repeated civil wars; finally the oligarchic Republic was replaced by a monarchy supported by a subordinate aristocracy, a professional army, and by an emergent bureaucracy. The second aim is to conceptualize some of these changes in terms of structural differentiation: this is the process by which an institution, previously charged with several overlapping functions, develops in such a way that these functions are taken over by other more specialized institutions. In this sense we can trace in present-day industrializing societies, for example, the emergence of specialized economic institutions and of a formal educational system, whereas previously such economic and educational activities were typically embedded in family organization. The concept of structural differentiation has been used notably by Smelser (1963), and by Eisenstadt (1964) in his analysis of historical bureaucratic societies. My own analysis owes a lot to both, and is, as the subtitle indicates, an attempt to see the changes which took place in Roman society during the Republic in the context of its evolution to a bureaucratic empire after 31 B.C.

CHANGES IN ROMAN SOCIETY, 200-31 B.C.

In 300 B.C. Rome was a city-state with an adult male citizen population of about 250,000 (census 294 B.C.: 262,321). It controlled central Italy through a series of alliances with neighbouring towns, which had varying degrees of autonomy and reciprocal rights in their dealings with Romans. Through a combination of aristocratic competition for honour and military glory, a general desire for booty, and inter-city political manœuvrings, Roman armies plundered, conquered, pacified, governed, and eventually settled the rest of Italy, Sicily, Spain, North Africa, Greece, Eastern Asia Minor, Syria, Gaul, and Egypt. The usual estimate of the total population of the empire at the end of the Republic (31 B.C.) is in the region of 50 million. Of these, about four million would have been citizens, including their wives and children.

The effects of these conquests were pervasive and uneven. The citizen army, for example, up to 107 B.C. consisted in principle of peasant land-holders, who originally served only in the summer fighting season. Increasingly, extended wars against foreign powers necessitated longer service; peasant-soldiers therefore neglected their holdings. But wars and the government of provinces brought wealth to Rome which could safely and prestigiously be invested only in land; at the same time prisoners of war were enslaved and so provided an alternative source of labour to the peasant-soldiers. Moreover, there were alternative occupations for Roman citizens both in the provinces and in the new concentrations of population which grew up at Rome and in Southern Italy, where much of the provincial booty and taxes were consumed. As a result of these processes, peasant land was bought up with war profits, the free peasants were dispossessed, and their land was concentrated into plantations. These plantations were cultivated by slaves and produced new capitalistic crops (e.g. wine and olives) for the growing towns, which themselves consumed and reworked other plunder of empire.

Thus while the duration and distance of wars from Rome increased, the number of peasants from which the army could be recruited diminished. In a particular military crisis towards the end of the second century B.C., soldiers were legally recruited for the first time without regard to property qualifications, even from the urban proletariat. This was the beginning of a professional army, in the sense that soldiering was separated from agricultural labour and was recognized as a full-time (if short-term) occupation. But the short-term service of the Roman army, recruited from an underemployed lower class – whether peasantry or proletariat – was significant. For it marked a transitional stage between the former peasant army and the fully professional army of the early Empire (after 31 B.C.). The fully professional army is tied to a stable relationship to the state by the regularity of its pay, by a career structure and the opportunity of promotion, by the chance of civilian employment on completion of service, possibly bolstered by a pension or bounty. The *assured* regularity of all these elements was missing in this transitional stage, for a Roman army was recruited by each military leader for each campaign (though there was in fact continuity) and pension rights (in the form of land allotment) depended upon political manœuvring between each general and the state. These uncertain expectations were only partly qualified by actual long- or medium-term service by soldiers re-enlisting with successive generals. The unpredictable outcome of these arrangements was one of the main factors in the instability of the army's behaviour during the last century of the Republic.

The Romans themselves associated their conquest of Syria and Asia in the beginning of the second century with a qualitative change in their life-styles. It was then that nobles began to dine off gold and silver and to be sharply differentiated in their life-styles from the proletariat. An occasional old-fashioned aristocrat continued to eat off wooden platters. The provincial revenues, derived from official war-booty and afterwards from taxes, were sufficient to finance other wars and provincial administration. No property taxes were levied in Rome or Italy after 167 B.C. Private profits from war and conquest were probably even greater than the public revenues. Not only victorious generals but also successive governors and public tax-farmers exploited provincials, often mercilessly. The flood of wealth to Rome was initially distributed according to existing status distinctions. Thus the rich became richer, the poor relatively, and in some cases absolutely, poorer.

In the early Republic (before 300 B.C.) the Senate had about 300 members and could easily monopolize nobility even in a relatively powerful Italian city-state. It was impossible for the same number to monopolize the wealth of the Mediterranean basin. Even when the Senate was doubled in size in 81 B.C., there were still very many wealthy men who were not senators. The social and political influence of such men was recognized and institutionalized in the creation (123-122 B.C.) of a second estate, of *equites* or knights, and the money base of their status was affirmed by the requirement of a minimum property quali-fication (HS 400,000).

The same movement which saw the creation of a second privileged estate saw the gradual demotion of the concept of citizenship. Once, as in other city-states, citizenship had been sufficiently a mark of quality to entitle a large proportion of the population to a share in the profits, just as citizens shared the duties of fighting. But as fighting became a specialized occupation, the empire burst the bounds of a city-state, and privilege was more marked by being a *senator* or *eques* and later a town-councillor (*decurion*) than by being a Roman citizen.

This said, it was a matter of relative deprivation. One only has to recall Paul's defence against physical punishment in Judea to see that in the provinces at least Roman citizenship was worth having. Certainly, in the period 125-90 B.C., Italians were eager to share Roman citizenship, and the Roman plebs was adamant in its refusal to grant it. It was afraid of the dilution of its privileges. The Italians eventually forced the issue and won their point after three years of bitter civil war (90-87 B.C.).

If they came to the city of Rome, citizens could exercise the right to vote. This privilege derived partly from the sense of membership typical of the city-state, but mostly from aristo-cratic reliance on the fighting power of the plebs; witness the quasi-military organization of the electoral bodies. The ancient military power of the plebs had been the basis of its power as arbiter between aristocrats competing in the elections to political office. One outcome of the plebs' strategic position was the notorious blandishments of bribery and public entertain-ment given by individual aristocratic patrons to their clients; and free corn doles from the state (public bribery) belong to the same syndrome.

As the rewards of political office and provincial governorship increased, competition between aristocrats for plebeian votes and for political offices was intensified and affected the norms and institutions regulating the pattern of competition. Aristocrats

had always competed; it was the mark of an aristocrat; but
in early Rome the competition for political office had been
generally contained within reasonable bounds; there was clearly
sufficient glory in subordinating individual to collective interest.
Besides, the stakes were relatively low; in the long run a
family's status depended upon electoral victories to consul or
praetor, but losing at any particular time was neither politically
nor socially disastrous. By the later Republic, the whole tempo
of political competition had changed. The influx of wealth
allowed those who had it to spend it as befitted the new aristocrat: in ostentatious consumption, and in largesse to social
inferiors who also acted as the electorate.

Just as the cost of aristocratic stylishness and of elections
increased, so did the political prizes associated with winning.
The profits of provincial governorships, and especially of conquest, formed the basis of many senatorial fortunes. Indeed,
without a fortune one could not be a senator. Wealth was added
to birth as a necessary condition of senatorial status. And this
requirement was later institutionalized in a minimum property
requirement (1 million sesterces). As a corollary to this development, losing an election involved loss of prestige, of social connexion, and of chance of a governorship. For some indeed this
meant the risk of social extinction, since provincial profits far
outweighed other respectable sources of money (e.g. by dowry
or inheritance). True, some senators engaged in business ventures, especially money-lending, but this was easier after ready
cash had been accumulated in office or through political influence. The costs and profits of winning office promoted the
habit of borrowing against the chance of being elected, and of
repaying creditors out of the profits, either in cash or in opportunities to participate in the spoils. One immediate by-product
of the process was the creation of a group of impoverished
nobles, who on one occasion attempted a general revolution (63
B.C.). Another product was the determination of electoral win-
ners that nothing should obstruct the exploitation of their
victory. The aphorism that provincial profits could be divided
into three parts, a third to pay advocates and defenders, a
third to pay the costs of court fines for corruption, and a third
for a personal fortune, reveals the regularity and the condonation
of such peaceful exploitation (Cicero, *In Verrem*, 1.14.40).

The military expansion of the period can partly be attributed to a similar search for profit and booty (treasure, slaves, taxes, and glory) which brooked little hindrance from the central government. For Roman administration followed the traditional pattern of investing each provincial governor with the total delegated authority of the Roman state – administrative, judicial, and military. His subordinates were not members of professional bureaucratic agencies, but were his own friends (*necessarii*) chosen *ad hoc*. The only limits to the governors' power were the typically short term of office (seldom over two years), and the possibility of subsequent indictment by injured provincials through their Roman patrons (and the governors' political enemies) and of consequent loss of status and exile. But in fact even extreme corruption went unpunished. This freedom of governors to exploit provincials, and of their political opponents to attack them for it afterwards, gave rise to repetitive bickering between aristocrats. It was symptomatic of the tension which was eventually organized in armed conflicts, full-scale civil wars, and the subsequent 'legalized' murder of political opponents (proscriptions) in 81 and 43 B.C.

Provincial magistrates, then, wielded huge authority. They operated at a distance from Rome which, given the poor state of communications and the absence of a state-employed supervisory bureaucracy, minimized such control as the central authority could exert over them. They therefore could accumulate money and establish loyalties, especially if they were left in command for long periods, as their military expertise occasionally dictated. It has been argued that it was fear of such a process which stopped the Romans from providing continual administration of the lands they conquered early in the second century B.C. If it was so, their fear was well founded. For the administration of the empire involved increasing the number of executive magistrates from 25 in 250 B.C. to 44 after 80 B.C., and even then their tenure was frequently prolonged to enable them to serve abroad afterwards. In the first century, as a part of the same process, the senate was doubled in size (81 B.C.) and aristocratic exclusiveness breached. The profits of provincial exploitation and the control of men and money in the provinces served as a springboard for rebellion and revolution and social change throughout the last century of the Republic.

Just as ineffectual as the delay in accepting the responsibilities of provincial administration were attempts at containing aristocratic competitiveness within traditional bounds by controlling patterns of acquiring and consuming wealth. In 218 B.C. senators were forbidden to engage in large-scale maritime trade. Nevertheless, the law was evaded, and aristocrats made money through trade, urban building, and money-lending. But there was always an aura of distaste about trade – at least, ideally. Witness the equivocal opinion of Cicero that trade was demeaning unless on a big scale (Cicero, *De Officiis*, 1.42), or Livy's statement that to senators all profiting seemed indecorous (Livy, 21, 63).

Similarly, by sumptuary laws, the senate tried, without success, to limit the display of wealth to traditional levels. Equally unsuccessfully, it tried to suppress the power of newly-made wealth with laws against electoral corruption. For magistrates had at their disposal not only powers of private patronage but of state patronage as well; it was one more weapon in the arsenal of rival politicians, until eventually the state provided either subsidized or free corn to great numbers of the free proletariat of Rome (by 46 B.C., the recipients numbered 320,000). With somewhat more success, the entrenched nobility lessened the impact of change by limiting the number of legitimate candidates for senatorial office. The lex Vilia annalis (180 B.C.) and Sulla's lex annalis (81 B.C.), for example, laid down the minimum age of 27 or 30 for first office (*quaestor*) and of 37 or 40 for the further office (*praetor*). Given the high rates of natural mortality then current, this must have had the effect not only of making people keep their turn, but of giving the restricted number of legitimate candidates for higher office a reasonable chance of election. One flaw in the system was the occasional need for a talented magistrate or general in a particular place; another was the occasional seizure of power against the formal rules by men of genius or ambition, such as Pompey, Caesar, and Octavian.

So much for the control of conflict between aristocrats themselves. Yet in spite of their differences, the old aristocracy collectively set its face against newcomers. Few were the men who gained entrance to the charmed inner circle. Indeed, the word for noble, *nobilis*, gained a new currency and was used to describe exclusively those aristocrats who had been consuls, or who had consuls as ancestors. But under the novel conditions of the later Republic, aristocrats had to be wealthy as well as well born; they had to be able to defend their wealth and their lives against political enemies, as well as gaining high office. Their number grew smaller, and it is a moot point whether their successful exclusiveness can better be seen as a gallant last-ditch defence, or as the reinforcement of a dam which only concentrated the several streams of opposition.

There is one more change in custom which I should like to discuss briefly. According to Roman myths about early times, marriage had once been an indissoluble union whose avowed purpose was the procreation of children. It had been a union between families to which the girl brought a dowry as a gift; she left the *patria potestas* of her own father and entered into the power of her husband or of his father. Several major changes seem to have occurred in this system among the upper class by the last century B.C. The size of dowries increased, the form of marriage changed to allow the girl's father to retain control over his daughter even after her marriage; he could withdraw her and her dowry from her husband. Marriage coupled with a dowry thus became a flexible if single tool of political alliance. Divorce was frequent in the first century B.C., and, from being pawns in the power game of others, women attracted strong elements of that power to themselves sufficiently often for it to be formalized in law. Thus they controlled their own property and initiated divorce with or without moral grounds. They competed with each other in dress, beauty, and expenditure. Nor did this affect their life-style only. Their reluctance to spoil their figures with large numbers of children was one factor which prevented the self-replacement of the aristocracy. But if the aristocracy did not replace itself, there were only two possible outcomes: social mobility, or the restriction of privilege to a diminished number of aristocrats.

STRUCTURAL DIFFERENTIATION

One of the main problems in analysing social change on such a large scale is that we have no body of theory which validates the selection of a single factor or set of factors as the prime cause of the change or as the determinant of the direction of change. Nor can we arrange the many possible causes in their order of importance. Without a theory we are left swimming in an ocean of possibilities; the only landmark is what 'actually happened'; and that is not so easily discovered as von Ranke hoped. Once ashore, we are open to the charge of retrospective determinism; all we try to explain is what happened, not what did not happen. I see no way out of these difficulties.

By underplaying the temporal sequence of factors, we can however concentrate upon the repercussions of change throughout the society considered as a system. We can hypothesize that changes in some sectors (e.g. the monetization of the economy, the relative professionalization of the army) throw other traditional social arrangements out of gear, and force adaptation, that is change. The change is thus 'explained' by the suggestion of incompatibility between two or more sets of social arrangements (e.g. between a monetized economy and a system of social control based upon unspecified mutual obligations); or by the suggestion of necessary concomitance between two or more sets of social arrangements (e.g. a professional army requires *regular* payment, whose collection and redistribution are likely to be bureaucratically organized). It is clear from the examples that the statements of incompatibility or of concomitance are not absolute, but may be more or less probable. Moreover, their validity depends upon a set of assumptions or parameters (i.e. the specification of the *ceteris paribus*) which it would be tedious or impossible to specify. Yet the approach, for all its apparent weaknesses, has advantages in that it acknowledges the adaptive, integrative aspects of social change without denying or neglecting the hitherto overemphasized elements of conflict in change.

One of the most obvious changes which occurred at Rome in the later Republic was the creation and institutionalization of spheres of conduct which had previously been relatively undifferentiated. One can point to the formalization of differences in stratification, the creation of the equestrian estate, and the growth in the number of slaves, freedmen, and provincials. One can point to the increased difference in the style of life of rich and poor, and the cultural homogeneity of the well-to-do, conquerors and conquered alike. One can point to the separate institution of the army, increasingly dissociated from the peasantry; to the economic institution of plantations producing new cash crops and quite distinct from the more or less subsistence peasant farming of archaic Rome. One can point to the growth of schools and of higher education in contrast to the old process of socialization at the side of the paterfamilias; and also to the emergence of the legal profession as a body of jurisconsults and pleaders, independent of religious and aristocratic priesthood. And finally one can point to the acknowledged separation of marriage from procreation, and of individualized love from marriage.

Not all these changes can be analysed on the same level; some of the newly differentiated institutions were acknowledged as separate by contemporaries; others (e.g. peasantry, plantations) spring partly from modern categories, but can also be confirmed by ancient evidence. In so far as institutions, such as the army, the legal system, the economy, became differentiated, their identity and relative autonomy were maintained by the creation of special roles, norms, and rules. In this way one can understand the formulation of their boundaries *vis-à-vis* other institutions, the legitimation of those boundaries and of the internal structure of the institutions.

Let us take as illustrations the development of the military and legal systems in the later Republic. When Hannibal invaded Italy in 216 B.C., the Romans sent out a large army under two consuls, who held command on alternate days. For traditionally, it was assumed that one aristocrat, *qua* consul or praetor, was as good as another at commanding troops and fighting battles; and it was thought that supreme power should not, if possible, be concentrated in the hands of one aristocrat. He might win too much glory. It is clear that the principle of leadership was not dictated by the demands of military tactics, strategy, or skill. In the event, this dual leadership gave Hannibal an advantage which he exploited. By the first century B.C., military leadership and the area of command, though affected by extraneous considerations, were also seen as specifically military problems. For example, it was realized that the most efficient way to subdue piracy in the Eastern Mediterranean was to overstep traditional land provinces and give one general immense resources and unified command of the whole area (67 B.C.). As a further example, Caesar is said to have chosen his lieutenants not according to their social origins but according to their skill (Suetonius, *Julius Caesar*, 65). The noble amateur was at least in part displaced. The long civil wars of the last century B.C. and the quasi-professional army which serviced them engendered 'professional' personnel at all levels, with specific skills, rules of conduct, and expectations.

Similarly, the legal profession in the last two centuries B.C. used 'professional' personnel, where previously the aristocratic priesthood had held a monopoly. We can trace the rise of non-aristocratic consultant lawyers (*iuris prudentes*) and of special pleaders (*causidici*) who, as orators, used highly formalized schemata for their speeches. Romans had had written law ever since the XII Tables (traditional date: 451 B.C.), but in this period the process of adjudication was further developed and institutionalized by the creation of permanent criminal courts, each specializing in different types of case.

Of course, when we speak of differentiation and autonomy, it is on the assumption that differentiated institutions are also integrated with significant parts of the overall value system or organization of the society. They may be more or less integrated, though, that said, there is no satisfactory theory which sets forth the criteria of relative autonomy. Similarly, modes of integration vary from, for example, power and subjugation to shared values and interests. It is the mark of the pre-industrial society that the degree of differentiation is limited by the reliance of institutions upon ascriptive modes of support; for such a society is organized to a large extent on the basis of kinship, locality, and hereditary status; this makes it impossible to create or maintain organizations based on achievement, impersonality, and bureaucratic efficiency. For example, although formal bureaucratic structures are set up, albeit with a great deal of effort, in pre-industrial societies, nevertheless the dominant form of personal interaction is based not on formality and impersonality which are two hallmarks of bureaucracy, but on clientship and personal recommendation, i.e. on ascription. Bureaucrats therefore have no choice but to compromise their formal behaviour and accommodate themselves to the informal ascriptive demands of their friends, enemies, and clients; the typical response is what we call corruption.

In this sense of limited differentiation we can understand that the legal system, like the military, was the locus of much non-legal activity; such activity has mostly in modern historiography been labelled 'political'. This is convenient but rather crude and misses some of the point, which is that the political sector was also, compared with our own society, relatively embedded in or enmeshed with other institutions. For example, the onus of prosecution for what we should call a criminal action often lay through a claim for damages by private claimants who, if they were to win cases against aristocratic defendants, needed aristocratic patrons. Thus the initiation of proceedings was much more the product of personal or 'political' enmities than it would have been if this duty had been entrusted to a consciously apolitical agency (cf. the Director of Public Prosecutions in England).

In spite of the degree to which legal and 'political' actions overlapped, the legal network of legislation and adjudication served as a distinct source of legitimacy, even in circumstances in which contending parties relied ostensibly upon force. Even in the period of repeated civil wars of the last century of the Republic (133-31 B.C.), political groupings tried to legitimate their behaviour by legalizing it. Caesar, for example, was faced with the prospect that he would be a private citizen for a short period between the end of his ten-year Gallic command and his entry on a consulship. In this time, by law, he was open to prosecution for maladministration and/or other offences, and might not have been able to take up the consulship. Both he and his opponents did their best to use or change the law to maximize their advantage. Law was thus an arena of political contention, but at the same time a point of reference, which was not by any means identical with political action. The behaviour of Caesar and his opponents was all the more striking in that they both had armies at their disposal – and soon used them to decide their rival claims to power.

There are, then, two points I want to stress: first, that the degree of differentiation is limited by the articulation of the separated institutions with the rest of society and by the modes of interaction (e.g. ascription) current in the society. Second, differentiated institutions by their very existence become points of reference for both conflict and alliance to other institutions and to their own personnel. An illustration of this tendency can be found in the repercussions following the creation of the second estate, the *equites* (knights), in 123-122 B.C. The *equites* were mostly landowners, but there was a very important element of tax-farmers, and perhaps of merchants. The upper limit of the estate was determined by the *de facto* hereditary exclusiveness of the senatorial order, and the exclusion of senators from trade. Its lower limit was set by a minimum capital requirement of HS 400,000. The formalization of these boundaries between the senate, *equites*, and plebs led both contemporaries and later historians to exaggerate the significance of the conflct of interests between the senate and *equites*; they have been seen as classes engaged in a class-struggle, and the end of their rivalry was envisaged by Cicero, for example, as a sound basis for constitutional government (*concordia ordinum*). True, the distribution of profits from provincial taxation was disputed by aristocratic governors and equestrian tax-farmers. Nevertheless, in most political disputes of the later Republic, senators and *equites* were thoroughly mixed in all groups, and very little of the history of the period can be understood in terms of such a class struggle. But it is important that the disputants often saw their situation, in terms of an unrealistic dichotomy.

Other conflicts were more broadly based in reality. There were those who favoured or who had interests in the maintenance of traditional patterns of behaviour; and there were others who exploited the emergent institutions as new sources of power. For it is inconceivable that the non-traditional beliefs and values which bolstered newly differentiated institutions could be evenly spread throughout society. This unevenness gave rise to conflict between, for example, the entrenched ruling group, the old aristocrats (*optimates*) and the also aristocratic populist leaders (*populares*). Whereas the one invoked tradition (*mos maiorum*) and the authority of the senate (*auctoritas*), the others advocated reforms ostensibly in the popular interest and had more frequent recourse to violence.

It is often argued that in industralized societies, change has become built into the social structure; it is regulated by specialized institutions (e.g. bureaucracies) and takes place within the framework of an overall consensus and ideology (e.g.

the rule of law, national consciousness). In pre-industrial societies by contrast, traditional forces are too strong to allow such a steady and persistent rate of change. In Rome at this period, one of the major determinants of the type and rate of change and of the instability induced by change was the tension between the traditional elements and the emerging specialized institutions. The newly differentiated institutions and their personnel, because of their very newness, had no established place or status within the society; and Rome like other traditional societies did not have at its disposal strong mechanisms for the regulation of change or for the reallocation of status. Yet the new men had to be placed. The first attempt was to assimilate the newcomers to traditional patterns. For example, it was laid down in 204 B.C. that advocates should not be paid fees, that is they should conform to the old tradition of the amateur, not to the new standard of the professional.

Similarly, the Senate reacted by stark prohibition to the increasingly extravagant life-style of the rich, to the importation of Eastern mystery religions, and to the introduction of Greek philosophy into school education. But it did not have available any executive establishment through which such prohibitions could be enforced. Indeed law for its efficient operation needs both executive personnel and a dominant body of consensus which condemns the law-breakers. Both were missing. Had these shortcomings merely affected life-style or religion or education, it would not have mattered much. But they affected the place in society of new institutions and groups such as the semi-professional army, and the impoverished aristocrats and very rich *equites*. What had presumably made Rome strong was her cohesion and reliance upon tradition. But what she lacked was a set of institutions with enough strength, flexibility, and support to mediate change, regulate the inter-action of the new differentiated institutions, and win consensus for the status allocated them.

One of the most serious symptomatic weaknesses of the senatorial government was its inability to control provincial governors. Typically, control was attempted through traditional mechanisms such as collegiate office and short tenure. The Senate relied upon the community of interest among its members, but this was effective only so long as the tasks confronting

governors were routine, or were under the immediate supervision of peers or superiors, or were undertaken in an atmosphere
of mutual trust. Even when these were missing, a professional
executive service specializing in certain areas of administration
could have acted as a brake upon the wide authority of governors. But such a service did not develop until Rome was ruled
by emperors.

CONSENSUS AND DISSENSUS

We have seen that the process of structural differentiation
involves the evolution of special roles, norms, and rules, which
enable each institution to maintain its autonomy. But this
autonomy was restricted by the continuing power of ascription,
locality, and kin groups. The tension between the emergent
specialized institutions and traditional patterns of behaviour
was reflected in the open conflict between those who favoured
or had interest in traditional authority and those who sought
to increase their power by exploiting the emergent institutions.
In addition to the competition which was endemic among the
ruling aristocrats, the process of structural differentiation engendered other conflicts both among the new institutions and
between them and the ruling elite. For the new institutions
had no established place within the society, and there was no
powerful mechanism within the traditional structure capable of
accommodating change on such a scale. There was no consensus
as to the place that these institutions should occupy; and the
initial reaction of the Senate, that they could be comfortably
assimilated to traditional patterns, was patently inadequate.

Yet even in their embryonic state the new institutions existed
as sources of power, both ideological and material, which stood
outside traditional alliances; as such they were new tools for
aristocrats already engaged in a struggle for power, and as
such they served to increase dissensus, which flared up in the
repeated political murders and civil wars of the last century
B.C. The process of structural differentiation thus made great
demands upon the political authority to establish a new consensus on the relations to be maintained between the traditional
and the new elements of the social structure. What needs to be
explained is the initial failure of Romans to establish this

consensus, and their eventual if partial success under the emperors.

One apparent cause of this failure was the exacerbation of the competition between aristocrats. Since the new institutions were not firmly placed in society, and because of their power, they were irresistibly engaged in the conflict for placement and the control over resources. This extra leverage splintered the traditional political system, by widening the arena and intensifying the tempo of conflict. Previously competition had been between only a small number of aristocrats, who virtually monopolized positions of power. Their rule was limited only by the arbitrament of the plebs whose services were required as soldiers. In the social sphere the stability of the ruling elite seems to have been based upon a system of unspecified mutual obligations, typified, for example, in the outright gift of the dowry. One was kept to the mark by tradition, shame, and the desire for good reputation. In the pursuit of political office these restraints were bolstered by the authority of the Senate (peers) and by short, collegiate tenure. But were such restraints and rules sufficient to contain the strong ideal of individual ambition?

Foreign conquests epitomized the pursuit of this ideal; for abroad it was allowed freest rein. But the repercussions bit deep. Let us take money as a paradigm. Money was first minted in Rome in the third century B.C., and flooded into circulation in the second century as the provinces paid taxes. It could not but corrode the system of unspecified obligation; for money is so much more storable and flexible. It is universalistic, in the sense that it makes obligations transferable; it mediates interaction between and inside much larger and more differentiated groups. Its influx increased the stakes of political competition and the number of competitors; the criterion of wealth was imposed on that of nobility, and nobles were exposed to the risk of social extinction. In such a situation the identity of aristocratic interest, and the constraints of tradition, shame, and reputation, lost their force. Distrust took their place, and weapons were used as they came to hand: clientship, bribery, murder, and civil war.

Just like the economic system, the military, educational, and legal systems, the systems of trade, religion, and stratification, to name but a few, all disrupted traditional patterns. The new professionals made their demands for recognition and placement, and competed for the control of scarce resources. Traditional alliances of kin groups and traditional loyalties to the state were rejected. Marriage and divorce were fashioned into more flexible tools of political alliance, just as friendship (*amicitia*) became a word which commonly identified cool common interest as well as affection. Yet these were only stopgaps.

It was the army which acted as the executor of this dissensus. And it was a victorious general, one of a succession, who founded the imperial bureaucratic state. Dissensus invited violence, but does violence precipitate centralized control? It did in Rome, possibly because a professional army with a strong hierarchy monopolized fighting; and combat was sufficiently institutionalized to give victory to the possessor of the battlefield at dusk. Thus victory could be quick and opposition afterwards minimal. Continual wars and political executions had destroyed many bastions of the old order. Add to this Augustus' insight that integration could be based on two main foundations. First, gradual reform was legitimated by an ideology of the restoration of tradition; and, second, a patrimonial bureaucracy was created which mediated the interests of emperor, aristocracy, taxpayers, and army.

REFERENCES

EISENSTADT, S. N. 1964. *The Political Systems of Empires*. New York: Free Press, Collier, Macmillan.
SMELSER, N. J. 1963. In Hoselitz, B. F. & Moore, W. E., *Industrialization and Social Change*. Paris: UNESCO.

ACKNOWLEDGEMENTS

I should like to thank Mr P. A. Brunt, Professor R. P. Dove, and Mr A. W. G. Stewart for their criticisms of this paper.

Edwin Ardener

Documentary and Linguistic Evidence for the Rise of the Trading Polities between Rio del Rey and Cameroons, 1500-1650

The early historical material for the area between the Cross River and the Cameroons Estuary is full of ambiguities. Dapper (1668) and Barbot (1732) between them imposed upon the seventeenth century a canonical scheme. Peoples such as Ambozi and Calbongos dominate the scene, and many of us have been tempted to try to interpret at its face value a system of toponymy which derives in part from a corrupt manuscript tradition, and in part from the compilation of a few independent sources into layer upon layer of variants. This paper attempts to unravel some of the tangle, and by the addition of as yet unconsidered sources to advance the matter a little further from the point reached in the original scholarly study by Bouchaud (1952), the standard work in this field.

I shall be primarily considering the early contact of European trade with the stretch of the West African coast from Rio del Rey to the Cameroons River, places now in the Federal Republic of Cameroon. Some indirect light is also thrown on the situation in Old Calabar. This is not a political study but a clearing of the decks for such a study: of the growth of the trading hegemonies of Duala and Bimbia, which led to the establishment by the end of the eighteenth century of mercantile spheres bounding that of the Efik. I have tried to establish more precisely the period in which this political dawn occurred. This attempt has been aided by new evidence for the presence on the coast of speakers of Bantu languages, specifically of Duala type – indeed we may now virtually say speakers of the Duala language – before 1665. Certain personages may now be said to be 'historical', one of whom stands near the head of the genealogy of the trading dynasties of the Duala people: the later Kings of the Cameroons River (Ardener, 1956, pp. 17-21).[1]

81

RIO DEL REY AND CAMEROONS

0 20 40
Miles

EFIK
(Old) Calabar
Old Calabar
Cross River
ISANGELE
Amutu
Rio del Rey
BALUNDU
Andokat
Rumby Estuary
KOLE
WOMBOKO
Mt. Cameroon
Fako Peak
BAKWERI
Cape Debundscha
Victoria
Bimbia Creek
ISUBU
Wovea Islands
I. of Fernando Po
BUBI
BAKOKO
DUALA
Douala
Dibamba River
Cameroons Estuary
MALIMBA

82

LITERARY SOURCES OF THE ONOMASTIC PROBLEMS[1a]

The Portuguese discovery of the Cameroon coast is usually linked with that of the neighbouring island of Fernando Po, on various good grounds. The island and the coast present the appearance of two mountain peaks only some 25 miles apart at their bases. The date of the sighting of the island itself is, however, never clearly stated in Barros (1552), who merely says that 'at that time' the island of Fermosa was discovered by one Fernam do Pó and that it now bore in Barros' day the name of its discoverer instead of this earlier name. The time referred to appears to mean 'in the contract of Gomes' (beginning in 1469) and not to the period of 1474 which has also been referred to as *'neste tempo'* just before. Bouchaud has clearly demonstrated by the weight of evidence that early in 1472 is the most likely date for the discovery of Fermosa by Fernam do Pó, and by implication of the opposing coast.[2]

There is no direct contemporary evidence concerning the area until the years about 1500, when the veil of secrecy concerning the Portuguese discoveries begins to lift. The *Esmeraldo de Situ Orbis* of Pacheco Pereira is here, as elsewhere, of great value and interest, but the standard English translation (Kimble, 1937) is misleading at precisely this point. The Esmeraldo was written at some time about or after 1505 (Basto, 1892, p. ix; Silva Dias, 1905, p. 4; Kimble, 1937, pp. xvi-xvii).[3] The information for our area may relate to 1503-1505, the time of Pacheco's second visit to India. Since he was governor at S. Jorge da Mina in 1520-1522 and since one terminus for publication is 1521 (the end of D. Manoel's reign), a date for the acquisition of hearsay information as late as this cannot be excluded (Silva Dias, p. 4), improbable as it is.

After an account of Rio Real (the joint estuary of the New Calabar and Bonny Rivers), and after mentioning minor rivers to the east in the Niger Delta area, Pacheco's Chapter 10 is entitled '... *da serra de Fernam do Poo*' (S. Dias, p. 124). Some confusion in the interpretation of this chapter comes from the fact that the Cameroon Mountain was at this time called 'the mountain range of Fernam do Poo' a name it did not lose for about a century.[4] This chapter therefore is concerned with both the *serra* (on the mainland) and the *ilha* (the island), and it is not therefore accurate to state as Kimble does (1937, note to p. 131), followed by others, that Pacheco says nothing concerning 100 miles of coast between the Rio de S. Domingos (in the present Eastern Nigeria) and the Cameroons River. Pacheco refers to *esta serra e ilha* (S. Dias, p. 125) – 'this mountain range and island' – as having been discovered by Fernam do Poo. Kimble, apparently unaware of this local peculiarity of nomenclature, was reduced to the translation: 'this island with its mountain range', taking the latter (as his note confirms) to be the peak of the island of Fernando Po itself. In what follows Pacheco refers sometimes to the *ilha* and sometimes to the *serra*. It is the *serra* (13,350 ft) to which he refers as being visible in clear weather from 25 and 30 leagues, not the lower eminence of the *ilha*. 'And the island at the mouth of this bay', he continues immediately (*this* referring still to the mainland in the Bay of Biafra), 'is very populous and there is in it much sugar cane and the mainland (*terra firme*) is five leagues distant; and a ship coming to the said land (*dita terra*) for anchorage will be in 15 fathoms a half-league from the shore. Slaves may be bartered there (*aly*). . . .'

Stopping here, we may note that *aly* refers to *dita terra* and the latter refers to the *terra firme* which is five leagues distant from the populous island with the sugar cane. We may rest assured therefore that what follows refers to the mainland and not the island. To continue:

'Slaves may be bartered there at eight to ten bracelets (*manilhas*) of copper apiece. In this country (*nesta terra*) there are many and large elephants, whose teeth, which we call ivory, we buy, and for one bracelet of copper one gets a big elephant's tusk [the elephants confirm that we are on the mainland and not on the island]; and in addition there is in this country (*nesta terra*) a fair abundance of malagueta of fine and good quality. There are many things in this Ethiopia which yield a good profit when brought to this kingdom.'

We have then clearly set the scene as the mainland at the *Serra de Fernam do Poo*: Mount Cameroon. This falls to the sea by way of a range of foothills and the spur of the Small Cameroon (5,570 ft), at a point comparable with the 5 leagues (the Portuguese league was 4 miles) from the *ilha* of Fernam do Poo of

Pacheco. There are elephants, and good-quality *afromomum* –
as at the present day. There are inhabitants, and they sell
tusks and slaves for a handful of manillas. The end of this
sentence is of great interest:

> '. . . e ha jente d'esta terra lhe chamam em sua lingoajem
> "Caaboo" e dentro no sertaão sincoenta leguoas da costa dó
> mar está hũa [corrupt text] linguoa que há nome "Bota".'[5]

The meaning of this sentence, so crucial, is in doubt: 'The people
of this country are called "Caaboo" in their language' (this is
clear) 'and in the bush 50 leagues from the sea-coast is a
[break] *linguoa* which has the name "Bota" '.

Kimble's translation of *linguoa* is 'language', and he suggests
an original something like: 'another people, called in their
language "Bota" ' (Kimble, p. 134). Basto (p. 111) suggests:
'*lingua de terra, ou baixo*', that is: 'tongue of land, or reef'.
Whatever this Bota was it is clearly stated to be 50 leagues
from the sea-coast at the *serra de Fernam do Poo*. In later
centuries a Bota was located *on* the sea-coast, and it is so called
today, although not in the vernacular of the inhabitants. Were
it not for this modern circumstance it would probably have
been generally assumed that the Bota in question was the
Serra Bota which Pacheco actually mentioned later at a distance
(by his own reckoning) of 48 leagues from the *Serra de Fernam
do Poo*, southward along the African coast, north of Rio Muni.
This range appears in the Strasbourg Ptolemy map of Africa
of 1513 (Santarem, 1899) as well as regularly in later sources.
The name means in Portuguese: 'the blunt range'. We are
then presented at the outset with at least the possibility that
the Cameroon *Bota* is a ghost name which acquired reality
through a long life in the travel literature. The same question
arises indeed for the *Caaboo*. These matters will be discussed
below. Here it is enough to make clear that Pacheco's text
concerning the *people* so called intends to locate them at the
mainland coast of the *serra*, not the *ilha* de Fernam do Poo.
This is further confirmed by the evident continuity of the coast
assumed in the next sentence:[6]

> 'Item. All the sea-coast from this *Serra de Fernam do Poo* to
> *Cabo de Lopo Gonçalvez*, which is eighty leagues, is densely
> populated and thickly wooded.'

After general remarks, including one on the presence of whales, he continues:

> 'Item. Two leagues from this *serra de Fernam do Poo* to the north-east is a river which is called *dos Camarões* [=Cameroons Estuary], where there is good fishing; we have not yet had any trade with the natives; great tornadoes accompanied by very violent storms are experienced on this coast, and as a safeguard you should furl sail while they last.'

The statement that the distance from the Serra de Fernam do Poo was two leagues suggests that a promontory near Bimbia Creek was the point on the mainland from which the measurement was made. Also it is to be noted that the Cameroons River was not yet the place to which local trade came. It has been necessary to consider carefully this authoritative Portuguese source for the condition of the Cameroon coast about 1500, because, although the interpretation given here was clearly made by Bouchaud, the English translation has helped to confuse the position for English-speakers.

Approximately contemporary with Pacheco's account is one by João de Lisboa, published in 1514 in his *Tratado de Agulha de Marear* ('Treatise on the Compass'). I have been unable to consult the Portuguese edition (Brito Rebello, 1903), and here rely on Bouchaud's French translation (1952, pp. 51-53). This source fills the geographical gap left by Pacheco. After the *Rio de sam domingo* (the Andoni river of the Niger Delta: Jones, 1964, p. 34), he names the *Rio da cruz* (the Cross River), and the 'anse de la pêcherie' or 'Fishery gulf': the *Angra Pescaria* of contemporary and later maps, at the entrance to the Rio del Rey. From Rio Real (the Bonny-New Calabar estuary) to the *Pescaria* the whole coast was wooded.

> 'Know [he says] that from this *pescaria* to the bar of the *Rio das Camaroys* [sic] there is a distance of 15 leagues. In this coast there is a mountain range which is called *serra de fernam do poo*, and if you wish to go to the *Rio dos Camaroys*, passing between the island and the mainland, you must navigate with the lead, because there are shoals.'[7]

Pacheco and João seem to be independent sources here, but, despite this early mention of the Cross River and of the *Pescaria* we need not question the conclusion, based upon Pacheco, that these areas at this early date did not attract a great deal of trade (Jones, 1964, p. 34). The *Pescaria* probably received its name because of the dotting of the sea by fishing traps on its bed, like those which are still a prominent feature today.

We next have to deal with a group of sources, in various languages, clustered round the name of Martin Enciso, who in 1518 appears simply to have translated into Castillian a manual written early in the same year by a Portuguese, Andreas Pires, whose own manuscript is in the Bibliothèque Nationale (Taylor, 1932). The latter was a pilot who had transferred his services to Spain. Enciso refers to the distance between Rio Real and a 'Cape of Fernando Po' (*cabo de Fernãdo polo*) as 30 leagues. To the west of this cape, he says, was the *rio de los santos* ('river of saints'), and to the east the *golfo d' l galo* (Enciso, 1518). The Cape would appear to refer to that point on the sea-shore at the Cameroon Mountain already referred to by Pacheco. This may be Cape Debundscha or, more probably, one of the points near Victoria. The *golfo d' l galo* probably contains a misreading of *delgado* (Port. 'slender') a term consistently used at the period of the Suellaba point at the entrance of the Cameroon River. The 'river of saints' may be the Rio del Rey or the Cross River.[8]

Enciso continues:

'These three rivers are large and have good entrances and the land is very hot. And it is a land of much gold. Here there is a fruit from palms which is called Cocos: and it is big and yellow. They make wine of it and it is also good to eat. In this country they make cloth of wool [=fibre] of palms in such a way that it is good to wear. And in all those lands they use that cloth. They have iron and steel' (ibid.).

The three rivers include the Rio Real, and so a long stretch of Eastern Nigerian coast is evidently included in the description. The land of coconuts (possibly confused also with palm-wine), and of raffia cloth, is possibly intended to be closer to Rio del Rey than to the Cameroon River. Very small amounts of gold have been panned in the Ndian affluent of the Rio del Rey estuary, but Enciso here may be fanciful. The statement of the possession of iron may be noted.

Ambos

The Enciso relation was itself pirated and translated into English (with almost no addition) by Roger Barlow, in an MS. dated to 1541, and published by Taylor (1932). A French version was made by Jean Fonteneau (alias Jean Alfonse) and Raulin Sécalart, pilots of La Rochelle in 1545. This uses French forms (translations and quasi-phonetic renderings) of the Portuguese names: we read of the *cap de Frenandupau*, *rivière de Tous les Sainctz*, and *l'ance de Jau* (= 'The gulf of the cock' = 'golpho de' l galo'). They try to adjust the cape of Fernando Po to the island, which they state to be full of cannibals. This bungled text becomes of interest because they also interpolate into Enciso in this passage certain remarks concerning a people they refer to under the name *Ambous* and like forms. They write:

'And turning to the coast, I say that the rivers are big rivers and along them grey pepper and malaguetta can be obtained. And the people of the country are called *Ambous*. And they are people *qui ont les plus grandz natures que gens du monde et sont puissantes et maulvaises gens*' (Fonteneau, 1545, Ed. Musset, 1904, pp. 337-338).

Then comes one of those confusions that bedevil all inquiries in this field. Of Cape *Lope Gonsalvez* (Cape Lopez in the modern Gaboon), the authors make the further statement:

'And at the said cape ... the nation of the *Ambons* [sic] finishes, the *Manicongres* people begin, who are continually at war with the *Ambos* [sic]. The *Ambos* eat them when they catch them being cannibals. The *Manicongres* for the most part are Christians. These Ambos have several kinds of wild beasts. The land is very hot' (op. cit., p. 339).

These latter *Ambos* were a people of the Congo area, who are mentioned by Pigafetta (1591): they are placed by Ravenstein between the coast of Congo and Anzica, and he identifies them with the Balumbu (Ravenstein, 1901, p. 191). The *Amboas* who appear on Pigafetta's map (1591, end) thus should be seen in relation to the Anzicos of the Congo basin near which they are placed, and not as in the hinterland of Cameroon near which the distortions of the map also place them. We are not, however, concerned here with the identity of the Congo basin *Ambo* (Doke, 1961, p. 6, identifies them with the Ovambo). Our difficulty is in deciding whether the Cameroon Ambo really existed. This is important, because, from the seventeenth century, their name is permanently with us.[9]

It must be stressed that ghost names of all kinds became attached to the West African coast, partly during the Portuguese period, but more especially during the seventeenth century. Numerous cartographical and route-book recensions of the names occurred in the early period, but the Dutch produced a kind of definitive series of terms which remained unamended virtually until the nineteenth century. Bouchaud has shown the probable purely graphic development of the shadow region of Biafra from the Mesche Mons of Ptolemy.[10] In any investigation of the toponymy the null hypothesis must be to assume a ghost name, and here the possibility of a deformation of the form *Caaboo*, given by Pacheco, cannot be excluded. We find a possibly intermediate form (*isolas canboas*) in Martines' map of 1567 (Santarem, 1899). Confusion with the Ambo of the Congo may have made the fixing of the form *Ambos* all too plausible. It must be said that the argument that *Caaboo* was a corruption in the reverse sense carries as great conviction. None the less, until recently there was no unequivocal evidence available that the term *Ambos* was ever actually applied to Cameroon in any early non-cartographic Portuguese source.

Luckily we now have the following reference, which at least removes doubt on this score. It is in a letter from Duarte Rodrigues (Roiz) to the King of Portugal, dated 10 May 1529 (*MMA*, IV, 1954, p. 144). The writer had been sent to the Congo, and was delayed there for six months. The letter advises the King about irregularities observed in the trade of S. Tomé, Axim, and Mina. In one passage he says:

'Your highness has a country in the *Ambos* which is between the island of *Fernã do Po* and the mainland, from which there comes much malagueta, and it seems to me that 30 or 40 moyos [1 moyo=822 litres] may be taken out, and, if the country became accustomed to it [the trade] there would be much more; this malagueta is denied to you because no factor of yours in the Island of *Santomé* has ever declared it to you;

I have informed you of it; and because my desire is great to serve you I rejoice in looking out for everything, and for this reason give an account to your highness, for it seems to me that in this I do you sufficient service. ... Today the 10th May, 1529,

Duarte Rojz.

Address: For the King our Lord.
    This letter is highly secret; let it be opened in front of his highness.

Vay de Colỹ'[11]

The name *Ambos* thus existed in 1529, and was applied to a spot somewhere between the island of Fernando Po and the mainland – clearly an island or islands, and thus probably either the islands in Victoria Bay or the island near Bimbia known as Nicoll Island. We have confirmation of the existence of the malagueta mentioned by Pacheco, and further evidence that the area was neglected by Portuguese trade at that time. This solitary contemporary reference to the Ambos in the Portuguese period, outside the shifting onomasiology of the maps and route-lists, enables certain hypotheses to be suggested. First, out of many corrupt forms, *Ambos* (plural) can now be established as not a ghost name. Second, the later references that relate the *Ambos* to islands off the coast can be given special weight, and the question whether the use of the name for the mainland by the Dutch was secondary can be raised.

A source which now comes into a certain focus is the *Hydrographia* of Figueiredo, which was licensed for publication in Lisbon in 1614. It says (folio 44, reverse) that from the island of *Fernam do Pâo* [sic] to the mainland was five leagues and that 'looking to the north you will see a very high mountain range, which is called *serra de Motão*, and which is above *os Zambus* which is a little island to the south of it'. He says that care should be taken not to go too much on the mainland without someone who knows the country, even if short of water,

'for all the people here are warlike, and there are no people acquainted with the Portuguese, except those of the *ilheo dos Zambus* which is half a league, and seeing people in this island do not go ashore, as they too are warlike people, but go two

leagues distant from the island so that the peak is to the east
of you. . . .'

This account is circumstantial, and if the common name of the
island was *os Ambos* or *'the* Ambos', the spellings *os Zambus*,
dos Zambus can be explained as an artifact of word juncture.
Figueiredo's account is now greatly strengthened. Of course, it
may be countered that the error in word division is not
Figueiredo's but that of Duarte Roiz, who was after all writing
from the Congo. There is also hovering in the background the
difficult shadow of Pacheco's *Caaboo*, which with its peculiar
doubled vowels has the look of a scribe's corruption for a word
of about the length of *Zambus*. If indeed *Caaboo* did not apparently re-emerge in the later seventeenth century in a Dutch
form, discussed below, we should already be well advised to
reject it altogether.

Before considering this question further, Figueiredo has a
further significance – the last of the major Portuguese sources,
he is also used as the basis of an early major Dutch source:
Dierick Ruiters whose *Toortse der Zee-Vaert* was published in
1623. When he reached the points in Figueiredo cited above,
he used the following forms:

1. '. . . eenen hooghen Bergh sien, noorden van u, ende werdt
   ghenoemt Monton, ofte Maton: 't is eenen Bergh gheleghen
   op Amboes'
2. '. . . 't eylant Amboes 't welck oock Zambus ghenaemt
   werdt.'[12]

In the first passage, *Amboes* has been substituted for the
Zambus of Figueiredo. In the second, it has been offered as an
alternative. Considering the corrupt forms of Figueiredo's *Motão*
in passage (1), Ruiters' emendations on their own have little
status. With the establishment of an independent Portuguese
form *Ambos*, however, it now seems more likely that Ruiters is
here emending from other, possibly oral sources (*oe* to represent
the *u*-like Portuguese *o*). The Dutch and Flemish definite articles
would not introduce the same ambiguity of word division (at
this point in its history Ambos soon ceases to be perceived as
in itself plural). Naber (1913 (2)) suggests, improbably, that
Zambus has a Portuguese etymology from the citrus *Djambua*,

Edwin Ardener

but on balance I think that the current Portuguese name was *os Ambos* and not *os Zambus*.[13] Further, the *Ambos* seem to have been people continuously associated with an island or islands off the mainland – islands, from Figueiredo's description, identifiable as one of those with which their name has always been associated in Ambas Bay off Victoria. There is no mention of any people called *Ambos* as living on the mainland in any early source. This situation was blurred by the writers of the succeeding period, as will be shown. If Figueiredo is anything to go by, the later Portuguese were already in doubt as to the form of the name.

Elements in the Dutch tradition

The Dutch *bouleversement* of the Portuguese position in the Gulf after the attack on S. Thomé at the end of the sixteenth century, culminating in the capture of S. Jorge de Mina in 1637, used a mixture of Portuguese maps and textual sources of different ages, and to some extent rationalized them. The Portuguese had already been under competition from the Spanish and part of the nomenclature which the Dutch popularized was derived from Spanish forms.[14]

In another part of Figueiredo's work, and not connected with the account already cited, which is an independent source, he gives for good measure a copy of Pacheco, slightly paraphrased, in which the doubtful portion in which Pacheco refers to the 'Caaboo' and 'Bota' is rendered as follows:

'... esta terra chamão o *Chaquim*, do cabo pera dentro no sertao cinco legoas està hum lugar a que chamão *Bòta*' (this is called *Chaquim*, and from the cape into the bush five leagues is a place which is called *Bòta*).[15]

This attempts to tidy up the lacuna in Pacheco, and puts the mysterious Bota only 5 leagues away and definitely inland. This version of Pacheco is of interest in the present context because of the blunder: *Chaquim*; by which the name of a well-known place in Dahomey is substituted for Pacheco's even then incomprehensible Caaboo. This was then copied by Ruiters in his *Toortse*, which says that the inhabitants called the coast *Chaquin* (sic). He rephrases the whole passage but refers to the malagueta and elephant's teeth of Pacheco, and says, still para-

92

phrasing, that trade takes place 4 [Dutch] miles inside the cape at a place named *Botas*, and that the natives like nothing but good arm- and leg-rings.[16] It is important to stress that Ruiters is not an independent source here. The line is direct: Pacheco, with Figueiredo's emendations, paraphrased by Ruiters. This point has to be established, because from Ruiters the two place-names *Chaquin* and *Bota* enter the Dutch arm-chair sources. By the time of Dapper and Barbot, the former has, I believe, become the *Cesge* which is coupled with Bota in these classical and misleading texts to give alternative names of an inhabited place near the Cameroon Mountain.

In view of the separate life of the nomenclature of the coast, it is a certain relief when an actual visitor appears – Samuel Brun (or Braun or Bruno), a Swiss surgeon on a Dutch ship whose account (published in 1624) was very influential.[17] In 1614 he reached Benin and then he says '. . . we went to the *Land von Ambosy* and *Camarona*, *Rio de Anckare* and *Rio de Ree*'. He has something to say on the economic life of the area and he is a valuable independent source.[18]

For our present purposes, we may note the form *Ambosy*, now with a suffix added to the original Portuguese plural form. The proximate source is said by Brun to be Spanish. We may however bear in mind the possibility of a 'feedback' of the very word *Ambos* in a form shaped by West Coast African traders or interpreters who, we may think, would by now be cognizant of the Portuguese usage. Brun it is, however, who first likens the Cameroon Mountain to the Peak of Teneriffe, and derives its name from the Spanish *Alta tierra de Ambosy*. All of which was lifted whole later by Dapper, broadcast by Barbot, and was being cited from Barbot by Burton as late as 1863.[19] Nothing illustrates more sadly the lack of corroborative value of so much of the literature on this zone. From now on, forms such as *Ambosy* and the like become firmly attached to the Cameroon Mountain itself, as well as remaining attached to the island or islands off the coast. The mountain ceases to be known as the Serra de Fernam do Poo before the end of the sixteenth century.

Bota and the Cameroon Mountain
Once again Figueiredo occupies a critical place. Where Pacheco talks of a people, called *Caaboo*, and a 'something', called *Bota*,

50 leagues away from the coast in the *sertão*, Figueiredo speaks of *os Zambus*, and, to the north of them, a high mountain called *serra de Motão*. If the *Caaboo* are possibly *Ambos* or *Zambus*, we may wonder if the *serra de Motão* is not the peculiar Bota. It is indeed nearer 5 leagues inland to the peak than 50. Once again there are no certainties. The considerable misstatement of numerals is not uncommon in the courses: thus Enciso gives the latitude of *Cap Fernam do Poo* as 'xl [40] and a half degrees' instead of 'iv [4] and a half' – the error may stem basically from a confusion between V and L in the MSS. of the period. Figueiredo himself corrects Pacheco's 50 leagues to 5 as we have seen above. I am of the opinion that Pacheco's inland feature was the Cameroon Peak and that this was what was called Bota. Whether it should have been *Motão*, while his own form was influenced by the *Serra Bota* of lower down the coast, may be left an open question. What may now be explained is why a name located by Pacheco far inland could also have been given to a point on the coast. The mountain and parts of the coast have often exchanged names.

We may now ask from what language, or languages, *Motão* or *Bota* were derived. The most conservative conclusion is to offer Portuguese etymologies. *Motão* may be a colloquial augmentative of *mota* 'mound', 'motte'. *Bota*, 'blunt' was already used elsewhere of mountains, as we have seen. It may be argued that Pacheco at least is sometimes reliable on local West African forms (*Jos*: Ijaw, *Ogane*: the Oni of Ife), but he does not clearly say that this is a local form. An alternative hypothesis, much less firmly based, is that these are Portuguese folk-etymologies, even possibly for the same word, from some local language. It will be worth while pursuing this hypothesis in order to demonstrate the ambiguities that hedge it round. *Bota* has frequently been taken to be of Duala, or other Coastal Bantu origin, and thought to mean something like 'catching of fish'.[20] The name seems not to be indigenous to the area. *Bata*, meaning 'a kind of net', seems more possible – since the other *Serra Bota* down the coast gives us *Bata* in Rio Muni. However, etymons from the language of the Bubi of Fernando Po are also possible, if *motão* and *bota* are to be linked.

In Fernandian dialects *b* and *m* are interchangeable, especially in the singular prefixes, as forms for this people's name

(=*mome*- in certain dialects) themselves exemplify. *Môte* means 'big' in Bubi (Tessmann, 1923, p. 153). The inhabitants of the present inhabited island in Victoria Bay claim to be of Bubi descent, and were already called *Boobees* in 1855. They now call themselves by a version of the name *Bobe* (Ardener, pp. 30-31). The Island and its neighbours have a continuous history of occupation after Dapper's account, and one of these is probably also the *ilheo dos Ambos*, as we have seen. It is, of course, plausible that the Portuguese should have taken Fernandians when visiting the mainland opposite. It may well be that the Bubi settlement of the island dates from this time, whatever the origin of the Bota/Motão nomenclature.

There are a few more speculative comments that might be made. The present indigenous population of the mountain (the Bakweri) refer to their 13,500-ft peak as *Fako* 'cleared land', in reference to the grass which covers its upper ranges. This is burnt spectacularly in the dry season at a time which Tessmann gives in the calendar of the Bubi as *ăsamôte*, which he renders as *ăsa* 'dry, burnt' and *môte* 'big'. The deity of the Cameroon Mountain among the Bakweri is *Êfásamòtè* a name which is translated in folk-tales as 'half-man' (Ittmann, 1953, p. 19; Ardener, 1956, p. 107). We may be dealing with a pre-existing topographical name and with an onomastic tale to explain it. We should not then assume that Bubi ever occupied the mainland mountain – only that the Bakweri were in contact with Bubi-speakers, possibly at the coast, during the time of their settlement of the lower slopes of the mountain. With great landmarks like Mount Cameroon, of course, the range at which independent names may be given extends very far.[21]

Calbongos

We now turn to the other important name of this time. Pacheco's *Caaboo* seem to be suddenly resurrected in 1668 as *Calbongos*. No form of this sort occurs in any intermediate source. We have in fact merely to contend with Dapper (1668) on this point, for the great vogue of the Calbongos in maps and compilations of the eighteenth century is due entirely to his work. This applies equally to Barbot's account, which adds nothing independently on this subject.

In a well-known passage concerning Rio del Rey, Dapper,

after referring to the trading settlement of a certain Samson (of whom more later) adverts to the nature of the land round the river, and then says:

> 'The people who live higher up the river, by them called *Kalbongos*, are bold men, but villainous rogues (De volken, die hooger de reviere op wonen by hen genaemt Kalbongos zijn kloeke mannen, maer snode guiten)'.[22]

Dapper is not referring to Samson's people but to a people 'higher up'. It is not perfectly clear by whom they are called Kalbongos – it seems to be by themselves. They are fishermen with filed teeth, wearing penis-sheaths and smeared with camwood. They swear an oath by sucking the blood from a cut in the swearer's own arm, a custom which (also) the people 'on the high land of *Amboises*, in *Amboises* and *Boetery* observe; whose inhabitants continually wage war against the blacks on the *Rio del Rey*'. We recognize here derivatives of the *Ambos* and *Bota* of our other sources. An account of the *Landschap van Ambosine* then follows, which we may pass over and come to the account of the Cameroon River. Dapper says:

> 'On the north bank of the river Kamarones live very many people, called *Kalbanges*, who wage war against those above (*tegen tie van bovenen*), there the trade takes place. These *Kalbangen* are subject to a head (*Opper-hooft*) named *Monneba*.'[23]

As we shall see, Monneba's village is certainly the modern Douala, and, taking into account other evidence to be given below, we can state with virtual certainty that speakers of a Bantu language of Duala type were established there by 1665. The *Kalbangen* of Dapper would certainly then have to refer to the latter.

Barbot (in Churchill, 1732) merely repeats Dapper on Rio del Rey and Cameroons. He tidies up ambiguities in his source. 'The nation of the Calbonges' are firmly described as 'inhabiting about the upper end of Rio del Rey'.[24] After passing by *Ambozes*, Barbot says:

> 'The lands opposite to the latter places, on the north of Rio Camarones, are inhabited by the Calbonges, and as I have

said before, extend to the upper part of the Rio del Rey, and are a strong lusty people very knavish and treacherous dealers, and miserably poor, continually at war with the Camarones Blacks, living higher on that river, governed by a chief of their own tribe, called by them Moneba. ...'[25]

Barbot here collates Dapper's *Kalbongos/Kalbanges* into one, and interprets them as different from the Cameroons inhabitants with whom they are at war. Later maps and globes collate both Dapper and Barbot, stating that the Calbongos are at war with each other.[26] It cannot be too strongly emphasized that we have one source here – that is: Dapper. Barbot merely appears to doubt that there are *Kalbanges* as well as *Kalbongos* (as well he might) and that Moneba's people were either.

First we must ask: what is the status of Pacheco's form? Unfortunately, Dapper and Pacheco tend to be used to give each other mutual support without either being firmly founded. As we saw, Pacheco's doubled vowels are suspicious.[27] They may be corruptions for other letters, as we have seen. *Caaboo* never turns up again in the Portuguese period. The Italian form *Isolas canboa* merges with readings of *Ambos*, and I incline to see the *c* as merely misread: for *d'anboa* or the like. The status of Pacheco's form is then in doubt, and it is best to leave it out of consideration and to discuss Dapper on his own merits. Calbongo might be a ghost form for *Calborch*, an early (perhaps the earliest) Dutch name for Old Calabar, a form of which Dapper gives as an alternative to (Oudt) Kalbarien. How Old Calabar got its name is a well-known mystery in its own right (see Forde, 1956; Jones, 1963). The Calbongos are possibly part of the same mystery.

There are, however, the following points: we are by 1660 at the head of several genealogies of the Cameroon Coast. As we shall see, Moneba is probably the Mulobe of Duala, who is genealogically placed as the son of the eponymous Ewal'a Mbedi of the Duala.[28] Behind the eponym himself stands, however, the unexplained *Mbongo*, a form which lies at the heads of the genealogies of many local peoples, for example: the Bakweri, in the forms *Mbongo*, *Nambongo*, and *Nembongo* (for others see Ittmann, 1953; Ardener, 1956, p. 22). The full honorific form for a 'person of the Bakweri tribe' is *mokpel'anembongo*.

97

Indeed there is no dearth of local forms at these genealogical levels to play the jingling changes on the Calbongo theme. The Kole (Bakolle), a people of the Cameroon coast close to the Efik, traditionally descend from a separate offshoot of the Duala migration under a brother of Ewale of Duala. With Kol'a Mbongo and Ewal'a Mbongo, we can almost keep Dapper's Kalbongos and Kalbanges.[29] It is clear that a halt must be called: too many here is too much. Suffice it to say that, with the form Mbongo at the back of so many tribal histories, Dapper's sources *could* have heard a number of forms like *Calbongo*. It may be that such a form lies behind the name of Old Calabar (*Calborch*), with which New Calabar from Kalabari would then be quite unconnected.[30] Finally, the inland peoples of the Rio del Rey may have looked, and behaved, as described by Dapper. This is a separate question from whether the name *Calbongos* was 'real'.

The weakness of the onomastic evidence

I have ventured thus far into the onomastic morass, in order to set out how treacherous is the field to those approaching it either from the literary remains or from local knowledge, unless armed with the profoundest scepticism. The excessive range of coincidence alone must at once deter and amaze. There is no place for simple equations. It can easily be seen how, by the erroneous procedure of taking the sources at their face value, and then of taking each subsequent quotation of a key source as independent confirmation, a picture such as the following was built up, and it lies implicitly behind many statements on this area: The Calbongos are non-Bantu. As Caaboo they still occupy the Cameroon Mountain c. 1500 (Pacheco), but by Dapper's time, c. 1660, they are being pressed back by the Ambos who are Bantu. The Calbongos by this view are vaguely felt to be Efik- or Ekoi-speaking because of the similarity to the name for Old Calabar. A romantic variant of this view was Massmann's (1910) who saw the Calbongos and Kalbanges as *Zwergvolk* – Pygmies. The indefatigable Avelot, in his treatment of the population of Gaboon, imposed from afar an order on this scene.[31] He identified both Cameroon and Congo *Ambos*, linking under this name ('*Ambou*') the Bakota and other peoples, whom he took to have preceded the Bakongo founders of the Congo kingdom, together with the Duala of Cameroon, in 'a period before the twelfth century' (!) (see Poutrin, 1930).

Upon the most charitable view, the literary sources are just not precise enough for this kind of thing. Onomastic evidence should, in any event, never be confused with evidence from other sources, even when the latter is relatively soundly based. The compulsion to provide nomenclature from an 'historical' source for patterns derived from other data, has bedevilled equivalent fields in European studies for many years ('Celts', 'Scythians', 'Belgae', and the like). The connexions of the north-western Bantu among themselves form a separate and complex study, which is not helped by attempts to attach shadowy labels to already shadowy hypotheses.

From the survey of this first set of evidence, I wish to bring out the following points: for the period from the Portuguese discovery until the seventeenth century we can rescue *Ambos*, and probably *Bota*, as current terms. The former was primarily associated with the islands in Ambas Bay; the latter was probably a name of the inland peak of Mount Cameroon, the main ridge of which formed the *Serra de Fernam do Poo*. Doubtless this could be confirmed or denied by careful search in Lisbon. The peak was in any event also called by the name of *Motão*. We cannot even say of what people the Ambos Islanders were. Bubi of Fernando Po were there in historical times. I have merely added speculative remarks that would keep as an open question whether the Bubi settlement dated from a period as early as the Portuguese discovery. Pacheco's Caaboo remain unconfirmed. Calbongos are part of some confusion of Dapper's. Later, in the seventeenth century, the term *Ambos* was certainly applied to the area next to Rio del Rey, but the application is purely secondary at that time. The most we may be permitted to ask is: whether the early sixteenth-century name for the home of the islanders was given to the Portuguese from any local source. Only the peoples of Fernando Po or of the Rio Real (Ijaw) are likely to have been in a position to propagate such a name so early. Although there is evidence that the inner gulf was widely known by names of which *Moko*, *Womboko*, *Mumoko*, and the like appear to have been variants, applied to overlapping places, it would be premature to connect these with the name *Ambos*, let alone with some single people.[32]

99

EARLY EVIDENCE FOR THE DUALA AND EFIK POLITIES

In Dapper (1668) occurs a famous statement concerning the river of *Kamarones* (the Cameroon River):

'In deze reviere worden by d' onzen ook slaven gehandelt, voor een en de zelve waren, gelijk in Rio del Rey. Zy gebruiken met die van de *Kamarones* een selve getal: *Mo*, is by hen een; *Ba*, twee; *Mellela*, drie; *Meley*, vier; *Matan*, vijf.' (In this river our people also trade in slaves for the same goods as in Rio del Rey. They use the same numbers as the people of the *Kamarones*: *Mo* is among them: one; *Ba*, two; *Mellela*, three; *Meley*, four; *Matan*, five).[33]

This is repeated by Ogilby (1670, p. 483), who mistranslates (or possibly amends) it to read that the speech at Rio del Rey is different, instead of the same, but gives the same numerals with slight copying errors. Barbot (p. 385) follows Dapper accurately. The numerals are of Coastal Bantu type (shown in Ardener, 1956, p. 17n.). It is to these that Johnston refers when he says (1919, p. 27): 'the numerals of the Bakwiri or Barundo at Ambas Bay (Cameroons) written down by some French or Dutch trader at the close of the seventeenth century are almost identical with the modern form'. The numerals are not really of these specific types, but more important: there is nothing at all in these sources to show that they were written down at Ambas Bay. Elsewhere Johnston (1922, p. 144-145) refers specifically to the 1732 volume in which Barbot was published. Doke (1961, p. 20) follows Johnston.

This evidence for Coastal Bantu numerals at the Cameroons River by c. 1668 has always been very useful. Dapper's further statement that the language was the same as at Rio del Rey could have been taken fairly seriously as evidence perhaps of the activity of the Bakolle offshoot of the Duala whose traditions start at the same period. It was not to be expected that any further light could be thrown upon this situation, but this can now be done. In an edition of Leo Africanus issued at Rotterdam by Arnout Leers, bookseller, in 1665, there begins at p. 289 a description of the coast of Africa to supplement Africanus' account of the interior. This description is without doubt a chief source for Dapper in this area, or one which drew upon a common source with him – possibly that account by Samuel Blommaert referred to in Dapper's own introduction. Leers' publication in any event clarifies much in Dapper. In particular it gives a vocabulary containing thirty-seven words and all the numerals from one to ten. Since this material has not previously been extracted I have included it in an Appendix to this paper.[34]

This section is headed (translated): 'Words, in the *Cameronis*, *Rio d' Elrey*, and the high land of *Ambosus*'. That description is pretty well what it is: the list contains a mixture of Bantu words, many now visibly of Duala type, and some Efik-type non-Bantu words, together with their meanings in Dutch (or possibly Flemish). The two languages are clearly separated in the gloss for 'water', for which two words are given: *amon* (=Efik *mmɔŋ*), and *mareba* (=Duala *madiba*, in which *d/r* are allophones). The numerals are of completely Duala type, with the exception of 'nine' which is an interpolation. The detailed linguistic interest of this list cannot be gone into here, but it establishes that, by 10 March 1665 (the date of Arnout Leers' preamble), Efik- and Duala-type languages were spoken in an area bounded by Rio del Rey, where Efik is now spoken, and the Cameroons Estuary, where Duala is now spoken. The likeliest conclusion is that Efik and Duala were spoken then as now at Rio del Rey and Cameroons respectively. Dapper's statement that Rio del Rey and Cameroons spoke the same language can now be seen to derive from the somewhat ambiguous heading of this word-list.

Since this is a mixed list, it is quite possible that some of the forms were collected between these extreme points – that is: from the highland of *Ambosus*. But the Leers vocabulary is not a jargon, that is: not a trade language of mixed origin. Nevertheless, it goes back to the period in which the Duala language, as we know it, was laid down. As Ittmann early noted (1939, p. 32), Duala contains many Efik loan-words, and two of them actually appear in this list, one in basically Efik form (*macrale* ≡ Ef. *makara*, borrowed as Du. *mokala*, 'European'), and one probably already in borrowed form (*tocke tocke* ≡ Du. *tɔkitɔki*, borrowed from Ef. *etuk etuk*, 'small, a little'). The preservation of *k* in *kinde*, 'go', is less typical of Duala than of the neighbouring Isubu – a people between the Duala proper and the Cameroon

I   101

Mountain, who formed by 1800 the rival trading kingdom of Bimbia. Yet the Bantu vocabulary as a whole shows none of the clear Isubu stigmata (see Ardener, 1956, pp. 33-36). Possibly the loss of *k* was less advanced in Duala at the time. Two Coastal Bantu entries appear in Barbot's Old Calabar list which, unlike that of Leers, *is* largely a jargon and dates from the last quarter of the century: *kinde nongue-nongue* (Barbot: 'go sleep') which would be *kɛndɛ nanga o nɔngɔ*, or the like; and *meraba* ('water'), cf. Leers *mareba* from *madiba*. In the corrupt context of Barbot's list these words are not evidence on their own for the presence of settled Bantu-speaking people at Old Calabar (even though some of such people were probably there): the rest of the list contains reduplicated forms of possibly Efik-Ibibio origin, as well as entries like '*Negro – A black*' and '*Basin – Basons*', and many hypochoristic or baby-talk forms. This is merely evidence that forms of Coastal Bantu were among the scraps picked up by Barbot's rather unsophisticated informant in the Old Calabar area.

On the whole, the linguistic evidence, old and new, confirms the present distribution rather than any other, and suggests that the Efik and Duala trading clusters were already separately established, meeting in the Rio del Rey and Old Calabar zone, by the 1660s. It is of interest that further west, for the Bonny-New Calabar area, Dapper gives the numerals 'one' to 'four' (*barre, ma, terre, ni, sonny*) which are appropriately in an Ijaw form (*gbere, mme, tere, ini, sono* – cf. Thomas, 1914, p. 21). They are clearly from that same reliable source that must lie behind Leers for the Efik and Duala words, suggesting the presence of a fairly accurate linguistic observer along the coast at the time.

Samson and Moneba
Given the refreshing solidity of Leers' source, we may turn to his trading remarks with interest. They are separately appended in a section called: 'On the Customs in *Rio Calbary* or *Rio Reaal*'. After a few words of advice on the payments to be made at New Calabar, he moves straight to the Cameroons River, and afterwards adds a few words on Rio del Rey:

'There is little [to pay] at *Rio Cameronis* so the following should be noted, otherwise the Negros will make demands as unreasonable as they usually do. When you are in the river off the village, which is four [Dutch] miles up, in order to trade, the chief (*oppersten*) *Monneba* comes on board. You give him one iron bar and two copper bars. He is satisfied with this – if you want to give more you can.

At *Rio d'Elry*, there is also little, so the following should be noted, as aforesaid. The chief (*oppersten*) there is called *Samson*. When he comes on board, if he is given a half measure (*mas*) of beads (*koralen*), with two copper bars, he should be satisfied: he will pester you for more in trade, but give as little as you can, or he won't think highly of you' (Leers, p. 313).

Clearly Samson of Rio del Rey counted for more than Monneba of Cameroon, but neither for very much: the next entry is for the Gaboon (*Riviere de Jambon*) where the king and four notables had to be given many more goods. The historical existence of Samson and Monneba is probably firmly based. The author names another chief (*Abram*) at Cape Lopez, the names of the Portuguese owning sugar mills at S. Thomé, and the names of 54 mills themselves. Once again, this was a meticulous reporter.

Old Calabar River, as we shall see, was not visited. The Rio del Rey was the trading-spot of the time, and Samson's people, it appears, spoke an Ibibio dialect. The present Isangele of Oron-Amutu seem to be their successors (see below). The trade of Duala must have been in its very early stages. Given this firm ethnic fix in the middle of the seventeenth century, we may now attempt to relate it to the trading situation some years before.

The nature of the European contact
Samuel Brun, in his account of his voyage of 1614 (op. cit.), described the trade of an area, as we saw, somewhat imprecisely bounded, but mainly covering the zone from Rio del Rey to the Cameroons River. The trade was both in *accory* – a stone of indeterminate nature (Fage, 1962) which was bought by exchange against cowries – and in slaves captured by the local people, and sold at a low price: three or four measures of

Spanish wine, or two or three handfuls of cowries (Brun, ed. Naber, pp. 32-33). Brun noted that they would be sold at 100 ducats apiece 1,000 leagues away. The picture here and else-where in Brun would suit the mountain area: fruitful soil, no palm-wine (both oil- and raffia-palms have been relatively scarce), and leaf-mat houses (very characteristic – for the volcanic soil does not compact to make mud walls). The im-pression is of the same kind of trade as that described by Pacheco a century earlier. By 1614 the trade was still unsophis-ticated, and almost laughably inexpensive. There are hints, however, that some regularity in the trade may have been beginning. Brun's ship bought four boys in the area for 9 measures of wine. They were offered by the 'towns' (*Staden*), a usage reminiscent of the later trader's terminology for the Cameroons River, and there is striking evidence to suggest that the people of this estuary were now known.

When Brun visited Cape Mount on the (Liberian) Grain Coast (Bouchaud [p. 84] – grossly misled by the Latin version, and followed by Mveng [1963, pp. 161-162] – places it in the Congo)[35] he found a king, Thaba Flamore:

> 'This king or Thaba Flamore spoke French, but his wife (called Maria by us Dutch) spoke good Netherlandish, black of body though she was. For another supercargo [*comes*≡ Dutch *kommies*] had brought her from *Camaronas*, desiring to keep her near him, and she learned the language from him. She afterwards became the wife of the Thaba, however, in this way: the Thaba was involved in a war six years since, and he asked this *comes* to take part in the fight with him, and in return he would give him eight *centner* [c. 8 cwt] of ivory. The *comes* did this with pleasure, as he was well acquainted with the Thaba. They went together into battle but the *comes* and a cabin-boy perished, and so the Thaba took the wife of the *comes* to himself.'[36]

This 'curieux petit roman colonial', to use Bouchaud's felicitous Gallic phrase, occurred, from Brun's dates, in the year 1608. The French had already a big establishment near Sestos by 1602 (Naber, p. 39 note), which would account for the Thaba's proficiency in French.

One senses that the contacts with the Cameroon coast still

had some of that amiability (soon to be lost) that marked the contacts of the Fernandian Bubi and the English in the early nineteenth century. Brun's voyage probably occurred when the Dutch had barely begun to exploit this part of the coast. In the description of Guinea, bound in with the voyage of Linschoten, published in 1596 at Amsterdam, the author recommended sailing straight from the Gold Coast to Cape Lopez or to S. Thomé.[37] The inner portion of the Bight of Biafra was probably not easily navigable until the seventeenth century. Pieter de Mareez, referring to about 1600, advises that it is necessary to leave Benin straight for Cape Lopez

> 'and to pass by all the rivers which are inside the bend (*destour*) because there is nothing profitable to do there, and if one happens to fall behind the island of Fernando Po, one is in danger of staying there all one's life without escaping' (Mareez, 1605, p. 93).

Sometimes, he adds, the wind would not even serve to reach Cape Lopez direct, and one ended up at the Rio d'Angra and Corisco Island at its mouth.

Indirect confirmation of this navigational problem, in the Portuguese period, comes from a report of João Lobato to King John III (dated 13 April 1529), dealing with the economic and social state of S. Thomé, under which, at the time, the Bight of Biafra nominally fell.[38] He is asking for gear to rig out ships for Elmina. Of one of them he says:

> 'The ship Toyro Santo, which is still in the shipyard, as I have written to Your Highness, and which I have made so that it can be rowed in order to go to the Island of Fernã do Poo (*fiz pera se poder remar pera hir á jlha de Fernã do Poo*) ... is not yet finished.'

There was a shortage of cables and anchors. It seems very likely that the Portuguese visits to the coast opposite Fernando Po also required the use of oars. This would explain the salience of the Cameroon Mountain coast nearest to Fernando Po in the early material, rather than the later emporia of Rio del Rey and the Cameroons River.[39]

After 1600 the technical difficulties were apparently less

important. In about 1618, not long after the time of Brun's visit to the area in a Dutch ship, Gaspar da Rosa, the Portuguese factor at Elmina, wrote that the Dutch had been undercutting the Portuguese for years along the Guinea coast with up to thirty ships, and that:

> 'the evil has gone so far that the Dutch in addition go with their ships to the trading ports of *Sam Thomé, Benim, Jabu, rio Forcado*, and *rio do Camarão*, where they obtain much cloth, cotton, fowls, accory and other precious stones for the coast of Mina, and ivory and pepper which there is in Benim, and no more trade remains for Sam Thomé than that in slaves, because these Dutchmen purchase the other goods. . . .'[40]

The reference to Cameroon and the accory for Mina are Portuguese confirmation of Brun's story, besides specifying the Cameroons River as a trading-place.

By the time of Leers' source, trade, as we have seen, has become regularized, with recognized middlemen and dues to pay at Rio del Rey and Cameroons River. There are now detailed sailing directions for passing up the Rio del Rey estuary. The writer makes a reference to the Old Calabar river under the form *Oude Calborch*, with the surprising statement that a great reef lies before its entrance which blocks the whole river so that it cannot be navigated.[41] Nothing could be more indicative of the critical date of this source. From Rio del Rey, the route down the Cameroon Mountain coast is given with detail on soundings. The mountain is called the *High Land of Bota*. On its coast is a trading place near a cape, from which the coast runs south-east to the Islands of *Amboises*. These are described as 'two small islands' between which it was possible to sail. They are now said to be merely a good spot for provisions but of little value for trade, and little visited. From here the sailing directions take us past the 'small' or 'old' *Cameronis* (the Bimbia River) and to the Cameroon estuary itself with minute directions to reach the trading-place of Moneba. Ivory in small quantities is obtainable in the estuary. There is no longer need to speculate upon the source of these directions, for maps of the type to which the Leers' source referred are in the Dutch Archives at The Hague. On a large-scale chart of the Cameroon Estuary, *Monna Baes dorp* (sic) is marked on the present site of Duala, and specifically on the later site of Bell Town. The creek at which ivory was picked up led westwards towards the present Mungo river, and thus to the mountain hinterland. On a collated map which includes material from this chart also, the Rio del Rey area is shown. Villages near the Rumby Estuary, as well as the *dorp* which was probably Samson's on the Andokat arm, are marked. The charts will be the subject of a separate paper.[42]

This cluster of sources with its cartographical, linguistic, and trading documentation clearly lay behind much later knowledge of the area. It confirms strikingly, once again, that the term *Ambos* and the like referred specifically to the islands, and not to the mainland, and gives further support to the hypothesis that Pacheco's *Bota* was the Cameroon Mountain.

When did this dawn of the new trading situation on the coast between the Cross and Cameroons rivers occur? For the position had developed spectacularly when Dapper received his charter to publish in 1668. His text follows the Leers source closely, but passes by Old Calabar without mentioning its unnavigability, and comes to the Rio del Rey, to the trading-place of Samson. But something is changed; Dapper amends his source (Ogilby's translation of 1670 is here adequate):

> 'At the Northerly shore thereof lieth a Township, over which (some years since) one Samson had the command; but driven out by those of Ambo, he hath ever since maintained himself by Robbing; for his village was so wasted by fire, that very few houses remained, and those all made of Palm canes [Dapper: *Palmitasbladen*: 'palm-leaves'] from the top to the bottom as well the Sides as the Roof.'[43]

If Samson had declined in the world, Moneba appears to have risen in fortune. His people are dubbed *Kalbanges*, as we saw earlier, a matter we may now ignore. They are, says Dapper:

> 'under a headman (*Opper-hooft*) called Monneba, who is taken to be the strongest of the princes round about. The village where this headman has his residence, lies upon a height, which has a very tidy cover of natural vegetation, and it is taken to be the pleasantest spot in the whole bight. There is an abundance of provisions such as yams, bananas, palm-wine

and bordon-wine [raffia-palm wine]. This bordon-wine is
like palm-wine, but is not so good because it grows in
swampy country. The houses are built in a rectangular
shape.'[44]

Dapper adds little on trade, but he notes the ivory that was
collected there. Other items he mentions seem to come in some
obscure way from the Leers' word-list (see Appendix).

For the zone between Rio del Rey and the Cameroons River,
we are offered a collation. Samuel Brun's terminology on the
'Highland of Ambosy' is substituted for the 'High Land of
Bota' of the Leers' source, and, together with Brun's remarks
on the Spanish and the Canaries Peak, it becomes, with Dapper
and Barbot, canonical. The trading-place of the Leers' source on
the mountain coast becomes: 'various villages, among others
one called Bodi or Bodiwa, otherwise Cesge'. *Cesge*, at least, I
have suggested to be a ghost-name ultimately from Ruiters (see
above). *Bodi* or *Bodiwa* is quite possibly a ghost from *Bota*.
Although only *one* village has these three names in Dapper,
Barbot turns it into three and, in later maps based on him,
three are accordingly marked. From Brun are lifted directly
references to the lack of palm-wine and to a certain *Gayombo*
drink, now ghosting its way through the literature as *Gajanlas*.[45]
'In the village Bodi', Dapper adds, possibly as if to mark a
change since Brun's day, 'there is trade in slaves but little
accory.'

Lastly Dapper contributes, from an unidentified source, an
independent section on the Islands of Amboises, which is classic
and need not be repeated in detail here. The inhabitants lived,
it may be noted, on the middlemost island of three, that is: the
one named on Admiralty charts to this day as *Ambas* (although
known as *Ndame* to the coastal peoples). The islanders spoke
Portuguese at the time, thus surely confirming that these were
the *Ambos* of the days of Portuguese supremacy. The tradition
from now on runs unbroken, through Barbot and the English
period of the eighteenth and nineteenth centuries, down to the
present day. After Dapper, the islanders take second place to
their neighbours of the Cameroons River in future contacts with
European trade.[46] The Isubu trading chieftaincy of Bimbia
began on another island in a creek on the edge of the Cameroons

Estuary – the 'small Cameroons' of Leers – for traders now preferred middlemen with organized contact with the hinterland, which the islanders could never have had. Some of their trade in ivory had been coming through the creeks from the Cameroons River (Dapper, p. 138), probably via the future Bimbia. Moneba's Duala-speaking trading-spot was to become firmly established. I believe the identification with Mulobe of Duala to be sound, and others of his dynasty can be identified in the second half of the eighteenth century when independent English sources begin for the area. But the standard geographies and the great maps of the time showed no advance. Indeed, nearly a century and a quarter after the Leers' publication, Moneba was still said to be ruling on the 'River Kamarones', in an English volume commemorating Captain Cook's voyages (Bankes *et al.*, 1787, p. 365).

Historical conclusions

Samson's decline at Rio del Rey was certainly succeeded chronologically by the development of Old Calabar. When Samson flourished, Leers' meticulous source thought the Cross River entrance was unnavigable. Barbot says that, on his first voyage in 1678, he met an English ship which had spent ten months in Old Calabar, and had obtained 300 slaves. In another well-known passage he records that, in April 1698, the *Dragon* collected 212 slaves and indulged in a valuable trade there, in which a long list of notables was involved.[47] The advantages of Old Calabar, as a trading-point, far outweigh those of Rio del Rey. For one thing, the Cross River Estuary leads to a real river, and an important one. Rio del Rey was in effect an anchorage in the eastern delta of the Cross, into which only minor streams ran. We do not have to visualize Rio del Rey rendered uninhabitable by attacks from the Cameroon Mountain followed by a retreat to Old Calabar, for slaving took place in Rio del Rey through the next century. Dapper's remark that Samson's village at Rio del Rey was burnt by people 'of Ambo' is however of interest. By *Ambo* is by now meant, as we have seen, the geographical area towards the Cameroon Mountain. Some degree of conflict on this coast is referred to by several writers of the seventeenth century. Samson's attackers may have been Bakolle congeners of the Duala movement. This is the parsimonious conclusion. Nevertheless it is probable that movement towards the estuary by the inland Bantu-speakers now known as Balundu and the like had begun by this time.

The Ibibio group known as *Effiat* (Forde & Jones, 1951, p. 89), who occupy fishing villages in the estuary of Rio del Rey, seem to have lost their foothold on the mainland, and especially on the Rumby Estuary, to these peoples, whom they call *Efut* and *Ekita*, and who called them in turn *Ifiari* or *Fiari* (Langhans, 1902). Efut mingled with Efik in the group known as Isangele to the north of Rio del Rey, and some became part of the population of Old Calabar (Forde & Jones, op. cit., p. 90; Forde, 1956, pp. 4, 121, 123).

The Ibibio-speaking Isangele population of Oron and Amutu villages were the traders of the later Rio del Rey, at the head of the estuarine system. Their traditions, as assembled by Anderson (1933), speak of movement to Rio del Rey from Enyong and the establishment of trade with the Portuguese, upon hearing of the success of Bonny; of contacts with the Balundu (the Efut who joined them); of fights with Ifiang cannibals to the north; and of the departure of trade because of an invitation by the chief of Obutong (Old Town, Calabar) to the Europeans. Samson's people seem to belong somewhere in this story, as may Dapper's wild up-river people. Later a group straight from Old Calabar (Archibong: Asibong) dominated this already mixed group.

In addition, Old Calabar acquired an 'extended family of Creek Town' (Simmons, in Forde, 1956, p. 71) called *Ambo*, and various personalities in Old Calabar had, in Antera Duke's time (c. 1785), names such as: Sam Ambo, King Ambo, and the like (see also Jones, in op. cit., p. 160, and elsewhere). The association of the Ambo family with the Cameroons seems to have survived into the nineteenth century. The name is said to be regarded by them as a foreign name of Portuguese origin (op. cit., p. 160) although their etymology is fanciful.[48] The name would rather have belonged to the pidgin used with the foreign frequenters of Old Calabar, to denote an origin from the general Cameroon area. Their own name *Mbarakom* is of interest and confirms this, as it appears to derive from the milieu of the Upper Cross River Bantoid-speaking peoples, and not from that of the coastal Bantu. Several inland movements seem to have been set off by the growth of Old Calabar as a trading-centre, which affected the whole Cross River Basin, and by the nineteenth century had touched the inland grassland plateau.[49]

Samson and Moneba are the earliest named coastal Cameroonians recorded, after Maria, the queen of Cape Mount. The period they inaugurate is broadly, in ethnic and linguistic respects, that of today. The widest limits for this appearance lie between 1614 (Brun) and 1665 (Leers). If Leers' source was really Samuel Blommaert (referred to by Dapper in his introduction as his own source), then the terminus 1665 may be pushed back. Blommaert was born in 1583, and made his first voyage to the Indies in 1603. His prime was from 1622 until about 1646, during which period he was influential in the Westindische Compagnie of Amsterdam.[50] The Leers' linguistic material is first-hand. If Blommaert was personally involved in its collection (which is not, of course, necessarily so) we may have to look back at least to the 1630s. The 1630s are also suggested by the possible date of the large-scale map of the Cameroons Estuary already mentioned.

If Moneba was Mulobe, with a floruit at A.D. 1650±15, his father Ewale, the supposed founder of Duala, and his grandfather Mbedi, would belong to a milieu datable to c. 1600. That would be about the time of the early informal contacts: the opening of the Rio dos Camarões to trade, and the Maria and Samuel Brun period. Jones (1956) has provided a useful insight into the interpretation of genealogies in the trading states. The lack of any tradition between the shadowy Mbongo (Ardener, 1956, pp. 22-23) and Ewale, son of Mbedi, would suggest, by the principle Jones uses for Kalabari, that the Mbongo tradition validates the origin of the Duala and their congeners, while the stories of Ewale, and of the other Mbedine lines, validate the dynasties that grew out of the trading contacts. Mbongo belongs to the 'proto-tradition'. The Mbedine events themselves (Dugast, 1949, pp. 10-21; Ardener, 1956, pp. 17-18, 20-21) can hardly have occurred later than some time in the sixteenth century (for their time-span will have been compressed) although we need not imagine that they had any great conspicuity. There is, traditionally, a movement from a place called *Pitti* above the Cameroon Estuary on the Dibamba affluent: the creek later known, indeed, as Moneba's Channel.

Other small ethnic groups attach their ancestors to the same movement, including the Kole who moved within sight of Rio del Rey and the Malimba who settled on the south of the Cameroons Estuary. These lengthy although exiguous movements (even the Duala numbered less than 20,000, three centuries later, while the Kole were numbered in hundreds) are surely to be accounted for by the response to the growing demands of that early trade mentioned by Pacheco at about 1500. This, mediated by the Ambos islanders at first, directly involved the Cameroons Estuary only later.[51]

The foundation of the Duala dynasties may then be securely pushed back to at least a century before Asmis' unsupported date of 1706 (Asmis, 1907, p. 85) – to which Brutsch (1956, p. 56), followed by Mveng (p. 140), gives a surprising weight – with its roots probably in the sixteenth century. Less securely, I would guess that the presence at Rio del Rey of an Ibibio-speaking element was no younger. The early mention of the *Pescaria*, in João de Lisboa, 1514, and the unbroken reference to it thereafter, suggests that the estuary presented much the same appearance as today. Today the fishing traps belong to Efik-Ibibio and to Kole. One or other people was probably old-established by c. 1500; the former are perhaps, in view of the preceding, more likely to have been first.

FINAL REMARKS

Of late, historians of Africa have rightly become very conscious of the problems of the use of oral tradition (Vansina, 1965). It may well be, however, that social anthropologists for their part still tend to underestimate the intricacies of the 'documentary tradition'. That completely uncritical use of documentary sources remarked upon by Professor Evans-Pritchard (1961) is becoming a thing of the past, but the course of the maize controversy reveals that it is not yet dead (Teixeira da Mota & Carreira, 1966, p. 79 note). The nature of the documentary tradition must of course be worked out, as far as possible, independently of hypotheses from other bodies of evidence, for in the field of African history cross-tainting takes place almost insensibly. Nowhere is this more likely than in the onomasiology. Thus the Basa have been sought in the Cameroons sources, because oral tradition suggested that they should be sought, although the onomastic variants upon which conclusions were based belonged to corrupt sources. For a sufficient and critical examination there can be no substitute for recourse to the original texts: even the best editions (and all translations) may let us down.

On the other side yawns a different pit-fall. Local knowledge, the social anthropologist's forte, may be dangerous (although slightly less so than lack of it). Etymologies do not necessarily become any more trustworthy because they are derived from local languages: their deficiencies may become merely harder to detect. I have offered some, because it is the duty of those placed to do so to offer a certain amount of controlled speculation. But the difference between this kind of etymology and that scientific kind which rests upon even fair linguistic evidence is, I hope, revealed by the valuable Leers' vocabulary given in the Appendix. It is a pity that those students who work, for example, among the linguistic fragments remaining in the toponymy of early Europe, do not, before applying etymologies to them, turn to us for evidence of the welter of conflicting possibilities that exists before the process of oblivion reduces the problem to more manageable proportions.

For political history this paper adds, I think, to the evidence for the great value of the genealogies of the trading dynasties of West Africa. They tend to open and shut like concertinas according to the chronologies offered, but I believe that Jones's attempt to separate the validating tradition of the dynasty from that part validating the origins of the ethnic group at large, does throw real light upon the foreshortening found so frequently in them.

NOTES

1. In this paper I have usually been compelled to make my own translations of European sources. Fortunately the language, often that of seafaring men, is usually very simple, and where it is not I have taken advice. I am especially indebted to Mr R. Cinatti, but must also mention the suggestions of Mr R. Feltham, Mr G. Stuvel, and Mr Cutileiro, on specific points. None of these is responsible for any errors that remain. Save for the rather elementary commentary on Pacheco, there is no point at which any interpretation of idiom could be, I hope, crucial.

Geographical forms and proper names when cited in a source in translation are in the form of that source. When not citing sources in quotation marks, standard spellings are used. Specifically the four basic forms: *Rio del Rey*, *Fernando Po*, *Cameroons River*, and *Cape Lopez* will be used. The name *Moneba* in certain sources has two *ns*, and so although I take the former as standard I also use the latter in those contexts.

I have tended to use the term 'Efik' for the Ibibio dialects of the Bight of Biafra. It may be that this is a misuse. I use the term to distinguish not Efik from other Ibibio dialects, but Ibibio-speakers in the present Efik area from speakers of Bantu languages.

1a. The status of onomastic studies in many fields is to be seen in, for example, the symposium edited by Blok (1966).

2. This part of Barros' text is reprinted in *MMA*, I, pp. 438-439. See also Bouchaud (1952, Chapters 3-4). The Portuguese *Camarões*, 'prawns', refers to the migrations of a particular species (Monod, 1928, p. 177; Ittmann, 1939, p. 5; Ardener, 1956, p. 42). But *Camarão* (singular) was a name also given to an island in the Red Sea (Ramos-Coelho, 1892). See also Note 14.

3. The edition of Silva Dias is used here. Bouchaud discusses Pacheco in his Chapter 5.

4. This is quite clear from all sources.

5. S. Dias, p. 125.

6. After the words *Aquy mapa*: 'here is a map' – an irony: for this important map, like all his others, is missing.

7. South of the Cameroon estuary was the *Cabo do Ilheo* ('Cape of the Islet'), which Bouchaud identifies with the western extremity of the islands which form the delta of the Sanaga River, south of Douala on the present Cameroon coast (Bouchaud, op. cit., p. 53).

8. Enciso (1518) – there is no pagination. Bouchaud (pp. 56-57) uses Barlow's English translation (mentioned below) which gives *de galo*, and so obscures the source of this folk-etymology (as if 'gulf of the cock'). On the *Rio de los santos* I am not absolutely happy, but it is clearly a river between the Rio Real (New Calabar-Bonny) and the Cape of Fernando Po.

9. Also on Jean Fonteneau, see Bouchaud (Chapter V, and notes). The accessible edition is Musset (1904). Pigafetta (1591), who was published at Rome, translated the work of Duarte Lopes, a Portuguese, into Italian. Pigafetta says that *le nationi chiamate Anziques* are bounded on the seaward side by *populi d' Ambus* (p. 14). I take Pory's (1600) description of the position of the Ambus to be a verbal description of Pigafetta's map, rather than an independent statement. Pigafetta is the source of the spelling *Ambus* on the Italian map in Brown's Edition of Pory, which otherwise owes a great deal to Ortelius' *Theatrum Orbis Terrarum* dated 1570. Of the Cameroon coast, Pigafetta says that the inhabitants of S. Thomé had commerce with those of the mainland who gathered (*si riducono*) at the mouths of rivers one of which was called after '*Fernando di Poo, cioè di Polue*' (Po was taken commonly to mean 'dust' – thus he is frequently called *Fernand Poudre* in French sources) who discovered it. There was an island opposite its mouth 36 miles away. The 'Fernando Po river' was probably the Cameroons River, but one doubts whether this name was actually used. It looks like an attempt to explain Pigafetta's own map in which the corrupt name *Serra de Bisenscias do poo*, referring to the mountain, is placed along the Cameroons River.

10. Bouchaud (pp. 170-171). He traces forms in the maps from *Biafra* and *Biafar* back through: *Biascar, Giafar, Maffra, Masra, Mascha, Mescha,*

Mesche. Bouchaud gives reasons for the rejection of other etymologies. The name became a 'kingdom' and later a city was created on the maps. Of late, some in Cameroon have wished to find the name *Basa* (an important people of Sanaga-Maritime) in the word.

11. *MMA*, IV, 1954, pp. 144-146. The document is now also listed in Ryder's recent guide (1965) as item 41, p. 12. (On the amount of a *moyo* see Mota and Carreira, 1966, p. 81n.) Mr Cinatti suggests to me that Roiz is complaining that the malagueta was denied to the king, not by peculation of the *feitor*, but by the failure of the latter to open up the market. This letter, and one to be cited later by Lobato of the same year, suggest an active period of interest in Fernando Po and the coast. There is a well-known document of 26 March 1500 by which the inhabitants of S. Thomé were accorded rights in perpetuity to trade on the mainland 'from the Rio Real [New Calabar-Bonny estuary] and the island of Fernam de Poo, as far as the country of Manicomguo, excepting that they cannot trade in the country where there is gold. . . .' (Text in *MMA*, I, 1952, p. 183; also Ramos-Coelho, 1892, p. 107; Blake, 1937, Vol. I, pp. 89-92). The bishopric of S. Thomé was established on 3 Nov. 1534, and comprised the coast of West Africa and South-West Africa. The area from Cape Lopes to the Cunene was excised as the Diocese of Congo and Angola, at S. Salvador, by the Bull of 20 May 1596.

12. Ruiters (1623). The Edition of Naber (1913 (1)) gives only part of the text. Further portions are cited in the notes to Naber (1913 (2)).

13. A derivation from Portuguese *zambos*, 'half-castes', would be better than Naber's: in that it is not excluded that the islands had a population of this type, although from Figueiredo's words this does not sound very likely. At most this significance may account for the faulty word-division.

14. The union of the Portuguese and Spanish crowns lasted from 1580 to 1640. The Dutch were, of course, in close contact with the Spanish Netherlands. The English name Cameroon(s) comes via Sp. *Camarones*. The name *Jamoer* appears in Dutch sources as an alternative for *Camarones* or the like. I take this to be a reading from Italian maps in which *gamaro* or deformities of it appear – being translations of *camarão* ('prawn'). Ruiters, by the way, gives another Portuguese name for Mount Cameroon, in addition to those already discussed: *Montegos*. Naber interprets this as (I translate): *monte*='mountain', *gos*, 'a measure of length' (see Naber, 1913 (2), p. 31, note). Portuguese *gos* derives from India, and ultimately from Sanskrit *gavyuti* (*DELP*) a measure of about 2 miles.

15. Figueiredo (op. cit., folio 57, reverse).

16. Ruiters (Naber, 1913 (1), p. 83).

17. Brun's surname is so spelt on the title-page of the German edition (which is also in his own words, from which the Latin edition of De Bry seriously departs). The edition is Naber (1913 (2)).

18. Bouchaud (1952, pp. 82-83) uses the Latin (De Bry) translation of Samuel Brun (1625), which unfortunately tidies up and even misrepresents the German text in many respects. For example, after the passage cited above, the German says in literal translation: 'The which two countries (*Länder*) received their names from the Spanish, since fine rivers or streams there flow down and into the sea'. The former says (according to Bouchaud, p. 82): 'These two appellations, borrowed from the Portuguese, were given to the streams which flow into the sea at this place because they are particularly pleasant and salubrious.' *Rio de Anckare* (Bouchaud, *Rio de Anchara*), from Portuguese

Angra, 'creek' or 'bay' is the usual name of the estuary of Rio Muni. It could also mean the *angra da pescaria* of Rio del Rey. Bouchaud states that here it means Ambas Bay. I think it does not: Corisco (see below) was the next land-fall at this time after the Cameroons River. The length of coast concerned is said by Brun to be '60 miles'. We must assume 60 Dutch miles, however, which will be more compatible with the distance from Rio del Rey to Corisco. Possibly Brun confused the names of the Pescaria and Corisco but visited both.

19. Naber (1913 (2), p. 32) gives Brun's words. His statement about the Spanish gives the form *La alt tierra de Ambosy.* Dapper (1668) copies it as *Alta terra de Ambosi,* and Barbot (1732) copies him as *Alta-Tierra de Ambozi.* Burton (1863, vol. II, pp. 235-237) copies this, but quite wrongly attributes the source to 'Mr Grazilhier' whom Barbot uses for a different part of his text. Barbot is cited in the Cameroons Annual Report (e.g. 1958) and so has acquired currency locally.

20. In Ardener (1956) and Ittmann (1956, 1957) the local versions of *Bota* probably stem ultimately from a Duala-European source. They are not used by the inhabitants of the present Bota Island and Bota Land. When *Bota* was applied in the seventeenth century to a point on the coast there is much to suggest that it was at a different point – near Cape Debundscha.

21. Tessmann thought to see Bubi influence on the Bakweri language, although his examples are not convincing (Tessmann, 1932, p. 119). Another etymology for the first element of *Efas' a mote* would be *masa* 'mountain' (var. *basa*). The Bubi call both their own peak and the distantly visible Mt Cameroon by this name, the latter being in Tessmann's time distinguished as *masa mo moa mbola*: 'Peak inside the *moa*' (Tessmann, p. 151) where *moa* is 'the view on the horizon'.

22. I cite the second edition of 1676, p. 137.

23. Op. cit., p. 138.

24. In Churchill (1732, p. 385).

25. Op. cit., p. 386.

26. Cf. the famous map reproduced at the end of Bouchaud (1952).

27. If they express phonetic care they render almost exactly the Yoruba greeting: *kábɔ́ɔ́* (some misunderstanding involving a Benin coast interpreter? That way madness lies!).

28. See Brutsch (1950, pp. 214, 216); Ardener (1956, pp. 18-20).

29. By the omission of Mbedi.

30. The *Kole (Kɔ̀lɛ̂)* offer the best centre for speculative derivations since their usual eponymous form Kol'a Mbedi was actually in use to describe them in the nineteenth century, as *Collambedi* (Hutchinson, 1858, p. 167). Since this would be heard as something close to *Kɔlambɛri*, the likeness to 'Calabar' is striking even if, as is all too possible, fortuitous.

31. Avelot's views may be found in Poutrin (1930, p. 49 ff.).

32. Bouchaud (1952) cautiously suggested Ibo or Abo as etymons. I (1956, p. 22) suggested the present *Bamboko* (through some form as *vato v' Amboko*). Mveng (1963, p. 175) follows me. I rejected the *Mbo* because this very active cluster never reached the coast. It is now possible to think that the name *Mbo* whose full form may appear in Bakossi Mbuog, is basically a place-name of the same origin as Womboko. This matter will be treated elsewhere without prejudice to the question of the origin of the Portuguese *Ambos*. These con-

fusing elements should be noted: According to *DELP*, *Ambó* 'from the Indo-Aryan' occurs in the Portuguese literature on the Indies as the name of a fruit tree ('. . . *arvores de fruitas . . . ambós fermozissimos . . . de grandes, e saborozos*') which occurred in Amboina. Dr Pocock informs me that *ambó* would be connected with Gujarati *amb*, Skt. *amr*: 'a mango'. The world-wide nature of the 'onomastic reserve' of the Portuguese language should not be lost sight of. Finally, a lady called Ana Ambó gave her name to the bay (*enseada*) at which the first Portuguese settlement on S. Thomé was made in 1486, under João de Paiva (Tenreiro, 1961, p. 59).

33. I cite the second edition of 1676, p. 135.

34. There is a reference to Leers' work, the only one which I have seen, in Naber (1913 (2); see the valuable note to p. 31).

35. There is an error (90 miles for 900 miles) in Bouchaud's text, p. 85, for the distance of Cape Mount from Angola, which has misled him, and indeed makes him take the story as evidence of a strong French presence in the Congo area at this early date. Naber's edition is quite clear on the point. Mveng further states this error on his p. 117. The reference to the *Staden* is also in neither author.

36. Brun's 'uns Teutschen' is translated as 'us Dutch' because he is clearly identifying himself with the Dutch interest. Bouchaud, followed again by Mveng, gives 'sixteen years' instead of 'six years'. The latinized text is also inevitably a more polished and over-explicit paraphrase of Brun's rather crude style.

37. Linschoten (1596, p. 1 of the Description).

38. See note 11.

39. Lobato's letter was written only a month before the complaint of Duarte Rodrigues. Lobato is given in *MMA*, I, 1952, pp. 505-518, and is listed in Ryder (1963, p. 12) as item 40. For a discussion of general reasons why S. Thomé and not Fernando Po became the centre of Portuguese power, see Tenreiro (1961, pp. 57-59).

40. The text is in *MMA* (VI, 1955, pp. 346-350). It is also quoted in Cordeiro (1881, p. 23), and listed in Ryder (1963, p. 79), as his item 965.

41. Leers (op. cit., p. 304). It is the first Dutch form for the name Old Calabar known to me. It is important to note that Leers' source refers to New Calabar only as *Rio Reaal*. It is Dapper who applies the name *Kalbarien* to both the *Rio Reaal* and *Oude Calborch* (he uses for the latter the alternative *Kalborgh* derived from Leers' source). The Leers' form *Calborch* may not be a folk-etymology (as if ending in *-burg* or *-borg*), but a form coincidentally similar to that of (New) Calabar and which was known first to the Dutch. One would ask the historians of the Delta when the name (New) Calabar (from Kalabari) was first used separately from Rio Real (Simmons gives a reference to 1650). It is certainly separated in the late Portuguese period, e.g. Garcia in 1621 separates a *rei de Calabar* from a *rei do Rio Real* (Cordeiro, 1881, pp. 27-28; Ryder, 1965, p. 79, item 965, says 1620).

42. These MS. charts present some difficulties because both are to some extent collations. (Hague, *Rijksarchief*: (1) *Marine* 2334, (2) Leupe 145. No (1) is also incorporated in No. (2), but rationalized, it seems, in the light of a Barbot-type description. No. (1) calls the Dibamba Creek *Monna Base Gat*: for *Monnabaes Gat*. The clear parallel with the name of the village (so: Monnaba's Creek) clears up the problems of later forms: *Monambascha* and the like, which have

been interpreted as Malimba and Basa in the past. The Basa may be looked for in vain in the sources.

43. Dapper, p. 137; Ogilby, p. 483. Ogilby is not a reliable source to use without reference to the original.

44. Dapper, p. 139. Ogilby more imposingly translates: 'The Town where he keeps his seat royal stands scituate on a Hill, very neatly Hedged about with Trees . . .' (p. 484).

45. Brun (Naber), p. 32, refers to a drink named *Gayombo* which he says is made from a 'certain root'. He says that the people made it. If, as Naber (1913 (2), p. 32) suggests, this is a reference to Gombo (*Hibiscus esculentus*) from which 'Gomba coffee' is made, the drink would be of West Indian origin and drunk perhaps by the African crew-men when short of palm-wine, not by the local people.

46. For the present inhabitants, see: Ardener (1956); Ittmann (1956, 1957); Ardener, E. and S. (1958).

47. Barbot (pp. 381, 383, 465); Forde (1956); Jones (1963).

48. From 'love'. The reference to 'Portuguese' origin is of no corroborative value in this context. The Portuguese were not at Old Calabar as we have seen. Whatever the implications of the following part of this paper for Efik contacts with Bantu-speakers elsewhere, I suggest that the term Ambo at Creek Town comes from the period of Barbot and later.

49. Mbarakom=Mbudikum, and the like, which meant at the coast the approaches to the inland plateau. The name is connected (in a complex way) with that of the Widekum area on the borders of the plateau (cf. Chilver 1961, p. 235). In all the early sources it may be noted that only two purport to refer to any far inland area. The first is the undoubtedly corrupt text of Pacheco concerning Bota. All probability is against the figure '50 leagues inland' being a real one, quite apart from other considerations already cited. For, in the words of Shakespeare's Henry V, 'who hath measured the ground?' We are not dealing then with the Babute (Wute), as Mauny and others speculate (Mveng, 1963, p. 105). The second is Ruiters (op. cit., p. 83 *et seq*.), who has a section called: 'Of white men, who dwell among the blacks, and continually fight with the *Negros*'. He says that 150 miles to the north-east or north-north-east of the Cameroons River 'live a race of people who in contrast to the *Negros* are not black but pure white . . .'. He adds that they wage fierce war against the Negroes who live there. Their people were so strong (or numerous) that, 'had they all their faculties', they would have overwhelmed all the Negroes. (Ruiters takes them to be albinos, whom he goes on to describe in accurate detail, with their physical infirmities.) There may conceivably be an echo of inland rumour here. The distance was probably inspired by some version of Pacheco's '50 leagues'. It sounds like someone trying to check Pacheco on the spot and getting a vague account of marauding white-men in the interior. At about Ruiters' period of reference, c. 1600, the Sefawa kingdom of Bornu, under Idris Alooma (c. 1580-1610), had Turkish military instructors, and 'Bornu influence was extended southwards towards the Benue' (Fage, 1962, p. 36). So into the purview of the Cameroon Grasslands: an area easily affected by disturbances on the Benue, and one that may have been at the head of its present dynastic histories at about this time (Kaberry, 1962, p. 285).

50. Kernkamp (1908, pp. 3-21). But the letters of Blommaert to the Swedish Chancellor Oxenstierna, 1635-1641, discussing the openings in Guinea for

Swedish copper and iron, omit the stretch of coast between Benin and Cape Lopez, just as do so many other sources of the time (op. cit., pp. 67 ff.).

51. The Bakoko branch of the Basa people are supposed to have been supplanted by the Duala, but doubtless the fishermen of both peoples had used the estuary for long before that. The sons of Mbedi must have merely jostled out a niche at the most favoured trading spot (Dugast, 1949, pp. 11-12).

Appendix

The Leers' Vocabulary, 1665

[Additions in square brackets]

Woorden, in de *Cameronis, Rio d'Elrey*, en't hooge Land van *Ambosus*.

[1]	Daby	Schip	[Ship]
[2]	Macrale	Blancke	[White man]
[3]	Inboe	Land	[Country]
[4]	Kende	Gaat	[Go]
[5]	Singa	Komt	[Come]
[6]	Edican	Komt hier	[Come here]
[7]	Ommele	Handelen	[Trade]
[8]	Bange	'k Wil niet	[I will not]
[9]	Jubaa	Stelen	[To steal]
[10]	Nanga	Slapen	[To sleep]
[11]	Tocke Tocke	Kleyn	[Small]
[12]	Ninne Ninne	Groot	[Big]
[13]	Fyne	't Is goet	[It is good]
[14]	Broucke	't Deucht niet	[It is no good]
[15]	Mareba	Water	[Water]
[16]	Amon	Water	
[17]	Moeye	Vuur	[Fire]
[18]	Masiotje	een Man	[Man]
[19]	Lobbesje	een Vrou	[Woman]
[20]	Oreyne	Vis	[Fish]
[21]	Wynba	Wine	[Wine]
[22]	Bolly	Bananese	[Banana]
[23]	Makonsje	Iniames	[Yams]
[24]	Obre	Iniames	[Yams]
[25]	Corca	Hoenders	[Fowls]
[26]	Jocke	Koebeesten	[Cows]
[27]	Marule	Oly de Palm	[Palm-oil]

[28]	Masange	Koralen	[Beads]
[29]	Malulle	Orangie past	[Orange paste]
[30]	Nigelle	Lavendel q^r	[see notes]
[31]	Poupe	Wit q^r	[see notes]
[32]	Macocke	Ysere staven	[Iron bars]
[33]	Longe	Kopere dito	[Copper bars]
[34]	Mabeusie	Beckens	[Basins]
[35]	Faye, Mes	Mes	[Knife]
[36]	Myse	Oogen	[Eyes]
[37]	Insou	Toebak	[Tobacco]

Tellinge

Moo	Een	[one]
Meba	Twee	[two]
Melelle	Drie	[three]
Menaey	Vier	[four]
Metany	Vijf	[five]
Metoba	Ses	[six]
's Jamba	Seven	[seven]
Lomba	Acht	[eight]
Sieyte	Negen	[nine]
d' Jon	Tien	[ten]

LINGUISTIC NOTES

(Efik forms from Goldie (1874); Duala from Dinkelacker (1914); for the latter, double tones only marked; *b.a.*='borrowed as'.)

1. This first word has no obvious explanation from local languages. Perhaps Duala *ndabo*, 'house' – referring to the ship's superstructure.

2. Efik *makara*, 'white man', *b.a.* Duala *mokala*.

3. Duala *mboa*, 'home'; Bakweri *mboa*, 'village'; Isubu *mboka*, 'dry land'.

4. Isubu *kɛndɛ*, 'go'; Duala *ɛndɛ*.

5. No explanation (*singome* in Barbot's list means 'show me').

6. Efik *ɛdi ken*, sing. *di ken*, 'come here'.

7. Duala, *ongwɛlɛ*, 'trade with'; *mongwedi*, 'trader'; Bakweri, *umwɛlɛ*, 'show someone (something)'.

8. Duala *banga*, 'to refuse'; *nabangi*, 'I refuse'.

9. Duala *jíba*, 'to steal, theft'.

10. Duala *nanga*, 'to sleep'.

11. Efik *ɛtük-ɛtük*, 'small, a little', *b.a.* Duala *tɔki tɔki*, 'the very first'.

12. Balundu *nɛnɛ nɛnɛ*, 'very big': Duala *ndɛnɛ ndɛnɛ*.

13. Efik *fɔn*, 'to be good'; spelling influenced by Portuguese or Spanish *fino*, or even by Dutch.

14. ? Error for Dioucke=Efik *diɔk*, 'to be bad'. (Too early for English 'broke'!)

15. Duala *madiba*, 'water'.

16. Efik *mmɔŋ*, 'water'.

17. Duala *wea*, 'fire'; Bakweri *mweâ*, 'lava stream'.

18, 19. These are inexplicable from local languages. Barbot's Old Calabar jargon contains *labouche* for 'woman' which resembles (19). (18) is probably Portuguese *muchacho*, 'boy'.

20. Uwet *ɛrɛnkemu*, 'fish' (Goldie): Andoni *iriŋ*, *iriɛŋ* (Thomas, 1914).

21. Isubu, Bakweri *mimba*, 'wine' [*Wynba=Mynba*].

22. Bakweri *mbɔ̌*, 'banana', Efik *mburo*, 'ripe plantain'. The Bakweri form implies earlier **mbɔ̀lɔ́*.

23. Not explained.

24. Kwa (Ekoi) *ɔbid*, *ɔbirɛ* or the like, 'cocoyams' (cf. Crabb, 1965).

25. Kwa *ŋkɔk*, 'fowl'.

26. Duala *nyaka*, 'cow'.

27. Duala *mŭla*, Bakweri *mauja*, 'palm-oil'. A form **màúlà* would lie behind.

28. Duala *misanga*, 'beads'.

29. Whatever 'orange paste' was, its name is only a doubtlet for 27, 'palm-oil', which is also an orange-coloured paste! Dapper mentions both 'orange and lemon pastes' among his trade-goods for Cameroons (p. 139). In Barbot (p. 384) they have become 'presses for lemons and oranges'. The Frenchman Labarthe as late as 1803 was still quoting Dapper for this area and (p. 184) he translates this passage as 'presses to extract orange and lemon juice'. What can be meant? Palm-oil presses? Pomade? Or just palm-oil? Shades of Ogilby's 'Thin beaten Bosses, which they use instead of Money' – to translate Dapper's *Boesjes* (=cowries).

30. This must be in full: *Lavendel Quispel-grein* – the phrase occurs in Dapper (p. 139) and is translated by Ogilby (1670, p. 485) as 'Violet beads'. Barbot seems to mean the same when he talks of 'bloom-colour beads or bugles' (p. 384). Labarthe (loc. cit.) talks only of 'lavender'.

31. This would mean presumably 'white beads'. I cannot offer equivalents for *nigelle* and *poupe* but suspect Portuguese *nigela*, 'black inlay', and *pombo*, 'dove-white' or the like.

32. Duala *mikɔkɔ*, 'iron bars' (sing. *mukɔkɔ*).

33. Unexplained.

34. Unexplained.

35. Bakweri *fao*; Duala *pɔ*, 'knife'. Cf. Efik *faka*, 'long knife' (Goldie, 1874).

36. Duala *misɔ*, 'eyes'.

37. ? Efik *nsuŋikaŋ*, 'smoke' (without ikaŋ, 'fire') seems to belong here.

Numerals

DUALA (Class 2/3)		EFIK (Goldie)
mɔ̌	1	*kiet*
mibǎ	2	*iba*
milalo	3	*ita*
minɛi	4	*inaŋ*
mitanu	5	*itiuŋ*
mutoba	6	*itiokiet*
samba	7	*itiaba*
lɔmbi	8	*itiaɛta*
dibua	9	*usukiet*
dôm	10	*duŭp*

Comments

Of 28 locally explicable forms, other than numerals: 11 are explicable from Duala, 6 may be from Bakweri/Isubu, 1 from Balundu, 7 from Efik/Ibibio, 1 Andoni, and 2 Kwa (Ekoi). Some of the forms or meanings suggesting Bakweri/Isubu (e.g. Notes 3, 4, 17) are not inconsistent with a Duala dialect. Nos. 18 and 19 must be interpolations from slaving jargon.

In addition, the numerals with the exception of 'nine' are without doubt Duala. They cannot be Bakweri (e.g. Bakweri: *lisamba*, 'seven', *wambi*, 'eight', *liomɛ*, 'ten'), or Isubu (e.g. Isubu *isaka*, 'ten'), or Balundu (all numbers after 'five'). Duala *dôm*, 'ten', with implosive *d* may even be represented by *D'Jon*. The numerals alone are clear evidence for the Duala language, properly so called, on the coast. Basa or the like can be ruled out. For 'nine' an interpolated derivative from Efik is suggested (interpolation of the Spanish for 'seven' is less likely). It is not a Balundu or Kwa form.

The Leers' list shows evidence of printer's errors even in the Dutch. The abbreviation 'qr' for *quispel-grein* is probably a misprint for 'qu'.

REFERENCES

ANDERSON, H. O. 1940. (ed. Goodliffe, F. A.). An Intelligence Report on the Isangele Community of the Kumba Division (1940) based on a Report by H. O. Anderson, A.D.O., 1933 (or 1934), *Buea MS*. Ae 35 (1080).

Annual Report on the Administration of the Cameroons. 1958. London: H.M.S.O.

ARDENER, EDWIN. 1956. *Coastal Bantu of the Cameroons*, London.

ARDENER, EDWIN & ARDENER, SHIRLEY. 1958. Wovea Islanders. *Nigeria* (59): 309-321. Lagos.

ASMIS, D R. 1907. Der Handel der Duala. *Mitt. aus den deutschen Schutzgebieten* **20** (2): 85-90.

BANKES, T., BLAKE, E. W. & COOK, A. 1787. *A New Royal Authentic and Complete System of Universal Geography . . .*, London.

BARBOT, JOHN. 1732. An abstract of a voyage to New Calabar river, or Rio Real, in the year 1699 . . . in Churchill (q.v.) (Vol. V).

BARLOW, ROGER. *A Brief Summe of Geographie* (see Taylor, E. G. R.).

BARROS, JOAM DE. 1932. *Asia*, reedição da edição *princeps*, Coimbra.

BASTO, RAPHAEL EDUARDO DE AZEVEDO (ed.). 1892. *Esmeraldo de Situ Orbis. Edição commemorativa da Descoberta da America por Christovão Colombo no seu Quarto Centenario*, Lisbon.

BLAKE, JOHN W. 1937. *European Beginnings in West Africa, 1454-1578.*

BLOK, D. P. (ed.). 1966. *Proceedings of the Eighth International Congress of Onomastic Sciences*. The Hague: Mouton.

BOUCHAUD, JOSEPH. 1952. *La côte du Cameroun dans l'histoire et la cartographie: des origines à l'annexion allemande (1884).* Douala.

BROWN, R. 1896. *The History and Description of Africa . . . by . . . Leo Africanus,* London (ed. of Pory, *q.v.*).

BRUN, SAMUEL (ed. Naber, S. P.). 1913. *Samuel Brun, des Wundartzet und Burgers zu Basel, Schiffarten . . .,* Basel, 1624, in *Werken Uitgegeven door de Linschoten-Vereeniging,* Vol. VI.

BRUTSCH, J. R. 1950. Les relations de parenté chez les Duala. *Etudes camerounaises* **3** (31-32), Sept.-Dec.

—— 1956. 1956 Anniversaires d'histoire Douala. *Etudes camerounaises* (51), March.

BRY, J. T. & J. I. DE. 1628. *Descriptio Generalis totius Indiae Orientalis et Occidentalis.* Frankfurt.

BURTON, R. F. 1863. *Abeokuta and the Camaroons Mountain.* Vol. II, London.

CHILVER, E. M. 1962. Nineteenth Century Trade in the Bamenda Grassfields, *Afrika und Übersee* **45** (4), June, 233-258, Hamburg.

CHURCHILL, MESSRS. 1732. *A Collection of Voyages and Travels, some now first printed from Original Manuscripts. . . .* London.

CORDEIRO, LUCIANO. 1881. *Viagens explorações e conquistas dos portuguezes. Collecção de documentos 1574-1620.* Lisbon.

CRABB, D. W. 1965. *Ekoid Bantu Languages of Ogoja.* Pt. I. Cambridge.

DAPPER, DR O. 1668. *Naukeurige Beschrijvinge der Afrikanische Gewesten. . . .* Amsterdam (2nd impression 1676).

DELP, *Dicionário Etimológico da Língua Portuguesa* (ed. Machado, José Pedro). 1st edition.

DIAS, AUGUSTO EPIPHANIO DA SILVA (ed.). 1905. *Esmeraldo de Situ Orbis. Edição critica annotada.* Lisbon.

DINKELACKER, E. 1914. *Wörterbuch der Duala-Sprache.* Hamburg.

DOKE, C. M. & COLE, D. T. 1961. *Contributions to the History of Bantu Linguistics.* Johannesburg.

DUGAST, I. 1949. *Inventaire ethnique du Sud-Cameroun.* Paris.

ENCISO, MARTIN FERNANDEZ DE. 1518. *Suma de geographia q̄ trata de todas las partidas & provincias del mundo. . . .* Saragossa.

EVANS-PRITCHARD, E. E. 1961. *Anthropology and History.* Manchester.

FAGE, J. D. 1962. An *Introduction to the History of West Africa* (3rd edition). Cambridge.

—— 1962. Some remarks on beads and trade in Lower Guinea in the Sixteenth and Seventeenth centuries. *Journal of African History* **3** (2): 343-347.

FIGUEIREDO, MANOEL DE. 1614. *Hydrographia.* . . . Lisbon.

FONTENEAU, JEAN (alias ALFONSE DE SAINTONGE). 1904. *La Cosmographie avec l'Espère et Régime du Soleil et du Nord* (ed. Musset, Georges). Paris.

FORDE, D. (ed.). 1956. *Efik Traders of Old Calabar.* London: Oxford University Press.

FORDE, D. & JONES, G. I. 1950. *The Ibo and Ibibio-speaking Peoples of South-eastern Nigeria.* London: International African Institute.

GOLDIE, HUGH. 1874. *Efik Grammar.* Glasgow.

GRENFELL, G. 1882. The Cameroon District, W. Africa. *Proceedings of the Royal Geographical Society* **10**, Oct., 586-595.

HUTCHINSON, THOMAS J. 1858. *Impressions of Western Africa.* . . . London.

HAIR, P. E. H. 1967. Ethnolinguistic continuity on the Guinea Coast. *J. African History* **8** (2): 247-268.

HARLEIAN COLL. 1745. *A Collection of Voyages and Travels.* . . . Vol. II, pp. 511-517.

ITTMANN, JOHANNES. 1939. *Grammatik des Duala (Kamerun) unter Mitarbeit von Carl Meinhof.* Berlin and Hamburg.

—— 1953. *Volkskundliche und religiöse Begriffe im nördlichen Waldland von Kamerun.* Berlin.

—— 1956. Der Walfang an der Küste Kameruns. *Zeitschrift für Ethnologie* **81** (2).

—— 1957. Der kultische Geheimbund *djengu* an der Kameruner Küste. *Anthropos* **52** (1-2).

JOHNSTON, SIR HARRY H. 1919, 1922. *A comparative study of the Bantu and Semi-Bantu languages.* 2 vols.

JONES, G. I. 1956. In D. Forde (ed.), *Efik Traders of Old Calabar.* London: Oxford University Press.

—— 1963. *The Trading States of the Oil Rivers.* London.

—— 1965. Time and oral tradition with special reference to Eastern Nigeria, *Journal of African History* **6** (2): 153-160.

KABERRY, PHYLLIS M. 1962. Retainers and Royal Households in the Cameroons Grassfields. *Cahiers d'Etudes Africaines* **3** (10): 282-298. Paris.

KERNKAMP, G. W. 1908. Zweedsche Archivalia uitgegeven door G. W. K. 1. Brieven van Samuel Blommaert aan den Zweedschen Rijkskanselier Axel Oxenstierna, 1635-1641. *Bijdragen en Mededeelingen van het Historisch Genootschap (Gevestigd de Utrecht)* **29**: 3-196.

KIMBLE, GEORGE H. T. (ed. and translator). 1937. *Esmeraldo de Situ Orbis.* London.

LABARTHE, P. 1803. *Voyage à la côte de Guiné.* . . . Paris.

LANGHANS, P. 1902. Vergessene Reisen in Kamerun, 1. Reisen des Missionars Alexander Ross von Alt-Kalabar nach Efut 1877 und 1879. *Petermanns Mitteilungen* 48 (IV): 73-78.

LEERS, ARNOUT. 1665. *Pertinente Beschryvinge van Africa ... Getrocken en vergadert uyt de Reysboeken van Johannes Leo Africanus.* Rotterdam.

LINSCHOTEN, JAN HUYGEN VAN. 1596. *Itinerario, Voyage ofte Schipvaert van Jan Huygen van Linschoten naer Dost ofte Portugaels Indien ... t' Amstelredam. By Cornelius Claesz.* Amsterdam.

LISBOA, JOÃO DE. 1514. *Ho Tratado de Agulha de marear....* Lisbon. In Rebello (1903).

LOBATO, JOÃO 1952. Relatório de João Lobato a D. João III (13.4.1529) Arquiva da Torre do Tombo, CC-1-42-90. *MMA* 1: 505-518.

MAREEZ, PIETER DE. 1605. *Description et Recit Historial du Riche Royaume d'Or de Gunea* [sic], *aultrement nommé la coste de l'or de Mina, gisant en certain endroict d'Africque. ...* Amsterdam.

MASSMANN, P. J. C. 1910. *Realienbuch für deutsche Schulen in Kamerun, A. Geschichte.* Limburg a.d. Lahn.

MONOD, TH. 1928. *L'industrie des pêches au Cameroun.* Paris.

MMA. 1952+. *Monumenta Missionaria Africana, Africa Ocidental,* Coligida e Anotada por Padre Antonio Brásio C.S. Sp., Lisbon.

MOTA, A. TEIXEIRA & CARREIRA, ANTONIO. 1966. *Milho Zaburro* and *Milho Maçaroca* in Guinea and in the islands of Cabo Verde. *Africa,* 36 (1), Jan., London.

MUSSET, GEORGE (see Fonteneau).

MVENG, ENGELBERT. 1963. *Histoire du Cameroun.* Paris.

NABER, S. P. L'HONORÉ. 1913 (see Ruiters).

—— 1913 (see Brun).

OGILBY, JOHN. 1670. *Africa. ...* London.

ORTELIUS, ABRAHAM. 1570. *Theatrum Orbis Terrarum.* Antwerp.

PEREIRA, DUARTE PACHECO (see Basto, Dias and Kimble).

PIGAFETTA, FILIPPO. 1591. *Relatione del Reame di Congo et delle circonvicine contrade tratte dalli scritti & ragionamenti di Odoardo Lopez Portoghese.* Rome.

PORY, JOHN. 1600. *A Geographical History of Africa. ...* London.

POUTRIN, M. 1930. *Enquête coloniale dans l'Afrique française occidentale et equatoriale. ...*

RAMOS-COELHO, JOSE (ed.). 1892. *Alguns documentos do Archivo Nacional da Torre do Tombo ácerca das navegaçoes e conquistas portuguezas ...* Lisbon.

RODRIGUES (ROIZ), DUARTE. 1954. Carta de Duarte Roiz a El-Rei (10-5-1529). Arq. da Torre do Tombo—CC-I-42-116. *MMA* **4**: 144-146.

ROSA, GASPAR DA. 1955. Lembranças de Gaspar da Rosa. *MMA* **6**: 346-350.

RUITERS, DIERICK (ed. Naber, S. P.). 1623. *Toortse der Zee-Vaert.* ... Flushing. 1623. In *Werken Uitgegeven door de Linschoten-Vereeniging*, Vol. VI, 1913.

RYDER, A. F. C. 1965. *Materials for West African History in Portuguese Archives.* London.

SANTAREM, VISCOMTE DE. 1899. *Atlas composé de cartes hydrographiques et historiques depuis le VIᵉ Jusqu'au XVIIᵉ siècle, pour la plupart inédites, et tirées de plusieurs bibliotheques de l'Europe.* ... Paris.

TALBOT, P. A. 1912. *In the Shadow of the Bush.* London.

TAYLOR, E. G. R. (ed.). 1932. *Barlow, Roger, A Brief Summe of Geographie*, London.

TENREIRO, F. 1961. *A Ilha de São Tomé.* Lisbon.

TESSMANN, GUNTER. 1923. *Die Bubi auf Fernando Poo.* ...

—— 1932. Die Völker und Sprachen Kameruns. *Petermanns Mitteilungen* **78** (5/6): 113-120; (7/8), 184-190.

THOMAS, NORTHCOTE W. 1914. *Specimens of Languages from Southern Nigeria.* London.

VANSINA, JAN. 1965. *Oral Tradition.* London.

WADDELL, REV. HOPE MASTERTON. 1863. *Twenty-nine Years in the West Indies and Central Africa.*

POSTSCRIPTA

(1) Since this paper was given in 1966 Dr Latham has drawn my attention to the evidence of John Watt, an English sailor kidnapped in 1668 near 'old Calabar', upriver of the Parrot Island anchorage (Harleian Collection 1745, 2, pp. 511-517). His account (which is reported inaccurately by Barbot, p. 381) shows slave-trading at Old Calabar only three years after Leers, strengthening the view that the latter source is older than 1665. The milieu was Kwa(Ekoi)-speaking, from two local words given by Watts: '*ebung*, a root like a turnip' = Kwa *ɛbid* (Goldie's) *ebut*: the vowel is centralized and the final phoneme unexploded), 'cocoyam' (cf. the plural in Note 24 of Appendix); and *Ajah*, a deity = *Eja*, an Ekoi fetish of bloody repute (Talbot, 1912, pp. 74-78). Kwa (Aqua) are an original component of the Old Calabar population (Forde & Jones, p. 89). The Kwa names of two foodstuffs in Leers shows their closeness to Efik-speakers already at Rio del Rey. (2) Hair (1967) has now independently published a general survey of the Guinea Coast, with some similar conclusions on the need for documentary research (he even, like myself, criticizes the European historians). His *Calbongo* < *Pongo*, one of the minor Mbedine peoples (Ardener, 1956), is linguistically and geographically improbable.

Martin Southwold

The History of a History

Royal Succession in Buganda

HISTORY IN BUGANDA

In this paper I attempt to give an analytical history of a process
of development that occurred over past centuries in Buganda:
the development of modes of succession to the throne. I shall
not, however, simply narrate the events in the order in which
they occurred: rather, I shall reconstruct the analysis in much
the order in which it occurred to me. The reasons for this
eccentric arrangement will emerge as I proceed: but, briefly, I
have chosen it in order to emphasize how little this history can
properly be regarded as a straightforward presentation of data.
I do not mean that it is not a factual account – indeed, I take
time to argue the contrary; but I do mean that it must not be
regarded as merely objective. Though I shall by the end have
presented an historical account, it is equally my aim to raise
and discuss problems of historical method.

This paper is concerned with a number of such problems. I
have neither the space nor the competence to give an adequate
general discussion of any of them; but at this I am not
abashed. It is one of the principal strengths of anthropology
that we discuss theoretical issues as they are raised by our
specific factual inquiries, and not in abstraction: I hope this
paper remains in this tradition.

The theoretical questions at which I shall glance are as
follows:

1. What is history? And what is *a* history?
2. What is it to do history, to write *a* history?
3. Why does one 'do history'? More narrowly, why have I
   done this history?
4. Can I do this history – do I have the means, that is, adequate
   historical materials?

5. Supposing I can write this history of Buganda and that
   history of Buganda – can I in any way propose to write
   the history of Buganda?

So far as possible I want to examine these questions in the
course of doing, that is of narrating, this history; but some
preliminary discussion is essential.

What is history? The answer, even as I understand it, is
complex: but let us begin with at least a minimal definition. I
understand by 'history': 'a factual account of what did occur
in times past – that is, of past acts, events, and situations'. The
account need not tell of all events that did occur, nor need it
be perfectly accurate. We term an adequate factual account
'history' in order to contrast it with fiction. Fictions which
might be mistaken for history we usually call legends or myths:
these are apparently accounts of past events, but, we believe,
the events did *not* occur.

What then is *a* history? Confining ourselves to a minimal
working definition, I propose: 'a factual account of what did
occur in times past: with specification of when, where, and to
and by whom'. Within such limits one might attempt to
present all the known facts concerning all the known events.
Most commonly, however, there is a still further selection of
events which are judged to be connected, by similarity of kind
and/or by causal or other explanatory connexions. This can be
described by saying that the history has a subject and/or theme,
which is the more prominent the more articulated and analytical
the account.

Let me define my present history in these terms. My subject
is succession to the throne; my theme is how and why the forms
of succession changed over time. The place, Buganda; the
people, Baganda and especially their kings. When? The events
described occurred over a period which ends in 1884; the period
begins at a time twenty-one generations of the royal dynasty
earlier – presumably, then, not later, and probably a good deal
earlier, than the year 1500 in our chronology.

Why does the period have these two termini? The beginning
is marked by the accession of the man some traditions describe
as the *first* king of Buganda: on this view, the beginning is
determined by what did occur, in relation to the chosen subject

of the history. (Strictly indeed, the first *succession* was that of the *second* king.) Other traditions speak vaguely of still earlier kings, but tell us nothing solid about their accessions: on this view, it is the nature of the sources which requires us to begin no earlier.

The posited end of the period is much more arbitrary: successions continued to occur after 1884, and the source material gets better, not worse. After 1884 the situation in Buganda was complicated in various ways as a consequence of the irruption of Europeans: therefore adequate analysis of later events becomes complex in itself, and is partly discontinuous with the analysis appropriate to the earlier period. Given limitations of my space, it would be uneconomic to attempt to deal with the later events.

What is it to 'do history', to write a history? This is probably the most subtle and difficult of all the problems: but at the simplest level the answer would obviously be 'to write a factual account of events, variously specified, which did occur'. I wish to observe, first, that one necessarily implies that events did occur approximately as described. But further I wish to stress that what events are described is determined in part by what did occur; but also, as the remarks above bring out, by human selection, and by chance and human failings. All sorts of possible facts have failed to get into our sources, and the sifting is probably not random. Let me pass however to the type of selection I have just illustrated: selection by me the historian. It was I who selected at least the later limit to the period, and it was I who selected the subject, the kind of event to be discussed. In so far as the account I give is analytical, such selection could disastrously bias the analysis. Briefly, though, I have in fact found that the events after 1884 do not demand radical revision of the analysis I give.

But selection of the subject, or the approach to it, could be most damaging. Buganda is a patrilineal society, and so I have tried to determine whether, or in what circumstances, a king is succeeded by his son, or his brother, or his grandson, or ...? But this could well be irrelevant, and any patterns that emerge quite adventitious.

Only a Prince of the Drum can reign; and this status belongs to those who are son or son's son to a former king. But the prince who was made king was chosen from among many by the leading commoner chiefs. There is sufficient evidence that a major consideration for the electors was the maternal affiliations of the various princes: for a prince is attached to, and virtually a member of, the totemic agnatic clan of his mother – which is always a clan of commoners. Understandably, clans tried to put their own 'sister's sons' on the throne. So it might be that the pattern of successions to the throne ought really to be explained in terms of the maternal affiliations of the princes and the relative political strength of the various clans concerned; and that the patrilateral connexions of the princes are largely irrelevant. I cannot be certain that this is not so. But since there were at least two dozen clans, it is hard to imagine that the ambitions of any one clan can have been sufficient to determine the choice of a successor; and the clear patterns of patrilateral relationship between successive kings that emerge from analysis cannot well be dismissed as purely fortuitous.

Similarly, when I went behind Roscoe's king-list to the facts given by Ganda authors, I noticed that I was counting as successors men who had actually won the throne by rebellion: presumably I was confusing data of two distinct kinds. However, I found that the basic patterns of relationship between successive kings were identical whether or not rebels were excluded. Reflection on the Ganda political system satisfied me that this was not surprising: that the men who would rebel successfully ought to be similar to those who would emerge from peaceful election.

Closer analysis of the cases of successful rebellion showed something further: that, in seven of the eight cases, these were men whose right to the throne was better than their expectation of getting it peacefully. They were men who could consider they had been, or would be, wronged. So put, this is just what one would expect of successful rebels: and it indicates that the cases of rebellion, so far from being irrelevant to the determination of rights to succession, might even be especially revealing.

These observations, then, illustrate the point that the contents and shape of a history are commonly, if not invariably, in large measure shaped by the interests, limitations, and thought-categories of the historian. It is not hard to see how this might invalidate the historical analysis: but naturally I shall not simultaneously present an analysis and explain why it is false! The dependence of the history on the historian will emerge still more in what follows.

SOURCES FOR A STUDY OF BUGANDA SUCCESSION

I will postpone discussion of why I have done this history, and pass on to consider whether I have the means, proper historical materials. My immediate sources are mainly a number of books written in Luganda by Baganda authors. One of these is presented as an historical chronicle; the others, though overtly dissertations on various aspects of Ganda custom, contain many historical statements and narratives, which can readily be extracted from their context. For convenience I refer to these sources as the chronicles, and their authors as the chroniclers.

In various ways it is a great asset to have such sources. For example, three of the chronicles were written soon after 1900 by Sir Apolo Kaggwa, a man of great ability and eminence: and no contemporary anthropologist could hope to collect material of such quality.

But the chronicles obviously depend on anterior sources: almost entirely on memories and traditions which the Baganda have transmitted orally. Except for events in the latter part of the nineteenth century which were also described by Europeans in Buganda, and for a very few earlier events which are illuminated by the similar traditions of neighbouring peoples, there is no external check on these traditions.

It is obviously crucial to establish that this material is essentially historical rather than legendary, if any attempt is to be made to write a history. But since the very existence of this symposium shows that we are not radically sceptical about the value of oral traditions, I need not now present a complete defence. One argument, however, is so closely related to the themes of this paper that it deserves consideration.

The chroniclers, as befits Baganda writing for Baganda, describe particularities, and infrequently offer any but the most restricted generalizations. But I am only partly a Muganda, and you are not even that: our concern must naturally be with statements of general import, comparatively and theoretically, and with particularities only as contributing to these.

Martin Southwold

I construct my history out of the chronicles, by bringing together facts, which are often found widely scattered, and by deducing from these further specific facts, statements of regularities, and specifications of exceptions to these regularities. Further, I ask why these things should have been as they seem to have been, and commonly find other facts which provide explanation. I thus relate together a great many facts, and produce a picture of past events richer and more articulated than anything explicit in the chronicles, and having a marked degree of verisimilitude and intelligibility. I hope that the latter part of this paper illustrates this.

Now when such analysis is applied to legendary materials, the result is typically to expose inconsistencies and implausibility and loose ends: this indeed becomes a reason for classing the material as legendary. Exactly the opposite occurs when the Ganda material is analysed: the already impressive consistency and sense of the statements in the chronicles are found to grow and deepen.

Since I am satisfied that my conclusions were not perceived by the chroniclers themselves, nor are merely read by me into the material as others read Bacon into Shakespeare: I see no way to account for the strength and complexity of the story implicit in the chronicles, except by relating it to the truth and complexity of real social events. Which in turn implies that the chronicles are factual accounts of what did occur. Q.E.D. It is precisely through attempting to do history that I have convinced myself that I have to hand the means to do history.

Yet, paradoxically, the very experience that persuades me that I can write *a* history of Buganda persuades me equally that I cannot write *the* history of Buganda. As I have indicated, my history is produced out of the chronicles by asking questions of them, and by selecting those facts that answer or relate to my questions. In producing my first historical essay, *Bureaucracy and Chiefship in Buganda*, which describes the decline in the power of the clans and the development of a sort of bureaucratic chiefship, I worked over the chronicles fairly thoroughly, and thought I had extracted most of their significance. Yet, when I came back to the same chronicles, with new questions concerning succession to the throne, I found an overwhelming wealth of information to which I had hitherto been quite blind.

How many more themes, perhaps more important than any I have yet followed through, may still remain embedded in the chronicles, awaiting the questions which will awake them from sleep?

To claim to write *the* history of Buganda is to claim to know all that can be known about the past, within the bounds set by the limitations of the sources. But this entails the further claim that one has asked of the chronicles all the questions that can possibly be asked, and this is a logical absurdity. *The* history of Buganda can never be written; what can and will be written is *a* history more significant than anything I have yet suspected.

I turn now to the remaining question, why does one 'do history'? Or more narrowly, why have I done this history? – since the answer to that is surely not typical, and may be interesting because of its oddness. When I began this investigation into succession to the throne I had no intention of writing history, except in a very simple sense. It was Dr Goody who asked me to contribute an essay[1] on the subject, and I took it that I was to make a report on this area of Ganda custom. Because of the changes in the rules of succession, to the throne and to other positions, which are attributable (largely) to Christianity, I found informants confused about what was indigenous Ganda custom, and I lacked observations of it in action. If I was to describe *Ganda* custom in this matter I would have to describe what it was before Christianity became influential: what it was, say, eighty years ago. It is in this simple sense that I expected the work to be historical: in its describing a situation as it was in the quite recent past.

I thought that I could do little more than to reproduce the statements on the matter that Roscoe made in his book *The Baganda*, published in 1911. But to pad my essay out I thought I would illustrate Roscoe's statements by citing instances in support.

Now Roscoe himself prints a king-list, on which all the kings and a few other princes are named, and numbered to indicate their order of succession to the throne. The genealogical connexions between these men are also shown; so too are the names and clans of the mothers of these men. The king-list I have presented with this paper is identical, except that I have added a few details – mainly the distinguishing of rebels. All the facts given by Roscoe's king-list can also be found, several times over, in the chronicles; and, one trivial error apart, Roscoe is confirmed entirely by the chroniclers. But they do not present the facts, as Roscoe and I have done, on a genealogical diagram, but embed them separately in narrative or other contexts. If Roscoe's diagram is studied intensively enough, certain patterns of succession emerge rather clearly though not easily: these patterns could never be seen from the facts as strung out by the chroniclers. Roscoe's genealogical arrangement is essential for revealing these patterns; but it is also very dangerous, for it implies that it is agnatic genealogy that determines succession, and as we have seen, this can be challenged. I shall show how in at least one respect I was misled by the diagram into trying to explain certain facts in terms of genealogy when in reality it is other facts, omitted from the diagram but included in the chronicles, which I believe provide the soundest explanation.

Now, when I examined Roscoe's king-list in order to find illustrations for his statements of custom, I soon found that several of his statements were not supported but were refuted by the facts; and further examination revealed regularities and patterns which were not reflected at all in Roscoe's statements. It became plain that I must set aside Roscoe's statements and analyse the facts afresh.

I was now, as I have recently come to understand, getting ensnared in the serious logical difficulties which infect our concept of custom. When we describe a custom in a certain society, we are sometimes referring to a regularity we have observed in conduct (more exactly, a regularity is our generalization of what we regard as similarities between numerous items of conduct); sometimes we are referring to a rule, professed as authoritative by members of that society; but most often we refer to an ill-examined combination of rule and regularity. This is not scientific, but is merely taken over from the assumptions of our culture (as of other cultures). Unless on our guard, we assume that for a stated rule there will be a corresponding regularity: and surely this is because to acknowledge that a rule is often not obeyed is seriously to weaken its coercive moral power. We tend also to assume that for every regularity of conduct there will be a corresponding rule. But as critical anthropologists we are aware that both assumptions are false. It is not uncommon to find rules which are often, even regularly, flouted, so that there is no corresponding regularity. Again, we know that regularities of conduct may arise otherwise than through following rules prescribing such conduct. In particular, a regularity may arise because the logic of a certain kind of situation is such as to lead any actor rationally pursuing self-interest to choose the same line of action. We must therefore distinguish between rule and regularity, look for each separately, and demonstrate rather than assume a connexion between them.

On the other hand, the naïve assumption of a connexion between rules and regularities is very far from baseless: it is hard to imagine a society where such a connexion is not largely realized in fact. The concept of custom, which normally implies both rule and corresponding regularity, is not thoroughly fallacious and unsound. On the contrary, the degree of mutual implication of rule and regularity is such that whenever we find a rule we should search for a corresponding regularity, and when we find a regularity (unless it is obviously to be explained otherwise) we should look for a corresponding rule.

But there is a further difficulty in the association of rule and regularity implied by the concept of a custom. A statement of rule is usually understood as timeless: it sounds odd to reply to such a statement by asking 'When?' This is because rules assert values, and values are atemporal: a value is not an event, and it is events which are referred to space and time. (Of course the fact that a value is held, or that a rule is propounded, is an event – but this is a different matter.) A statement of regularity, however, is only a generalized statement about a finite number of events, and events are placed in space and time. It is not logically odd to ask 'When?' in reply to a statement of regularity. But in anthropology the temporal reference of statements of regularity is rather easily overlooked, because the events from which we deduce regularities are essentially synchronic: if we are talking about the same time, then distinctions of time are excluded. If one does ask 'When?' the answer should normally be 'In the ethnographic present': and the ethnographic present is not a present of time, contrasted with past and future, but the present tense of habitude. Thus the logical incompatibility of atemporal rules and temporal regularities does not obtrude itself.

A statement of custom, such as is the stock-in-trade of anthropologists, is therefore normally understood as timeless. If an anthropologist states, as a matter of custom, 'My people do such-and-such' and you reply by asking 'When?', your question will be regarded as impertinent – at least in the sense of 'not pertinent'. This is because statements of custom refer to atemporal values and synchronic events.

But there is a more fundamental reason why our statements of custom are implicitly timeless. Dr Beattie entitled his introduction to social anthropology, *Other Cultures*, and with good reason: because social anthropology grew out of an interest in other cultures, and this interest still largely shapes our subject. To the extent that this is true, it is the otherness of cultures that draws us to study them, and that shapes many of our questions. Now I suggest that when otherness becomes the focus of concern, distinctions of time are naturally excluded. If I am comparing Ganda culture with British culture, distinctions of time within that culture will only distract. The same principle manifests itself in the fact that in Omaha systems of kinship terminology members of the mother's lineage are not distinguished by generation: as we all know, this is because it is the distinction of that lineage from our lineage which the terminology is stressing.

Thus I suggest that the fundamental reason why anthropology is so uneasy in dealing with social change and other temporal processes is because of its concern with culture (i.e. customs), and particularly culture in its otherness. Is it not significant that when we do attempt to deal with social change it is precisely to the extent that the culture is no longer purely other, it is part of our own colonial culture? I suggest also, as this appears to me to be subjectively true, that our interest in the pre-colonial history of the societies we study is a function of our personal involvement in those societies, through the acculturation that we undergo in doing fieldwork. This is not, however, how I became involved in this history that I am discussing in this paper.

I had begun by regarding Roscoe's statements as statements of custom, referring both to rule and regularity, which I did not then distinguish. Nor did Roscoe distinguish: some of his statements have the grammar of statements of regularity, some that of statements of rule, and at least one is entirely ambiguous. But I found that I had to revise Roscoe's statements in the light of the regularities I deduced from the king-list.

I had intended to write an article about custom: but now I found myself forced to write history. Simply because successions to the throne are events which are necessarily far from synchronic: if I was to examine sufficient of such events to establish regularities, I had to consider events spread over a considerable span of time. Logically, of course, the assumption of timeless custom might have held: in fact, however, it did not.

REGULARITIES AND IRREGULARITIES IN FRATERNAL SUCCESSION

The most striking regularity which emerged from study of the king-list was that fraternal succession to the throne was rather common; indeed, within a period of eight successive generations, very common. There were nineteen kings in these eight generations; of these, eleven came to the throne in succession to brothers (including first cousins). Differently expressed, in one of these eight generations there was no fraternal succession; there were three generations in each of which one fraternal succession occurred; and four generations in each of which two fraternal successions occurred. One could hardly require more impressive evidence of a regularity – particularly since no system can practise succession through brothers only.

This was particularly striking because it has been consistently overlooked, and even denied. None of the chroniclers and none of my informants stated that fraternal successions were common or customary; and the two best of the chroniclers, Kaggwa and Nsimbi, make statements which are inconsistent with about half of the cases (I enlarge on this below). Mair (1934, p. 180) states bluntly 'The Kingship went in direct descent from father to son', which is plainly incorrect. Roscoe (1911, p. 232) recognizes that fraternal succession did occur, but his statement about it seems quite inadequate: 'In some instances the succession was carried on through a brother of the King, in cases where the King's sons were too young to rule, or when, for some reason, a prince was rejected'.

But in spite of this, the regularity was apparent; and I asked myself whether it was possible to assume that there was a corresponding rule. Indeed it was. I had had good informants on the rules governing succession among commoners to clan offices – which resembled, they had said, those governing succession to the throne. In succession to clan offices, other things being equal, a brother, or even an agnatic cousin, was preferred to a son. They also told me (as is confirmed by Kaggwa, 1905, p. 198) that in choosing the personal successor and principal heir to any deceased, it used to be the rule that a brother or still more remote agnate was preferred to an own son. To choose an own son was considered as 'repudiating kinship' (*kuboolagana*), and the more remote relative was preferred in order to keep kinship alive. This rule had been changed, in favour of own sons, by Kabaka Muteesa I (reigned c. 1860-1884), because, with the development of trade, there came to be more heritable property than hitherto, and people were unwilling to see such property pass outside the family. A similar change in succession rules among the neighbouring Basoga is described and explained in similar terms by Fallers (1956, pp. 86-92). Thus it seemed to me altogether probable that there had been a similar rule favouring fraternal succession in the royal house also.

But now I faced a further difficulty. Fraternal succession to the throne was, as I have said, regular over a period of eight generations; but this was preceded by a period of ten generations, and followed by a period of three generations (a fourth generation began in 1884 and should not be counted) in which fraternal succession did not occur at all. There were therefore two changes in the pattern of regularity, and at this point my study became inescapably historical.

There were three possible hypotheses to account for these changes. First, the changes in regularity had perhaps resulted from changes in rules. If not, then either: second, the rule throughout preferred fraternal succession, but there were special reasons why it did not occur in the first and third periods; or else, third, the preference throughout was for filial succession, and there were special reasons for the frequency of fraternal succession in the second period.

I thought that the best places to look for clues would be in the historical circumstances immediately surrounding the points of change. The first period ends with Nakibinge (K8, i.e. the eighth king): and the circumstances of his reign were most dramatic. Bunyoro, then much the more powerful kingdom, attacked Buganda, routing her army and killing the king, and then overran the whole country. The Banyoro soon after withdrew – according to their own traditions, on the warning of an oracle. Nakibinge was presumably killed while still young; at any rate he left only three sons, all infants, the eldest of whom, Mulondo, was chosen to succeed.

The trouble about this information is that it is too rich: it can be used to support various hypotheses, and it took me a long time to determine what I think was the crucial factor.

Dr C. C. Wrigley had pointed out to me that some facts in the chronicles raised a suspicion that Mulondo (K9) was really an invader from Bunyoro, and therefore the founder of a new dynasty – and in the circumstances this would not have been unlikely. This might then, I reasoned, have accounted for a change in the rules of succession at this point. But even if the suspicion were stronger than it is, the theory would be inadequate, since there is no reason to regard the Banyoro as more devoted to fraternal succession than the Baganda themselves. More fundamentally, I considered that any supposition of a change in custom, including rules, must be excluded by Occam's Razor, at least until all simpler hypotheses had been rejected.

Now, with regard to the first change in the pattern, Dr Goody drew my attention to the fact that in the dynasty of the sultans of Turkey there had also been a period of only filial successions, followed by one in which fraternal successions became common; and that there too the change had occurred after a sultan had died young in battle, leaving only very young sons. The parallel was highly suggestive; but I could not see what it was in the situation of orphan princes which would cause a change to fraternal succession.

I began to see the light when I examined the two cases of succession by first cousins – Kimbugwe (K13) and Ndawula (K19). As I have said, among commoners cousins were favoured successors in order to keep the bonds of kinship alive; and at first I supposed that this was the reason that cousins had been chosen in the royal house. But when I examined the facts more closely it appeared that the succession of both of these kings was attributable rather to matters of personal character.

It will be seen from the king-list that Ndawula (K19) succeeded his first cousin Tebandeke (K18), who was son of Mutebi (K15). I have not space here to go into all the details, which are fascinating and illuminating. But, summarily: Mutebi was a bad king; there was good reason to expect that Tebandeke would repeat his father's faults, and in the event he did so, and was a still worse king. When he came to the throne Ndawula explicitly and forcefully dissociated himself from such tendencies. I suppose that Ndawula was chosen because the chiefs had had enough of the misbehaviour of Mutebi's family, and for this reason passed over the brothers and the son of Tebandeke. That comparable factors would explain the succession of Kimbugwe emerged only at the end of a difficult and intricate analysis, which I can present more usefully at a later point.

There was therefore no reason to think that the desire not to repudiate kinship had ever led to the choice of a cousin as successor. But, among commoners, this desire is also the rationale for the preference for a brother as successor; if, among royals, it had not led to the choice of cousins, perhaps also it had not led to the choice of brothers. And indeed this seemed reasonable. We have seen how, among commoners, the preference for a brother as successor came to be set aside when the increase in value of heritable property caused people to be unwilling to see the succession pass outside the family. But in the royal house the value of the succession had always been very great: one would then expect that the ideal preference for brothers would have become ineffective much earlier.

I therefore began to consider more seriously Roscoe's proposition that it was considerations of relative age that in fact sometimes led to the choice of a brother to succeed. The chronicles sometimes tell us the approximate age of a prince at a certain point, or at roughly what stage of his father's reign he was born; they also commonly tell us whether or not a king reigned long or to an advanced age. When this evidence is pieced together it does appear that at six of the fraternal successions the princes of the next generation were probably still young; and that in each of the other five cases there were more or less obvious reasons why the sons should have been passed over.

To my surprise and reluctance I found myself led by the evidence to suppose that Roscoe was probably right after all. And once I had agreed that relative age might well have been the crucial factor, I could see why fraternal succession began to be practised after the death of Nakibinge. It is when military requirements are most pressing that it is most necessary that a king shall be a mature man; and the Baganda could not have missed this point after the experience of trying to recover from a military catastrophe, under the child-king Mulondo.

This explanation fitted the fact that fraternal successions had not occurred in the earlier period. There is no record of Buganda having engaged in any major war in these earlier reigns; and, as we know from the traditions of the western peoples that Bunyoro at that period was heavily engaged further west, this is understandable. The fact that many of these earlier kings are stated or implied to have reigned to a great age also implies that generalship was not essential among the king's duties. It is also related that under Nakibinge the Baganda conquered a large part of the county of Ssingo; and since Ssingo is good cattle country, and marches with Bunyoro, this probably explains why the Banyoro then rounded on their southern neighbour.

Fraternal successions did not occur in the third period because Ssemakookiro (K.27) instituted a policy of butchering the royal brothers. One also finds that each or the last three kings (Ssuuna II to Mwanga II) is noted as having been remarkably young when he came to the throne – Ssuuna indeed was only twelve years old. Now, Dr Beattie tells me that from about the middle of the eighteenth century Bunyoro went into relative decline under a succession of weak kings. The Baganda must have realized this when, under Ssemakookiro's elder brother Jjunju, they conquered the very important province of Buddu from the Banyoro (although Professor Anthony Low informs me that the Banyoro had lost control of Buddu, by its secession, before this).

FRATERNAL SUCCESSION AND MILITARY LEADERSHIP

Thus the changes in regularity concerning fraternal succession parallel changes in Buganda's relations with Bunyoro; and this is intelligible if fraternal succession is determined by considerations of relative age, and these are significant because of their military implications.

But if the relative youth of sons explains why a brother is preferred as their father's successor, it is less intelligible why after this yet a third brother should be chosen to succeed. But one then observes that when a third brother does get the throne he does so as a rebel – the one exception in four cases is Ssuuna I (K11). One also sees that when a third brother does reign, he is regularly deposed by rebellion of a prince of the next generation. Kyabaggu (K25) is not an exception: he was murdered by rebellious sons, who were then defeated in civil war by Jjunju (K26). The only real exception is, once again, Ssuuna I. This pattern of rebellion and counter-rebellion is perfectly intelligible. Equally, one sees that sons do not successfully rebel against the second of a set of brothers to reign – the only exception is Kateregga (K14).

Now observe what a concatenation of oddities centre upon the succession of Ssuuna I (K11) and the next few kings:

1. Ssuuna I is the only third of a set of brothers to succeed peacefully. This is all the stranger when one finds that Ssekamaanya, the senior prince of the next generation, was almost certainly a mature man at the time.
2. Ssekamaanya (K12) is the only king peacefully to have succeeded a third brother.
3. Ssekamaanya was succeeded by his cousin. His son Kateregga is definitely stated to have been only a lad at the time, but Ssekamaanya had brothers; moreover these were full brothers, and I shall later show that the claim of full brothers was particularly strong.
4. His son Kateregga (K14) is the only prince to have rebelled successfully after only one fraternal succession.

Of course, a great deal of analysis is necessary to produce these facts, and to relate them together as constituting one problem. But even after the issues have been clarified in this way, it is not easy to see where the solution might lie. Eventually I perceived that the first three oddities, at least, would be explained if Ssekamaanya and his brothers had had a very weak claim to the throne. But had they? – there was not the slightest hint of this in the chronicles.

Another analysis suggested a clue. When I tabulated the maternal clan affiliations of every king, I noticed that Ssekamaanya was the only king to have been born from the Civet-cat clan. Now this in itself was a little odd, since the Civet-cat clan was one of the most important of all. Could it have been that there was a bar of some kind against kings of this clan?

I then recalled that the chronicles say that before Kintu, the first king, came to Buganda, the country was ruled by Walusimbi, the head of Civet-cat clan, and that one of his titles was 'Buganda' (Nsimbi, 1956, p. 194). Roscoe (who is not always accurate) goes further and says (1911, p. 145) that this clan-head was king of Buganda, and that he was deposed by Kintu but allowed to retain the title of king (*kabaka*). The chroniclers also say that when Ccwa I, the second king, disappeared and the throne was vacant, 'Walusimbi ruled as king' (Nsimbi, 1956, p. 195); and further that when Kimera, the third king, returned from Bunyoro to take up the throne, Nakku, who was daughter to Walusimbi and widow of Ccwa 'informed him of all the matters to do with ruling the Kingdom of Buganda' (Kaggwa, 1908, p. 26). In reality, Kimera was most probably a Nyoro prince and the real founder of the dynasty; and the stories about him and about Kintu (allegedly the first king) may really be a doublet. But on any interpretation there seems a firm tradition that Walusimbi was an autochthonous ruler before the arrival of the first king. When we recall the ritual opposition and separation between the king and the (successor of the) autochthonous ruler in other societies, it becomes probable that in Buganda it might have been thought improper to have as king a prince attached to, virtually a member of, the clan of Walusimbi.

Although this is not conclusive, it fits very well with the facts that have raised the problem. Not only does it explain why Ssekamaanya's succession was delayed, it also explains why Ssekamaanya himself was succeeded by his cousin Kimbugwe (K13) in preference to his brothers; since these were full brothers, they too were members of Civet-cat clan.

It seems then that Kimbugwe, like Ndawula (K19), the only other first cousin to succeed, achieved the throne rather because of the disqualifications of more obvious candidates than through any concern with keeping kinship alive. Let us now try to explain why Kateregga (K14) successfully rebelled against him. Kimbugwe had a son, Prince Kamyuka, who was of course

143

second cousin to Kateregga. Now even among commoners, where the desire to keep kinship alive has some effect, I have the impression that succession by a second cousin is unusual: and it is easy to see the difficulties to which such a practice would give rise. Among the royals, where as we have seen the desire to keep kinship alive seems to have been ineffective, succession by a second cousin would have been most unlikely. Hence if Kateregga got the throne, Kamyuka would have been virtually disqualified; and conversely. Now we are specifically told that 'when Kamyuka grew up he was very very handsome, and his father loved him much'; we also learn that at the time of the rebellion he was at least old enough to bear arms (Kaggwa 1901, pp. 27 and 29). Given the structural situation, it would have been surprising if Kimbugwe had not been plotting to arrange for his own son's succession, and for Kateregga not to have seen this as fatal to his own chances. We are also informed (though the chronicler tells a different story to account for this) that when he raised rebellion Kateregga said to his men, 'Kimbugwe has repudiated kinship with me, I am not his agnate'. I suggest that the repudiation of kinship that Kateregga really had in mind was his own prospective exclusion from the succession. (A similar situation could not have arisen in relation to Ndawula, since he had so arranged things that Tebandeke's only son was disqualified from succeeding.)

So far then, it appears that the facts bear out Roscoe's statement in more detail than he can have known. But if the king-list is studied further, a new fact will be seen to emerge. Of the eleven fraternal successions, three were by half-brothers, two by first cousins, but six by full brothers (I reckon Mawanda (K22) as full brother to Kikulwe, since, though they did not have the same mother, their mothers were sisters (Kaggwa, 1908, p. 63)). Moreover, these full-brother successions occurred in the latter part of the period: indeed after the reign of Kateregga (K14) all fraternal successions were by full brothers – except for that of Ndawula (K19) to Tebandeke, which we have already discussed, and that of Kikulwe (K21) to Kagulu. Now Kagulu was such an extraordinarily bad king that, uniquely, the whole nation rose in revolt against him. So this is once again a special situation (and anyway Kaggwa, 1905, p. 45, records him as without full brothers).

Moreover, the attribution of fraternal succession to military necessity wears a little thin for the generations after Kateregga. For he is recorded as having made substantial conquests from Bunyoro – as are several later kings. In the military circumstances that this might imply, was it *necessary* to choose a brother as successor? Could it not be that a full brother as such was the rightful successor irrespective of any other considerations?

This hypothesis fits the facts even better than would appear from the king-list. As I remarked earlier, every king who is known to have had a full brother was in fact succeeded by him – of the exceptions to this, only one (Ccwa I – K2) lacks suitable explanation. It might well be that other full brothers who lived but did not reign have dropped out of the record. On the other hand, we can be confident that none of the sons of Nakibinge had full brothers: for their father died while they were still infants, and until a child was weaned (at the age of three) there was a taboo on intercourse with the mother. Again, even if Kagulu (K20) had truly had full brothers, they would not have succeeded since the maternal clan was held guilty of part of the offences for which Kagulu was deposed. Thus half-brother succession occurred only when no full brother could have succeeded; and as we saw earlier, a similar statement can be made about the cases of succession by first cousins. Thus it may well have been that succession by a full brother was the preferred mode.

Moreover, there is positive evidence that this was so. It is, to be sure, only circumstantial, and depends on critical analysis of a series of odd and apparently absurd stories that I lack space to relate. In brief, it appears that elder full brothers are commonly recorded as hating their younger full brothers, and/or as knowing full well they were plotting rebellion; that they refrained from killing their rivals even when they had them fully in their power; but that they attempted to contrive their 'accidental' deaths through ramshackle plots, which are paralleled only by the contrivances by which Ssemakookiro (K27) tried to bring about the death of his son Kamaanya, whom he had informed was to be his successor. Again, the words and the deeds of each member of two pairs of full brothers (Jjuuko (K17) and Kayemba (K18); Namugala (K24) and Kyabaggu

(K25)) show that each of them regarded the succession of the younger of the pair as automatic. Finally, there are several striking expressions of the identity of full brothers: e.g., Jjuuko and Kayemba are said to have reckoned themselves to be twins in the womb of their mother (Kaggwa, 1905, p. 43).

Since one case alone must suffice for illustration, I will describe the clearest of all. Namugala (K24), on learning that his full brother Kyabaggu was seeking to kill him by sorcery in order to get the throne, called Kyabaggu to him, mildly reproached him, and then abdicated in his favour, saying 'I have no wish to fight with thee; all that is ours is thine: I have relinquished the kingdom for thee, therefore eat it' (Kaggwa, 1901, p. 59).

There is then evidence of some regularity of full-brother succession, and a marked suggestion that full brothers succeeded by right. But to suppose a corresponding rule is difficult. Nowhere have I found a hint of such a rule – and since maternal affiliation is quite irrelevant to succession among commoners, we can find no analogy in that direction. More seriously, the two best authorities, Kaggwa and Nsimbi, appear to deny even the regularity – let alone the hypothetical rule. Kaggwa describes how important duties concerned with protecting the Kabaka from rivals were customarily entrusted to his maternal kin 'because they are the most diligent in taking care of him, and [because] the female parentage is not wont to bear twice' (Kaggwa, 1905, p. 121). Nsimbi (1956, p. 251) remarks that Nanteza was the mother of the two kings Jjunju (K26) and Ssemakookiro (K27), and that this is the origin of the proverb 'The wild banana does not bear twice, except for that of Nanteza'. Yet it is plain that this proverb is flatly untrue; and Kaggwa's statement (which may also be a proverb) is at least an equivocation. Nevertheless it is easy to demonstrate the impressive honesty and concern for truth of both these chroniclers.

If the cases of full-brother succession are examined more closely, it can be seen that younger full brothers usually succeeded as rebels; that the elder brothers found it impossible to defend themselves effectively against them; and that the quarrels between such full brothers were peculiarly horrible – Kaggwa several times condemns what happens, and a number of the events transparently symbolize desecration of the very bases of kinship (blood and the womb).

At a more analytical level, it is evident that the choice of the prince who should be king was determined partly in terms of right, derived through his paternity, partly in terms of the strength of his politico-military support which was organized through his maternal connexion. In an elegant fashion, the two possible lines of filiation intersected to indicate the man who, as maximizing both right and might, was best fitted to be king. Ideally (and the statements of Kaggwa and of Nsimbi may be taken as expressing this ideal), this should have indicated a unique choice, under whom the nation should unite. It should further have guaranteed every king the indubitable (because self-interested) support of one of the clans; and further, because successive kings should have been of different clans, it should have both focused the interests of all clans on the kingship, and ensured the circulation of the supremacy through at least the major clans. But the possibility of full-brother princes was a serious flaw – almost a fallacy – in this system. It is not difficult to see how the wretched events that were in fact associated with full brothers arise from this basic flaw. Nor is it unreasonable to suppose that the Baganda are unwilling to perceive these events as a pattern precisely because they disrupt the most basic structure of their political system. I think it would be unjustified to say that there was a rule of full-brother succession; rather, such succession resulted from an unwelcome loophole in the rules.

SUCCESSION AND THE POWER OF THE KING

I might have chosen to present the events I have described in chronological order. In that form they would have been less intelligible and less interesting. More seriously, such a presentation would have been misleading, since the really significant facts are deductive, and cannot fairly be presented along with gleanings from the chronicles as if they were established and settled. Their status arises from and rests upon the analysis I have presented. Nevertheless, I may usefully conclude by summarizing what seems to me the trend of developments.

We are ill informed about the first seven reigns of the dynasty, and some of what is recorded is almost certainly fictitious. But there is no reason to doubt that fraternal successions did not in fact occur. This fits reasonably with the apparent tendency of these kings to reign well into old age, which in turn fits with the absence of military pressure from Bunyoro, allowing the kingship to have remained (as I surmise) relatively undeveloped as a military and governmental institution.

The military catastrophe in the reign of the eighth king explains why fraternal succession should have been favoured in following generations; and this precedent perhaps facilitated the later successions by full brothers, dysfunctional though these were.

But in various ways fraternal succession made rebellions more likely. By preserving brothers as potential mature and strong successors, potential rebels were also preserved. Third brothers were apt to rebel lest they lose their chance of the throne; but this in turn provoked counter-rebellion from the filial generation. Younger full brothers were particularly dangerous, since their claim to the throne was exactly as good as that of their elders, and apparently for that reason their elders were unable to curb them. Finally, the fact of fraternal succession tended to inflate the number of princes – their sons and grandsons – eligible for the throne and therefore rivals for it. Under Kyabaggu (K25) this had become such a problem that he invited the princes to fight among themselves for the throne, apparently in order to thin them out, since he had no real intention of abdicating; and even so he was later slain by a revolt of ambitious princes, which developed into a series of particularly bloody civil wars. Eventually Ssemakookiro (K27) – one of the few kings whose deeds are familiar to most Baganda – achieved the throne, and instituted the reforms which prevented both fraternal succession and successful rebellion for several generations.

Curiously Kaggwa, unlike Roscoe and most Baganda today, did not see the measures instituted by Ssemakookiro and followed by his successors as customary – he shows no awareness even of a regularity. Nevertheless it is broadly true to say, as Roscoe does (1911, pp. 188-189): 'To avoid the danger which was often caused by princes rebelling, King Ssemakookiro (allowed his mother to)* put all his brothers (except three)* to death as soon as he had several sons born to him, and thus the succession to the throne was secure. . . . The custom thus established of putting princes to death as soon as a new king had secured the succession was carried out until Mutesa's reign.' (The passage is more accurate without the phrases distinguished by asterisks.) A further important innovation was that these later kings each nominated one of his sons to succeed him, typically a notably young prince.

No one could have known better than Ssemakookiro the havoc caused by rebellious princes; nor does it seem coincidental that the introduction of these ruthless reforms occurred when the dangers from Bunyoro had sharply declined.

But these reforms had further effects that Ssemakookiro probably did not foresee. Presumably young princes were nominated as heirs-apparent to minimize the danger of successful rebellion by any of the king's sons. But to weaken all rivals was to weaken all successors: and hence when these young and inexperienced princes came to the throne they found themselves dominated by the chiefs, and particularly the Katikkiro – as is described in detail for Muteesa I (K30) and Mwanga II (K31). There was grave danger too that the prince nominated by his father to succeed might turn out to be incompetent – as Mwanga II was. Thus these reforms, designated to free the king from the dangers of his royal kin, were likely eventually to subject the kingship to the commoner chiefs, which is not surprising if the kingship is seen as the pivot of a balance between the royal house and the commoner chiefs. The first Katikkiro to benefit substantially from this effect held office from 1889 till 1926, and for most of that time was far more powerful than the Kabaka himself. He was Sir Apolo Kaggwa: and perhaps this is why Kaggwa as chronicler failed to present Ssemakookiro's reforms as initiating a new set of customs.

There seems at least a tenuous parallel with a development in European history which has been remarked by Professor Gluckman. In Buganda, as in Europe, as the nation, the government, and the kingly office became more powerful, measures were taken both to specify more narrowly who should succeed to the throne, and to deal more harshly with rebels or potential rebels. The immediate effect was vastly to strengthen the power of the king; but the long-term effect was to make the kingship itself subordinate to powerful commoners.

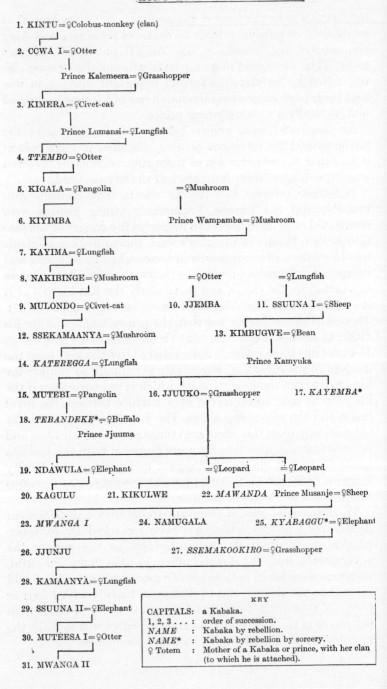

1. KINTU = ♀Colobus-monkey (clan)

2. CCWA I = ♀Otter

Prince Kalemeera = ♀Grasshopper

3. KIMERA = ♀Civet-cat

Prince Lumansi = ♀Lungfish

4. *TTEMBO* = ♀Otter

5. KIGALA = ♀Pangolin   = ♀Mushroom

6. KIYIMBA   Prince Wampamba = ♀Mushroom

7. KAYIMA = ♀Lungfish

8. NAKIBINGE = ♀Mushroom   = ♀Otter   = ♀Lungfish

9. MULONDO = ♀Civet-cat   10. JJEMBA   11. SSUUNA I = ♀Sheep

12. SSEKAMAANYA = ♀Mushroom   13. KIMBUGWE = ♀Bean

14. *KATEREGGA* = ♀Lungfish   Prince Kamyuka

15. MUTEBI = ♀Pangolin   16. JJUUKO = ♀Grasshopper   17. *KAYEMBA**

18. *TEBANDEKE** = ♀Buffalo

Prince Jjuuma

19. NDAWULA = ♀Elephant   = ♀Leopard   = ♀Leopard

20. KAGULU   21. KIKULWE   22. *MAWANDA*   Prince Musanje = ♀Sheep

23. *MWANGA I*   24. NAMUGALA   25. *KYABAGGU** = ♀Elephant

26. JJUNJU   27. *SSEMAKOOKIRO* = ♀Grasshopper

28. KAMAANYA = ♀Lungfish

29. SSUUNA II = ♀Elephant

30. MUTEESA I = ♀Otter

31. MWANGA II

KEY	
CAPITALS:	a Kabaka.
1, 2, 3 . . . :	order of succession.
NAME :	Kabaka by rebellion.
*NAME** :	Kabaka by rebellion by sorcery.
♀ Totem :	Mother of a Kabaka or prince, with her clan (to which he is attached).

NOTE

1. See Southwold (1966). In that paper I give a fuller and more detailed account of matters here dealt with somewhat summarily.

REFERENCES

BEATTIE, J. H. M. 1964. *Other Cultures*. London: Cohen & West.

FALLERS, L. A. 1956. *Bantu Bureaucracy*. Cambridge: Heffer.

GLUCKMAN, M. 1965. *The Ideas in Barotse Jurisprudence*. New Haven: Yale University Press.

KAGGWA, SIR A. 1901. *Basekabaka be Buganda* (The Kings of Buganda). (I refer to the edition of 1953, Kampala and London: Uganda Bookshop and Macmillan.)

—— 1905. *Mpisa za Baganda* (The Customs of the Baganda). (I refer to the edition of 1952, Kampala and London: Uganda Bookshop and Macmillan.)

—— 1908. *Bika bya Baganda* (The Clans of Baganda). (I refer to the edition of 1949, Kampala: Uganda Bookshop and Macmillan.)

MAIR, L. P. 1934. *An African People in the Twentieth Century*. London: Routledge.

NSIMBI, M. B. 1956. *Amannya Amaganda n'Ennono Zaago* (Ganda Names and their meanings). Kampala: East African Literature Bureau.

ROSCOE, J. 1911. *The Baganda*. London: Macmillan.

SOUTHWOLD, M. 1961. *Bureaucracy and Chiefship in Buganda*. East African Studies No. 14, Kampala: East African Institute of Social Research.

—— 1966. Succession to the Throne in Buganda. In J. R. Goody (ed.), *Succession to High Office*. Cambridge: Cambridge University Press.

E. R. Cregeen

The Changing Role of the House of Argyll in the Scottish Highlands

ARGYLL AND THE HIGHLANDS

The house of Argyll – the senior branch of the clan Campbell – has always been a subject to stir controversy and passion in the Scottish Highlands. Their immense power and territorial possessions have been regarded by their enemies, who are many, as the fruits of evil deeds. Their very success in emerging triumphant out of the violence and treachery of the clan feuds of the sixteenth and seventeenth centuries argues in some eyes an unmatched proficiency in guile. As the head of a clan whom one of its enemies characterized as 'a race that craves ever to fish in drumlie (muddy) waters' (Gregory, 1836, p. 375), the house of Argyll has attracted a more than ordinary share of distrust and hatred.

It is the aim of this paper to assess the role which was played by the house of Argyll in the Highlands, mainly from the sixteenth to early nineteenth centuries, and more specifically between 1680 and 1806. This role, it will be argued, had a basic consistency over the centuries, yet it evolved, presenting different aspects in successive periods. First as agents of the Scottish Crown in destroying the overmighty Macdonalds, next as Protestant reformers and leaders of rebellion in the seventeenth century, then as pillars of the Whig party and preservers of the eighteenth-century Establishment, finally as leaders of an economic revolution and pioneers in the creation of a new system of social relationships in the Highlands, the earls and, later, dukes of Argyll appear in many roles. But all are in fact aspects of one constant role, that of drawing into the mainstream of modern life an area still in the sixteenth century politically and culturally autonomous, 'the Hieland, where nane of the officeris of the law dar pass for fear of thair lyvis'.[1]

This led to political, religious, economic, and social revolution, the absorption of the Highlands into the world of ideas and institutions that was emerging in England and the Scottish Lowlands. The tradition of the house of Argyll, whose members were almost without exception men of great native ability and energy, was to initiate, to lead, and to control the revolutionary process.

The question whether, under different leadership, the Highlands might have fared better in the coming to terms with the modern world, is bound to be asked. It is not possible to answer it, but it is part of the argument of this paper that the attitudes which the house of Argyll aroused in the West Highlands in the early and middle stages of its career, when the process of extending law and order went hand in hand with their own territorial aggrandizement, remained as a legacy of mistrust and hostility; and that this legacy proved an almost insurmountable obstacle to the Argylls when in the eighteenth century they launched programmes of economic reform that required trust and cooperation from their tenants. Thus in a very significant degree the earlier role of the house of Argyll in the West Highlands shaped, influenced, and impeded the later developments of a new enlightened role.

The subject is a historical one, and the writer has based this paper in a wholly orthodox way on printed sources and unpublished documentary material.[2] Nevertheless, it is, in intention at least, something other than an essay in the writing of orthodox history. It is hoped that it may serve to provide some kind of bridge between history and social anthropology. The approach remains fundamentally that of an historian, but the subject is one familiar to social anthropologists – a traditional society involved in rapid change. Until the eighteenth century, the Scottish Highlands preserved a way of life comparable with that of many present-day peoples in undeveloped countries. They felt the effects of the economic and social revolutions one to two centuries before most of Africa, Asia, and Central or South America. Their experience will, it is thought, be found relevant to social anthropologists concerned with social change.

This study has been influenced by the writer's interest in comparative social history and by an acquaintance, however limited, with the works of modern social anthropologists. The germinating effect of this brief union encourages the hope that more permanent collaboration between the two disciplines will prove extremely fruitful. In the meantime, social anthropologists who recognize their influence in aspects of this paper are thanked; there is little likelihood that their paternity can be formally disentangled and recognized.[3]

THE HOUSE OF ARGYLL AS AGENTS OF THE CROWN IN SUBJUGATING THE WEST HIGHLANDS

The house of Argyll rose to power and pre-eminence by service to the Scottish Crown. Their original lands were, in the Highlands, the barony of Loch Awe, a compact but by no means extensive territory in the centre of Argyll, held in the late thirteenth century by the founder of the clan, Colin Campbell, after whom the later heads of the clan have taken their Gaelic title, MacCailein Mor ('the great son of Colin'). His son, Sir Neil, married the sister of King Robert I and was among the Bruce's strongest supporters in his contest with Baliol and the English king, Edward I.

Throughout the fourteenth and fifteenth centuries the barons of Loch Awe showed an unwavering loyalty to the Scottish Crown and were rewarded with titles and grants of land. Successive barons were thus able to endow younger sons with land, and in this way cadet branches (lineages tracing their descent in the male line) arose, scattered in an ever-widening circle around the original barony – the Campbells of Inverawe, of Lerags, Stronchormig, Loudon, Barbreck, Ardkinglas, Glenorchy, Breadalbane, Auchinbreck, and others.

In 1457 the earldom of Argyll was created and bestowed on Colin Campbell of Loch Awe, who moved his seat to Inveraray on the shores of Loch Fyne. Here it has remained. The house of Argyll continued to thrive and expand in the sixteenth century. The earls held the highest offices of state, intermarried with leading families in Scotland (while their daughters were frequently married into the chief Highland families), acquired fresh lands, established new cadet branches. Their control of the mainland of Argyll grew with each accession of land and each new branch established.

The late fifteenth and sixteenth centuries were crucial in the rise of the house of Argyll. First the Earls of Argyll became the

155

royal agents or lieutenants, charged with 'daunting' the West Highlands, in other words reducing them to obedience. Second, they formed their close and important link with the new Presbyterian order in the Church. These two developments set the earls on the course and cast them in the role that governed their descendants for several generations and created the image of an unscrupulous, power-loving family.

The daunting of the West meant, in fact, the destruction of the clan Donald, the great rivals of the Campbells. The clan Donald, through its numerous branches and allied or dependent clans, controlled the Hebrides and much of the coast of the western Highlands as the Campbells now controlled the main core of Argyll. Macdonald himself, since 1345 bearing the title 'Lord of the Isles', ruled what was virtually an independent kingdom that extended in the fifteenth century over a third of the area of Scotland. Regarding himself as the heir of the Celto-Norse kings of the isles, he kept royal state at his court, levied men, galleys, and prestations from his large empire, gave charters to land, negotiated treaties with foreign powers, and employed his vassals, the western chiefs, as his officials (Mitchell, 1900, pp. 344-345). The destruction of this native empire was as desirable and necessary to the Scottish Crown as it was to the house of Argyll.

The first commission of lieutenantry, to carry out the forfeiture decreed against the fourth Lord of the Isles, was given to the first Earl of Argyll in 1475. The work of destroying the Macdonald power was virtually completed by 1607. Only fragments of their extensive lands remained. The earls had done their work well. Nothing survived of the confederacy of the clans which Macdonald had united under his aegis.

With the forfeiture of the last Lord of the Isles, his empire had begun to crack. The subject chiefs and various branches of the clan Donald, once the authority of the Lordship had gone, lost all cohesion and plunged into savage feuds with one another. These were skilfully fomented by the central government and by its agent Argyll. It was indeed this use of diplomacy and stratagems rather than open violence that won the Campbells such hatred. The utter barbarity of the history of the Highlands from roughly 1475 to 1625 was largely the result of the 'daunting of the Isles' and the destruction of the Macdonald lordship.[4]

The Argylls were well repaid for their pains. It was they who eventually turned to their advantage the power vacuum left by the fall of Macdonald, first by acquiring from the Crown the lion's share of the Macdonald's possessions in mainland Argyll (Knapdale in 1493, and their rich Kintyre lands in 1607) and distributing them among their clansmen and allies, second by extending their control and overlordship over many of Macdonald's former vassals.[5]

The expansion of the house of Argyll did not end with these acquisitions. It continued through the seventeenth century, particularly as a result of the long-headed policies of the eighth Earl (and first Marquis) of Argyll, and his son, the ninth Earl. Nearly the whole of the Maclean lands were annexed by the ninth Earl c. 1680 in consequence of his father's earlier purchase of Maclean of Duart's debts. This territorial gain extended to half of Mull, a great part of Morvern, the island of Tiree, and part of Coll. Meanwhile a timely loan to Cameron of Locheil made him a vassal of the Earl of Argyll.

By their destruction of the Macdonald lordship, while acting as agents of the central authority, and by exploiting the opportunities of territorial aggrandizement which this gave, the house of Argyll had thus, by the end of the seventeenth century, roughly quadrupled their estates. Their rent-paying property land was not less than five hundred square miles. Besides this, the Earl of Argyll was overlord or feudal superior of most of the chiefs and land-holders in Argyll and of some in Inverness-shire, extending over an area of something like 3,000 square miles. As hereditary sheriff of Argyll, the earl represented the law of Scotland in the West Highlands and was charged with the administration of justice, and as the Crown's lieutenant (soon to become hereditary lord-lieutenant of Argyll) he had control of its armed forces and ample powers to use them with impunity.

Having built up its agent to such a towering strength, it was essential to the Crown that the house of Argyll should remain faithful.

The house of Argyll as leaders of the Reformed Church
The conflict that eventually destroyed the alliance between the Stuart kings and house of Argyll sprang from religious difference.

The Earls of Argyll identified themselves with the Reformation of the Church from the middle of the sixteenth century and played a leading part in establishing the Presbyterian order. Whether in fact greed for Church lands and revenues was among their motives (and they were beneficiaries in the secularization of the lands of Iona and other Church property) is irrelevant here. The eighth Earl and Marquis appears to have held sincere evangelical religious beliefs and placed himself at the head of the Covenanters. More than any one man in Scotland it was he who brought about the break with the Crown in 1638, which led to the great Civil War and involved England, Scotland, and Ireland in conflict. For twelve years the Marquis, by his authority over the Committee of Estates, directed the course of events in Scotland.

Both the Marquis and his son, the ninth Earl, died on the scaffold, the Marquis for the part he had taken in the Civil War and his son for raising a rebellion in the West in 1685 in concert with the Duke of Monmouth's rising in south-west England. Their estates and titles were forfeited, but in each case they reverted to the heir.

The Revolution of 1688 finally expelled the Stuart dynasty and established the Protestant Succession. The accession of the Hanoverian dynasty in 1714, through the timely intervention of a group of nobles of whom Argyll was one, finally sealed the triumph of the Whigs. These two events also established the house of Argyll in a position of unassailable power in Scotland. In 1689 the tenth Earl administered the Scottish coronation oath to William and Mary at Westminster. In 1701 he was created first Duke of Argyll. In the following half-century the dukes of Argyll enjoyed for long periods almost complete control of political power and patronage in the northern kingdom.

Thus in the seventeenth century the house of Argyll had assumed a new role, that of creating and leading a new order in Church and State. It had brought about the dissolution of their traditional close alliance with the Scottish Crown, but by forging a new alliance with the Presbyterian cause and eventually with the Whig party it had maintained the Argylls, through many vicissitudes, as the controlling force in the West Highlands and the agents of the central government. After 1688 the interests of the government and those of the Argylls were as inextricably linked and as interdependent as they had been under the Stuart kings. Without the loyal support of the Argylls the new dynasty and the Whig interest would be left without their staunchest ally in the Highlands. Ironically, had it not been for the Argylls, there would probably not have been a Jacobite cause in the Highlands.

'Disaffection to the Family'
The whole Highland region was a hot-bed of Jacobites for more than a generation after 1715. The risings of 1715, 1719, and 1745 had their beginnings and their warmest support here. A Stuart restoration, at least in Scotland, appeared at times within the bounds of possibility. In these circumstances the existence in the south-west highlands of a solid core of fervent Whigs, attached to the Argyll interest, was of crucial import-ance.

The most zealous Jacobites in the West were the Camerons, the Macdonalds, the Stewarts of Appin, some of the Macleans and others who had suffered from the expansion of the Clan Campbell. Indeed, the political and religious alignment in the Highlands was decided in the seventeenth and early eighteenth centuries by clan relationship. The fact that the Campbells were anti-Royalists was sufficient reason to swing their enemies over to the king and to turn into passionate adherents of the Stuart cause in its downfall clans which in previous times had shown little regard for the monarchy. Envy, deprivation, and hopes of revenge, besides altruism and loyalty, were active ingredients in the Jacobite cause.

The phrase 'disaffection to the Family' occurs frequently in Argyll estate documents of the eighteenth century. What is implied was that the 'disaffected' were followers of another chief and hostile to the interests of the Argylls. The very fact of having engulfed great tracts of land belonging to other clans necessarily meant that, short of wholesale deportation, most of the people living on the Argyll estate owed their allegiance to a chief who was not their landlord.

To counteract this, the newly annexed lands had been partially settled by colonists either belonging to the clan Campbell or allied to it. In Kintyre in the mid-seventeenth century the Marquis settled not only his own clan and dependants but

Covenanting Lowland gentry and farmers (McKerral, 1948). His successor, the ninth Earl, in annexing the Maclean lands, assigned them in extensive tracts on 'tack' (lease) to gentry of the clan Campbell and one or two reliable Macleans. The actual colonists were the sub-tacksmen of the principal tack-holders, and were normally kinsmen of theirs. The sub-tacksmen, with their sub-tenants and servants, moved into the annexed areas as outposts of the clan Campbell and part of the security system whereby the house of Argyll maintained its hold over these scattered and deeply hostile territories.[6]

A petition submitted to the third Duke in 1749 by John McLauchlan of Kilbride reveals something of the danger which the original settlers ran. It is clear from this that they themselves undertook the task of seizing their lands from the old possessors. McLauchlan's grandfather had been assigned the Garvellach islands in the Firth of Lorne on a 'wadsett' (which was a sort of mortgage, secured in land and redeemable by the owner, in this case the ninth Earl), 'and although he met several obstructions yet at length he forcibly obtained possession of these islands which for several years made no return to the family of Argyll.' This indicates that until McLauchlan seized them, the Earl's annexation of them had been purely titular and he had not succeeded in collecting any rents.

'Although the McLeans did for some time smother their resentment on account of my grandfather's having thus dispossessed them, yet at length a band of them came fully armed under cloud of night and in hostile manner and most riotously plundered and carried off the whole effects and bestial on these islands to the value of 3,000 marks, and after destroying the houses and byres, stript the possessors of their vivers and left their wives and children stript naked and exposed to the inclemency of the weather. . . .'

Over the whole of the annexed Maclean lands acts of overt hostility such as this, as well as innumerable acts of secret revenge ranging from cattle-maiming to arson and stealing of the rents, were going on fifty years after the actual annexation. Indeed, the position of the tacksmen in Morven became so untenable that it was hopeless to let farms to any but the original occupants, the Camerons.

Clan structure and land-holding

To appreciate the social revolution which the house of Argyll introduced in their estate in the eighteenth century, some notion must be given of the traditional clan structure and its relation to land tenure.

Until land became commercialized in the Highlands, its function was purely to support the chief, his clan, and dependants. A chief reckoned his wealth not in sheep, cattle, or acres, but in the size of his following.

His following was made up of his clan and 'dependers'. The inner core of the clan consisted of the chief's immediate kinsmen, the gentry of the clan or *daoine uaisle*, generally known in the eighteenth century as 'tacksmen'. They depended on the bounty of the chief to provide them with land and originally enjoyed their benefices, usually one or two extensive farms, without leases and over several generations. In the seventeenth century, the custom of granting land on a long lease or 'tack' became common (though it was frequently resisted by the gentry themselves as hedging in their prescriptive right to land), and led to the use of the term 'tacksmen' for these tenants of high social status.

In a large and powerful clan such as the clan Campbell, tacks of enormous extent are found given to men of importance who besides being the heads of lineages were, like the Campbells of Ardkinglas and of Lerags, 'feuars' or proprietors of estates in perpetuity, conferred on them by ancestors of the Dukes of Argyll.[7] In such cases as this, they established kinsmen as their sub-tacksmen of their tack-lands.

The *daoine uaisle* were the chieftains of the clan, responsible for organizing the clan as a fighting force. They were essentially a military caste, for whom prowess and courage were the ultimate values, and war and cattle-raids a way of life. In default of opportunities of serving their chief at home they sought employment in the Continental armies, where they were known for their proud bearing and ferocity. They despised manual work, but dealing in cattle, being in a sense a natural extension of the cattle-raid, was regarded as an acceptable pursuit for tacksmen. The work of their farms was performed by servants and sub-tenants.

The bond uniting the *daoine uaisle* to their chief, the representative of the founder of the clan, was extremely close. In the early seventeenth century Lord Lovat, chief of the Frasers, would not allow any of his kinsmen to live on the lands of any other chief, for 'there was no earthly thing he put in ballance with them; they were his ammunition, his guard, his glory and honour, and few could compare with them' (Grant, 1930, p. 506). On their part, they were usually completely devoted to their chief, but this devotion had to be reciprocated by the chief. A chief who lost the clan's lands through folly or who failed in his duties of hospitality, generosity, or protection, could be removed or killed (Grant, 1930, pp. 518-522).

The clan proper included commoners, most of whom lived on the lands of the gentry as sub-tenants or as servants, but a proportion of the clan lands always appears to have been let out directly to small tenants, who occupied their holdings at will, without a lease, paying their rents partly in kind, partly in money, and partly in service.[8] They were known as 'common tenants' since they occupied a farm 'in commonty', several of them sharing the arable land, grazings, peat, and other appurtenances of the farm, and re-allotting the arable at frequent intervals. A tenant's holding was made up of pieces of land ('rigs'), not compact and enclosed but scattered about the infield in the manner known as 'run-rig'.

Reciprocal rights and duties united the chief and the commoners. Many commoners claimed kinship with the chief and combined complete obedience to their chief with an immense pride and dignity.

> 'The Highlanders walk nimbly and upright, so that you will never see, among the meanest of them, in the most remote part, the clumsy, stooping gait of the French paysans or our own country fellows, but on the other hand a kind of stateliness in the midst of their poverty. They have a pride in their family as almost everyone is a genealogist' (Burt, 1754, Letter XIX).

The commoner, like the tacksman, followed the chief in war and paid a rent in money, kind, and services of various sorts, but in the commoner's case the services involved physical labour. The chief, on his side, was obliged to furnish land, see his people through scarcities and other hardships, and protect them against the government and other enemies.

Precise definitions of rights and duties and of relationships generally in the Scottish clan are extremely difficult. The data which a social anthropologist would regard as an indispensable basis for his work are frequently completely lacking. Nevertheless, one can see running through Highland society the controlling principle that kinship carried inescapable obligations and indisputable claims respecting land. Tacksmen and tenants could claim to be maintained in land by the chief and near kinsmen could expect to enjoy their farms undisturbed for a long period.[9]

The kinsmen and dependants of tacksmen and small tenants could equally expect to be maintained in land by these tenants. Throughout the eighteenth century small tenants continued to observe the custom of sub-letting a considerable part of their diminutive holdings to their relations. Reporting on this to the fifth Duke of Argyll in 1771, one of his chamberlains wrote: 'This practice has proceeded so far as to reduce possession (i.e. holdings) in Tiry to the smallest possible division, to such a degree indeed that the separate possessions of the small tenantry do not pay at a medium 30/- rent'. The same report explains to the new Duke: 'Besides these [rent-paying tenants] there are a number of sub-tenants in the islands, for the Duke has not a tacksman in the run-rig farms of that estate whose portion of land is not sub-let in whole or part to his children or other relations for their support.'

A clan, however, was never simply a group of kinsmen dwelling together and tracing descent from a common ancestor. Besides those who bore the chief's surname and were related to him by blood ties, there were often families that had adopted the name as a means of protection in troubled times (as, for example, the MacGregors after their proscription in 1603) or out of deference to the chief or in return for a bribe. There might also be septs of a different name owing allegiance to the chief and enjoying protection and favour from him. Among these were normally his functionaries – his harper in early times, his piper, seanachie (genealogist), bard, henchman (who was often his foster-brother), his armour-bearer, purse-bearer, and so on.[10] Thus the MacMhuirich family were hereditary seanachies of the Clanranald branch of the clan Donald (and earlier of the Lord of the Isles), the MacCrimmons were the pipers of the MacLeods of Dunvegan, and the MacColls were hereditary bodyguards to the Stewart chiefs of Appin. They were rewarded for their services by enjoying an unbroken succession to particular lands.

The chief of a clan might include among his followers the representatives of ancient local families too weak to stand alone in the ruthless conditions of the sixteenth century. The struggles of the great clans induced the weak to seek protection from the strong and give 'bonds of manrent', promising to follow and obey the chief and to bring presents at stated times in return for the chief's favour and protection.[11]

Fugitives and broken clans, and their descendants, went to swell a chief's following. They would be especially welcome if, like the MacUalrigs who settled on Glengarry's land, they enjoyed a reputation as bonny fighters and daring caterans.[12]

Septs such as these, not related by blood to the chief, would frequently have their own chieftains and serve under these in the clan's war array. They enjoyed the possession of land under the clan chief, though possibly this land had formerly belonged to them outright before they were absorbed in his following.

Clansmen and dependers alike shared the obligation of giving presents at stated times to the chief and of paying 'calps' (their best beast) to him at their death. This last obligation of heriot, found in many societies, present and past, was the hallmark and diagnostic of subordination to a chief.

The Scottish clan in its larger sense was thus heterogeneous in composition. It was based as much on a binding lord-vassal relationship such as occurs in all feudal societies as it was on kinship. But in spite of its varied make-up and origin, the clan was remarkably homogeneous as a body of people owing loyalty and obedience to a chief, living under his authority and protection, and identifying itself with the traditions and family pride of the chief.

The Duke of Argyll was chief of the clan Campbell and feudal superior of many vassals holding their estates from him in return for military services and on other terms. From among his clan and his vassals he could muster well over five thousand men in the early eighteenth century. But it has been shown earlier that his estates harboured numerous tenants who, while they might grudgingly admit that he was landlord, were followers of other chiefs. This was a familiar enough situation in the Highlands,[13] but for the ducal house of Argyll in the eighteenth century it raised problems of a wholly new kind.

GENERAL HISTORICAL TRENDS IN THE HIGHLANDS IN THE EIGHTEENTH CENTURY

It is commonly held that the old Highlands died on the field of Culloden in 1746, and that the subsequent statutes abolishing hereditary jurisdictions, military followings, Highland dress, and the rest destroyed the clan system. This is a naïve and superficial view, which a study on any part of the Highlands would show to be false.

What destroyed the old Highland social and political structure was its growing involvement in the general cultural influence of their neighbours to the south, that is England and the Scottish Lowlands. This influence, expressed in speech, manners, clothes, religion, political sympathies and activity, trade, seasonal migration, and so on, was at work in the Highlands long before 1745 and reached its climax considerably after.

Already by the end of the seventeenth century much of Argyll had, through the activity of the house of Argyll, adopted the Presbyterian order in the Church and the Whig politics of its leader. In areas of the Highlands and islands further north, the new Church was even more powerful. A new economic outlook can be seen in the estate management of a number of the Campbell lands and further north, of the Mackenzies, long before 1745. Floods of impoverished Highlanders are found seeking work in the Lowlands in periods of crop failure. Highland chiefs are found selling their poorer tenants as indentured labour in the American colonies (Grant, 1959, pp. 404-409). If in the period following 1745 there seems to be a speeding up of change in the Highlands, it is because the whole of Britain, indeed of Western Europe, was passing into a more active phase of development, with everywhere a sharp upsurge in population growth, a rapid expansion of trade and industry and techno-logical mastery, the emergence of an industrial proletariat and of a class of entrepreneurs rich and energetic enough to challenge the landed interest.

Thus the passage of the West Highlands, under the leadership of the house of Argyll, into the mainstream of modern political and religious development, which has been noticed already, was paralleled in the eighteenth century by a process of economic and social assimilation. The whole economy of the Highlands was radically changed so that its near-independence became almost total subordination to the demands of Lowland industry. By the early nineteenth century, the economy of the West Highlands was almost wholly directed towards supplying cattle and sheep, wool, kelp, and labour to the southern towns.

This abandonment of an economic condition approaching, though never attaining, self-sufficiency created rural problems of a kind familiar in the enclosure movements of France and England. The disappearance of ancient farm-towns was accompanied by an unaccustomed mobility, by the rise of new villages, by an intensified activity in coastal areas (associated with fishing and kelp-burning), and by the emergence in many areas of what was in effect a rural proletariat, engaged in wage-labour, kelp manufacture, and fishing, and occupying little or no land.

The disintegration of the traditional social structure was accompanied by the growth of a new system of relationships based on commercial values. The chief became the landlord, treating the land no longer as a means of supporting a warlike following but as a source of revenue and as a commodity to be bought and sold. The clansmen, released from their military services and labour dues, became simply rent-paying tenants, or, losing their stake in the lands, turned to wage-earning employment or emigration (or to seasonal migration).

With this, new attitudes developed. For the chief, now frequently a non-resident landlord, with a son at Eton and a daughter doing 'the season', the claims of vassals and clansmen became irksome and irrelevant. They for their part gradually lost their affection and loyalty for the chief and looked to improve their condition elsewhere.

It can be argued that the legislation that followed Culloden hastened the procession of change by pre-disposing chiefs to accept the values of the militarily successful and politically

dominant South. Samuel Johnson, whose account of his Highland journey in 1773 contains probably the most profound
analysis of the social changes taking place, saw the chiefs as
turning to wealth and display in compensation for the loss of
their power.

'The chiefs, divested of their prerogatives, necessarily turned
their thoughts to the improvement of their revenues, and
expect more rent as they have less homage. . . . When the
power of birth and station ceases, no hope remains but from
the prevalence of money.'

This seems profoundly true, but it is to be understood not
simply in the context of 1745 and its aftermath but in the whole
preceding century. Macleod of Dunvegan's financial embarrass-
ment and his demand for higher rents dated from his becoming
a member of Parliament in 1741 (Grant, 1959), and many
another Highland chief was lured away, first from his estate,
then from his clan, by becoming involved in English politics
and society after the Union. It was this spectacle that made
Dr Johnson declare: 'Sir, the Highland chiefs should not be
allowed to go further south than Aberdeen. A strong-minded
man like Sir James Macdonald may be improved by an English
education, but in general they may be tamed into insignificance.'
If Robert Redfield, following Toynbee, is right in seeing the
Scottish Highlander as one of the three primitive peoples
accepted as equal partners by the Western world, the credit, or
the responsibility, must go to the chiefs, who showed an almost
indecent haste in assimilating the southern culture (Redfield,
1953, p. 45).

THE HOUSE OF ARGYLL
AND ITS NEW ENTREPRENEURIAL ROLE

In the eighteenth century the role of the Duke of Argyll in the
Highlands is no longer in the political and religious spheres a
revolutionary one. With the triumph of their cause through the
events of 1688 and 1714, their role is that of maintaining the
established order against Tories, papists, Jacobites, and the
disaffected generally. They take the lead in destroying the
threat from the Stuarts in 1715 and 1745.

But, true to their family tradition as pioneers and innovators

they assume a new revolutionary role as leaders of economic
and social change. They are found introducing agricultural
improvements in the early decades of the eighteenth century.
They revolutionize the whole basis of land tenure on their
estate before 1740. They build a castle at Inveraray in the new
Gothic style, one of the earliest examples of this fashion in
Britain, and lay out parks, gardens, and woodlands. They build
new towns and villages, found industries, promote the construction of roads, piers, and canals, and encourage schemes of
re-settlement in the Highlands to prevent emigration. One after
another, with remarkable consistency, the eighteenth-century
dukes pursue this new economic policy, making Inveraray the
main focus of change and 'improvement' in the West Highlands.

It was natural that the Argylls should assume a pioneer role.
Their political activities made them normally resident in
London, so that their visits to their Highland estates were
usually confined to a few summer months. Their social activities,
tastes, and expenditure were those of the great Whig magnates.
The possession of five thousand fighting men as a personal
following no doubt lent a certain romantic grandeur to the
Duke of Argyll in the eyes of his peers, but the spending of five
thousand pounds a year in cash was more necessary if the Duke
was not to appear down at heel among the Russells, the Stan-
hopes, and the Pelhams. A perennial need for revenue characterized the estate management of the Dukes of Argyll in the
eighteenth century.

The new economic role of the house of Argyll was in one
sense an aspect of their more general political role. Although
the execution of their programme of agrarian reorganization
was sometimes, as will appear, in conflict with immediate
political objectives, both stemmed from the same underlying
philosophy. When, in his instructions to the Chamberlain of
Tiree in 1756, the third Duke, requiring that tenants should
henceforth pay a part of their rents in spun yarn and that their
womenfolk should spin diligently, wrote: 'I'm resolved to keep
no tenants but such as will be peaceable and apply themselves
to industry. You'll cause intimate this same sobbath after
sermon', he was speaking as a good Whig. In the schemes for
'civilizing the Highlands' which occupied the Duke and his
friends in Government after 1745, projects for linen factories

in remote areas, associated with the cultivation of flax and domestic spinning, bulked large. The economic virtues of hard work, thrift, and sobriety were constantly urged upon the Highlanders, and were regarded by the Duke and his friends as an excellent antidote to Jacobitism and disaffection, which thrived in idleness and intemperance.

The encouragement of such virtues, however, went beyond a purely political purpose. Industrious, sober, and enterprising tenants were required if the estate was to yield a steadily increasing rental. This would be beneficial not to the Duke alone, but also to the tenant. Thus, the fifth Duke, later in the century, when pursuing his programme of abolishing the joint farms, appealed to the spirit of private enterprise and wrote to the Chamberlain of Mull: 'My own wish is that these farms should be divided into sixteen different possessions so as every man may have his own separate farm to manage and improve in his own way, and the skilful and industrious may reap the benefit of their labours and knowledge, and at the same time be examples to others.'

Introduction of a new tenurial system
Until the period of the second Duke of Argyll (1703-1743), the famous 'John of the Battles', contemporary and rival of the Duke of Marlborough, the tenurial structure of the Argyll estate was, in spite of rent rises, indistinguishable from that of any other large Highland estate. The second Duke dramatically changed the whole basis of land tenure. First in Kintyre, about 1710, then on his other lands in 1737, he offered tacks (leases) of farms in open auction to the highest bidders – whoever they might be.

The Duke's agent, Duncan Forbes, Lord President of the Court of Session, declared war on the tacksmen, convened the inhabitants (sub-tacksmen and sub-tenants) of the various districts, and 'acquainted them with your Grace's favourable intention of delivering them from the oppression of services and herezelds [heriots] and of encouraging them to improve their farms by giving them a sort of property in their grounds for nineteen years by leases, if they showed themselves worthy of the intended favour by offering frankly for their farms such rent as honestly and fairly they could bear'.[14]

By skilfully driving a wedge between the tacksmen and their
dependants, Forbes succeeded in raising the rents substantially
and letting most of the farms either to the previous sub-
tacksmen, who were gentleman-farmers, or to joint tenants.
The increases in rent were obtained, according to Forbes,
without adding to the tenants' burdens, since their labour
services to the former tacksmen had been abolished. The com-
mutation of rents in kind followed.

Almost at a single stroke of the pen, clanship and vassalage
ceased officially to count in the tenurial system of the largest
Highland estate, and this a decade before the '45 Rising. In
future, the deciding principle in the allocation of land was to
be a commercial one. At first, the public auction, with open
competitive bidding, was customary. By mid-century the bad
consequences of the system were recognized, and in its place
the third Duke introduced a system of private offers, which
permitted other factors besides the financial one to be given
weight, in particular the willingness of candidates for farms to
undertake certain improvements.

Competition had been established as the ruling principle in
the allocation of land. The ancient tenants could no longer
presume on long attachment or kinship to the family of Argyll,
but must make good their claim by offering high rents, substantial improvements, and the certainty of prompt payment
of rent. Clansmen must submit their offers on the same terms
as the rest and trust that, other things being equal, their
attachment and that of their ancestors to the house of Argyll
would sway the issue. A proposal for a farm is submitted thus
by John Campbell, 'tennent in Ballinoe in the island of Tirrie'
in 1755:

'Humbly sheweth – that the said John Campbell, his father
and grandfather have been tennents in the said island since
your Grace's family obtained the property thereof, and were
the first Campbells who settled in it. As I have four sons,
three whereof are married but have no possessions, I humbly
propose for myself and sons to take a tack of Kilchenichmore,
one of your Grace's farms in the said Island, and to pay yearly
thereof, including cess and teinds, seven pounds, eleven
shillings sevenpence farthing sterling.

May it therefor please Your Grace to consider the premises
and grant such answer to the above proposal as to your Grace
shall seem fit.'

In practice, as will be shown, claims of kinship and loyalty
continued to influence estate management, but their scope was
much restricted. In the long run the new criteria being applied
to tenancy on the Argyll estate winnowed away many of the
ancient families. Some emigrated to the American colonies and
established their whole following of sub-tenants and dependants
there, surviving in some cases to come forward as loyalists in
the War of American Independence with offers of service from
themselves and their body of followers.[15]
Others succeeded in retaining their lands, at any rate for a
period, but their function, if not their outlook and values, had
changed. They were no longer the military leaders of the clan,
counsellors of the chief, and masters of a numerous sub-
tenantry, but gentleman-farmers, owing an insecure possession
of their land to the efficiency with which they promoted the
improvement of the estate.
Dr Johnson found them a harassed and vanishing class, and
lamented the disappearance of their feudal virtues, their lavish
hospitality, and the cohesion which they had given to a society
which he saw becoming polarized and deprived of its native
leaders.[16]
In place of the *daoine uaisle*, one increasingly finds the large-
scale tenant farmers of the late eighteenth and the nineteenth
centuries. They graze cattle and, later in the century, sheep, for
the Lowland and English markets, apply themselves to the
improvement of their extensive holdings, and rarely have sub-
tenants. This new type of enterprising farmer and dealer is
typified by the family of Gregorson or MacGregor who, in the
second half of the eighteenth century, acquired the lease of
several large farms in Mull and Morvern, was tenant of the inn
at the ferry between the island of Mull and the mainland of
Argyll, and gained the monopoly of transporting cattle from
this important grazing area to the mainland. This concentration
of economic opportunities enabled Angus Gregorson to pay the
fifth Duke larger rents than any other tenant on the Argyll
estate.

Local depopulation frequently resulted from the grazing activities of the new tacksmen. Cattle and sheep required fewer hands than did cultivation. The Gregorsons devoted one of their Morvern farms to grazing cattle in the 1770s; the estate census of 1779 shows it sparsely populated in comparison with the crowded populations of neighbouring farms. One of them, Innimore, for example, the only farm still retained by the Camerons on the Argyll estate, had a population of forty-five souls, joint tenants and their servants, all of them bearing the surname Cameron. In Morvern generally, grazing farms maintained on the average no more than twenty-two people in 1779, in contrast with the traditional mixed arable and grazing farms, where the population averaged fifty-six people. This contrast between densely populated farms and depopulated grazing farms became sharper as sheep-farming spread in the later years of the century.

Between the new tacksmen and the small tenantry there was not the close attachment that had bound together the *daoine uaisle* and their dependants, even where the original families remained. The divergence of interest became clear in times of war. For the first time military recruitment became difficult in the Highlands. 'A military spirit prevails much among the gentlemen of this country; they wish to keep the men, but their lands give so much more rent by stocking them with sheep that they cannot withstand the gain.'[17]

The second Duke's new leases had established a larger body of direct tenants on the estate than had existed previously. It was clearly intended that the former sub-tacksmen and small tenants should benefit from the removal of the tacksmen. Indeed, the second Duke saw himself as their protector.[18] What were the actual results of the competitive system on this tenantry in the long run?

The population of the Highlands was increasing fast from about the middle of the eighteenth century. This fact, combined with the extension of the cattle industry and the arrival of sheep-masters, who bid strongly for farms, meant a steadily increasing demand for land and consequently rising rents.

Rents were pushed up even higher than they need have been by fierce rivalry between different clans. The rent of the Garvellach islands, mentioned earlier as occupied by McLauchlan of

Kilbride, an ancient follower of the Argylls, rose when the lease was open to competitive bidding, from about £14 in 1749 to £42 in 1757, owing to traditional antagonism between the two contending parties, McLauchlan and MacDugald of Gallanich. Such situations, in which clan feuds expressed themselves in ferocious bids and counter-bids instead of in pitched battles and cattle-raids, were occurring over much of the Argyll estate until the end of the eighteenth century.

Tenants were often ruined by the competition for land. More than half of the small tenants on the Argyll estate who received leases from Forbes in 1737 lost them through insolvency and other causes within a decade, and in general small tenants held from year to year, at the landlord's will, throughout the century. There is a general and extreme instability in the occupancy of the farms, steadily rising rents, and a rapid turnover of tenants. In 1779, for example, the rent of farms in five Kintyre parishes stood at about 250 per cent of the level of rents in 1720. In this period of half a century the surnames of the tenants, in all but seven of the fifty-five farms which were examined, changed. In the north of the estate this kind of instability existed and was due to political as much as to economic causes, but in Kintyre it stemmed largely from sharp competition for land and from an estate management that did little to aid or retain long-established tenants.

One cannot generalize too broadly about the changes in social structure which entry into a world of competition brought about. There are differences between one district and another and between one period and another.[19] In areas suitable for grazing, the generally rising price levels of cattle and sheep favoured extensive farming. It is in such areas, particularly Mull and Morvern on the Argyll estate, where gentleman-farmers were dominant and where extreme differences in wealth developed. In Tiree, less congenial to graziers, the gentry played a less important part. Here economic conditions and estate policy combined to bring into existence a new class of crofters. In Kintyre, where barley for distilling was an important crop, and where, moreover, the existence of the busy port of Campbeltown produced an interpenetration of trade and agriculture, with greater prosperity than was common in the Highlands, the new social structure was characterized by a class of middling tenant-farmers who bridged the gap between the impoverished small tenantry and the gentleman-farmers.

A rising population, combined with agrarian changes on the whole favouring an extensive agriculture, tended to create a large landless class, unknown before in the Highlands. Emigration overseas or to the new Lowland industrial towns drained off large numbers, but war conditions and the movement of prices in the last two decades of the eighteenth century and the first two decades of the nineteenth century created new incentives to expand the fishing industry and the production of kelp from seaweed. Lairds sought to discourage emigration in these circumstances. Farms were divided into individual crofts for the support of fishermen and kelp-burners. In this period, for the first time, the crofter emerges as the characteristic inhabitant of the coastal areas and the western islands, neither wholly a farmer nor wholly a labourer or fisherman, taking the place of the traditional 'common tenant' and inheriting many of his characteristics. Threatened by insecurities of a new kind and largely deprived of the moral support of a strong and stable culture, he clings all the more passionately to his meagre holding and is suspicious of all change.

Conflict and compromise in the ducal role

Competition had come to stay and its long-term effects were revolutionary. But it would be mistaken to think of clanship as irrelevant to the Argyll estate after 1737. Reference has been made to the instability of tenancies. Thus of sixty-one farms in Mull and Morvern for which information is available, thirty-nine changed hands wholly or in part between 1744 and 1779. But of the twenty-two farms where the tenant's surname at these two dates is unchanged, twenty-one are in the hands of tenants of the name of Campbell. Could free competition produce such a remarkable result, or are other influences at work?

The claims of clanship, spurned in 1737, reasserted their importance for a number of reasons, political, economic, and personal.

Ironically, the clan Campbell had never been more vitally important to their chief than in the years following 1737. Jacobitism was rife, a rising was preparing to overthrow the

Hanoverians, and the disgruntled Campbell colonists were threatening to leave Mull and return to the mainland. The new landlordism of the ducal house was placing in peril the police and security of the estate, perhaps even the stability and safety of the government. Without the backing of his clan the Duke's traditional role as guarantor of peace and order in the West Highlands could not be sustained.

The third Duke in succeeding his mercurial brother in 1743 showed a sound appreciation of the crisis. A leading member of the clan expressed the hope of the Campbell gentry that he would 'restore that old intercourse of duty and tenderness which subsisted between the heads of that family and their friends in the country'.[20] (In this context 'friends' would have its still common Scottish significance of 'kinsfolk'.) Already a number of the native clans in the annexed northern lands had regained their former holdings by outbidding the colonists. The third Duke answered the situation by making political loyalty a pre-condition of tenancy on his estate.

The instructions to his various chamberlains in 1744 contained the following clauses:

> 'You are to treat with the tenants of that part of my estate under your management for tacks of the farms where the possessors are under bad character or are not affected to the Government or my interest, and in farms that are not now under tacks you are to use your endeavours to introduce tenants that are well-affected to the Government and my family, and as I am informed that my lands are rather too high-rented in these countrys, so that there may be a necessity of some abatement of rent, I do approve that those abatements be chiefly given in those farms where you can bring in people well disposed to my interest.'

In another instruction the Duke wrote: 'I would have it made a condition of the tacks that every tenant should take the oath of allegiance and a promissory oath never to raise or encourage any rising in rebellion against the present Government.'

These measures and the elimination of numbers of the Macleans and nearly all the Camerons from holding tacks on the estates for their participation in the 'Forty-five' restored the Campbells to their holdings and made sound politics in future an essential condition of tenancy. Conversely, it turned the large tenants into collaborators with the Dukes in schemes of improvement. They began to apply themselves to fulfilling the conditions contained in their leases concerning the enclosure of the land, the planting of trees, the draining of mosses, the building of slated houses, etc. But they scrupulously preserved their character of gentleman-farmers, doing no manual work themselves. Their shaken loyalty to the family was restored. In proposing a scheme for enclosing the woods in Mull and Morvern against depredations in 1771, one of the fifth Duke's officials recommended that the upper tenants should act as a sort of unpaid police: 'These tacksmen may be chosen for their integrity and attachment to the family. They can be found among the Campbells that are called gentlemen farmers on that estate.' Thus kinship and politics continued to have a potent influence on the management of the Argyll estate for more than a generation after the great reorganization of 1737.

The cohesion of the clan Campbell under the third Duke showed itself not only in the relations between Duke and tenants but in the close alliance that the Duke maintained with that numerous body of Campbell lairds who were his vassals in Argyll. For about a generation after 1743 they enjoyed a halcyon time. Under the aegis of their powerful protector and patron they had no rivals to fear in the West Highlands after 1746. They dominated Argyll politically by their near-monopoly of magistracies and Commissionerships of Supply (their Achilles' heel was their lack of freehold voting rights, since most of the property in Argyll was held direct by the Duke, not the Crown). Their web of intermarriage linked together branches of the Campbells into closer unions and maintained the integrity of their properties. Their solidarity is evident, too, in business partnerships and in mutual guarantees of credit.

In return for their solid political support (no more than a handful of Campbell lairds ever went over to the Jacobites), the Duke rewarded them amply out of the enormous store of his patronage, though he diplomatically kept open a channel of army promotions for the Macleans and other Highlanders, as a means of converting them into loyal subjects of the king.

The alliance of Duke and vassals went beyond politics into

economics. Enterprising Campbells initiated and promoted ducal improvements at Inveraray and over the estate at large. The almost hereditary positions which several ancient families occupied in the estate administration gave them influence over it. Innovations in animal breeding, agricultural practice, and tree-planting at Inveraray spread quickly to other estates in Argyll. Cattle of finer breed from the Duke's parks were, for example, sold chiefly to Campbell lairds with a view to improving the West Highland breed.

The Duke's new castle at Inveraray and his general style of life undoubtedly influenced the West Highland lairds. One notes the spread of a fashion for new country houses, parks, and other embellishments; for town houses, carriages, and servants in livery; for English and Lowland ways and often ruinous expense.

New enterprises, underwritten by the Duke, for developing the economic potential of the Highlands, offered the Campbell lairds opportunities of getting rich: timber contracts for the iron furnace established on Loch Fyne in 1754; a spinning school and factory set up at Inveraray (and later a woollen factory in the neighbourhood with the shareholders all Campbell lairds to a man); a whaling company at Campbeltown; and other such ventures.

The third Duke played a dual role – half traditional chief, half modern landlord and entrepreneur. An estate management based on dispassionate economics was still impossible. Competition for land operated within the limits set up by political security and family alliances. Economic enterprises were much in the air, but benefited mainly the Campbell lairds and gentleman-farmers and their friends.

There can be no doubting the benevolent intentions of the third Duke for the welfare of the inhabitants of his lands in general. Circumstances, however, still forbade the development of an economic role independent of political connexions. For the inhabitants of the former Maclean lands the role of the Duke of Argyll remained still that of 'daunting the isles' and dividing the spoils among his clan. The effects of this slow backwash from centuries of aggrandizement into the era of Improvements can be studied in more detail in one of the old Maclean possessions acquired by the house of Argyll.

Tiree: a case-study in resistance to the improving movement
A great improving landlord could, one might have thought,
afford to snap his fingers at mutinous small tenants and improve
them whether they liked it or not. The history of the island of
Tiree, however, may be cited as a case-study in ducal intentions often frustrated by native resistance. A small, flat, wind-
swept Hebridean island, lying open to the gales of the Minch,
destitute of the shelter of a single tree, but favoured with good
light soil and a long growing season, Tiree had been wrested by
the Argylls from the Macleans of Duart, circa 1680. The whole
island had been set in tack to Campbell of Ardkinglas, who had
sub-let it to kinsmen and friends. In 1737, in the reorganization
of the estate, Ardkinglas lost his tack but several Campbells
gained farms and continued to hold them, usually as absentees.
Tacks of several farms were also gained (or regained) by cadet
houses of the Macleans resident in Tiree. More than half the
farms were in the hands of common tenants and continued to
be even after they had lost their short-lived leases.

In this isolated island, cut off for months on end from communications with the outside world, the influence of a handful
of resident Campbell colonists was negligible. The mass of small
tenants continued to adhere strongly to the Maclean gentry,
their *daoine uaisle*. The Duke's Chamberlain of Tiree, arriving
in 1745 to recruit soldiers for the government, had to retreat
in alarm before menacing crowds of islanders. The ringleaders
were arrested after the Rising and gaoled for a time at Inveraray
and on their return to Tiree were excluded from holding lands.
They gathered on Scarinish, the only farm in the island not in
the Duke's possession, and by their turbulence and conspiracies
turned it into a veritable Cave of Adullam. The Duke was forced
to buy this farm, but disaffection and dispute continued to
work against the Argylls and to frustrate 'any instructions
your Grace is pleased to give relating to the policies of that
island'.

Between 1737 and the end of the century the instructions of
successive dukes to their chamberlains in Tiree range over a
wide variety of 'improvements': the construction of a harbour
and roads and the provision of wheeled transport (hitherto
unknown in Tiree as in most of the Highlands); the drainage of

peat-mosses and the building of sea-walls to preserve the land from inundation; the division and enclosure of farms and commons; the improvement of blood-stock and grain seed and the introduction of new crops; the founding of new domestic industries; schemes for training craftsmen, encouragement for fishermen, and much else.

The social situation in the Highlands urgently demanded economic reforms and expansion. A population crisis was already boiling up by the early seventies,[21] and emigration appeared to many observers the only hope for the prolific Highlanders. In Tiree, the overcrowding of the farms was serious by 1770 and acute by 1790. Yet it is not apparent that the ducal improvements attracted support and cooperation outside the ranks of the higher tenants. The pace of reform was in practice extremely slow. In particular, schemes for expanding manufactures and fishing and abolishing the joint 'run-rig' farms, made practically no progress in the eighteenth century.

The very qualified success of the improving dukes in Tiree was typical of the situation in the Highlands in general. Faulty planning, inadequate investment, and, most of all, distrust go far to explain the lack of success of the programme of economic reform in Tiree.

There was a need for planned reforms of a type that would readily be incorporated into existing practice and that were suited to the climate and environment in general. An excellent example of good planning was the experiment in exporting salt barrelled beef from Tiree, initiated by the third Duke in 1750. Cattle exported alive from the island frequently fell victim to the disease red-water, and hence this branch of the island's industry could not develop. The experiment overcame this problem, and considerable quantities of salt beef were being exported ten years later.

Some aspects of the planning, although admirable in principle were less fortunate in practice and could not be assimilated. An experiment in growing sown grasses and clover, begun on an improving lease in 1737 on one of the farms, proved wholly successful and should have revolutionized the constant problem of winter feeding. It was not followed up, however, and this for the good reason that because of the general lack of fences there was nothing to prevent cattle and other animals from straying promiscuously throughout the island. Fencing clearly must precede other innovations.

The islanders were not hostile to reform as such. They were intensely practical and had to be convinced of the value – for them – of a given innovation. They showed themselves capable of selecting and adapting from the series of improvements that issued from Inveraray. Thus, in the early years of the nineteenth century, when the fifth Duke sent wheeled carts to the island, the islander accepted them, but first replaced the spoked wheels by solid wooden wheels, better adapted to travelling through sand.

Inadequate investment is also an element in accounting for the slow progress of economic development in Tiree. A massive expenditure of human labour was required if the pitifully low material standards of the islanders were to be raised at all significantly. They needed a safe harbour and seaworthy boats if their isolation was to be broken down and if trade and fishing were to be developed. Problems of transport within the island demanded roads and carts, and these did not exist. No important advance in agriculture could be expected without capital outlay in drainage and fence building (not necessarily the separate enclosure of individual holdings, but the fencing of arable land and sown pastures against straying animals).

The dependence of the islander on outside assistance was acute: for example, the island had no timber of any kind, and every boat spar, house beam, and agricultural implement was made of imported wood. They possessed no crowbars, gunpowder, or carts necessary for obtaining stone and building masonry walls, and there was no mason in the island. They had practically no peat, and derived most of their supplies from the island of Mull. (Their absence for several weeks in early summer each year while they cut and transported the peat imposed limits on the crops which they could grow with advantage. Crops needing close attention and weeding were of no interest.) They had no effective corn-mill and were dependent on hand-querns of prehistoric type or on the services of the little mills on the Ross of Mull, twenty-five miles away.

Capital outlay of the kind and quantity required could take the form of specialist services provided by the dukes, and this indeed was given; advice on new crops, expert surveys and reports, the provision of skilled craftsmen, etc. But a vast amount of labour and materials was also indispensable. The labour could be provided in the island but would be available only if the islanders felt it worth their while. It is clear that the third Duke utilized the public labour services due from tenants to carry out specific works of public utility, but did not offer sufficient incentives to small tenants to improve the farms. Leases for a reasonable period of years, and rents fixed at a moderate level to permit tenants to carry out basic improvements, were the minimal requirements.

It is in fact the case that rents on the Argyll estate were, under the fifth Duke of Argyll, among the most moderate in the Highlands. But even moderate rents could be excessive in conditions of poverty; and it appeared that rents absorbed 50 per cent of the revenue of the island in 1794 (Cregeen, 1964, pp. 35-39 and 39n.). All the dukes of the eighteenth century spent lavishly on their new houses, estate offices, parks, and other amenities, and often strained the resources of the estate in meeting these costs. Even the fifth Duke had to be restrained in this respect by his agent, James Ferrier. It was only at the end of the fifth Duke's time that leases were offered to small tenants in Tiree, with incentives to carry out improvements.

Perhaps the fundamental cause of lack of economic progress in Tiree was the mistrust and hostility which the mass of the islanders felt towards the house of Argyll and which was the legacy of the Argylls' historical role. Open resistance was rare after 1745, but there is evidence of conspiracies, of a sullen apathy towards the landlord's enterprises, and of malicious joy when any of them failed. A whole century after annexation by the Argylls, the islanders remained determined followers of the Macleans: 'The small tenants of Tiry are disaffected to the Family', read an official report to the fifth Duke in 1771; 'In this disposition it is thought that long leases might render them too much independent . . . and encourage them to that sort of insolence and outrage to which they are naturally prone and much incited by their chieftains of the Maclean gentry.' Similar statements were made by the same officials concerning the Mull and Morvern population.

It was a vicious circle. Small tenants were disaffected and must not have leases. Without leases they would never cooperate in improving their farms. If the run-rig farms remained unimproved, while population rose, poverty would increase and resentment would continue – and leases would be as far away as ever.

Some of the most necessary improvements were thus defeated by the antagonism of the islanders, who regarded them as Campbell tricks to deprive them once again. This distrust, and the fear of additional burdens, kept agriculture down to a remarkably unproductive level. The whole attitude of the times is reflected in the saying, still current in the island: 'Mur b'e eagal an da mhail, bheireadh Tiridhe an da bharr'[22] ('But for the fear of double rent, Tiree would yield a double crop').

The fifth Duke (succeeded 1770, died 1806) attempted a wholesale solution of the economic and demographical problems in Tiree, but like all his contemporaries he had no use for the run-rig farm with its joint tenants. In his sweeping scheme of reform he planned to endow the more industrious and better-off joint tenants with modest-sized, compact individual farms. The surplus tenants and the cottars – the 'supernumeraries' as he called them – were to be removed and settled in new fishing villages which he was to create on the coast and receive small crofts and other assistance provided they fished. The scheme was impeccable in theory. In practice, it was a total failure. The spirit of resistance spread through the island and a plan of emigration was set on foot. The Duke seized the first pretext to withdraw the plan.

The Duke's attempt to abolish the joint farms had provoked the most bitter resistance. Why was this? There was more to it than simply conservatism and aversion to change. The joint farm represented a very practical adaptation to circumstances of material poverty and extremely low technology. Jointly the 'fellowship' of the farm could survive where isolated a single tenant would be at a disadvantage. It assured to each tenant the material advantages and greater security, as well as the comradeship, of a larger working unit. Further, it lent itself to the maintenance of a kinship system in which all near relatives enjoyed rights to a share in the land. Those whom the Duke had unwarily designated 'supernumeraries' were, in many cases, close kinsmen of the tenants, who in the customary system could expect to receive a portion of the farm.

182

The fifth Duke's plans threatened, by the bodily removal of the 'supernumeraries' to new villages, to destroy the tenaciously held kinship system. By aiming at the abolition of the run-rig farms, he touched the nerve-centre of the traditional Highland socio-economic system. These were to survive for many years to come alongside the new crofts which he carved out of the coastal farms.

In his last three years the fifth Duke saw a gleam of hope in events in Tiree. To solve the problem of overcrowding, due to a multiplying population and static supplies of land, the Duke took over the farms of the large tenants, including the absentee Campbells, and divided them into crofts and individual farms for the small tenants and cottars. In addition, he offered long leases to those who undertook improvements. For the first time for a hundred and twenty years, the islanders' hostility to the house of Argyll began to wane. Presented with clear signs of being assured a stake in the land, they reacted with un-accustomed vigour, adopted new systems of cropping and new techniques, and even began to divide up run-rig farms into individual holdings (Cregeen, 1964, pp. 73-78, 87, 92-94).

THE HOUSE OF ARGYLL DEVELOPS AN INDEPENDENT ROLE

In the closing two decades of the eighteenth century, the house of Argyll, in the person of the fifth Duke, shook off its traditional political role in the West Highlands and finally emerged as head of a purely economic organization and as spokesman of a general Highland interest distinct from that of the clan Campbell.

Jacobitism was no longer a live issue. The need for a government watchdog to overawe the West Highlands had gone. The fifth Duke was the first of his house since the Middle Ages to be free from this political role. Although he was a soldier by training and a stalwart supporter of government, the fifth Duke was primarily interested in estate-management. From his London residence he directed the ploughing and sowing, composting and marketing, of his demesne farms in the Highlands with the most exacting attention and passionate interest, and later in life settled at Inveraray and devoted himself wholly to the delights of rural life.

It is in his time (1770 to 1806) that the Argyll estate finally emerged as an economic organization, its operations mainly determined by price levels. There is little left of its character as a tribal and feudal kingdom. Important changes take place in the make-up of the tenant body, in the composition of the feuars, and in the character of the estate administration. All reflect the decline of kinship ties and political motivations, and the dominance of more purely economic stimuli.

Economic considerations determined the choice of tenants much more than under the third Duke. By this it is not meant that the largest rents always carried the day. Rents might indeed be reduced for tenants of the right calibre, and stability of occupancy was given an important place. Nevertheless, the position of the Campbell tenants decayed in this period. In particular, they suffered through the creation of small tenancies and crofts in coastal areas.

Dramatic changes were also taking place in the composition of the Duke's feudatories, that deeply entrenched body of Campbell proprietors whose alliance with the house of Argyll had long been of crucial importance in enabling the Argylls to fulfil their traditional role in the Highlands. In the closing years of the eighteenth century, the ranks of these ancient families were being thinned by bankruptcy. The Duke's agent wrote to him in 1797 of

'the bankruptcy of so many of the old familys of Argyllshire whom your own goodness has led you to regard as so many parts of yourself: Dunstaffnage, Glenfeochan, Gallanoch, Inverliver, Ederline, are all irretrievable, and this day I have had a meeting with the creditors of Comby, who by an injudicious interference with his credit . . . for the support of the others has brought himself into very great pecuniary difficulties. . . . In my last letter I noticed that some good is to be expected from ill. Here your Grace is about to lose a number of hereditary captains, who were ready to attend you to the field . . . but in their places you are to expect persons of more placid dispositions whose study will be to introduce industry and manufactures into the country and to convert it from a warlike into a rich one.'

The involvement of Comby in an attempt to save the credit

of his fellow Campbells is of a piece with the solidarity of this remarkable body of kinsmen-lairds. Like climbers roped together, the fall of one could bring a whole team down.

Their days of influence in the administration of the Argyll estate were numbered too. The administration had always been entrusted to leading Campbell families. With the increasing absence of the head of the Argyll family, the Chamberlain of Argyll, as the chief official, enjoyed greater authority. Each October, the Duke, with his Receiver General, would meet the Chamberlain and his colleagues or deputies at Inveraray to audit their accounts, hear business, and leave fresh instructions. Such instructions are usually fairly brief, and the Chamberlains retained a wide discretion of day-to-day administration. Though most of their business was concerned with the granting of tacks and the collection of rents and feu-duties, it also meant deep involvement in politics. Before and after the 'Forty-five', the Chamberlain of Mull and Morvern maintained a regular correspondence about the state of the country and the progress of disaffection with the Duke's Edinburgh agent, Lord Milton, who was also the effective head of government in Scotland. (It was Milton whom the Duke of Cumberland described as 'as able and willing a man as there exists, but too much of an Argyll man to be trusted with all that will be necessary after this affair'.)

After the abolition of the system of tacksmen in 1737, the administration had to be expanded in order to deal with matters that had previously been part of the tacksmen's duties. A great many small tenants were now directly under the estate administration. By the mid-eighteenth century there were separate chamberlains for each major district of the estate. As schemes of economic development and agricultural reform got under way, the duties of the chamberlains became more multifarious and exacting. The instructions given to them were increasingly long and detailed, their content more and more economic. Like the noble stewards, the *upravitelyi* of contemporary Russian landed estates, similarly submerged in the rising tide of commercial estate-management until eventually forced to give way to serf-born managers, the Campbell chamberlains appear more and more out of their depth (Confino, 1963, pp. 43-44; Indova, 1955, pp. 48-50).

Sweeping changes took place under the fifth Duke. His agent in Edinburgh, James Ferrier, who was a paragon of business efficiency, carried out a drastic reform of the financial system. Under a steady fusillade of criticism the older chamberlains retired. Their places were taken by a new type of official – men with greater skill in accountancy, law, and practical farming, without pretensions to landed estates, and without clan and family ties with the Argylls. After 1800, only one Campbell remains in the five chamberlainries of the estate. The fifth Duke's own personal attention and the management of the estate combined with these changes to turn the Argyll estate into an efficient, modern economic engine instead of a semi-tribal political kingdom.

The fifth Duke had no obligation except to make the estate profitable, and it would seem that the evolutionary process of the house of Argyll was complete, beginning with power, ending with profit – a neat if disappointing development. This, however, was not the end of the story.

The fifth Duke, for all his love of economy and his passion for efficiency, was a man of broad humanity. While running his own Highland estate, he was very conscious of the crisis in which the whole Highland region was becoming involved. He saw that if the future of the Highlands was to be other than that of a colonial territory, supplying raw materials and labour to the Lowland industries, there had to be a master-plan to channel the benefits of the Industrial Revolution into the Highlands. He discouraged emigration as a solution and instead advocated the fullest exploitation of Highland resources.

There was scarcely a single enterprise in the Highlands in which the fifth Duke did not take a leading part. His sanguine hopes included new industries, roads, canals, fishing villages, and a score of other schemes. The new sheep farms would be linked with woollen factories and would employ the displaced population. He was elected first president of the newly formed Highland Society, and was recognized as one of the great exponents of Highland affairs in his day.

In the evolution of its role in the West Highlands, the house of Argyll had outgrown its identity with the interest of a particular clan or a particular political interest, and had finally, in the crisis of the early nineteenth century, claimed a general role as protector and leader. In this role, however, the fifth Duke enjoyed little success. He found himself fighting against the tide of events, a situation in which no member of his house had ever found himself for very long.

The house of Argyll had always been in the forefront of change. Its role in the West Highlands had been that of innovator. Its representatives had been leaders, successively, of political, religious, and economic revolution, and they had drawn the West Highlands out of isolation and independence into the mainstream of events. This has been their essential role in the West Highalnds. Their attempts, in the era of the new landlordism, 'to introduce industry and manufactures into the country and to convert it from a warlike into a rich one' were doomed not to succeed.

After the collapse of kelp and agricultural prices in the 1820s, the Highlands, with a population in some areas double or even triple the level of 1750, faced a future of dire poverty, famine, and massive emigration. Their fate was to become sheep-walks and sporting estates, supporting a dwindling and aged population. Being in the mainstream was to mean, in actual terms, economic decline and cultural decay.

In considering the whole development of the Highlands, one is bound to ask whether it need have resulted thus; and whether it was simply the penalty for the lack of mineral resources; or whether, in the crucial years of the eighteenth century, when chiefs transmuted themselves into landlords and went after strange gods, some subtle alchemy turned the souls of the Highlanders against the modern world. The attempts of the lairds, in the words of a manufacturer writing to the Chamberlain of Argyll in 1750, 'to make a people distinguished by bravery appear with additional lustre by industry' were almost uniformly disappointed.

The ardour and energy of the Highlanders and the strength of clanship were pressed into the service of the Crown and created the new Highland regiments.[23] They were the basis also of numerous settlements formed in the American colonies. One wonders that the modern economic development of the Highlands ignored the immense potential in this tremendous head of steam represented by the clan spirit and the cooperative genius of the joint tenantry of the run-rig farm.

NOTES

1. From a royal document of 1527, quoted in Haldane (1952), 10n.

2. The main documentary sources are the Argyll muniments at Inveraray Castle and the Saltoun Collection in the National Library of Scotland. Detailed references to documentary sources are not given here, but the more important ones appear in my volume in the Scottish History Society's publications listed in the bibliography.

3. I should, however, like to make special mention of my debt to Professor Meyer Fortes and his colleagues, notably Dr Audrey Richards, in the Department of Social Anthropology at Cambridge. Here I recently spent four terms generously sponsored by the Nuffield Foundation, and gained valuable insights from seminars and discussions.

4. Gregory (1836, pp. 287-290, 354-355, and *passim*). The population of the Highlands was very probably expanding in the sixteenth century, as it was generally in Western Europe (Slicher van Bath, 1963, pp. 78-79), and creating conditions likely to produce land disputes. But the problems this raised would have been more satisfactorily managed and the worst barbarities avoided had it not coincided with the deliberate destruction of the ordered system of government and the political and social equilibrium represented by the Lordship of the Isles, and had not clan feuds been systematically encouraged by government and the Argylls.

5. The Mackenzies were the northern counterpart of the Campbells, supplanting the Macdonalds and their vassals in much of the north-west mainland and in Lewis.

6. In the early eighteenth century there were eight principal tacksmen who rented the extensive lands formerly belonging to Maclean of Duart in Mull, Morvern, Coll, and Tiree. Under them were several scores of sub-tacksmen occupying one or more farms and sub-letting to their sub-tenants.

7. The distinction between those whose tenure of land was limited to a tack and those who had secured a feu and could therefore normally not be removed was to assume a crucial importance in the eighteenth century.

8. The earliest example of a farm let directly to joint tenants is in 1718 on the Dunvegan estate, but it was a common practice both on the Argyll estate and the Duart lands at least as early as the late seventeenth century.

9. Lands might be taken from a tacksman's family on its becoming remote from the main line of chiefly descent. This could gradually swell the number of ordinary clansmen, but it also meant that *daoine uaisle*, threatened with dispossession, had a strong incentive to encourage war with neighbouring clans and to seize their land.

10. My attention was drawn to this fact by the Rev. Wm. Matheson, University of Edinburgh Celtic Department.

11. Examples of bonds of manrent are printed in C. Innes (1851-1855, pp. 80-97, 196-208).

12. The Macualrigs (the name is variously spelt) were descended from Walric Kennedy, a fugitive from Galloway. They were greatly prized by their adopted chief, Glengarry, and lived at Lagganachadrom on his lands. In 1740 a band of them carried out a particularly audacious raid and stole horses and cattle from the glens in the immediate vicinity of the Duke of Argyll's castle at Inveraray. (Information from documentary sources and from Rev. Wm. Matheson.)

13. In my account of the clan I have assumed that the chief possessed land of his own to maintain his followers, but many cases occurred where, through forfeiture or other causes, the chief's resources of land were insufficient and part of his clan lived on another chief or landlord's lands. In these circumstances, however, they usually continued in allegiance to their own chief.

14. Forbes's report is printed in Appendix A to the Crofters' Commission Report of 1884.

15. Governor Gage of North Carolina was sure that he could recruit a thousand Highlanders for the Crown if Allan Macdonald of Kingsburgh (Flora Macdonald's husband) were appointed major and his son-in-law, captain, because 'they have most extensive influence over the Highlanders here, great part of which are of their own name and family' (Graham, 1956, p. 158). These were not emigrants from the Argyll estate, but they illustrate the way in which Highland clanship was transplanted to the colonies.

16. Samuel Johnson (1775). His remarks on the tacksmen form an eloquent plea for the preservation of this class. 'If the tacksmen be banished, who will be left to impart knowledge or impress civility?' He notes that a growing burden of hospitality was falling on the ministers as the tacksmen disappeared. In the nineteenth century the tacksman's role as social leader and educator was largely taken over by the minister.

17. Statistical Account, vol. IV, p. 575 and footnote.

18. In his instructions to the Chamberlain of Argyll in 1729, the second Duke wrote: 'You are to enquire into the condition of the sub-tennents of Glenaray and Glenshyra, and particularly to examine what rent each pays for his possession to my tacksmen . . . and if they complain of any abuses, you are to protect and redress them as far as lawfully you can'.

19. Socio-economic change in general (but not religious change), affected the south-west Highlands before the north-west, probably largely because of their proximity to the new industrial areas. Already by the end of the eighteenth century, prices and wages in South and Mid-Argyll approximated to those of the Clyde towns. Not only economically but in speech, manners, dress, and outlook these districts were changing rapidly through the influence of the Lowlands. In this process, seasonal migration played a highly significant role. That this has not been sufficiently appreciated is mainly due to the fixing of attention solely on the alienation of the upper classes of Highland society from their traditional culture. In fact, the seasonal journeys of young Highland men and women to the Lowlands, which had reached massive proportions by the 1790s (in Argyll probably the majority were engaged either in Lowland employment or in fishing), were perhaps equally important in bringing social change.

20. Letter of Archibald Campbell, laird of Knockbuy, to Stonefield, 2 Feb. 1744. The original is in the Stonefield Papers, Scottish Record Office.

21. The introduction of potato-cultivation c. 1750 must have had a great deal to do with the falling death-rate and consequently rising population. In Tiree, a population rather over 1500 in 1750 had risen to 2,776 in 1802 and 4,453 in 1831. Holdings inevitably became fragmentary, and poverty appears to have been getting worse in the first half of the nineteenth century. In spite of emigration and of many cases of local depopulation, the population of the Highlands may have doubled in the century after 1745.

22. I am indebted to members of my Extra-Mural class in Tiree for this information, and in particular to Mr Allan MacDougall, Cornaigmore.

23. The second and third Dukes of Argyll had much to do with introducing the policy of establishing new Highland regiments as a means of strengthening the Army whilst channelling off Highland disaffection. A chief with a numerous following had little difficulty in obtaining a command, and Highlanders assisted their chiefs in this matter by offering to enlist under him (Stewart, 1822, p. 119 and footnote). The chief of the Duart Macleans, Sir Allan Maclean of Broloss, obtained a command through the third Duke's good offices; but the Duke's motives were not disinterested, for he was aware that many of the Macleans had Jacobite sympathies and would be better out of the way. In 1797 the government recurred to the same idea, and Henry Dundas wrote to the fifth Duke that whatever reasons there were before for proscribing clanship, they had now ceased, and 'much good, in place of mischief, may on various occasions arise from such a connection among members of the same family and name'.

In 1803 the fifth Duke proposed to extend the same plan to naval recruitment and wrote: 'Proposed to the Highland Society to raise a fund by subscription or otherwise for the education and support of midshipmen, being the younger sons of heritors of small estates, who must all speak the Erse [Gaelic] language. When these young men become officers, especially when they obtain command of King's ships, the lower classes, whose natural prejudices prevent their entrance into the Navy, will be induced to engage in the service under officers who speak their language and with whom they may have some clannish connection and protection.'

REFERENCES

This list contains a selection from the works that have been found useful in addition to those referred to in the text.

ADAMS, M. I. The Highland Emigration of 1770. *Scottish Historical Review* 16: 280-293.

—— The Causes of the Highland Emigrations of 1783-1803. *Scottish Historical Review* 17: 73-89.

ALLARDYCE (ed.). 1888. *Scotland and Scotsmen in the Eighteenth Century*. Edinburgh: Blackwood.

ANDERSON, J. 1785. *An Account of the Present State of the Hebrides*. Edinburgh: C. Elliot.

ARGYLL, DUKE OF. 1883. *Crofts and Farms in the Hebrides*. Edinburgh: David Douglas.

BATH, B. H. SLICHER VAN. 1963. *The Agrarian History of Western Europe*. London: Arnold.

BOSWELL, J. 1941. *Journal of a Tour of the Hebrides*. Everyman's Library. London: Dent.

BURT, E. 1754. *Letters from a Gentleman in the North of England*. London: S. Birt.

CONFINO, M. 1963. *Domaines et Seigneurs en Russie vers la Fin du XVIIIe Siècle.* Paris: Institut d'Etudes Slaves.

CREGEEN, E. R. 1964. Instructions of the 5th Duke of Argyll to his Chamberlains. Scottish History Society.

CROFTERS COMMISSION REPORT, 1884.

DARLING, F. F. 1955. *West Highland Survey.* Oxford: Oxford University Press.

FERGUSSON, SIR JAMES. 1951. *Argyll in the Forty-Five.* London: Faber & Faber.

GRAHAM, I. C. C. 1956. *Colonists from Scotland.* Ithaca, New York: Cornell University Press.

GRANT, I. F. 1930. *The Social and Economic Development of Scotland.* Edinburgh: Oliver & Boyd.

—— 1935. *The Lordship of the Isles.* Edinburgh: Moray Press.

—— 1959. *The Macleods.* London: Faber & Faber.

GRAY, M. 1957. *The Highland Economy, 1750-1850.* Edinburgh: Oliver & Boyd.

GREGORY, D. 1836. *The History of the Western Highlands and Isles of Scotland.* Edinburgh: Longman.

HALDANE, A. R. B. 1952. *The Drove Roads of Scotland.* London: Nelson.

HANDLEY, J. E. 1953. *Scottish Farming in the Eighteenth Century.* London: Faber & Faber.

INDOVA, E. I. 1955. *Krepostnoye Khoziaistvo v nachale XIX veka.* Moskva: Akademia Nauk USSR, Institut Istorii.

INNES, C. 1851-1855. *Collectanea de Rebus Albanicis.* Edinburgh: T. G. Stevenson.

JOHNSON, S. 1825. *A Journey to the Western Islands of Scotland.* Glasgow: R. Griffin.

KNOX, J. 1785. *A View of the British Empire, especially Scotland.* London: J. Walter.

KYD, J. G. 1952. Scottish Population Statistics. Scottish History Society.

LANG, A. (ed.). 1898. *The Highlands of Scotland in 1750, from MS. 104 in the King's Library.* Edinburgh: Blackwood.

MACDONALD, A. & MACDONALD, A. 1896-1904. *The Clan Donald,* 3 vols. Inverness: Northern Counties Publishing Co.

MACDONALD, J. 1811. *General View of Agriculture in the Hebrides.* Edinburgh: S. Doig & A. Stirling.

MACFARLANE, W. *Genealogical Collections.* Scottish History Society, Vols. 33 and 34.

MCKERRAL, A. The Tacksman and his Holding in the South-West Highlands. *Scottish Historical Review* **26**, 10-25.

MCKERRAL, A. 1948. *Kintyre in the Seventeenth Century*. Edinburgh: Oliver & Boyd.

—— 1953. *The Clan Campbell*. Edinburgh: W. & A. K. Johnston.

MACPHAIL, J. R. N. 1914-1920. *Highland Papers*. Scottish History Society.

MARTIN, M. 1703. *Description of the Western Isles of Scotland*. London: Andrew Bell.

MITCHELL, D. 1900. *History of the Highlands and Gaelic Scotland*. Paisley: A. Gardner.

NEW STATISTICAL ACCOUNT OF SCOTLAND. 1835-1845. Vol. 4. Edinburgh: Blackwood.

PATON, H. (ed.). 1916. *The Clan Campbell*. Edinburgh: Otto Schulze & Co.

REDFIELD, R. 1953. *The Primitive World and its Transformations*. Cornell: Cornell University Press.

SMITH, J. 1805. *General View of the Agriculture of the County of Argyll*. London: Richard Phillips.

STATISTICAL ACCOUNT OF SCOTLAND. 1790-1798. Edinburgh: William Creech.

STEWART, D. 1822. *Character, Manners and Present State of the Highlanders of Scotland*. Edinburgh: Archibald Constable.

WALKER, J. 1812. *Economical History of the Hebrides and Highlands of Scotland*. London: Guthrie & Anderson.

WILLCOCK, J. 1903. *The Great Marquess*. Edinburgh: Oliphant, Anderson & Ferrier.

ACKNOWLEDGEMENTS

The writer wishes to acknowledge his debt to His Grace the Duke of Argyll for making possible this piece of research, for much help and encouragement, and for permission to incorporate material from the Inveraray Castle archives in this paper. The writer's thanks are also due to the National Library of Scotland for permission to make use of the Saltoun papers, and to its staff for their willing assistance. The constructive suggestions and criticisms of colleagues have been invaluable and are gratefully acknowledged.

R. E. Bradbury

Continuities and Discontinuities in Pre-colonial and Colonial Benin Politics (1897-1951)

This paper sketches the broad outlines of Benin political history between the years immediately before 1897, when the independence of this ancient West African kingdom was abruptly terminated, and 1951, when Nigerian regional and national politics had begun to make a direct impact on its internal affairs. Despite their subjection to alien rule and the destruction of their traditional framework of government, the Benin (Edo) people – especially the residents of the capital – displayed an unflagging appetite for the game of politics. Their exuberant and fluid factionalism and their tendency to internal, unstable dichotomization constantly taxed the wits of their colonial over-rulers, whose ability to understand and control these processes was limited by their lack of adequate information about Edo political culture. On several occasions the British officers on the spot found that the 'native authority' recognized by the government as the instrument for the implementation of its objectives, had become transformed into an unpopular 'ruling' clique, to which they themselves were assimilated; and from which, in order to avoid a complete breakdown of order, they had, sooner or later, to withdraw their support.

One approach to the explanation of these insurrectionary crises would be to regard them simply as responses to alien rule. Certainly, determined resistance to regulations and measures imposed from outside Benin society is a component of all of them. But to adopt this starting-point is, I believe, to take too negative a view of the political skills and propensities of the Benin people themselves. In this paper I try to account for the pattern of political conflict and the course of political change by looking at them from the 'inside', that is in terms of the pursuit, by the Edo themselves, of individual and group interests, in an environment of changing structures, goals, and opportunities. I also attempt to explore the ways in which the effects of external impulses to change (political, economic, educational, ideological, etc.), are shaped and modified by concepts, norms, and strategies derived from the pre-colonial polity and from successive phases of interaction and accommodation between indigenous and exotic structures.

GOVERNMENT AND POLITICS IN
NINETEENTH-CENTURY BENIN

The late nineteenth-century Benin polity has been briefly described elsewhere (Bradbury, 1967). Here we can do no more than point up some of its salient characteristics. From its apogee in the sixteenth and seventeenth centuries, the Benin state had suffered a prolonged decline, interrupted by periods of resurgence. Immediately before the British conquest the king's writ still ran, however uncertainly and intermittently, over an area considerably wider than that of the Benin Division, which the British were eventually to demarcate as his successors' sphere of competence; and which roughly corresponded to what I have called the Benin Kingdom proper, that is, the core area of the Benin empire (Bradbury, 1967, pp. 3-4). We need be no more precise than this because the politics with which this paper is concerned are essentially politics of the capital. Though some village chiefs may be regarded as having been marginal to it, the pre-colonial political class was, to all intents and purposes, wholly resident in Benin City (Edo), which contained perhaps an eighth of the kingdom's quarter of a million or so inhabitants. The rest of the population was distributed through several hundred villages with populations ranging from a dozen or two to as many as four thousand souls; a typical village might have four or five hundred people. Between the political life of the village (Bradbury, 1957, 1967) and the capital there were marked discontinuities. A villager who wished to participate in the direction of the nation's affairs had to leave home and seek advancement through one of the various hierarchies located in the capital. It was by no means impossible for an able and enterprising man to do this, but villagers started at a considerable disadvantage compared with the sons of the king's chiefs and retainers, in terms both of family wealth and influence and of opportunities to acquire political and administrative expertise in the normal course of growing up. Thus the political class, and *a fortiori* the political elite within it,[1] were in large measure self-perpetuating.

Family continuity must be clearly distinguished from descent-group eligibility for office. As compared with most African states (even nineteenth-century Buganda or Dahomey) corporate descent groups played a negligible role in Benin political organization. Inheritance and succession were patrilineal, but lineages were shallow and weakly corporate. Land – the basic resource – was vested not in kin groups but in kin heterogeneous ward and village communities. In the absence of corporate rights to resources, a marked primogenitary emphasis in the rules of inheritance and succession – including succession to the minority of political offices that were hereditary – served to weaken rather than to strengthen kin-group solidarity. Neither at the village nor at the state level were political roles conceived in terms of the representation of descent groups.

The conduct of public affairs was vested in the *oba* (king) and the titled members of a number of tiered and opposed chiefly orders. Three orders – the *uzama*, the *eghaebho n'ore*, and the *eghaebho n'ogbe* – stood out in prestige and authority above the rest.

The *uzama* comprised six hereditary nobles and (in principle) the *oba*'s heir-apparent (*edaiken*). The hereditary character of their offices, transmitted by primogeniture, set them apart from the other orders, whose ranks were filled by royal appointment. Originators and custodians of the kingship, guardians of sacrosanct custom, the six nobles were looked upon as the 'elders' of the state. We may describe them as the king's peers. In their own villages, just outside the inner walls of the capital, they enjoyed relative immunity from interference by the *oba*. On the other hand, they participated less in the day-to-day conduct of public affairs and were less powerful as a group than either *eghaebho* order. Nevertheless, their prestige and moral authority carried considerable weight, especially in times of national crisis. Individually, one or two of them had important executive functions – especially the *ezomo* who, as one of the two regular commanders of state armies, was always a force to be reckoned with.

For commoners the *eghaebho* titles constituted the pinnacles of political ambition. They were the object of intense competition which all freeborn men (except the *oba*'s agnates, heirs to hereditary offices, and subjects of the *uzama*) were, in principle, free to enter. Formal qualifications for a title had normally to be acquired by initiation into and promotion through the grades of one of the associations of palace retainers. Once a man reached the senior untitled grade (*uko*), he was eligible to apply to the *oba* for a title, either in his own or another palace association, or in the *eghaebho n'ore* order. Within each association, individual titles were grouped into two tiers (*eghaebho n'ogbe* and *ekhaenbhen*); and in each tier titles were arranged in a single hierarchical series. Promotions from one title to another could be sought either within or across the boundaries of orders and associations. Few men reached the highest ranks without first having held one or more lesser titles. An alternative route to *eghaebho n'ore* titles lay through the *ekaiwe* association and the *ibiwe nekhua* order, membership of which was reserved for descendants of the *oba*'s daughters (Bradbury, 1967, p. 27). While it was not impossible for rich men whom the *oba* wished to favour to acquire the essential formal qualifications summarily, progress to the top was normally long and arduous. It was also expensive, for each advancement required the payment of substantial fees to the *oba* and members of all the non-hereditary orders, and the provision of costly entertainments. On the other hand, a title brought its holder influence and prestige, the ability to dispense patronage, a range of secular and ritual competences, rights to tribute and labour, a share in the revenue of the holder's order, and other perquisites.

Each retainer association had a range of functions within the *oba*'s palace – the care of royal regalia, the commissariat of the king's household, the care of his wives and children, etc. As well as administrating these functions, the palace chiefs, especially the *eghaebho n'ogbe*, played a major role in the day-to-day conduct of public affairs. In the king's name they despatched retainers to the villages on a variety of fiscal, political, and ritual missions; regulated the conduct of overseas trade; managed state revenue; organized the services of special occupation groups, and so forth. The senior *eghaebho n'ogbe* – *unwague, eribo, ine n'ibiwe, osodin, esere* – were in a position to wield great personal power and patronage and to exert influence on the *oba* himself. Together with the king, the *eghaebho n'ore* and, on occasions, the *uzama*, they constituted a state council which met frequently to take major policy decisions, try capital cases, and hear appealed disputes.

Formally senior, as an order, to the *eghaebho n'ogbe* – the prestige ranking of titles across order boundaries was a different matter – the *eghaebho n'ore* had fewer routine administrative roles. Although they were appointed by the king and exercised authority in his name, they were looked upon as the defenders of the commonalty against the threat of palace autocracy. Their leader, the *iyase*, was 'the *oba*'s first subject'. It was he who inducted all new title-holders in the king's name. As a military commander, his rank was at least equal to that of the *ezomo*. On the other hand, he was regarded as the champion of the Edo and he had a unique right to challenge the king's actions in public. In the 'conscious model' of the Benin polity it was the *iyase* who was most likely to emerge as the leader of any anti-*oba* or anti-palace faction. In dynastic traditions major political crises are repeatedly expressed in terms of personal confrontations between *oba* and *iyase*. The continuing effectiveness of the *eghaebho n'ore* as a constitutional check on the power of the *oba* and the palace was, in part, a function of their ritual roles. The mystical compact between the *oba* and his subjects, on which the legitimacy of the political order depended, could not be maintained without their cooperation (Bradbury, 1967, pp. 25-26).

This elaborate configuration of unitary and segmented orders, graded associations, and tiered and opposed hierarchies, with the politico-divine kingship at its centre, constituted both the enduring framework of government and the arena in which the political game was played. As an overall pattern of government, evolved over several centuries, sanctified by tradition, and constantly reaffirmed in ritual, it was, as far as we can tell, never seriously challenged. Its structural details and operational rules were, of course, subject to revision through the interplay of conflicting interests and environmental factors; but both oral traditions and the accounts of visiting Europeans suggest that

P   197

its main outlines had remained remarkably stable. As a political arena it offered wide scope for intrigue and competition, and all the available evidence suggests that factional alignments were extremely fluid. Each corporate segment of the political elite was jealous of its collective interests and strove to defend and expand them *vis-à-vis* other segments and the king himself. On the other hand, segmental solidarities were subject to the weakening influences of intensive internal rivalry (see below) and of cross-cutting interests and obligations. The character of the non-hereditary title system was itself such as to promote individualistic opportunism. The fact that the great majority of these appointive titles constituted a single promotional system made loyalty to a particular segment contingent upon personal ambitions and opportunities. The *oba*, the 'establishment' within the various hierarchies, and individuals looking for advancement all sought to manipulate the system to their own advantage. It was necessary for the ambitious young politician to enter into alliances in many directions. Bonds of kinship, affinity, and friendship cut across the boundaries of chiefly orders and served as a basis for political cooperation and intrigue. There were, too, certain corporate interest groups which, though marginal to the political order itself, had important implications for it. The most significant of these were a number of trading associations, each of which controlled one of the routes along which European goods, obtained at riverside beaches in exchange for palm-oil and other local products, were transported to inland markets; the return traffic being in beads, slaves, and other commodities for internal consumption. Participation in this trade, open only to initiated members of the associations, constituted one of the principle sources of economic support for the Benin political elite. Chiefs invested their spoils of office in slaves purchased at the hinterland markets, whom they placed in villages and forest camps to farm for them. Detailed accounts of the operation of these associations are difficult to recover but it is clear that they cross-cut the chiefly orders and that their interests were potentially in conflict with those of the *oba* and the chiefs of the *iwebo* association who were responsible to him for the regulation of the riverside trade.

Furthermore, while many governmental functions were

segregated as between orders and associations, some of the most important ones were distributed among chiefs of several or all the orders. There were, for example, two alternative military commands. The *ezomo* (*uzama*) had as his deputy the *ologbose* (*eghaebho n'ore*); while the *iyase* (*eghaebho n'ore*) was seconded by the *edogun*, head of the *ibiwe nekhua* order. Again the *unwague* and *eribo*, as heads of the *iwebo* association, regulated overseas trade, but their assistants were recruited from other palace associations. The functions of territorial administration were much more widely dispersed. Title-holders of all orders were each assigned one or a number of scattered villages for which they were responsible to the *oba* for the levying of tribute and labour and for military recruitment; and from which they drew labour and tribute for their own support. But the power of 'benefice-holders' over their villages was limited by the fact that the *oba*, through his Palace Chiefs, could send his retainers into their villages on a wide variety of missions. This dispersal of functions was clearly designed to prevent concentration of particular kinds of power in particular segments, but it also implied a complex ramification and interlocking of interests. One should not, therefore, expect to find that the pattern of political conflict directly mirrored the formal group structure of the political elite. Documentary and oral sources both present evidence of a fluid factionalism, in which political alignments were as likely to cross-cut as to coincide with formal cleavages.

In its mystical aspect the kingship supplied the ideological keystone of the political system. The continuity and integrity of the polity depended upon (*a*) the commitment of all sectors of the population to the belief that their well-being depended on the proper deployment of the *oba*'s own divine energy, and of his ritual authority as the intermediary with his predecessors; and upon (*b*) their acceptance of the need for the king, chiefs, and people to cooperate in ensuring that these functions were fruitfully deployed. Every title had its ritual roles and the higher a chief's rank the more indispensable his ritual functions. The economic support afforded by the people to the political elite was given in token of their performance of these functions. Villagers strove to defend themselves against the exploitative proclivities of chiefs and retainers by playing them off against each other; they did not challenge the legitimate basis of their authority.

The condition of the polity at any particular time was a function of the interaction of these ideological factors with the pursuit of group and individual interests. In the political process the king himself played a crucial role. According to his skills and opportunities (which were variable at different stages of his career as well as contingent on environmental factors), he could be a near autocrat, the instrument of a palace oligarchy, or a judicious statesman maintaining an equable balance of power. For brief periods effective power might lie with a faction setting itself up in opposition to the palace, but this was a situation conducive to violent conflict. Unless it succeeded either in bringing the *oba* over to its side or in placing its own candidate on the throne, such a faction would have difficulty in retaining popular support for very long.

The *oba*'s capacity to exercise personal power depended on his ability to maintain a balance between competing groups and individuals within the political elite; and (the two factors were closely related) his success in keeping open multiple channels of communication with other sectors of the population. The flexibility of the appointive system and the subtle distribution of segregated and dispersed competences bear witness to the relative success of kings, over the centuries, in preserving their freedom of manœuvre. In their struggles with the chiefs they were hampered by the fact that their mystical roles confined them within the palace. On the other hand, the *dignitas* and mystical authority of the kingship, and the existence in Benin City of numerous groups of ritual functionaries and craft specialists whose interests were closely bound up with those of the *oba*, constituted built-in advantages. The king's power was constrained by the interplay of immutable 'constitutional' conventions with political and environmental factors. There is no room to catalogue these constraints here; a few examples must suffice. Thus, while the king alone could confer vacant titles and create new titles, a title, once conferred, whether by the reigning king or his predecessor, could not be taken away. Again, by such techniques as refusing to accept title fees or simply by refusing to collaborate with the new title-holder, the chiefs had the collective power to render his appointments ineffective. Within limits the *oba* could confer favours on his supporters by altering the ranking of titles within hierarchies but the uppermost titles in each order remained sacrosanct, by virtue of age-old tradition and their indispensable ritual functions. He could seek to alter the distribution of power by re-allocating administrative competences, but the limits of expediency in this respect were set by the need to maintain a viable balance between the expected and actual rewards of political competition. An *oba* who transgressed such basic rules of the political game as these risked consolidating the chiefs against him. By boycotting his councils and his rituals they could render him politically ineffective.

Major political crises occurred when the 'normal' scatter of counterbalancing sectional and personal interests gave way to a radical dichotomization of the political class around particular crucial issues. From oral tradition, European chronicles, and the testimony of old informants, three recurrent types of crisis can be discerned. In two cases the nature of the polarization is clear. The first of these was *succession conflict*. In nineteenth-century Benin the rule of legitimate primogenitary succession was universally acknowledged. In theory the reigning king made his rightful heir apparent by conferring on him the title *edaiken* and establishing him in his own court at the village of Uselu. In practice – either because they feared that a designated successor might constitute a threat to their own tenure, or because they found some other political advantage in leaving the issue in doubt – king after king failed to do so. The result, in each case, was a struggle for the throne between two sons of the king, who sought to justify their respective claims in terms of conflicting criteria of legitimacy. Each candidate proceeded to build up a faction by seeking two kinds of support: (*a*) by assembling a personal following of 'strong', ambitious younger men, recruited on the basis of friendship, clientage, matrilateral kinship, affinal ties, etc.; and (*b*) by seeking the patronage of influential chiefs in each sector of the political elite. It was necessary to do this because the wide dispersal of power (particularly in respect of military and territorial-administrative functions) made it impossible for any single order to determine the succession. This dispersal of power and authority was reflected in the ceremonial procedures by which the kingship was transmitted, the head of each major order having an indispensable function to perform (Bradbury, 1967, p. 30). In practice the succession was determined by the relative strength of the factions mobilized by the rival brothers, tested, if necessary, by armed conflict. Two of the last three successions of the pre-colonial era were settled by civil war.

The second type of major crisis, which we can characterize as a struggle between the *old guard* and the *new men*, was a direct consequence of the first. As we shall describe a particular struggle of this type below (p. 206) we need say no more about it here.

It is much more difficult to determine the nature of the polarization process in the third type of major conflict that we wish to distinguish. Oral traditions, and the one contemporary account of a crisis of this type (Nyendael, in Bosman, 1967, p. 466, and the present writer's note, p. 574), invariably describe a contest for power between the *oba* and one chief or a group of chiefs, leading to the formation of dichotomous factions and often to civil war. Some of these confrontations are explained, in very general terms, as being due to the *oba*'s disregard for his chief's prerogatives, or vice versa; others as resulting from a particular tyrannous or outrageous act on the king's part; still others as issuing from a personal quarrel between the *oba* and one of his chiefs. No major confrontations of this sort appear to have occurred in the late nineteenth century and folk memories of earlier crises are too vague to allow us to determine the detailed composition of the opposed factions. In some cases the evidence appears to point to a contest between the *eghaebho n'ore* and a palace clique; in others it seems more likely that the factions cut across the chieftaincy orders. In all these crises, however, one must infer the presence of issues of sufficiently wide concern to provide common ground between groups and individuals whose interests were 'normally' divergent. We are not concerned, in this paper, to speculate about what these issues might have been. However, broadly analogous confrontations, consciously assimilated by the Edo themselves to the major conflicts recounted in dynastic traditions, recur during the colonial period. In the following pages one of our aims is to analyse the process of dichotomization as it appears in these conflicts and to identify the issues involved.

BENIN POLITICAL HISTORY, 1897-1951[2]

The interregnum, 1897-1914

Benin City (Edo) fell to a British military force on 17 February 1897. Leaving aside the complex antecedents of this débâcle, we need only note that the immediately precipitating event was an attack, some six weeks earlier, on a British delegation *en route* to seek negotiations with the *oba*; its main declared purpose being to persuade him to remove embargoes which he had placed on external trade. *Oba* Ovonramwen fled from his palace as the troops approached and remained in hiding in the bush until the following August, when some of his chiefs, who had made their peace with the British, persuaded him to submit. At his 'trial', which began on 1 September, no evidence was forthcoming to indicate that the *oba* had been personally responsible for the massacre; indeed witnesses unanimously asserted that he had tried to restrain his chiefs from attacking the white men. After the trial the stated intention of the Consul-General, Sir Ralph Moor, was to make use of the *oba*'s authority. He told him that 'he could no longer order the people about as before, but that proper villages would be apportioned to him, with servants, food and all other necessaries as for a big chief, for he would probably still be the biggest chief, that position depending on his ability to govern. At the same time the Consul-General proposed to take the king and two or three other chiefs with their wives and servants on a tour for a year or so to Calabar, Lagos and the Yoruba country to see how other lands were governed' (Ling Roth, 1903, App. III). These proposals aroused the *oba*'s deep mistrust and on 9 September, the day appointed for their further discussion, he failed to appear. When a party was sent out to apprehend him he tried unsuccessfully to escape, whereupon Moor not only ordered his banishment to Calabar but announced that he would never again be allowed to return to Benin.

Ovonramwen's banishment removed any possibility that the old political order might be reconstituted as an instrument of British rule. The various hierarchies and structural oppositions of the traditional polity had all been defined with reference to the kingship, and with its elimination they collapsed. The charred ruins of the royal palace were left deserted, and the

203

palace associations, which had been the chief mechanism for recruiting, training, and allocating administrative personnel, as well as for channelling competition for power, ceased to have any meaningful existence. Since most important titles had been in the king's gift they could no longer be filled when their incumbents died. Even the heirs to hereditary offices required the *oba*'s approval before they could rightfully assume their fathers' titles. The kingship rituals, one of whose principal functions had been to reaffirm, and maintain support for, the distribution of authority and precedence, were abandoned.

In these circumstances, we should not expect to find anything like the degree of continuity between the pre-colonial and colonial political systems that has been described for such kingdoms as Zaria (Smith, 1960) where the colonial rulers were able to carry out their policies through going concerns. The first British administrators at Benin had to construct an administrative *bricolage* (Lévi-Strauss, 1962, p. 26 ff.) out of their own meagre resources of personnel and the fragments of a shattered indigenous polity. At the outset they had very little information about the interior of the kingdom or its outlying territories to the north and east. The establishment of effective authority over these areas was a lengthy process, involving the constant threat and frequent use of force, but it could not have been accomplished at all without the more or less willing cooperation of many of the Benin City chiefs who had exercised authority under Ovonramwen. The need to maintain the authority of these chiefs was a constant theme of early policy statements.

On taking office, the first Resident was instructed to ascertain who were the 'reliable' chiefs and to enrol them in a central Native Council which would advise him on custom, sit with him in judicial hearings, and help to set the government's economic, educational, and other policies in motion.[3] From the British point of view, the chiefs constituted an unstructured aggregate whose status as a ruling class was evident from their possession of titles, wealth, and influence. Most of the early council chiefs were, in fact, of *uzama* or *eghaebho* rank, but they were not chosen, or accorded authority, with reference to their specific placement in the traditional orders of chieftaincy. It was, indeed, to be many years before the British began to obtain even an approximate understanding of the structure of the traditional polity; and even if they had understood it they could not have operated it in the absence of a king. The basis on which the council chiefs were selected, therefore, was simply the Resident's assessment of the capacity of individual chiefs (and some non-titled men) to command obedience and respect, and of their willingness and ability to carry out his orders. Some of the older chiefs, who failed to win the confidence of the new rulers, or declined to adjust themselves to the new order, faded into obscurity. It was those who most rapidly perceived the personal advantages to be gained from cooperation that emerged as the new elite, and prominent among them were some of the ambitious younger politicians of Ovonramwen's reign, men whose fortunes were rising before the débâcle, and who had avoided becoming too deeply implicated in the massacre of the British officials.

Outstanding among these latter was a man called Agho.[4] He had been intimately associated with Ovonramwen from childhood, for the latter, as Prince Idugbowa, had been placed in the care of Agho's father, Ogbeide Oyo whom *Oba* Adolo had made *ine n'ibiwe*. In the early 1880s Idugbowa, tired of waiting for his father to designate him as the official heir (*edaiken*), had defiantly established himself in a house at Uselu, close to the Edaiken's palace, a gesture which affirmed his determination not to be deprived of the throne which, as the oldest son, he regarded as his birthright. From Uselu he proceeded not only to curry favour with the senior chiefs who would have a major voice in the determination of the succession, but also to build up a strong personal following of young ambitious men who would fight for him if the need should arise. For it was clear that he would be opposed for the throne by his younger brother, Orhokhorho, whose claim rested on the fact that, unlike Idugbowa, he had been born after his father's accession. In the ensuing struggle which reached its climax after Adolo's death in 1889, Agho's role might perhaps best be described as that of a manager of Idugbowa's faction. In the event civil war was averted. After his father's death Idugbowa made his determination plain by repeatedly marching through the capital at the head of a large, vociferous force – a gesture which probably helped to speed agreement among the most influential senior chiefs that he was the rightful heir.

One of a newly enthroned *oba*'s prerogatives was to create one or two new titles in each order of chieftaincy, which he could use to reward his most active personal supporters. For Agho, Ovonramwen coined the title *obaseki*, placing it third among the *eghaebho* of the *iweguae* association. This was easily the highest rank accorded any of the new titles. Agho's assignment to *iweguae* was an important strategic manœuvre. It was in the *iweguae* section of the palace that the *oba* had his living quarters and his personal commissariat. Thus his security depended to a considerable extent on the loyalty of the *iweguae* chiefs. That Ovonramwen mistrusted them is evident from the fact that for some two years after his accession he is said to have refused to live in *iweguae*. It was only when the ranks of that association had been thinned out by a series of ruthlessly executed manœuvres, that he consented to do so.

The sequence of violent episodes that marked the early years of Ovonramwen's reign, and which resulted in the deaths of a considerable number of chiefs and palace retainers, partly reflected the *oba*'s determination to root out any lingering loyalty to his brother. An overlapping, and longer-term source of conflict was the struggle for ascendancy between the 'old guard' of senior chiefs surviving in office from the previous reign and the 'new men', Ovonramwen's personal clients (known as *iguomore*, lit. 'I come with the child' – i.e. the new *oba*), who were now impatient to reap the highest rewards. The *oba*'s position between these two factions was a difficult one. He was strongly obligated to the senior chiefs who had ensured his peaceful accession, and highly dependent upon their political and administrative experience. On the other hand he could not afford to ignore the importunities of his personal followers, whose support he needed if he were to obtain any freedom of action in the face of the power of the entrenched old guard. The dominant political personality at the beginning of his reign was Egiebo, the *unwague*, head of the *iwebo* association and the most senior palace chief, a man of formidable character and influence whose backing had been eagerly sought by both rivals for the throne. While lending support to the *iguomore* in their efforts to dislodge other established chiefs, Ovonramwen was at pains to remain on good terms with the *unwague*. By 1895, however, the latter had so overplayed his hand in seeking to make the *oba* the instrument of his own power as to incur the hostility of his own *iwebo* chiefs. Accusing him, among other misdeeds, of plotting with the British, and possibly assuming that the *oba* would be glad to be rid of him, they eventually waylaid and assassinated him. Ovonramwen demanded immediate vengeance and, when four of the *eghaebho* of *iwebo* had been killed or had committed suicide, it was to *Obaseki* Agho's influence that the remaining conspirator turned in seeking reconciliation with the *oba*. The effect of this insurrection within the *iwebo* association had been to create five vacancies among the senior palace positions. These afforded the *oba* new opportunities to exercise his patronage and opened up possibilities of promotion to the *iguomore*. Agho, as the recognized leader of the new men, was now in an enviable position, and by the time of the débâcle, though by no means first in formal rank, he was certainly one of the most powerful palace chiefs.

Obaseki fled with the *oba* before the British advance on the capital, but he soon returned to Benin and made his submission. Some accounts say it that was the *oba* who sent him back to try to negotiate a settlement. However this may be, it is clear that by the time the *oba* gave himself up the old patron-client relationship between them had been substantially reversed, for by then Agho was already beginning to impress the British by his influence and ability and he was soon to become a key member of the Native Council. It was in *obaseki*'s house that Ovonramwen spent his last few weeks before his banishment and during that period Agho seems to have behaved quite correctly towards him. Once he had gone, however, *obaseki* wasted no time regretting the past but devoted his energies to securing the leadership of the new order. So adroit was he at handling the new regime that the other chiefs soon requested that he should be treated as their intermediary with the Resident. By March 1899, the latter was writing in his Quarterly Report that the Native Council worked well and regularly.[5] Chief *Obaseki* took the lead in everything and was a most intelligent man with influence among the other chiefs. Though allegations of extortion and oppression were frequently made against him in subsequent years, and in October 1899 there was even a suggestion that he might have to be exiled, this favourable view of him is repeatedly echoed in the judgements of successive administrators.[6] And he continued to be an indispensable instrument of British rule almost up to his death in 1920.

Before 1897, the *oba*'s domains had been divided, for limited administrative purposes, into many units – villages, village groups, sub-chiefdoms – responsibility for which the *oba* assigned to a wide range of chiefs and non-titled retainers. During the interregnum the British authorities adapted this system of territorial administration to their own requirements. The degree of continuity that was maintained is a matter for further investigation but it would appear that while, initially, some of the chiefs who had controlled particular areas for the *oba* managed to secure recognition as 'paramount chiefs' over those same areas, in other cases those warranted as paramount chiefs had had no previous authority over the areas assigned to them. As chiefs died, or were replaced on grounds of incompetence or tyranny, more and more administrative units came to be concentrated in the hands of a relatively small number of chiefs and non-titled men who enjoyed the patronage of *obaseki* and the confidence of the British officers. Thus, throughout the interregnum, there was a tendency for administrative areas within the Benin kingdom to become consolidated into larger units. The acquisition of paramount chieftaincies was to be a major object of political competition throughout this period, for they afforded their holders unprecedented opportunities for personal aggrandizement.

Though it bore a superficial resemblance to the pre-colonial pattern, the interregnal system of territorial administration operated in an entirely different context of structures and values. Before 1897, a chief's rights and obligations as a territorial administrator constituted only one of a configuration of roles conferred on him with his title. Fulfilment of his other roles, both ritual and secular, took up a great deal of his time and interest, and involved him in a network of structural loyalties and oppositions that placed restraints on his dealings with the villages entrusted to him. As I have noted above (and see Bradbury, 1967) alternative channels of communication between the *oba* and his subjects could be utilized from both ends to check the power of the territorial chiefs. Again, while the interests of the *oba*, his chiefs, and his people were often in conflict, they shared a common set of beliefs and values and subscribed to a single political ideology (see above p. 199). The authority of the territorial chiefs, though often abused, was legitimate because it derived from the king and was designed to fulfil the purposes of the kingship. The rules of the political game and the limits of expediency were widely understood and ultimately sanctioned by the forces of political competition operating within a framework of common value orientations.

In the interregnal situation these rules and limits were no longer effective; the guidelines of political behaviour had to be drawn afresh. For an evolved polity, with built-in checks and balances, the British substituted a monolithic administrative pyramid in which the paramount chiefs occupied the middle ground. As the agents of alien conquerors, motivated by un-familiar goals and values, they lacked the legitimacy accorded by the ordinary Edo to their pre-colonial counterparts. On the other hand they enjoyed the determined support of their new masters who, while holding a monopoly of effective force, were greatly dependent on them for the implementation of their policies. 'It is imperative that you uphold the power of the Beni Chiefs and force obedience of their orders and of those of the Native Council . . .' wrote the Consul General to the Resident at Benin in 1899.[7] The Resident passed on the message to his officers: 'The most important point to bear in mind is that the power of the Benin City chiefs must be upheld and the terri-tories worked through them and officers should always be accompanied by one of the chiefs when visiting the country'.[8]

At this time, internal security was still a problem. *Ologbose*, the chief who had led the attack on the massacred British officials, was conducting a guerilla campaign only forty miles away, and in many parts of the *oba*'s territories British rule was still being met with spirited resistance. The Consul General was hardly less exercised by fears of the encroachment of the Lagos Government on the one hand and the Royal Niger Company, on the other, on his own sphere of authority. But the long-run consideration underlying the government's deter-mination to bolster up the chiefs' power was an economic one. Long before the massacre had provided a justification for 'punitive' action, commercial interests in the Delta had been urging the British Government to open up the hinterland to them by taking over Benin, and the government was increasingly inclined to heed their representations. Certainly the Benin chiefs were expecting a British attack long before the massacre, which was itself the outcome of their anxieties. In the excitement of military action the primacy of commercial interests was never lost sight of. Moor's first instructions when Benin City had fallen defined the objects of the administration as pacification, winning the confidence of the natives, and the opening-up of trade.[9] From a perusal of the records of the early years of British rule, it is clear that the first two objectives were regarded primarily as a means to the third.

Attempts to promote economic development were soon under way. Metal currency was introduced; languishing markets were revived; the Edo were encouraged to tap wild rubber and collect other natural products; collective village rubber plantations were established; everybody was encouraged to trade freely in palm kernels which had formerly been a royal monopoly; and timber concessions were allocated. The paramount chiefs and council chiefs (frequently the same men) were assigned a vital role in making these policies known and promoting their implementation; as well as enforcing new regulations such as those devised to control the working of wild rubber. Generous inducements were held out to the chiefs for their active cooperation. They were permitted to collect tribute at an official rate (in 1902) of 5 yams per household and a goat for every 10 households.[10] They were assigned a generous proportion of profits accruing to village communities from a variety of sources. In the early stages these consisted mainly of rents imposed upon Urhobo immigrants who, from 1897, began to enter the Benin kingdom in large numbers to exploit its oil-palm resources; and on 'native aliens' and European firms who set up trading establishments. To rents were subsequently added timber royalties and the profits of village rubber plantations.

Another source of income derived from the chief's duty to recruit carriers and labourers for road-building and other purposes required by the government. Of the money allocated to the chiefs to meet the costs of these services, one-third was paid to the labourers, another third used to provide food for them, while the chief himself retained the remaining third.

These, at any rate, were the official proportions. It is unlikely that they were often adhered to. The chiefs were also encouraged to set an example in taking up new productive enterprises. Seedlings were supplied to them for the establishment of private rubber plantations and their servants received training in the working of both wild and domesticated rubber. The estates which many of them laid down have continued to furnish their heirs with a regular income up to the present day. The chiefs were important to the administration then, not only because they already possessed authority, but because it was considered that their enrichment was the most direct path to economic diversification, and the expansion of trade. By tying part of their income to the profits accruing to villages under their control, it was thought that they would actively stimulate palm-oil and rubber production. Another example of this policy is the attempt in 1898 to promote intensive cotton-growing. American seed was distributed to many of the chiefs, who were to supervise its cultivation, either directly or through the agency of headmen of their subject villages; but this scheme proved unsuccessful.

While many of them cooperated wholeheartedly in these schemes and derived great benefit from them, the paramount chiefs did not confine their activities to the promotion of economic development. Freed from the manifold traditional obligations associated with their titles, they devoted their close and continuous attention to the management of their benefices, in which they were allowed great latitude. They did not, of course, enjoy complete security of tenure. Chiefs were occasionally removed from office for misappropriation of funds, general incompetence, or excessive exploitation. Villages taken away from one chief were assigned to another, usually one of those who had proved most capable and competent according to the government's standards. Political action took the form, in these circumstances, of competition between the chiefs for government favours; and conflict between the chiefs and their subjects.

Administration officers spent a lot of time assessing the validity of complaints made by villagers against the paramount chiefs. The truth was often difficult to establish. Residents were naturally reluctant to dismiss chiefs who had proved their usefulness; and competence in terms of the government's

211

objectives was not necessarily incompatible with self-aggrandizement at the expense of the unfortunate villagers. Edo informants confirm that personal relations between government officers and a few trusted chiefs were more intimate at this period than in any subsequent phase of colonial rule. The great strength of the paramount chiefs lay in the breadth of their administrative roles which gave them a high degree of control over the flow of communication between the villages and the government.

Provided he did not directly defraud the government (or was not found out defrauding it), a paramount chief's capacity for survival depended largely on his ability to judge (*a*) how far he could carry his exploitation without provoking a general revolt in his benefice; and (*b*) where his over-rulers would draw the line between the necessity of maintaining the chiefs' authority and their responsibility for protecting his subjects from oppression. The second condition was closely dependent upon the first. That is, the test for determining when a strong chief had become an intolerable tyrant was the degree of unrest that his *ultra vires* actions provoked. The most 'reliable' chiefs were those whose exploitative activities were sufficiently selective for them to retain a reasonable amount of support among their subjects. It was when complaints became too general, when a chief exercised too little discipline over his agents, and particularly when a strong local leader emerged who was prepared to challenge the chief's authority, that the government was forced to conclude that a change was due.

We may take as an example the disturbances at Urhonigbe, a large village in the south-east corner of the Benin Kingdom, between 1909 and 1914. In 1909 the Urhonigbe people were in general revolt against their paramount chief (*P.C.I*) whom they accused of extortion, slave-dealing, and general oppression. The government's decision to remove him was no doubt influenced by the fact that he had failed to obtain either carriers or government tribute from Urhonigbe for some years; that is, the authorities were as much concerned with his administrative incompetence as with his alleged tyranny. The revolt was led by the priestly headman (*A*) of Urhonigbe whose aim was to get it declared a separate administrative unit with himself as paramount chief. However, the government preferred to appoint *P.C.II*, a non-titled paramount chief, who already held other

benefices. Unrest soon broke out again and *A* was, with government approval, carried off to *P.C.II*'s house at the capital.
After six months he escaped and resumed his activities. By 1913
obaseki was warning the District Commissioner that serious
trouble was threatening in Urhonigbe. The people were said to
be 'swearing juju' against both the paramount chief and the
D.C. himself. Complaints poured in and they are worth quoting
in summary form:

> The chief was said to have bought three slaves and placed
> them in the house of one of his agents at Urhonigbe. He had
> taken 30 women from the town and married them by force.
> He was always ordering the people to go and haul logs with-
> out payment. One day when they heard the D.C. was visiting
> the town they collected three cows to present to him but the
> chief objected to this and took them away. He asked the
> people to bring out their idols and make juju for him against
> anyone who tried to take the town away from him. He left
> his brother *E* in charge of the town. Every nine days they
> gave him 600 yams. The women were called upon to carry
> these to Abraka where they were taken in canoes to the
> coast for sale. *E* collected fines and sent them to the chief.
> 264 people were fined amounts of £2 to £10 to have their
> cases settled by the chief. They did not receive their share of
> timber royalties. A town on Urhonigbe land had paid £100
> rent but the chief had kept it all. They did not want him
> but wanted their own court in Urhonigbe.

The truth or falsity of any one of these charges is now beyond
verification, but it cannot be doubted that exploitation of this
kind was common in interregnal Benin. The reactions of the
government are interesting. Following an investigation by the
D.C. in March 1913, 'grave charges' were made against *P.C.II*
in the Supreme Court and his deposition was recommended.
Subsequently, however, the charges were withdrawn 'for
political reasons' and the Lagos authorities refused to approve
his deposition. *A* was removed from Urhonigbe. Otherwise
nothing further was done and the matter remained in abeyance
until it was overtaken by the extensive administrative changes
which accompanied the restoration of the kingship in 1914. In
the meantime *P.C.II* kept away from Urhonigbe, his personal

agents left the town, and it remained in the hands of the local elders. On the other hand he was allowed to retain his benefices in other parts of the kingdom.

The pattern of conflict between villages and their paramount chiefs is clearly illustrated by the Urhonigbe affair. The outlines of political competition and conflict among the Benin City chiefs are, however, much more difficult to discern. At one stage in the Urhonigbe investigations the D.C. had recommended that *P.C.II* should be replaced by another increasingly trusted chief, *B*. However, this recommendation was withdrawn when suspicion arose that *B* had himself been intriguing with the dissident elements in Urhonigbe against *P.C.II*. The wealth and power to be gained from benefice-holding and the highly unequal and arbitrary distribution of these advantages inevitably created resentment and intrigue within the indigenous elite of Benin City, but it does not appear to have resulted in the emergence of factions, or of a radical polarization.

It will be recalled that in 1897 the first Resident had initiated a Native Council of chiefs. The first proposal had been that it should consist of only five members so as 'to give the chiefs some incentive to become members'. In the event a dozen or more were appointed by the end of 1897, most of them *uzama* or *eghaebho*, but including one or two lesser title-holders; and to these the *oba*'s two eldest sons were added. In 1900 a second rank of 'minor chiefs' had been created. There were about fifty of these who formed a roster from which court members were chosen. At this time there were sixteen 'head chiefs' (the number was later to be increased to a limit of thirty) who sat in turn as court Vice-President for a month each. From time to time promotions were made from second to first rank. However, after the earliest years, when it was called upon to advise on such questions as to what to do with Ovonramwen's wives and slaves, there is no evidence that the Council ever acted as an effective advisory or policy-making body. The impression that emerges from administrative records and oral traditions is that the administrative officers came to rely more and more heavily for their information and for the implementation of their decisions on a very few chiefs, among whom *obaseki* was by far the most prominent. This interpretation is confirmed by various brief surveys of Benin administrative history prepared by administrative officers during later periods of reorganization. Thus the Acting Lieutenant-Governor reported to the Governor in 1920: 'At the outset the original seniority of the chiefs was to a great extent maintained, but gradually *obaseki*, owing to his capacity and ability, took senior place, was recognized as the senior Paramount Chief and practically all Government orders were issued through him. Rule was direct and he was regarded as the mouthpiece of Government . . .'.[11] My own oral inquiries largely confirm this view, though it is clear that some administrative officers established close personal relations with chiefs other than *obaseki* and used them as a check on his advice and activities.

The absence of overt factional politics is attributable to the fact that in the post-conquest situation, the main concern of the British was to establish the habit of obedience to their orders. The *oba* had striven to rule by manipulating competition between individuals and groups arranged in a complex configuration of opposed hierarchies and cross-cutting interests and obligations. The Resident, having direct access to overwhelming force, had no need of such subtleties; his interests were best served by the suppression rather than the encouragement of competition for power. *Obaseki* was able to dominate the centre of the stage for so long because the monolithic administrative structure made no provision for the emergence of a focus of opposition to him. However, the old political norms and habits were not dead, only dormant. Waiting in the wings was the uneasy figure of Aiguobasimwin, Ovonramwen's eldest son, always regarded as an object of some suspicion if never a serious threat.[12] The government's decision in 1914, to try him out in a leading role, enables us to present the next stage of Benin history as an unfolding drama, rather than as a series of mechanically repetitive episodes.

The restoration and the reign of Eweka II, 1914-1933
Ovonramwen's death, at Calabar in January 1914, conveniently coincided with the amalgamation of the Northern and Southern Provinces into the Colony and Protectorate of Nigeria. Lugard was Governor in Lagos, indirect rule was in fashion, and 'the opportunity was taken to inaugurate (at Benin) a native administration on the lines of those which had proved successful

in the Northern Provinces' (Burns, 1929, p. 217). Indirect rule demanded that there should be a 'native authority' and, to this end, the government was prepared to restore the kingship, at least for a trial period.

Aiguobasimwin's right to the throne was never strongly challenged by his nearest brother, Osuanlele, as it would probably have been in pre-colonial times. His only serious rival was the *obaseki* who would not have turned down the opportunity of founding a new dynasty. James Watt, then Resident at Benin, would certainly have welcomed the accession of the government's most trusted agent had there been any chance of legitimizing it. However, it was soon made clear to him that any such move would be strongly resisted by the chiefs and the people.[13] Dynastic continuity was the first axiom of Edo political values, and there was almost universal agreement that Aiguobasimwin was the only acceptable candidate.

The British aim was not simply to rehabilitate the pre-colonial Benin polity. In fact they made very little effort at this point to discover how it had worked. The organizational model they had in mind was derived from the developments which had taken place in the Northern Nigerian emirates where Lugard had worked out his concept of indirect rule. Those responsible for setting up the native administration recognized that this model would require adaptation to local conditions, but their reference was as much to the interregnal administrative structure as to the traditional political system. They made it clear to Aiguobasimwin that they had no intention of transferring to him the power which had been acquired by *obaseki* and the other elite chiefs of the interregnum. On the contrary they would continue to rely upon – and expect him to rely upon – the experience and advice of these chiefs.

The restoration made it possible to begin making new appointments to the titles that had fallen vacant on the deaths of those who had held them in 1897, and thus to bring about a somewhat closer correspondence between traditional precedence and *de facto* influence and prestige. The senior titles naturally went to the elite chiefs and inevitably, Agho became *iyase*, 'the *oba*'s first subject', the previous *iyase*, Okizi, having died in 1901. The *oba* later told Talbot that it was he who had suggested to Resident Watt that Agho should be made *iyase*,[14] but it is unlikely that he did so unprompted or without misgivings. Agho himself had a decisive voice in the first allocations of other senior titles and *iyase* is certainly the one he would have chosen for himself. The 'prime-ministerial' aspect of the *iyase*'s traditional role made Agho's accession to the title very appropriate in British eyes, but this appointment meant a great deal more to the Benin people than it did to the government. The officials at Benin certainly foresaw the danger of a personal struggle for power between Agho and Aiguobasimwin but it is unlikely that they were aware that, in the 'conscious model' (Lévi-Strauss, 1963, p. 281) of the traditional polity, *oba* and *iyase* occupied polar positions around which political factions were, sooner or later, bound to coalesce. Reaffirmed by the particular circumstances and consequences of the restoration, this conceptual polarity was to remain a significant factor in Benin politics over the next forty years.

In July 1914 the government presented its proposals for a Native Administration to the *oba*-designate and principal chiefs. There would be a small council of chiefs to advise on the formulation and implementation of policy, and suitable chiefs would be selected to staff judicial courts. The *iyase* would be president of the Native Court and the *oba*'s chief advisor. In place of the still fairly numerous districts administered by paramount chiefs, Benin Division would be divided into four large consolidated Districts, each under a District Chief (later called District Head) who would also be president of the courts in his district. Benin City would be divided into Quarters, each under a Quarter Chief who would take charge of sanitation, the maintenance of order, and the collection of rates. The system of remuneration was to be rationalized. Fees, fines, market dues, timber royalties, rubber receipts, rents, and the proceeds of a direct tax on all able-bodied men would form the revenue of a Native Treasury from which the salaries of the *oba*, the *iyase*, and council, court, district, and quarter chiefs and other administrative expenses would be met.[15]

This programme was substantially put into effect over the next few years, though not without strong opposition to some of its features. In particular, the chiefs firmly resisted the principle of direct taxation for they saw that it would not be to their advantage to have the tax obligations of individuals too rigorously defined. Only in 1920 was direct taxation to become an established fact; in the meantime a system was devised whereby villages were assessed to pay fixed annual sums. The other major proposals were in operation by 1916. However, I am not so much concerned here with the detailed, time-table of administrative reorganization as with the un-planned currents and rhythms of political behaviour that were unleashed by the restoration.

Aiguobasimwin was installed on 24 July 1914, styling himself Eweka II, after the founder of the dynasty. His accession met with popular acclaim. Gifts poured in from the Benin villages, and from some outside what the government now regarded as his domain. The palace was rebuilt with voluntary labour and resumed its place, in the popular mind, at the centre of the kingdom's affairs. The chiefly orders and palace associations were reconstituted and a body of retainers assembled; wives were recruited for the *oba*'s harem and women to be their servants. The elaborate network of ritual relations between the *oba* and his chiefs and subjects was reactivated and some of the rituals of divine kingship began to be performed again, if in attenuated form. The *oba* himself was embarrassed by some of the spontaneous responses to his accession and had constantly to consult the administrative officers as to what customary practices were still permissible.[16] The British welcomed (with reservations) the enthusiasm with which people renewed their services to the *oba*. It was recognized that Eweka needed to acquire popular respect and prestige if he was to be a useful symbol of the authority of the Native Administration. However, they could neither foresee nor fully control the degree to which the dormant behaviour patterns of the old political culture would be reawakened.

At Eweka's accession the government reserved all rights in regard to policy-making and the allocation of administrative responsibilities. The *oba* was permitted to make the first formal nominations for positions on the councils and for the district and quarter headships, but it is clear that allocations were worked out in consultation with the administrative officers and the elite chiefs of the interregnum. The district chiefships were, in the government's view, the key to efficient administration; and, from the chiefs' standpoint, the most desirable prizes.

Inevitably they were assigned to the *iyase* and three other chiefs, now all of senior *eghaebho* rank, who had proved themselves most 'useful' during the interregnum. These four, together with three other *eghaebho* and an *uzama*, were also appointed to the *oba*'s council. The nine Quarter Chiefs included three or four of sub-*eghaebho* rank but few, if any, were the *oba*'s personal clients.

The *oba* was conscious, from the outset, of the obstacles to the establishment of his personal authority presented by the continuing dominance of the interregnal oligarchy. In this respect his position was broadly analogous to that in which Ovonramwen had found himself at the commencement of his reign, when confronted with the power of the chiefs appointed by his father, Adolo. Eweka's capacity to manipulate the situation was, however, much less promising than Ovonramwen's had been. The accession of the 'reliable' chiefs of the interregnum to the district and quarter headships, and the presence of an overriding authority determined to make full use of their experience, were bound to strengthen and perpetuate their hold over him. Before his installation the *oba* had privately urged the Resident that two men should be appointed to look after each district so that they would check each other's activities. The chiefs, he suggested, would not tell the truth because of the bribes they would be offered in the villages. He begged the government to support him lest the chiefs should overthrow him as they had (in his view) overthrown his father.[17] Some heed was taken of the Edaiken's representations. In 1915, it was decided that tax should be collected by village heads and handed over to the District Chief in the presence of the *oba*'s representative. The headman and District Chief would each receive a percentage and the latter would hand the balance to the *oba* to be paid into the Treasury. Nevertheless, given the compactness and size of their new domains and the fact that they were now supposed to reside in their districts and to be presidents of district courts – all radical departures from pre-colonial practice – the district heads were in an even stronger position than they had been as paramount chiefs. Though their roles were now officially defined in more bureaucratic terms there was, in fact, little to stop them treating their districts as personal fiefs.

The *oba* naturally responded to the weakness of his position by trying to build up a personal clientele. There were, in Benin, men who had achieved wealth and influence in various ways without securing administrative competences and some of these were prepared to ally themselves with the *oba*. They included, for example, some who had been resident in the Benin trading post at the Yoruba town of Akure at the time of the British take-over, and who had since returned to Benin but continued their commercial relations with the hinterland. Another potential source of support for a 'king's party' lay in the fact that there were now a number of ex-paramount chiefs whom reorganization had robbed of income and prestige. By restoring the kingship but denying the king effective authority, the British created a nucleus of great symbolic potency, around which the grievances of the dispossessed chiefs and other traditional title-holders lacking government appointments could crystallize. The *oba* could and did hand out titles to men whose support he wished to acquire. Soon after his accession he submitted a list of 'household chiefs' which the government approved, though no provision had been made for integrating them into the new administrative order. Titles without official competences were, however, of little value. The *oba* might, perhaps, make recommendations for court membership and minor posts in the Native Administration but his powers of patronage compared unfavourably with those of the chiefs who, during the interregnum, had gained the government's confidence.

As the situation develops, in the early years of Eweka's reign, it is possible to identify five main sets of political interests, those of:

1. the administrative officers, concerned with maintaining order and with the development of an administrative organization which would be effective in implementing its policies;
2. the district chiefs and their clients and agents;
3. the *oba*, his palace staff, and others, such as ritual specialists, men (and women) of a traditionalist outlook, whose standing in the community was closely bound up with the *oba*'s authority and prestige; and the *oba*'s personal friends and clients, bound to him by various social ties and

common interests and by their opposition to the elite
chiefs whose power constituted an obstacle to their own
commercial and political ambitions;
4. the ex-paramount chiefs, intent on recovering their former
sources of income and prestige;
5. the general populace in the capital and the villages, seeking to defend itself against exploitation and the demands
of the government.

The story of the years 1914-1929 is one of a constant struggle
between the *oba* and the district chiefs, with the remaining chiefs
and the people being drawn by structural and personal loyalties
and interests into partisanship of one side or the other. The
position of the British representatives on the spot is complicated. The new policy measures which they sought (or were
required) to introduce provided fuel for factional dispute. On
the one hand, they were bound to give their support to the
indigenous ruling clique whose interests favoured acquiescence
in these measures; on the other, to act as mediators in the
conflicts that resulted. They have to be seen not merely as
external manipulators but also as participants in internal
political processes over which they had only limited control.

In July 1915 the Resident, Benin, felt able to recommend
confirmation of the *oba*'s and the *iyase*'s appointments. In his
view, Eweka had done his utmost to rule his people wisely and
follow the advice given to him. Confirmation would add to his
prestige. The *iyase*, for his part, had served the *oba* as loyally
as he had served the government, although he was now second
man instead of first.[18] By December of the same year this sunny
picture was beginning to be clouded. The reduction in the number of administrative officers caused by the outbreak of war in
Europe had led to a widespread rumour that the white men
were leaving Benin. After some carriers had been taken to
Duala it became very difficult to recruit any more. The *iyase*
assured the government that everything was all right, but also
advised that it would be prudent for the administrative officers
to take chiefs on tour with them. The Resident reported: 'The
oba has been loyal and useful but has not exercised enough
control over his household and messengers and unauthorised
persons claiming to be his messengers who have been claiming

things from the villagers. People under the impression that they are serving the *oba* do not see why they should also serve the chiefs.' The Resident felt that the trouble was partly due to the fact that the chiefs had important duties to perform, opportunities for extortion and no recognized income[19] – the district head system was not yet operative.

Evidently the villagers were beginning to resume their customary method of self-defence, that is, by playing off one set of officials against the other. In their eyes the palace emissaries were to be set off against the territorial administrators as they had been before the British arrived; and, in this matter, the *oba*'s interests tended to coincide with those of the villagers. His predecessors had striven to retain their freedom of action by keeping open alternative channels of communication between themselves and their subjects. By 1916, when the district head system had become operational, it was obvious to Eweka that he was not going to find it easy to emulate their example. The government's organizational model made no provision for overlapping spheres of competence. It accepted the desirability, if the *oba*'s prestige was to be maintained, of his retaining some direct links with his people and receiving some customary services from them; but these activities could not be allowed to interfere with the operation of the monolithic administrative structure which the British saw as best suited to the attainment of their objectives. The chiefs, for their part, regarded themselves as responsible directly to the administrative officers, a view which fitted in well with the latter's own wish to exercise as much personal supervision over them as possible.

This issue, in various guises, is a constant theme throughout the era of the district headships. The chiefs regularly complain that the *oba*'s emissaries tell the villages not to serve them. The *oba*, in return, accuses the chiefs of keeping his messengers out and of preventing villagers from making appeals to the *oba*'s court. Definition of the competences of palace staff took a long time to achieve. Along with the introduction of district headships went the first official recognition of village headships, both hereditary and non-hereditary. Legitimation of the succession to these headships was recognized to be the *oba*'s prerogative and this involved such matters as the presentation of village chiefs to the people by the officials of the palace associations. The *oba*'s right to send his representatives to village rituals could hardly be gainsaid. Indeed, as we shall see, the *oba*'s *failure* to fulfil his ritual obligations was later to be interpreted as an anti-government plot. It was also accepted that the *oba* had the right to expect his people to contribute to the cost of state rituals, by providing animals for sacrifice. These contributions had always been paid for (with nominal sums) and, in time, the role of the *oba*'s itinerant 'buyers' was to be regularized, and the 'price' of particular animals fixed. On the other hand, if palace officials were to visit the villages for these purposes, how could they be prevented from intriguing against the district heads?

Given the European value-orientations of the administrative officers, the royal harem provided the *oba*'s enemies with plenty of ammunition. In the old days one of the tasks of the *ibiwe* association had been to recruit large numbers of wives for the *oba*. By no means all of these entered into actual marital relations with him; many of them were given to loyal subjects as a reward for their services. When Eweka became *oba*, the *ibiwe* chiefs resumed their traditional functions of arranging marriages and seeing to the upkeep of, and maintenance of discipline in, the harem. As a result, there were endless allegations of women being kept there, or married off, against their will. The *oba*, in return, complained to the government that chiefs took away his wives and encouraged their followers to seduce them.

Certain actions by administrative officers did nothing to ease Eweka's position. In 1917 Resident Watt, angry about delays in the construction of a bridge, instructed the *oba* to order members of his palace associations to carry cement. The *oba*, according to his own explanation, pointed out that such work would be contrary to the customary dignity of his retainers. Nevertheless he was obliged to carry out the Resident's commands. The consequence was that his retainers, accusing him of weakness in not protecting them from humiliation, ceased to attend the *oba*; the audiences which he had given in the palace each evening to hear complaints no longer took place.[20] The novelty of having an *oba* again was beginning, by this time, to wear thin. The dispossessed paramount chiefs became increasingly aware of the *oba*'s impotence to right their grievances. According to Eweka's own version, they blamed him not only for the fact that their benefices had been taken away from them but even for the loss of their slaves – though this was due to the general abolition of slavery by the government in 1915. Other chiefs, including those entitled by Eweka himself, found that their expectations of administrative competences and perquisites remained unfulfilled.

The *oba*'s increasing isolation and frustration are reflected in an anonymous letter received by the Governor in July 1918.[21] The writer – whom the Resident divined (probably correctly) to be a palace servant – complained of the ill-treatment of the *oba* by the 'whitemen and native chiefs' and requested His Excellency to come to Benin to set matters right. When the *oba* talks, the letter goes on, the white men and chiefs always disobey him. Young men always try their very best to obey him. Since he became *oba* he has not done any wrong or abused the law. Yet the chiefs have told the white men that they do not want the villages to serve the *oba* again, that he should not be allowed to send messages to the villages. The writer begs His Excellency to raise the *oba* above all kings in Nigeria.

It was inevitable that the general malaise should manifest itself in a form familiar in Benin dynastic traditions, a direct confrontation between the *oba* and the *iyase*. The conflict took on traditional forms of expression. In August 1918 allegations were made that the *oba* had sent to the Yoruba town of Ondo for a 'native doctor' to 'make medicine' to protect him against the *iyase*. The native doctor alleged that the *oba* had told him that the *iyase* was taking his wives away, combining with the white men and all Benin to accuse him of taking their slaves and property, and taking half of all the presents sent to him. According to the doctor's own version, he had remained at Benin four months making medicines – but had drawn the line when the *oba* asked him to use his arts to kill the *iyase*. The Resident refused to credit the last part of the story, preferring to believe that the doctor had, in fact, tried to blackmail the *oba*.[22] However, there is evidence that the *oba* felt obliged to conciliate the *iyase* at about the time when these events were alleged to have taken place. Eweka himself was later to refer to an occasion when he had gone to the *iyase*'s house and knelt at his feet to beg forgiveness[23]; and the Resident reported that, about the same time, the *oba* had asked the *iyase* to assure him that all was well between the two of them.[24]

Despite an interregnum of 17 years, the ideology of divine kingship retained enough force for it to be a factor in political conflict. In November 1918 the administrative officers were perturbed by the general disquiet generated by the *oba*'s failure to perform *ugie-erha-oba*, the annual festival in honour of his father's spirit. Deaths and disasters were being blamed on the omission of these rites and the government's anxieties were increased by the approach of an influenza epidemic. When asked to explain why he had not performed the rite, the *oba* blamed it on the *iyase*'s refusal to take part – on the grounds of his having become a Christian. The Resident regarded the whole affair as a plot to arouse resentment against the *iyase* and the government. There may well have been some truth in this view but the political motivations were probably not all on one side; to boycott the palace rituals had always been one of the sanctions that disaffected chiefs could employ against the *oba*. The exasperated Resident was moved to suggest that Agho should give up the *iyase* title and take the style Chief Counsellor, while retaining his offices of District Head and President of the Native Court. Another, purely ritual *iyase* might then be appointed, so that the festivals could go on.[25] This suggestion was hardly likely to appeal to either Eweka or Agho, but it is indicative of the government's tendency at this time to think of the kingship as having purely symbolic utility.

The *oba*'s feeling that the *iyase* and the administrative officers were in league against him is readily understandable. The latter tended to regard the *oba-iyase* conflict as being a mere clash of personalities. Commenting on the affair of the native doctor, the Resident gave it as his opinion that: 'the political situation in Benin is that the *oba* is a weak man and, being in a position of hereditary authority, jealous of anyone under him whom he recognised as being stronger, wiser and better than himself'. He lent himself 'to the counsel of flatterers' and resented any restriction on his power by the government. That he was required to deal with the villagers through the District Heads was resented by the *oba* and his followers. The *iyase*, on the other hand, was loyal to the *oba* because (said the Resident) he believed in that way he was being loyal to the government. It was he who was making the administration a success.

In fact the *oba* was privately warned, about this time, that if he did not mend his ways he would follow in his father's footsteps. With the scales so heavily weighted against him it is not surprising that Eweka seems to have decided that it would be safer to join the *iyase* than to go on fighting him. He requested the Resident to mediate between them and, seven months after the *ugie-erha-oba* affair, their rapprochement had so far progressed that, as we may read in the 1919 annual Report: 'In mid-June Benin City went on fete when two of the *oba*'s daughters were married – Iyashere (*iyase*) married the second, Edogun the third'. Fulfilment of the custom whereby the *oba* was bound to give a daughter (ideally his first daughter) in marriage to the *iyase* helped to cement a mutually profitable partnership between Agho and Eweka. The *oba*'s position was much ameliorated and Agho, with the Resident in one pocket[26] and the *oba* in the other, had reached the crowning point of a remarkable political career. However, as we shall see, by 'capturing' Eweka he had both overreached the tolerable limits of his personal power and undermined the king's own legitimate authority.

Believing the clash between Agho and Eweka to be mainly a question of personalities, the Resident was delighted to see them reconciled. The festive atmosphere created by the royal weddings added to the government's optimism and it was now felt safe to press on with the plans to introduce direct taxation. This, however, was the spark that was needed to set fire to the smouldering resentment of the dispossessed and deprived sectors of the political class. Furthermore, it was an issue on which the latter could be assured of popular support.

In July 1920, Chiefs Esogban and Oloton sent a petition to the Governor on behalf of the titled chiefs of Benin City.[27] Their opinion was that the native administration since 1914 had been wholly bad. The Government had obtained their consent to (what the chiefs were now calling) the joint rule of the *oba* and the *iyase* by promises of power and emoluments. Since then 81 principal houses had been abandoned and were in ruins. The chiefs condemned the behaviour of the *oba* and the *iyase* in similar terms. Both had used their power to exact private tribute and free services from all the villages. The *oba* had taken the chiefs' former household slaves and set up new villages with them to work plantations for him. Others he had given to his daughters on their marriages to the *iyase* and *edogun*, and still others to the *iyase* himself. The chiefs demanded the abolition of the district head system; the restoration of their villages to the paramount chiefs; the removal of the *iyase* from the permanent vice-presidency of the Native Court, and the rotation of all court vice-presidencies among the chiefs; and the abandonment of the new 'head taxes'. Perhaps most significantly of all, they demanded that all administrative matters should be publicly discussed at *Ugha-Ozolua* (the great courtyard which housed the shrine of the fifteenth-century *oba*, Ozolua). They objected strongly to the *oba* and *iyase* (as they put it) arranging things privately with Resident Watt at his bungalow. Later on a supplement to this petition was presented,[28] giving lurid details of the misdeeds alleged to have been perpetrated by the *oba*, and especially by the *iyase*, against the inhabitants of a number of villages; and demanding that the *iyase* be suspended pending negotiation.

The government was greatly perturbed. Having helped to paper over the cracks between the *oba* and the *iyase* only a year or so before, it now found itself faced with a concerted revolt by the other chiefs and the villagers against the combined power of the *iyase*, the *oba*, and the Resident. About this time P. Amaury Talbot replaced James Watt as Resident. With characteristic industry and curiosity, he set out to make himself familiar with the whole history of the Benin administration. One detects at this point an entirely new spirit of inquiry, a genuine desire to come to grips with the realities of the political situation.

In the new crisis the fragility of the *oba*'s compact with the *iyase* was soon revealed. In a letter to the District Officer dated 30 August 1920, Eweka, recalling the glory of his predecessors, gave vent to his feelings of humiliation and resentment:

'The *iyase* is ordering me at which I am not pleased because I do not want anyone but the British Government to command me. A servant cannot command his master . . . [The *iyase*] has many times come to the *oba*'s house and boasted

227

that his orders surpass the *oba*'s . . . I am deprived of my boys by the *iyase* and have to attend farm myself to keep my wives and children.'

In the light of the chiefs' complaints against the *oba* himself, this last lament must be regarded as an exaggeration. The *oba* also had his own proposals for the future. He asked that the warrant chiefs should be made presidents of the district courts, and the *oba* himself President of the Benin Native Court. He also wanted to take over the *iyase*'s district and to have all communications to the government passed through himself. For Agho he prescribed a pension. Meanwhile, he recommended that he should be suspended, a proposal which the District Officer found 'preposterous' – it would throw the whole N.A. into chaos.[29] Talbot, however, was less committed to the long-standing dogma of Agho's indispensability.

Agho's downfall came with dramatic suddenness. In a report dated 6 September, Talbot described a meeting which he had had with the *oba* and all the Benin chiefs except the *iyase*.[30] Every one of them, District Heads included, supported the *iyase*'s suspension. Since there was no one to speak for him, Talbot inferred, he must have abused his power. Though very capable, he was dictatorial and arrogant. His power rested entirely on his favour with the European.

Indeed, it might seem that his life depended on it, for, on 9 September, the day Talbot's report left Benin, Agho died. Yet, Talbot's last remark fails to do justice to the political acumen and nerve that Agho had already demonstrated before 1897, and proved through more than twenty years of colonial rule. His loss of favour with 'the European' was a concomitant, not the cause, of his downfall, which, as we have seen, was the outcome of factional conflict generated in the intercourse of different political cultures. However, Talbot did see more clearly than his colleagues that the symbiotic relationship between Agho and successive Residents, which had been effective before 1914, was incompatible with post-restoration political realities. In retrospect, we recognize that *obaseki*'s supremacy during the interregnum had seemed unchallengeable not only because he enjoyed overwhelming external support, but also because his role and its structural context were alien to Edo political experience. The British were no less determined to uphold his authority after 1914, but the confrontation between *oba* and *iyase*, and the opposition between district chiefs and palace retainers which the restoration engendered, could be more readily assimilated to the traditional political culture. Hence, pre-colonial political norms and tactics, suppressed during the interregnum, re-emerged with Eweka's accession. The environment in which they operated was, however, very different.

The most salient difference lay in the drastic curtailment of the functions of the indigenous political elite – particularly in respect to policy-making and the control of effective force. The Benin chiefs found that, by political action, they could influence the details and timing of administrative structures and measures, but the taking of major policy decisions was out of their hands. In this situation, ambitions and interests were narrowly focused on intense competition for administrative competences which, though in some respects more differentiated, were much less widely dispersed than they had been before 1897. The stability of the pre-colonial polity had depended, to a considerable degree, on the maintenance of an elaborate structure of competition for titles which carried well-defined expectations of competences and rewards (Bradbury, 1967). After 1914 the traditional chiefly orders were reconstituted, but they had lost their corporate governmental functions, and placement in their hierarchies was no longer consonant with the distribution of administrative roles and perquisites. Whereas, in the nineteenth century, there had been a single organizational model and a common normative framework, in terms of which individuals and groups could formulate their interests, alternative and contradictory models were now available. To the 'traditional' model there had been added the 'interregnal' and the 'Northern' models, and these were differentially valued by various interest groups. Each group, while selecting favourable elements from all three models, tended to formulate its major objectives in terms of one or another of them. In crude terms, the *oba*, his palace staff and ritual functionaries, and the villagers, were wedded to pre-colonial norms and structures; dispossessed paramount chiefs conceived their interests to lie in a return to the interregnal pattern of administration; while the District Heads and their clients had nothing to lose by acquiescing in the modified Northern model favoured by the government as an instrument of rationalization. In the absence of an underlying consensual framework, the contradictions inherent in this plurality of conceptual means to the attainment of opposed interests led, through a series of factional realignments, to a 'revolutionary' confrontation. Reduced essentially to the *iyase*, the Resident, and the *oba*, the ruling oligarchy found itself implacably opposed by a coalition of dispossessed and deprived interest groups able to mobilize mass support. The government, forced to withdraw into its mediatory role, at this point perceived the need for a new structural synthesis.

In the continuation of his report on the meeting described above, Talbot went on to suggest what changes needed to be made in order to give the Native Authority a chance of success. The government, he said, ought to take full advantage of the Benin people's respect for the kingship and the traditional hierarchies. He described the *oba* as 'shy, loyal and above average ability and intelligence'; he had had a lot of responsibility and too little power and his position needed to be strengthened in every way. Talbot also envisaged a more active role for the *oba*'s Council which ought, in his view, to be composed of 'the most important of the capable chiefs' – a reversal of earlier formulations. The District Heads had had too much power and required closer supervision. By hiving off their judicial competences it would be possible to provide posts for more of the discontented chiefs.

Talbot's report led to further inquiries by the Lieutenant-Governor of the Southern Provinces. To a meeting of the *oba*, the Benin chiefs, and some of the more important village heads, Lieutenant-Governor Moorhouse presented the alternatives of 'making indirect rule along the lines of the Northern Emirates work, or reverting to direct rule'. The chiefs expressed themselves in favour of retaining a form of Native Authority with the *oba* at its head, but wished to enlarge the Council by the addition of more of the *uzama* and *eghaebho*. They also demanded an increase in the number of Districts, with District Heads to be appointed for one year only; and they urged the abolition of direct taxation and a return to the old system of 'tribute and labour'. The Lieutenant-Governor eventually recom-

mended a Council of up to sixteen chiefs; that the number of
Districts should be increased to six; and that in each District
four to six village chiefs should sit in turn as court presidents.
These proposals were substantially put into effect and though
modified from time to time remained the basis of administration
for the rest of Eweka's reign.

Agho's death, the administration's recognition of the need to
make more use of the *oba*'s authority, the creation of more
council, judicial, and executive posts, and the growth of the
Native Administration bureaucracy gave Eweka wider scope
for exercising patronage, and greater freedom of political
manœuvre. From this point onwards the *oba*'s traditional
prerogative of conferring titles was somewhat more congruent
with his ability to reward their holders with worthwhile posts.
Consequently there was rather more *de facto* correspondence
between the traditional ranking structure and the distribution
of government-recognized competences. The *oba*'s Council
started to play a slightly more positive role. With the encouragement of administrative officers, it began to meet more regularly
and to submit proposals for the revision of customary laws to
meet modern requirements; and also to make demands for the
improvement of public services. A summary of the recommendations (by no means all heeded) of a meeting of council
chiefs and district and quarter heads in 1922 provides a
fascinating glimpse of the intermingling of old and new values
and objectives:

'Whoever commits adultery with the wife of an *uzama* or an
eghaebho should be fined £30. The ancient penalty was
death. [?]

In the old days a master could give a wife to his faithful
servant and take her away again if he should prove unfaithful.
The chiefs want to revive this practice without being accused
of slave-dealing.

In the old days if anyone was accused of harming a town
he was liable to make sacrifices. This has now been stopped
and the chiefs want it to be allowed again.

In the old days witches were sent to live in [particular]
villages. Nowadays they are allowed to remain in the town
i.e. with unfortunate consequences. [The next *oba* was to

231

build, on the outskirts of Benin City, what can only be described as a row of almshouses for destitute witches.]

The forestry laws are bringing great inconvenience to towns and villages.

More standpipes are required in Benin City.

The prices of foodstuffs should be fixed, e.g. yams at 10 for 1s; a she-goat 10s etc.

More European firms should be encouraged to trade at Benin.

Benin should recover all its old villages now in other Divisions.

Any person who assaults a titled chief should be imprisoned.

The *oba* recommends that the sale of liquor should be checked by the introduction of licences; and that all-night meetings should be made illegal.'

The reorganization of 1920 did not, of course, eliminate strife between the *oba* and the District Heads, with the palace staff and the villagers playing their customary roles. However, though the District Heads still dealt directly with the administrative officers and retained almost feudal power over their districts, none of them was able to acquire anything like the monopoly of British trust that had been Agho's; and the *oba* was better equipped to defend himself. The reorganization had by no means removed all the grievances of the ex-paramount chiefs, but as Eweka's reign progresses, the pattern of conflict takes on what I would regard as a more normal aspect. There are numerous violently expressed disputes between the *oba* and particular chiefs, especially District Heads, but they do not add up to a crisis of dichotomous, breakdown proportions. More than at any other time during the period with which we are concerned, the administrative officers of the 1920s managed to avoid identification with a narrow ruling faction.

Conscious of the threat which any *iyase* potentially constituted, yet bound by custom to appoint one, the independent *oba*s of Benin had hit upon the idea of conferring this title on men of independent wealth and influence who were not previously deeply involved in the politics of the capital. Some, for example, were wealthy traders operating on the fringes of the

Benin sphere of influence. By appointing an 'outsider' *iyase*
the *oba* hoped to enjoy at least a 'honeymoon' period of good
relations with him and perhaps also use him as an ally against
the restricting power of the senior palace chiefs. Eweka followed
this precedent by giving the *iyase* title to Okoro-Otun, a man
who, though of part-Edo descent, had been brought up by his
mother's people, who were Ekiti Yoruba; and who, having
become a successful freelance warrior and trader, eventually
settled in Benin, some say at Eweka's invitation. To the end of
his life Okoro-Otun is said not to have been able to speak Edo
without mixing it up with Yoruba, but as *iyase* he served
Eweka loyally. However, there was no guarantee that the
loyalty of an *iyase* towards the *oba* who appointed him would
be extended to his heir – as tradition shows, and as Eweka's
son was to discover by experience.

Akenzua II (1933-) and the Benin road to party politics
Eweka II died in 1933 and was succeeded by his son *Okoro*
Edokporhogbunyunmwun, who adopted the style Akenzua II.
Akenzua, who was in his early thirties, was widely hailed as a
new type of natural ruler, carefully trained for the task of
leading his people along the path of enlightenment. After attend-
ing local schools he had been sent to King's College, Lagos, where
he achieved both academic and sporting success. On leaving
school in 1918 he was appointed a transport clerk in the Benin
Native Administration and later on served as his father's
secretary. In 1928, after spending two years at Abeokuta,
where he was sent to study the working of a native administration at that time regarded as one of the most advanced in
southern Nigeria, he was given a District Headship. In the
meantime his father, with government encouragement, had
invested him with the title of *edaiken* and he took up his
residence in the heir-apparent's court at Uselu. Akenzua's
accession was accomplished without overt dispute – a fact
which must be accounted for partly by government acceptance
of the rule of primogeniture at its face value (which permitted
formal training of the successor); and partly in terms of the
restraints placed on intra-dynastic rivalry by the British
conquest, which had put the kingship itself in jeopardy. Unlike
their nineteenth-century analogues, Akenzua and his father

had remained on terms of intimacy and mutual trust and the political environment in which they lived served to identify rather than oppose their interests.

Akenzua immediately substantiated his progressive image by disbanding his father's harem and freeing girls betrothed to his father from their obligation to marry himself. He dispensed with many of the palace attendants, urging them to go out and earn their living, and devised a form of clothing for his formerly naked pages. At the same time he demonstrated his devotion to the dignity of his office, and his accession promoted a new bout of cultural reconstruction. His succession rites – his father's funeral and his own installation – were performed with a splendour and attention to customary detail not seen in Benin since the 1897 débâcle.[31] A little later he had his mother posthumously installed as Queen Mother and built a mausoleum for her remains. He also reconstituted the order of Body Titles (*Egie-Egbe*), whose members represented physical and metaphysical components of his person and took it upon themselves to share his spiritual burden.

His familiarity with his father's and his more remote predecessors' predicament in the early years of their reigns made Akenzua well aware that he would have to work hard to establish his authority; and he had the additional burden of promoting the acceptance of new government policies and regulations which were rarely universally popular. Although he had not been engaged in a contest for the throne, his accession brought forward a new generation of young ambitious men, his friends and associates, many of whom, like himself, had had a considerable amount of formal education. According to precedent he created new titles for some of these followers, while others were appointed to vacant titles; and he began to recommend them for positions on the council and courts and in the native administration. The older chiefs inevitably saw these new developments as a threat to their own security and it was not long before they began to show signs of reaction. By 1935 this clash of interests was manifesting itself in the familiar guise of a quarrel between the *oba* and the *iyase*, which took the overt form of a dispute about traditional prerogatives.[32] The *oba* objected to *iyase* Okoro-Otun's appearing in the streets wearing a beaded head-dress and preceded by a ceremonial scimitar (*ada*). According to precedent the *eghaebho* were permitted to display these marks of rank only on particular ceremonial occasions. Under pressure from administrative officers, Okoro-Otun surrendered his beaded crown and undertook not to use the sword illegally again. This was by no means the end of his differences with the *oba*, but at this point it is necessary to signal the emergence of a new interest group.

As a result of the introduction of schools and new economic opportunities over the previous thirty years, there was by this time a growing intelligentsia of teachers, clerks, and civil servants whose literacy gave them access to Western political ideologies; and – overlapping with it in interests and personnel – a new commercial elite of transport owners, rubber and timber producers, middlemen, traders, and the like. Many of these were sons of the original paramount chiefs – in this sense the economic policies of the early administrators had paid off. The *oba* himself belonged to the intelligentsia and so did some of his closest associates, but there were others who saw the growing power of the palace clique as an obstacle to their own interests. Soon after Akenzua's succession an organization calling itself the Benin Community presented a petition to the government which was uncompromisingly anti-traditional in tone. It demanded that the *oba*'s Council should be opened to Muslims and Christians (who had been excluded because they refused to undergo title-taking rituals) and the abolition of customary rules limiting, according to rank, the height of houses and the use of *iroko* wood in their construction. More startlingly, it demanded the introduction of individual ownership of land and the election of Quarter chiefs by ballot.

At this point, then, it is useful to distinguish three fairly clearly defined sectors within the Benin political class:

1. The 'old guard' of titled chiefs (especially the District and Quarter Heads) who had come to power in Eweka's reign.
2. The *oba*, his retainers and functionaries, and his 'new men'.
3. What we may call the radical modernist element. Over the years an independent-minded ascetic named H. O. Uwaifo was to prove the most uncompromising exponent of this point of view.

Despite the fundamental divergence of their interests, the older chiefs and the anti-traditionalists were to find a surprising amount of common ground during the later part of the 1930s in opposition to the power of the palace, and to government-inspired measures and regulations which the *oba*, as Sole Native Authority, was required to support and implement.

By the 1930s the District Head system had outlived its administrative usefulness. Wage labour had replaced levies of labourers and carriers. Direct taxation on the basis of nominal rolls was well established and tax clerks rather than quasi-feudal lords were required for its collection. Similarly, the increasingly complex regulations concerning such matters as sanitation, the felling of trees, the planting of permanent crops, etc., could be enforced more efficiently by officials of the appropriate Government and Native Administration departments. The abolition of the system was also consonant with the new phase of indirect rule ideology which insisted that native administrations and judiciaries should be based on authentic indigenous institutions. Throughout southern Nigeria district officers were being instructed to conduct inquiries into these institutions and to make recommendations for administrative reorganization based on their findings. By 1936 Macrae-Simpson, in his Benin Division Intelligence Report, duly recommended that the District Headships should be abolished. He proposed the constitution of village and village group councils which would be responsible to the *oba* for local affairs and which at a later date might be represented on a central state council. The Quarter Headships of the capital would be replaced by a form of administration based on the traditional wards. Macrae-Simpson also made proposals for the reform of the Native Authority. When he made his report the Council consisted of the *oba*, nine District Heads, ten Quarter Heads, and seven other chiefs who, together with the *oba*, also constituted a court of appeal. Claims to places on the Council had long been presented in terms of placement in traditional hierarchies and, though the criteria of membership had never been clearly defined, only three members were below *eghaebho* rank. With more information at its disposal than ever before, the administration began to draw with increasing explicitness on its own model of the nineteenth-century polity. Macrae-Simpson proposed the enlargement of the Council to include *all* the *uzama* and *eghaebho* – a total of about fifty-four chiefs.

Not all these proposals were put into effect. Indeed, the process of reorganization took several years to complete and it was achieved only after prolonged political turmoil. The District and Quarter Headships were, however, immediately abolished and their incumbents experienced the same kind of deflation that had been the lot of the ex-paramount chiefs twenty years before. They remained on the Council, with increased salaries, but this was no compensation for their lost prestige and perquisites. The *oba*, to whom the village chiefs and headmen were now directly responsible, and who had a big say in the running of the administrative bureaucracy, stood to gain from this reorganization. For this reason, and because he was the sole recognized instrument of British policy, he was bound to become the object of the grievances of the dispossessed chiefs.

It will have been noted that Macrae-Simpson's recommendations took no account of the views of the anti-traditionalists. The increased power of the *oba* and the entrenchment of the principle by which access to office was by way of preferment to traditional titles were clearly against their interests.

The dispossessed chiefs and the modernists were drawn closer together by their common opposition to a series of administrative measures affecting the interests of both groups. The first of these was an attempt, in 1937, to control the indiscriminate planting of permanent crops, which partly originated in complaints by villages close to the capital of an alleged shortage of farming land due to the reservation of large areas of forest, and to the setting-up of extensive rubber, cocoa, and palm-oil plantations by residents in the capital. In the past there had been no shortage of land and the citizens of the capital had a recognized right to establish farms anywhere, either in the forest or, by arrangement with the elders, on land belonging to villages. The curtailment of these rights by a regulation which stated that permanent crops could be planted only with the *oba*'s permission, was construed as an attack on this right. The new regulation might have been expected to bring the *oba* the consolation of support from the villages. However, the villagers, who had developed the habit of planting up every food farm with permanent crops after the completion of the yam and cassava harvests, were equally opposed to them. A more serious issue, which threatened a general insurrection in the capital, arose out of the government's decision that it would be more equitable, and more profitable to revenue, if the water rate in Benin City were to be calculated on an assessment of the size of houses; hitherto a flat rate had been levied. The furore that ensued has since become, under the name 'The Great Water Rate Agitation', one of the legendary landmarks of Benin political history. The details of the dispute are less relevant here than the fact that it served to cement the two groups opposed to the *oba* into an effective coalition; and to polarize the residents of the capital into pro- and anti-palace factions.

The members of the Benin Community had quickly learned to pursue their quest for participation in the administration in the guise of appeals to traditionalist sentiments. Thus, when the *ezomo* alleged that the *oba* was transgressing the prerogatives of the *uzama* by awarding titles to his subjects, the modernists were vociferous in their support. The strategy of their attack on the *oba*'s position is illustrated by the following quotations from a Benin Community address of welcome to the Lieutenant-Governor in February 1938:

'There is a set of puppet chiefs of no substantial means who have gained appointments by their close relationships and domestic services to the *oba*. . . .

'The people of Benin City are at the mercy of the villages for their farming rights. . . .

'The *iyase* is the Prime Minister, the mouthpiece of the natives and without plebiscite he moves the great majority of the war chiefs and the whole community.'

The *iyase*, himself returned to the fray, complaining among other things that the *oba* had refused to admit his sons to the palace associations, and demanding the return of his confiscated headdress. However, Okoro-Otun, though a useful symbol of opposition, was no Agho, and on this occasion the government gave the *oba* firm backing. He also retained a solid basis of support within the political elite. In reply to the Benin Community's allegations, thirty-five council chiefs and ten others petitioned the government,[33] defending Akenzua and pointing out that all his troubles were due to his being made the tool of government policy. Allegations were also made around this time about the subversive activities of his opponents, who were said to be inciting villagers against tax-collectors, enrolling them as members of the Benin Community, and collecting subscriptions. This is the first sign we have from Benin of the emergence of anything resembling modern party politicking.

The struggle between the palace clique and the opposition coalition, which gained increasing popular support, grew to alarming proportions. A sensation was created by the discovery of paraphernalia of sorcery in the Residency garden. As was the custom in times of serious crisis, the *oba* sent chalk and kola nuts to many important priests 'for the purpose of appeasing the gods in the interests of all the people generally'. He also expressed his determination to uphold his authority by creating a number of new titles, each one reaffirming the supremacy of the kingship. Eventually, however, the administrative officers found themselves forced to listen to the representations of the Benin Community, which requested permission to produce its own Intelligence Report. This request was granted and the proposals made in the Benin Community Intelligence Report formed a basis for discussion in the preparation, by H. F. (later Sir Hugo) Marshall of an Intelligence Report on Benin City.

Out of all these activities there emerged, in 1940, a new organizational model which sought to take account both of the hierarchies of the traditional polity and of the desire of the new elites to participate in the government. Benin City was divided into 24 wards, each with its own (somewhat informal) council responsible for preparing nominal rolls and collecting tax. There was also to be a Benin City Council of forty-eight members, composed entirely of two representatives from each ward (to be chosen by consensus rather than direct suffrage). The City Council was empowered to make rules for the government of the capital and had control of its own funds, subject to the overriding authority of the *oba* in Divisional Council. The Divisional Council was to consist of seventeen senior chiefs (three *uzama*, six *eghaebho n'ore*, three *eghaebho n'ogbe* from each of three palace associations, and the *ihaza*, head of another order), twenty-four ward representatives, and representatives

239

of village groups throughout the Division. The Native Authority was now to be not the *oba* alone but the *oba*-in-Council.

This new pattern of government persisted, with modifications of detail, through the war years. The *oba* remained in a strong position, still able to exercise considerable patronage and retaining his right to make all land allocations in Benin City. The basis on which title-holders were selected for the Divisional Council still remained a source of grievance and of petitions, and served to create both solidarities in excluded orders and dissension within those represented. For the next major crisis, however, we have to move on to the post-war period.

By 1947 the modernists were again in revolt against what they described as the *oba*'s autocratic behaviour. The measures of popular representation which they had achieved in 1940 had, in fact, given them very little control over either policy-making (which, in effect, remained with the British) or the bureaucratic machinery of the Native Administration. Once again, as in 1920 and the 1930s, the polarizing issues were supplied by the government, this time in the form of increases in taxes, licences, and summons fees. The approach of a new crisis was signalled in a predictable manner. *Iyase* Okoro-Otun had died in 1943 and the *oba* had been in no hurry to name a successor. Now, in 1947, the Benin Community Taxpayers Association (a successor to the Benin Community) began a vociferous campaign for the appointment of an *iyase* who would voice the popular will and curb palace autocracy. The TPA had, as its core, many of the men who had led the campaign for popular representation in the late 1930s and it also obtained the support of title-holders who had failed to secure official positions, dismissed former employees of the Native Administration, and others who, for personal reasons, were antipathetic to the *oba*. The modernists proceeded to mobilize popular support by appealing to traditional values and precedents. The argument that only an *iyase* could defend the Edo against the combined power of the white men and the palace clique had wide popular appeal and the outcry against the *oba*'s failure to fill the title was soon almost universal.

The *oba*, with his father's and his own earlier experiences in mind – and with all Benin tradition confirming the inevitability of such experiences – was determined not to be forced to appoint

an *iyase* against his will. In an attempt to put an end to the
oba/iyase polarization factor, once and for all, he not only
refused to confer the title but announced his decision to abolish
it. 'It is my prerogative to abolish any title; this prerogative is
inalienable', he asserted in the *Nigerian Spokesman*, 11 November 1947; and he went on to give reasons for his action. Every-
one believed, he said, that whoever was made *iyase* must
become the *oba*'s enemy. 'The accursed name of *iyase*, not the
character of the holder of the title, was the cause of the *iyase*
becoming the arch-enemy of the *oba*.' In the old days, he
continued, the *oba* could send a troublesome *iyase* to war –
from which he was not expected to return – but this was now
impossible. The *oba* went further. In place of *iyase* he proposed
to create a new title, with the same privileges and rank (but
without power or authority), which would be conferred automatically on whoever proved worthy enough to marry the
oba's eldest daughter. The new title was to be *obadeyanedo*,
which can be approximately translated: 'the *oba* overshadows
the Edo'.

It is widely conceded in Benin that the *oba* had always
enjoyed considerable freedom in awarding titles, creating new
titles, and even, within limits, in altering the order of precedence between them. Nevertheless, it appears to be the case
that all the *uzama* titles and the uppermost titles in each
eghaebho order have remained unchanged for centuries; and
that their inviolability was one of the cardinal rules of the
Benin political game. The widespread passionate reaction to
Akenzua's attempt to abolish the *iyase* title helps to confirm
this interpretation. Within the next few weeks he was subjected
from all sides to a barrage of attack and abuse. Some went so
far as to demand his deposition and rumour had it that his
immediately junior brother was preparing to replace him. Mass
demonstrations took place in Benin City. Petitions poured in
from organizations of expatriate Edo in virtually every major
Nigerian town. With a mass insurrection threatening, the
government no longer found it possible to give the *oba* its
support. Virtually isolated, and under pressure from chiefs and
administrative officers, Akenzua was forced to retreat. On 17
February 1948, he announced that, in order to comply with the
wishes of his chiefs, he had decided to confer the *iyase* title on

a man who at that time was *esogban*. The *esogban* was a very old
man, illiterate and nearly blind. He had been a warrant chief, a
member of the Judicial Council and Native Authority Treasurer.
Acceptable to many of the chiefs, he was hardly likely to appeal
to the modernists. Faced with a renewed outburst, the *oba* had
once more to retract and, under great pressure from the government, he eventually consented to give the title to the nominee
of the Taxpayers' Association.

The new *iyase* was the epitome of the new elite. A rich farmer
and timber-producer, he had for many years served as the
Resident's Clerk. His name was Gaius Obaseki and he was a
son of Agho, who had been made *iyase* thirty-four years before.
The new *iyase* was a man of great enterprise, charm, and ability,
and, like his father, he quickly gained the confidence of the
British administrators. With his appointment came a complete
reorganization of the Native Authority, which was henceforth
to be defined not as '*oba*-in-Council' but as '*oba* and Council'.
The *oba* was to be the President of the Divisional Council with
the *iyase* as Chairman. There were to be two other ex-officio
titled members, the *esogban* and *eson* (both *eghaebho n'ore*),
and seventeen other chiefs to be elected by the palace associations. A further sixteen chiefs, who had been members of the
old Council, were allowed to remain as ordinary members.
In addition there were to be sixty-four members elected to
represent wards of the capital and administrative areas of
Benin Division. The most significant new development, however, was the creation of a number of Committees (Administrative, Staff Discipline, Finance, Income Tax Appeals) to
oversee the Native Administration bureaucracy, members of
which were to be elected by the Council. Finally the *iyase* was
also to be Chairman of the Benin City Council.

It immediately became evident that, in practice, the Native
Authority was going to be not the *oba* and Council but the
iyase and Council. Immediate steps were taken to lower the
oba's dignity and curtail his prerogatives. The Council voted
to reduce his salary from £1,800 to £800 p.a. and passed a rule
forbidding him to confer any title without the Council's
consent. The *oba* was not a member of the crucial Administrative Committee and henceforth he was to have no control
over appointments to the courts or administrative services.

All the Committees were, in fact, dominated by the modernists. Some of these men brought great energy and ability into the running of the Native Administration and the administrative officers frequently expressed delight at their efficiency. The *oba* seemed almost as impotent as his father had been after the 1914 restoration. However, as events soon showed, the pendulum of power had swung too far for the new regime to maintain its legitimacy for very long.

Signs of a reaction began to appear as early as October 1948, with the formation of a new organization called the Reformed Benin Community, which the *oba* himself described as consisting of 'dynamic youths and progressive aristocrats'. At a meeting of this group he read out a letter from a youth, calling his attention to 'what is a great menace to the Binis, particularly the youths. This is Ogboniism which dominates the Council. Remember, this is not Yorubaland'. The *oba* agreed with the writer that the *ogboni* had no place in the Benin Constitution and could not be allowed (as he put it) to pollute the political system.

The *ogboni* referred to here is not the indigenous Yoruba earth cult of that name (Morton-Williams, 1961) but the Reformed Ogboni Fraternity of the Christians, which had had its origin about the time of the First World War among a group of prominent Yoruba Christians in Lagos and Abeokuta. It is probable that the R.O.F. was partly modelled on freemasonry (certainly Masonic signs are used in the paraphernalia of the Benin Lodge) and intended to perform a similar function, though it also incorporated features of the indigenous *ogboni* that were felt not to be inconsistent with Christianity. It shared with both the old *ogboni* cult and freemasonry a great stress on secrecy. An R.O.F. Lodge had existed in Benin at least since the early 1930s, recruiting most of its members from the educated and commercial elites, though some of the older chiefs were induced to join by their educated sons. Before 1948, however, it had never been considered to have any direct political significance. That it now began to be perceived as a menacing and sinister cabal was due to the fact that its head, the *oluwo*, was none other than the new *iyase*; while other members of the new ruling elite (including the *oba*'s two immediately junior brothers) were also office-holders in it.

243

In order to make the nature of this organization clear, it is worth summarizing several clauses from its printed constitution:

8. No political topics shall be discussed in the Lodge nor can the Lodge concern itself in politics.

9. All members or initiates shall regard themselves as 'children of one another' and shall act towards one another as such wherever they meet.

10. Members of the Fraternity are in duty bound to help one another in distress, to succour in adversity, warn against danger, and be charitable under all circumstances.

16. Implicit obedience is required by all members to the laws, regulations, obligations and orders given in Council by the *oluwo*.

23. Admission into membership shall be by payment of a fee and initiation. . . .

I have no means of knowing whether Clause 8, barring political discussion, was adhered to in the Benin Lodge before the reorganization of the Native Authority in 1948. However, the high degree of overlap between the *ogboni* elite and the new ruling clique made it inevitable that the R.O.F. should, from this point onwards, become an important, and more or less overt, factor in Benin politics. Given the control now exercised by prominent *ogboni* over the administrative bureaucracy, the other clauses which I have quoted clearly take on a political significance. Within a year of Gaius Obaseki's appointment as *iyase* and Chairman of the Councils, the Taxpayers' Association had become firmly identified among the general population as a front organization for the Ogboni Lodge, though some of the more active members of the Association were not, in fact, *ogboni*. The feeling grew, not only among the ordinary villagers, but also among the educated men in the capital and other towns, that they had been betrayed. Having joined the general outcry for an *iyase* to defend them against a palace clique, it now appeared that they had only succeeded in placing even greater power in the hands of a more dangerous oligarchy operating from the secrecy of the Ogboni Lodge. The R.O.F., which had gone unnoticed for many years, took on sinister and fearful implications. It was a secret cult, with mysterious initiation rites, and in the old days such cults had never been allowed to operate in Benin City. Moreover, it was an alien cult, associated with the Yoruba, and had no place in Benin culture.

By 1950 the great majority of the Benin people, both in the capital and the villages, believed themselves to be at the mercy of an oppressive oligarchy. It was widely believed that all Council members and most court judges, police, and native administration officials of all kinds – sanitary inspectors, forest guards, and the like – had all been initiated into the R.O.F., and were, therefore, able to use their positions to exploit and oppress without fear of retribution. Those who had refused to join, it was believed, had all been ousted from their posts. Some of the British administrative officers, too, were alleged to be *ogboni* (European membership was in fact not unknown). Whatever the exact degree of truth in these beliefs and allegations (I cannot go into the evidence here) it is possible to say that they were by no means entirely unfounded.

Up to about 1951 most administrative officers were unwilling to believe that the anti-*ogboni* outcry was in any way spontaneously generated. They preferred to see it as a deliberate plot by the *oba* and reactionary chiefs, and by disgruntled ex-employees of the native administration, to recover their positions. In the course of time they were forced to revise this view. Nevertheless, such motivations were bound to be present, and the impetus towards organized opposition to the Ogboni-T.P.A. group naturally came first from those most closely affected. Two distinct organizations emerged:

1. *Aruosa*
   This was an attempt by the *oba* to found a national church of Benin. Its doctrines and beliefs were drawn entirely from Benin religion – the *oba* himself wrote a creed, scriptures, and 'hymns' – but its forms of worship owed much to the example of Christian church services. *Aruosa* – which had been founded at the end of 1945 – was developed as a focus of Edo values in opposition to the alien *ogboni* cult. It gained some success, mainly among older people, and played a part in the mobilization of anti-*ogboni* sentiments.

2. *Otu-Edo*

This organization, which grew out of the Reformed Benin
Community had, in 1950, been transformed into something
like a modern political party. Its early meetings had been
convened and attended by a heterogeneous collection of
chiefs, priests of royal cults, and other traditionalists, and
of young ambitious men who were opposed to the ruling
clique for various reasons. Although the *Otu-Edo* expressed
their opposition to the *ogboni* in terms of their loyalty to
the *oba*, Akenzua himself circumspectly avoided overt
participation in their activities. The leadership of the
Otu-Edo was taken over by a former civil servant, H.
Omo-Osagio, who had spent many years in Lagos. He
had long been a close associate of the *oba*, who had
conferred two successive titles on him, and also appointed
him a priest of *aruosa*.

By 1951 the population of Benin Division was divided into
two clear-cut factions. All quarrels and disputes, all clashes of
interest, tended to be interpreted in terms of the opposition of
Otu-Edo and *ogboni*, *oba* and *iyase*. Families were divided.
European administrators were assigned by the Edo to one side
or the other, according to which way their sympathies lay, or
appeared to lie. Edo expatriate organizations also split into
factions, though the majority of Edo 'abroad' were now as
vociferous in their loyalty to the *oba* as they had been in
condemning him three years before; and at home many of those
who had vilified him three years before gave him their unstint-
ing praise. In the Benin villages war songs were sung and the
exploits of the great warrior *obas* of the past were recounted.
Purveyors of medicines purporting to give protection from
gunshot and matchet toured the villages and did a roaring
trade.

Into this highly charged situation we have to introduce a new
factor. Although there were already Benin members of Dr
Azikiwe's N.C.N.C. (National Council of Nigeria and the
Cameroons), the rapid growth of nationalist politics in post-war
Nigeria had had relatively little effect on Benin internal affairs
– except in so far as it helped to spread ideas about democracy
and party organization. In the summer of 1951, however, the

first elections were to be held to the Western Nigerian House of Assembly. In the Region as a whole, the contest lay between the N.C.N.C. and Awolowo's newly formed, Yoruba-based Action Group. The clear-cut division of Benin into two political camps, and the obvious numerical superiority of the anti-*ogboni* sympathizers, provided a rich opportunity for a few men who aspired to enter national politics. Although several of them already had affiliations with the nationalist parties, they directed their attentions to turning the *Otu-Edo* itself into a modern political party and the three men who were chosen as its candidates campaigned almost wholly on the local issues of destroying the power of the *ogboni* and restoring the *oba* to his rightful position.

Shortly before the regional elections, elections were held for a new Benin Divisional Council, and, in these, *Otuo-Edo* candidates were universally successful. The end of *ogboni* domination unleashed a wave of violence throughout Benin Division. By this time there were a few *ogboni*s in most villages. Many of these were now driven out and some of their homes burnt down. The *iyase*'s compound in Benin City became a temporary refuge camp for fleeing *ogboni*s. In a few places there were serious riots and the Resident was obliged to call on the *oba*'s assistance to restore order. The Divisional Council and its powerful Committees passed entirely into *Otu-Edo* hands and immediate steps were taken to restore the *oba*'s dignity, by raising his salary and reaffirming his prerogative of conferring titles. The *iyase*'s downfall was as abrupt as that of his father, thirty-one years before. Though still ex-officio Chairman he was no longer to be seen at Council meetings.

The introduction of direct suffrage and regional self-government and the development of named political parties, were to have far-reaching effects on the pattern of political conflict at Benin, and this is therefore a convenient point at which to draw a halt. It is worth noting, however, that this latest confrontation between *oba* and *iyase* was to have implications for Western Regional and National politics in the 1950s. In the course of the 1951 local and regional campaigns at Benin, the *Otu-Edo* had become associated with the N.C.N.C. and the Taxpayers' Association/*ogboni* with the Action Group. Its association, in the minds of Edo electors, with the *ogboni* helped to put the

Action Group at a permanent disadvantage in Benin. This, indeed, was one of the reasons why Omo-Osagie, who proved himself a brilliant political campaigner, was able to deliver the *Otu-Edo* majority vote to the N.C.N.C. with predictable. regularity.

CONCLUSIONS

The outstanding landmarks of Benin political history in the period with which we have been concerned are the periodic 'reorganizations' – i.e. the redistributions and redefinitions of the competences allocated by their colonial rulers to members of the Benin political class; and the confrontations between ruling cliques and opposition coalitions that alternate with them. Reorganizations are motivated (*a*) by the government's searching for more effective administrative machinery for the implementation of its policies and (*b*) by the necessity of containing internal political conflict and of coming to terms with demands on the government which can no longer be safely ignored. A proper treatment of the first set of motivations would have involved us in the task of relating the government's actions at Benin to its general policies for southern Nigeria as a whole – a task which the present writer is not qualified to undertake. In so far as we had assumed rather than analysed British objectives, the interpretation of Benin political history offered in this paper is necessarily incomplete and distorted. However, the aim was not to write a comprehensive political history but only to throw some light on the way in which political concepts, norms, and habits evolved in the traditional polity come through into the colonial period and, by interacting with new objectives, opportunities, and administrative structures, help to shape the course of political change.

The continuities to which I have sought to draw attention reside not in the formal framework of government, which was subject to a sequence of disjunctive, non-repetitive changes, but in the style and structure of political competition and conflict. I refer not merely to the enduring appetite of the Benin political class for factional intrigue but, more specifically, to the persisting relevance, in a changing environment, of a model of political conflict which is expressed in terms of such binary oppositions as: *oba/iyase*, *oba/edo*, Palace/anti-Palace, capital/villages, territorial chiefs/palace emissaries, and 'old guard'/'new men'.

In analysing the political events of the immediate post-restoration period (p. 229 above) I drew attention to the co-existence of contradictory organizational models in terms of which various sectors of the political class formulated their divergent interests and objectives. The administrative structure arrived at in 1920 (which appears to have afforded a reasonably viable balance between palace and anti-palace groups) was followed by the imposed 'centralized bureaucratic' model of the mid-1930s and the 'representational' model formulated by the modernists and essentially given approval by the government. These, in their turn, served as the basis for the crystalliza-tion of new interest groups. My purpose here is to point out that the tactics used to forge alliances between divergent interest groups, and to amass support for demands made upon the government and upon the ruling clique who were its agents, draw to a considerable degree upon the pre-colonial conscious model of political conflict. By espousing the traditionalist causes of the *ezomo* and the *iyase* as well as defend-ing the interests of the population of the capital (in regard to the permanent crops and water-rate ordinances) the modernists mobilized the support of both the former District Heads and the general population for their assault on the combined power of the government and the palace oligarchy. In their second major campaign after the war they again rallied widespread support by demanding that the *oba* fulfil his obligation to appoint an *iyase*.

In these and other examples, the enduring potency of the implicit rules of the pre-colonial political game as rallying points for concerted political action is manifest. By presenting the *oba*'s alleged disregard for the *ezomo*'s prerogatives, his failure to appoint an *iyase* and his attempt to abolish the *iyase* title as transgressions of immutable rules, the anti-traditionalists were enabled to advance their own interests and thus to push for-ward the process of political development. Similarly, the attack of the ruling *ogboni* clique on the king's prerogatives and its own lack of, and contempt for, traditional legitimacy were the main targets of the successful campaign of the *Otu-Edo* in 1951, which, on the one hand, restored the *oba*'s authority and, on the other hand, launched its leaders' careers in national politics.

Finally, I draw attention to the structure of the political process that unfolds between one reorganization and the next. With the possible exception of that of 1920, each major reorganization generates a powerful ruling clique and a scatter of divergent interest groups. While the particular nature of the interests involved varies from one cycle to the next, these groups can regularly be categorized as 'dispossessed' (former paramount chiefs, former District Heads, former N.A. employees), 'deprived' (titled chiefs who have failed to secure competences, unrepresented commercial and educated elites), and 'exploited' (the 'ordinary' people of Benin City and the villages). Groups of the first two categories are similarly motivated by their desire for competences and employment but may be divided in their espousal of different organizational models. Sooner or later, however, they unite and secure the support of the exploited groups in terms of shared opposition to specific administrative measures (especially fiscal innovations and increased taxes) introduced by the government and implemented by the ruling elite. This opposition, we have suggested, gains effectiveness in so far as it is capable of being expressed in terms of traditional norms of conflict. The noisy confrontation that ensues between the opposition coalition and the government-backed ruling clique is resolved when the government is forced to adopt a more neutral stance from which it can negotiate and regulate a fresh distribution of competences. At this point the cycle recommences.

If this 'unconscious model' of a competitive process is accepted as valid, the question must be asked: What are its historical limits? Certainly one might expect to have to discard it for the period after 1951 when the political struggle lay between named, enduring local parties affiliated to nationalist parties contesting for power at the regional and federal levels. But the problem I find more absorbing is whether a study of the processes leading to confrontation crises during the colonial period can help us to ask the right questions about the precolonial confrontations to which the Edo themselves conceptually assimilated them. Further consideration of this problem must await another opportunity.

NOTES

1. I use the term 'political class', following Bottomore (1964, p. 8) 'to refer to all those groups which exercise political power or influence, and are directly engaged in struggles for political leadership'. 'Political elite' refers in this paper to those who actually hold offices and especially, so far as the traditional polity is concerned, to titled chiefs.

2. Much of the material relating to the colonial period was obtained from the Benin Provincial and Divisional Offices in the early 1950s. At that time I did not envisage writing a historical narrative and my ignorance of historiographic techniques was even greater than it is now. Consequently my notes are very inconsistent in respect of the identification of sources. Where possible I quote file numbers or indicate the nature of the source document in the notes below.

3. P.2/97. C. & C.C. to Res. Benin 25-3-97.

4. This brief account of the political conflicts of Ovonramwen's reign and of Agho's role in them is constructed from oral testimony, and in particular that of the late Chief Eghobamien, who was Agho's paternal nephew and a young servant to Idugbowa both at Uselu and, after his accession, in the palace.

5. P.15a/99.

6. In 1914 Resident James Watt described him as 'by far the ablest native chief whom I have ever met'. BP. 16/14, 5-10-14.

7. P.7/99, 7-3-99.

8. P.24/99.

9. P.1/97, Moor to Res. & officers, Benin, 14-3-97.

10. BP. 16/14.

11. CC.2884/12; BP. 1/1914; BP. 842/14; Rpt. by E. D. Simpson, D.C. 25-3-13.

12. On several occasions Aiguobasimwin had been rumoured to be plotting for the return of Ovonramwen, especially in 1906 when fears of widespread insurrection led to troops being brought in. On the other hand, both Aiguobasimwin and his brother Osuanlele were accorded chiefly status and competences during the interregnum.

13. See Talbot's brief survey of Benin political history under British rule dated 7-9-20.

14. Ibid.

15. BP. 16/14, 8-7-14; and other papers dated 1916.

16. BP. 679, August 1914.

17. BP. 16/14, Edaiken to Governor's Deputy, 19-7-14.

18. Watt to S.S.P., 22-7-15.

19. Watt to S.S.P., 10-12-15.

20. *Oba* to Res., 28-11-18.

21. BP. 13/1918.

22. R. 1/18(c), Res. to Lt. Gv., 17-8-18.

23. Ibid. *Oba* to Res., 24-11-18.

24. Ibid.

25. Ibid. Res. to S.S.P., 11-10-18.

26. In his Annual Report for 1919 the Resident referred to the *iyase* as the only District Head who required no supervision.
27. BP. 462/20, 28-7-20.
28. Ibid., 12-8-20.
29. BP. 462/20, D.O. to Res.
30. Talbot to S.S.P., 6-9-20.
31. *Nigerian Daily Times*, 15-4-33.
32. BP. 1103, 15-8-35.
33. BP. 1472, 12-2-38.

REFERENCES

BOSMAN, WILLIAM. 1967. *Description of Guinea*. London: Cass.

BOTTOMORE, T. B. 1964. *Elites and Society*. London: Watts.

BRADBURY, R. E. 1957. *The Benin Kingdom. . . .* London: International African Institute.

—— 1967. The Kingdom of Benin. In D. Forde and P. Kaberry (eds.), *West African Kingdoms in the Nineteenth Century*. London: O.U.P. for International African Institute.

BURNS, A. C. 1929. *History of Nigeria*. London.

EGHAREVBA, J. U. 1960. *A Short History of Benin*. Ibadan: Ibadan University Press.

—— 1947. *Concise Lives of the Famous Iyases of Benin*. Lagos: Temi-Asunwon Press.

LAWAL-OSULA, U. M. (ed.). 1949. Benin Native Authority: New Constitution 1948.

LÉVI-STRAUSS, C. 1962. *La Pensée sauvage*. Paris: Plon.

—— 1963. *Structural Anthropology*. New York: Basic Books.

LING-ROTH, H. 1903. *Great Benin, Customs, Art and Horrors*. Halifax: F. King & Sons.

MACRAE-SIMPSON, J. 1936. Intelligence Report on Benin Division. Unpub.

MARSHALL, H. F. 1939. Intelligence Report on Benin City. Unpub.

MORTON-WILLIAMS, P. 1960. The Yoruba Ogboni Cult in Oyo. *Africa* **30** (4): 362-374.

SMITH, M. G. 1960. *Government in Zazzau*. London: O.U.P. for International African Institute.

UWAIFO, H. O. 1959. *Benin Community Intelligence Report on Benin Division*. Oshogbo: F. M. S. Press.

Ian Whitaker

Tribal Structure and National Politics in Albania, 1910-1950

This study is not based primarily upon field research. It attempts to make social anthropological sense of the very extensive and uneven travel and historical literature on Albania, to distil from this formidable corpus a picture of the traditional social structure of the country, and to apply this as an analytical tool to understanding, at least in broad outline, the main political developments in Albania between 1910 and 1950. This type of analysis cannot, of course, compare with the rich harvest of elucidation garnered by first-hand field research. But since recent political changes in Albania have effaced or drastically altered the traditional structure of society, field research is likely to be of little help, and the choice is between the kind of anthropological history offered here and nothing.

The first part of the paper discusses the traditional social structure of the Ghegs, the more northerly of the two ethnic groups which make up present-day Albania. The second gives a much shorter résumé of the contrasting social conditions of the other main group, the Tosks, who occupy the south. These attempts to disentangle the main lines of traditional Albanian society are then applied in a brief analysis of recent political history up to 1950. Finally, in a short appendix, I make some comments on the sources that have been utilized.

THE TRADITIONAL SOCIETY OF THE GHEGS

'I am an old man, and I have seen that when men go down to the cities to learn what is in books they come back scorning the wisdom of their fathers and remembering nothing of it, and they speak foolishly, words which do not agree with one another. But the things that a man knows because he has seen them, the things he considers while he walks on the trails and while he sits by the fires, these things are not many, but they are sound. Then

253

when a man is lonely he puts words to these things and the words
become a song, and the song stays as it was said, in the memories
of those that hear it.'

'Gheg clansman from Thethis to Rose Wilder Lane, 1921'

The Ghegs of northern Albania present the only true example
of a tribal system surviving in Europe until the mid-twentieth
century. In these remote valleys with very inadequate communications has survived a group of people whose whole life
was organized in terms of kinship and descent. The clan, *fis*,
was a group of people all of whom claimed descent from a
common male ancestor, who may often have been fictitious.
The genealogies of individual persons would be carefully remembered, showing a link by male descent with the founder of
the clan, who might have lived thirteen or fourteen generations
earlier (Durham, 1931, p. 155). The clan of Berisha claimed the
longest genealogy, stretching back to 1370 and perhaps 1270,
according to the calculations of Baron Nopcsa (1912, p. 248),
but such putative pedigrees need not be accepted as true.
Indeed the account of the founding of the three allied clans of
Mirditë, Shalë, and Shoshi would confirm such a suggestion.
The common ancestor of these three clans, it is alleged, died a
poor man, leaving three sons. The first took the saddle (*shalë*),
the second the sieve (*shoshi*), while the third left empty-handed,
saying as he went 'Good-day' (*mirë-dita*) (Durham, 1928, p. 25).
The social importance of this origin-myth lies in its providing a
rationale for the alliance of the three clans, and it is interesting
to note that at one time they did not normally intermarry. As
Milovan Djilas (1958, p. 5), discussing the clan myths of
neighbouring Montenegro, has written:

'Every such fabrication is based on some truth, on facts so
reasonable and easily comprehended that even their fabricator
comes to believe in them.'

Ideally the clan was an exogamous unit. Frequently two clans
would exchange brides over several generations, as was the
case with Hoti and Kastrati, and with Vukle and Selca. In
this way an alliance was perpetuated, and the resulting consanguinity was not recognized socially since the connexion was
through women, and, as the Albanians put it: 'A man has blood,
and a woman kin' (Hasluck, 1954, p. 25).[1] In the case of one of

the largest clans, Mirditë, the subgroups (*bajraks*) formed two intermarrying divisions, men of Orosh, Speç, and Kushnen marrying Fan and Dibrri women, as well as women of the Christian *bajraks* of Selita and Kthellë in Mati, and the women of Lurë, before a blood-feud prevented these alliances (Coon, 1950, p. 28).

In practice, the rule of exogamy has been steadily breaking down, and unions within related groups have become permitted. Marriages between people of Shalë and Shoshi, for instance, were rationalized on the ground that the division of the clans took place a hundred generations ago, and in the less warlike Muslim areas a link more distant than seven generations was usually not regarded as a barrier to marriage. This trend away from clan exogamy is documented by the series of Ghegs measured by the physical anthropologist Carleton Coon (1950, p. 11) who found in 1929-1930 that, of 1,102 persons examined, 1,058 (96 per cent) had parents from the same clan, 11 (1 per cent) were the progeny of inter-clan marriages, while the remainder were children of at least one non-Albanian Gheg, or of a non-Gheg. At the same time as the rules concerning inter-clan marriage were being relaxed, however, the Catholic priests in Northern Albania seem to have been attempting to secure a recognition of the canonical laws relating to consanguinity, which would preclude a marriage between persons related in the female line, unless a dispensation was procured.[2]

Professor Coon asserted that the exogamous system was considered by the Ghegs to be superior, since, by bringing in wives from a distance, local rivalry for the same girl would be precluded, and the clan would moreover have fewer contacts with the girl's family to give rise to tensions. This would only be the case if brides were selected from outside groups at random, which, we have seen, was not the case. It is, however, true that the greater the distance from which a bride was obtained, the smaller the chance of frequent contacts between the husband and his in-laws. Such an institutionalized avoidance seems to have been common in Northern Albania, and it is significant that in those few villages of Mirditë where people from several clans lived together, there was a rule of village-exogamy, preventing a man from having close relatives of his bride within easy distance of his own home.

The household

The household (*shpi*) formed the basic unit of Gheg society. As elsewhere, this was based on a marital link, but unlike the practice in much of European society, the descendants of a couple would continue to live under a man's parental roof, and in this way extended families, often consisting of several brothers and their descendants, would form a single residential and economic unit. This system was of course common to much of the Balkans – the South Slav term *zadruga* being generally used in the sociological literature to denote this type of organization. The need for mutual defence in this politically disturbed region is often adduced as one of the main factors for the survival of this large familistic unit. The common ownership of the means of production was also an additional factor of importance. Family honour is, however, a basic value in Albanian society, and any explanation of the extended family among the Ghegs must take account of this cosmo-philosophical element. So fundamental was the unity of the household that when, in the famine following the Balkan Wars, the Albanians were the recipients of relief, they expected each family to get equal shares, regardless of the number of members (Durham, 1914, p. 101).

The household might extend to include scores of people all living within the same building complex. Mrs Hasluck (1954, pp. 29-30) records one in Zdrajshë which contained 95 persons in 1923, and another in Shalë with 70 inhabitants 'even more recently'. In Mati in 1944 a local chief, Çen Lezi, had sixty people living within his household. Such a household would be ruled by an elected 'master of the household' (*zot i shpís*).

This household head was chosen from the older adults, although in some cases he might have been nominated when somewhat younger by his predecessor. Primogeniture was taken into account when making this appointment, but a knowledge of the law, as well as general administrative ability, counted for more. His duties included ascertaining that the fields were tilled and the flocks cared for, allocating different people to different tasks. A semi-permanent division of labour, according to individual skills, would be evolved in the interests of efficiency, and this gave rise to minor technical specialization. The master of the household also had control of the family exchequer. He had the sole right to buy and sell land in the name of the family, but he did not receive more than other persons if the family group broke up and its property was distributed among its members. In this field of husbandry there were only two limitations to his power: the shepherd had the final say as to which sheep were to be disposed of, and the ploughman had the right to lend, and even to sell, the teams of plough-oxen.

The master of the household usually went to market himself to trade on behalf of the group, and it was his responsibility to see that all the members of the household were properly dressed and fed, and that the family had proper provisions with which to entertain guests. He paid the taxes, and purchased a rifle for every youth in the family who was of military age. This rifle was the only piece of personal property owned by the average Gheg male, which he might sell or pledge as he chose. A woman, however, always received a small personal gift of money (*pekul*) when she left her family to marry, and this remained hers, to be disposed of as she wished, and not to be alienated by the family into which she married. The only material reward the master of the household received was finer clothes and a horse, with which to maintain family honour in contacts with outsiders. Yet he was personally responsible for outside damage done by members of his household, and had himself to find compensation in the event of a lawsuit. He was, however, shown great personal respect, nobody speaking to him first or addressing others in his presence without his permission. He had the right to beat culprits within the family, or to starve them into submission. When his physical powers declined he might nominate a deputy, who would represent the family at market, and who might gradually assume the full duties of the master.

Within the marital family – a man and his wife and children – the husband had the power to chastise his wife, but he could not direct her work: this was the privilege and responsibility of the mistress of the household. She was the feminine counterpart of the master – the housekeeper. She was appointed by the master and her task was the domestic running of the household: she never worked in the fields like other women. She was not necessarily the master's wife – in fact the turnover of holders of this position was much swifter. She was never under forty years of age on appointment, since the younger women were needed for work in the fields, and at about fifty her duties became too onerous, and she would be superseded. She had to be impartial, never favouring her own children.

The 'brotherhood' and the village

In a wider social context the 'brotherhood' (*vëllezëri*; occasionally *mëhallë*, more correctly a neighbourhood) featured as an important cooperating unit. This comprised a group of households which had common descent and which might have developed from a single unit. The common descent and close residence ties of its members promoted a stronger degree of solidarity than was characteristic of the clan. Where a household split up, the original master retained authority not only over his own household, but also over that which hived off from it. He became the elder (*plak*) of the 'brotherhood' and his descendants would retain this paramountcy.[3] In many villages the total male population constituted a single brotherhood; but where several such kin groups resided together in one village, the head of the strongest usually acted as village headman (*kryeplak*), although heads of other brotherhoods might act as junior headmen. Among the headmen of several villages within a region, one was usually chosen as a chief elder for that area. This was less a hereditary position than one to which a person was appointed on a basis of personal qualities and the nature of his family. The elder had no special financial privileges, living in the same style as other men of his village, and he was not given any enhanced valuation in the blood-feud. Only in legal disputes, when an oath was sworn, was the elder given greater status, ranking as twelve ordinary jurors.

The village elder was expected to show the same paternal interest in his village that the master of a household showed in his home. He would represent the villagers in issues before the authorities, and he would represent them at larger assemblies where it would be impossible for every clansman to attend. In the case of a dispute between members of the same brotherhood, the brotherhood elder would act as arbiter; where members of different brotherhoods were in disagreement, the respective elders would consult together.

The clan and bajrak

Next above the elder, with a larger if specialized field of authority, stood the *bajraktar*, the military leader of the clan. The title is taken from the Turkish word *bajrak*, a standard; and indeed in each case the office derived ultimately from a person who had received an original standard for valour in battle. Some such *bajraktars'* offices date back to acts of gallantry performed as many as 400 years ago. Some clans had as many as five *bajraktars*, the senior in original appointment taking precedence.

The office of *bajraktar* was inherited in the male line, but a man might choose which son should succeed him, according to merit. An elder brother who was passed over would, however, lose the right of succession for his descendants, except in most exceptional circumstances. There was a sort of regency when the nominal *bajraktar* was still a minor. The *bajraktar's* functions were primarily military; he would warn his tribesmen of impending war, but he would also negotiate with the central authorities in time of peace.

He would be assisted in administration by the local headmen we have described, but he would often find himself being called upon to judge some civil issue. In oath-taking, a *bajraktar* counted as twelve men, and peace made in his presence was particularly binding. The *bajraktar's* office was not above the law itself, as a case among the Kryeziu clan in 1908 demonstrates. On that occasion a *bajraktar* and several headmen were fined a total of 100 rams and an ox by a plenary session of the clan composed of one man from each house, for having given prejudiced judgements. The only sanction, however, against a *bajraktar* taking bribes was a supernatural one. But his personal gain as a judge was generally not great; usually a meal and a fee (perhaps a sheep). *Bajraktars* in fact were not so much judges as arbitrators: their authority did not extend to imposing fines on individual clansmen. Such penalties had to be imposed by an assembly. When called upon to act in a civil case the *bajraktar* would name his fee and select a pledge – either money or an object – which would serve as a guarantee both of payment of the fee and of submission to the judgement. In minor issues an elder might be called upon to act as judge, and he would usually be from the litigants' own village. He might ask them to guarantee in advance to accept his judgement, and if in the event this was not done, the case would be referred to a village assembly, which might in addition fine the offender for breach of this contract. Where a particular elder's judgement was not accepted, however, there were devices for submitting the issue to reconciliation by another elder, to a maximum of three such hearings. The judge had a definite interest in seeing litigation concluded since his fee was fixed, and did not increase in relation to the time spent on the case.

In time of war the *bajraktar* received double or triple pay from the Turks. The *bajraktar*'s office derived its main authority from antiquity, and where there were several *bajraks* within one clan some rivalry was inevitable. Conflicts might also arise between a *bajraktar* and the heads of prominent, and genealogically senior, lineages of the same clan. One such case is recorded from Lurë, where there were two rival leaders to the Muslim *bajraktar*, Hakik Aliu Meta. In this religiously mixed clan considerable opposition to the *bajraktar* was offered by the Catholic Zef Doçi of Lurë e Vjetër and by the Muslim Ibrahim Gjoçi of Kreje. This strife persisted from the 1920s for some twenty years, the size of the respective retinues varying considerably (from 300 in 1926 to 32 in 1935 in the case of Gjoçi, and 4 in 1926 to 400 in 1935 in the case of the *bajraktar*). Factionalism of this sort was encouraged by the central political authority, which took advantage of the situation by rewarding pliant men with appointments as army officers on half-pay, or with scholarships. Displeasure would be signified by rewarding members of the rival faction. Difficulties would be most easily avoided where there was one *bajraktar* to the clan, but this was not always the case. We have seen the Mirditë had five, divided between two exogamous sections, while the *bajrak* of Pukë actually had members of seven different clans (*fis*) all owing allegiance to the one *bajraktar* (Coon, 1950, p. 50).

With the exception of Lumë the *bajraktars* represented predominantly Catholic clans, or clans which had been Catholic. In the non-tribal areas of Central Albania, such as Shpet and Martanesh, the *bajraktar*'s office was handed from family to family. In this connexion we must also consider the clan assembly (*kuvënd*), which was convened at his order, and over which he presided. The assembly, which afforded one of the few occasions for the clan to act as a unit, comprised all its elders.[4] It might be summoned by the *bajraktar* to discuss urgent matters of public importance, and it could have considerable executive and judicial power, as when in February 1912 the men of Miriditë met in *kuvënd* and condemned to death all the males of the Fan *bajrak*, notorious for their evil-doing. In all, 17 persons from five years old upwards, were shot by their fellow tribesmen as a result of this decision (Durham, 1928, p. 75).

The earliest recorded *kuvënd* was in the fifteenth century, when Lekë Dukagjini, who codified the traditional law, is said to have debated legal points with Skënderbeg (the great culture hero of the Albanians) himself at a *kuvënd* of the men of Northern Albania. Usually the clan was brought together on the basis of one man from each household. The assembly would be presided over by the person calling the *kuvënd*. It might decide on joint action, as when in 1855 and 1862 Mirditë attacked the Montenegrins after an assembly had approved the action. Clan *kuvënds* were called in 1908 to decide whether to accept the Young Turk constitution. Again in 1942 a *kuvënd* of all Mati was convened by the sub-prefect of that area in the (vain) hope of enforcing obedience to the Italian-controlled government of that time (Hasluck, 1954, p. 154).

The decision of the *kuvënd* would be binding, and a continuing dissenter would have no course of action other than to go into voluntary exile. It seems, however, that the authority of the assembly might vary and at the beginning of the twentieth century we have a tantalizing glimpse of a situation where it appears to have been flouted:

'In certain districts, notably Shala and Shoshi, an active radical party has sprung up lately called *Dielmnii* (youth), which has elected its own head and refused to recognize the hereditary right in council of the Bariaktar' (Durham, 1910, p. 464).

Unfortunately we are told no more.

Sometimes adjacent clans met together to resolve common problems, and at other times a new point of law, not apparently included in the traditional Canon, would be debated.[5] Certain crimes against society were also judged at a *kuvënd*: these included sacrilege, breach of the law of hospitality or of a truce (*besë*). Attendance was compulsory, absence being punished by a fine. When several clans were represented, that of Hoti always took precedence, apparently by ancient right.[6]

Small-scale assemblies to discuss the affairs of a unit smaller than the clan were also convened, generally twice a year. These might be at the level of a brotherhood, and would be presided over by the appropriate elder. These assemblies were, however, more concerned with purely domestic questions, such as wood-cutting or irrigation rights, or the use of common grazing, rather than wider political or clan issues.[7]

Where there was no *bajraktar*, authority and the right to call and preside over a *kuvënd* were vested in an hereditary chief. The Mati provide one of the classic examples of such a system, power being mainly held in the hands of the Zogolli family. Here factions, not *bajraks*, were the units, and authority was concentrated in the hands of four feudal lords (*beys*). Mati is, however, perhaps best described as a clan confederacy (*farë*), rather than as a single unit, since several different descent groups amalgamated for action. It was from this particular confederacy with its continual intrigues that the figure of King Zog emerged. His early acquaintance with such factionalism was to stand him in good stead in his later political life. Steinmetz (1905, p. 39) reports that the Nikaj clan had four hereditary chiefs whom he called *kren* (i.e. *krerë*?), who sat in council with the *bajraktar*.

The most famous confederacy of all, and one with greater stability, was that of Mirditë, ruled by the Gjomarkaj family who were styled Hereditary Captains (*Kapedan*) of Mirditë.[8] The head of this family was accepted as the source of all knowledge of the traditional Canon, and was the ultimate Court of Appeal. Indeed the authority of the Gjomarkaj family is carefully enshrined in the Canon itself: clause 1126 in Father Gjeçov's codification reads:

'The base of the Canon is the House of Gjomarkaj.'

(Gjeçov, 1941, p. 261)

In the vagaries of fortune that reduced the power of the Captains of Mirditë,[9] the Bishop acted as a final arbiter, not on account of his knowledge of the law, but because of his recognized probity.

The chief would therefore draw unattached *bajraks* or small clans into his confederacy,[10] and as leader enjoyed influence rather than authority. The solidarity of the group would depend upon the skill with which he could manipulate the situation, and upon the degree to which he could call upon some personal acknowledgement of power. When, as occurred upon occasion in this politically unsettled country, an unworthy or weak chief ruled, it was possible to depose him, or at least to expedite his abdication. Thus Zog's elder half-brother was deposed from the chieftainship of Mati after seven years' rule, on suspicion of dealing with the Serbs, and he was replaced by his brother, then a mere youth. One of the young chiefs of Dibër, who wasted the family substance in Italy, was encouraged to resign his responsibilities to a younger brother, which he did (Robinson, 1941, p. 51; Amery, 1948, p. 132). When the chief was too young, or in exile, a sort of regency might be established. Thus when the later King Zog succeeded to the Mati chieftainship, his mother, the future Queen Mother Sadijé, governed in his absence (Lane, 1923, p. 306; Redlich, 1936, p. 98). This was clearly very exceptional, however, for women were not normally permitted such authority. When the chief of the Kaloshi clan was in exile with Zog some decades later, the chief's authority and duties were divided between his son and his half-brother (Amery, 1948, p. 135). We do not hear how effective this was.

We see, therefore, that the power even of the chief was subject to some supervision and control by his clansmen, and there is some truth in Villari's (1940, p. 17) description of the Albanian clan as a sort of 'small aristocratic republic'. As the founder of Albania as an independent state, the Tosk landowner Ismail Qemal bey Vlora, declares (1917, p. 143), the clan was certainly not a feudal unit:

'. . . feudalism is incompatible with that sense of personal honour and independence which is characteristic of the Albanian, and which is carried to such lengths that the humblest consider themselves the equals, man for man, of the highest'.

The Canon of customary law

We must at this point mention the Canon of Lekë Dukagjini, the traditional body of law by which Gheg society was regulated.

This is a series of injunctions, which were for several generations passed down by word of mouth. They were reputedly originally formulated by one Aleksandër Dukagjini, probably the third of that name, who died in 1479[11]; he is said to have been excommunicated by Pope Paul II in 1464 for his most unchristian code. But probably all that he did was to codify and add to the existing customary law, as well as to enforce it more rigidly. Almost five centuries later Father Shtjefën Gjeçov (1874-1929) travelled through Northern Albania, and made his superb collation of the existing versions, most of which were conserved orally.[12] Variations in the law were at this time very few, largely because in the nineteenth century a mixed court of chiefs and government officials (*Djibali*, or *Fibal*) sat in Shkodër to consider amendments to the Canon (Skendi, 1953, p. 231). This may be considered to have been a sort of supreme *kuvënd*, and was probably recognized by the tribesmen in spite of its alien characteristics, at a time when the authority of the Captains of Mirditë was in temporary eclipse. It was the Canon (*kanún*) of Lekë Dukagjini which, over the centuries, gave continuity to Albanian custom, and the codified version that has come down to us deserves to be ranked among the great legal documents of the world for its clarity and logic.

Throughout this period, the mechanism by which order was enforced was the blood-feud (*gjakmarje*). Inseparably connected with this was the high value placed by the Ghegs upon family and lineage honour. Honour is the principal value of traditional Northern Albanian society: something prized above personal liberty, or even life itself. As the Albanian writer Christo Dako (1919, p. 33) puts it:

'What profit is life to a man if his honor be not clean? To cleanse his honor no price is too great. Blood can be wiped out only with blood.'

The feeling of the people of this part of the Balkan peninsula for the name and honour of their families and kin groups has been well expressed by the Montenegrin Milovan Djilas (1958, p. 106):

'The word "blood" meant something different in the language I learned in childhood from what it means today, especially the blood of one's clan and tribe. It meant the life we lived, a life that flowed together from generations of forebears who still lived in the tales handed down. Their blood coursed in all the members of the clan, and in us too. Now someone had spilled that eternal blood, and it had to be avenged if we wished to escape the curse of all those in whom the blood once flowed, if we wished to keep them from drowning in shame before the other clans. Such a yearning has no limits in space, no end in time.'

Analysis of the traditional Albanian epic songs (*këngë trimnijë*), shows significantly that the majority deal with blood-feuds provoked by offended family honour (Skendi, 1954, pp. 85, 87). These songs are of great sociological importance, since they reveal the Canon of Lekë Dukagjini in operation: for the people themselves, of course, they served as a powerful weapon of propaganda. Thus it was that family honour and prestige helped to perpetuate the blood-feud.[13] The Ghegs were always ready to defend their honour, and in its defence to shoot at the slightest provocation. 'When an Albanian has not got himself in hand, he has a revolver in it', as Ndoc Gjeloshi, one of the group who attempted to assassinate King Zog in Vienna in 1931, succinctly put it (Swire, 1937, p. 219).

The blood-feud and social control
The mechanism of social control by which family honour was maintained was the blood-feud. The slightest reflection on a man's family, either on his kinsmen or his ancestors, was an offence against honour, for which the one really satisfactory revenge was murder. Descriptions of Albania are full of accounts of the taking of people's lives for what often appear at first sight as trivial reasons. Such deaths invariably gave rise to a blood-feud between two clans that might go on for decades, a life being exacted first on one side, then on the other. The immediate cause of such a train of killings may seem trifling. Frequently, however, not only honour but property rights and subsistence were ultimately involved; and any affront to honour, no matter how petty, would be evaluated in terms of the state of the relations between the parties concerned. In one recorded instance, a fight between dogs belonging to shepherds from two different clans, the Onuzi and the Doçi, who had met

265

at the common boundary of their pastures, led to the death of one dog spitefully killed by one of the shepherds of the other side, and to the death within a few minutes of eighteen of the bystanders, a situation that gave rise to a blood-feud that raged for years until it was at last settled by the express intervention of the Sultan (Hasluck, 1954, p. 78). Hecquard mentions (1858, pp. 85-89) another feud that started in 1853 over pasture rights between two villages near Podgorica, the modern Titograd, an Albanian region now incorporated in Yugoslavia.

Another blood-feud arose over a boundary dispute between the Gashi and Krasniqi tribes: 124 men lost their lives in two days over this issue (Hasluck, 1954, p. 102). One of the better-documented blood-feuds was witnessed by Mrs Rose Wilder Lane (1923, pp. 9, 11, 30-31), the American traveller, in the spring of 1921 during her visit to Shalë. She found Shalë and Shoshi in feud with each other over the abduction of a married woman. One final instance of a feud which I wish to quote concerned a case in Shëngjen, where a man was engaged in a bitter quarrel with the family of his sister's former husband after she had been repudiated by her husband (Peacock, 1914, pp. 134-137). An action of this sort provided the most public challenge to an individual's family honour. As Julian Amery, whose profound knowledge of the Albanians was gained through his participation in guerilla warfare there, observed (1948, p. 8):

> 'Under anarchy, however, as in international relations, the importance of a crime lies less in its intrinsic character than in the challenge which it represents to the victim's prestige. All crimes, therefore, be they murder, rape, theft, or merely insult, are of equal weight. Prestige, however, can only suffer from a public slight; and it was said among the Albanians that though a rough word in company would often lead to a feud of years, a blow unseen by third parties might well be forgotten.'

There were, moreover, supernatural sanctions spurring a man on to seek revenge:

> 'The blood feud was a central fact in the life of the people – not merely vengeance, but an offering to the soul of a dead man' (Durham, 1928, p. 162).

And again (*ibid.*, p. 170):

> 'Nothing is too bad for a man who fails to set at rest the soul of his kinsman.'

When a violent death occurred, the natural avenger was the dead man's brother. Such revenge might be effected at a meeting deliberately sought, or in ambush. Occasionally a group of friends or servants might accompany the avenger on his mission of revenge, but any death caused by these persons would be 'credited' to the man who had asked them to accompany him. The main rule of the feud, however, was that women should not be involved, and hence no woman could take part, or be deliberately killed. The only possible exception to this was when, if all a woman's brothers had been killed in a feud, she might, if she had no husband, take their place. Then by swearing perpetual virginity, and by assuming man's clothing, she could be treated socially as a man, and kill and be killed.[14] Only in Malësia e Madhe, however, could such a sworn virgin (*virgjëréshë*) inherit from the last of her brothers – elsewhere everything went to the nearest male heir.

The rules of the blood-feud were carefully regulated by customary law. This provided that nobody might kill surreptitiously without leaving some article to identify himself as the author of the murder. Nobody of course would normally wish to kill anonymously, since one of the main purposes of the blood-feud – the public retrieving of family honour – would thereby be thwarted. After a murder was committed, within 24 hours any member of the murderer's clan might be killed in revenge 'whilst the blood is boiling'.[15] Thereafter the feud lay between the two households, although this restriction was never too strictly observed. As soon as other clansmen became involved, the feud between the two clans became general and any member of the one might fall a victim to vengeance taken by any member of the other. The ideal was to exact vengeance as quickly as possible; public opinion spurred the avenger.

The normal rule of the blood-feud would be a life for a life, with the qualification that the victim must be adult, but not enfeebled, and physically fit to carry a rifle. Only in the district of Lumë was the rule different: in that region social stratification was apparent, and where a man killed a social superior, the rule was two lives for one. Only if a woman was killed in error might another woman's life be taken, and in such cases there might be additional claims for the male children that the victim might have borne.

Property was never damaged in a feud, and in this sense a woman was counted as property: 'a sack for carrying things'. A corpse was never robbed. Only when murders occurred within a clan might the offender's house be burned down by his fellow clansmen, and he himself be expelled and his livestock slaughtered to prevent his return. In such an instance the greatest wrong was the breach of clan solidarity which resulted.

The blood-feud might rage on for years until one side lost so many men that further killing became impossible. Then the feud might be settled by the payment of blood-money, the family with the greatest number of deaths receiving a sum of money for each person killed whose death had not been revenged by an equivalent killing on the other side. The acceptance of blood-money, however, was always considered a sign of weakness: it was hardly an honourable way to retrieve honour. In fact, only in Mirditë was it commonly accepted; elsewhere it was spurned, only to be received in the less heinous cases, such as accidental murder, or when an animal killed somebody. In Shalë blood-money was only accepted if a death was unavenged for seven years; in Berisha it had to be paid within two years (Durham, 1909, p. 189); in Mati it was not accepted at all (Durham, 1928, p. 31). In the calculation of blood-money no account was given to the age of the victims, but women were valued at half-price.

In some areas a person who committed a murder might voluntarily exile himself to prevent his fellow clansmen from becoming involved in a feud, and such a person might remain away until the victim's family agreed to compound their vengeance by accepting blood-money. Enforced exile by one's own clansmen for such serious offences as sacrilege, breach of the laws of hospitality, or the violation of a truce, also occurred, as we have seen. These, however, were offences against the clan, and were dealt with by cutting off the offender permanently from membership of the group. The land of such exiles, unless their return was envisaged, was redistributed among their heirs (other than their descendants).

Not all feuds were resolved in this way, however. Cases are

known of a man remaining indoors to avoid retribution for as long as twenty-five years. Ippen (1907, p. 17) mentions a pair of brothers at Bshkashi near the Mati river, neither of whom had left the house for twelve years. In such circumstances women and children had to till the soil. Indeed, this is often stated to be the origin of the Albanian usage whereby the heavy agricultural work is undertaken by women while the men remain indoors. Throughout Northern Albania, however, manual labour is generally despised as suitable only for women, fighting and its preparations being true men's work. An alternative to this immurement was for a man who was feuding to have a permanent bodyguard, the course followed by Shefqet bey Vërlaci, one of the foremost politicians in Albania between the World Wars. Such a procedure was only open to the wealthy; Peacock (1914, p. 115) mentions a Central Albanian landowner who took refuge with his bodyguard in the town of Shkodër. A further means of protection in the blood-feud was for the men concerned to accompany a guest or a foreigner. The law of hospitality was stronger than the law of revenge, and no murder might be committed in a guest's presence.[16]

Innumerable travellers testify to the hospitality of the Ghegs. A benighted traveller might claim supper and shelter from any house he wished. With hospitality went protection, and a man who did not avenge a guest, if the latter were inadvertently killed, would be universally despised. Djilas (1958, pp. 14-15), writing of Montenegro, well describes the double disgrace involved when his paternal grandfather was murdered at his own godfather's table. This duty of protection applied not only while the guest was in one's house, but until he received hospitality from another, or until sundown of the day on which he left, whichever was the sooner. A guest who was attacked was enjoined to call out the name of his host.[17] Because of this concern for the safety of one's guests, nobody might enter the house of another when the occupants were not at home. The safety bestowed by the stranger was equally inviolate. Mrs Lane (1923, p. 247) was somewhat shocked to find that she had been accompanied throughout her travels in Shoshi by a Shalë man then at feud with Shoshi, but who had complete protection while in her entourage, since she was both a woman and a guest. The breach of these rules might be punished communally, as when a man from Fan was shot by the village, his own brother firing the first shot, for having killed his own guest. A similar case was reported from Bucaj in 1884 (Steinmetz, 1904, pp. 45-46; Schìrò, 1941, p. 291).

Responsibility for revenge
The blood-feud did not operate inside the clan. In cases of murder within the clan, the matter would be referred to a *kuvënd* called to judge the issue. If a man killed his son, father, brother, paternal uncle, paternal uncle's son, or brother's son, he was held to have 'killed himself'; the victim's blood was lost and he was not avenged. The murderer might be the dead person's nearest relative, and hence the man who would normally avenge him. If there were a nearer relative, bloodmoney might be claimed. Only when a murder occurred as the result of property being coveted might the community intervene, and expel the offender in the public interest. Some affines might undertake revenge, but only exceptionally

'. . . for marriage relationships were always contracted to secure a valued friend, and no Albanian in his senses ever threw a friend lightly away' (Hasluck, 1954, p. 212).

An adulterous wife might be avenged by her brother's clan unless she was taken in adultery and killed with her lover. If the paramour only was killed, he might be avenged by his family. A woman had the right to protection from her family throughout her life – her husband had only obtained her services in marriage, and not her life. Her rights in her clan of birth could not be alienated; and her kinsmen afforded her a standing assurance of vengeance. Miss Durham (1928, p. 148) found 'a strong belief that a woman's nearest and dearest is naturally her brother', and Djilas (1958, p. 311) has put this sentiment among the Montenegrins more forcefully:

'There is nothing finer or more delicate in this land than a sister's love. . . . But Montenegrin women love their brothers – even their cousins, if they have no brothers – with a love that combines a feminine feeling at its purest and subtlest with a primeval determination to preserve the breed from which one has sprung. . . . A sister will quarrel with her brother, but she will never break with him. She does not share with him in the property. The family has no obligations toward her, or she toward it. She simply gives and accepts love and goodness. Her love is surer than any other except the love of blood-brotherhood'.

Every woman was allowed to visit her former home once a year.

In the case of a betrothed couple a fiancé might avenge his future bride if she was killed by her own people to prevent the marriage. Here, however, the issue of family honour was involved. Exceptionally a maternal uncle might avenge his nephew, since he would be entitled to certain fees at the wedding of his niece, and in return had this contractual obligation to avenge the girl's brother. This was not a reciprocal duty, however, since no man avenged his mother's brother. Similarly, step-brothers (by different fathers) might avenge each other, thus bringing a third clan into the dispute. A few public servants, such as the field-guard, or a priest, or the Muslim *hoxha* could be communally avenged.

The termination of feud

The blood-feud could be terminated by a priest calling together the protagonists at Christmas and adjuring them to 'Give their vengeance to Christ' (Matthews, 1937, p. 122). This does not seem to have happened very often, however. Indeed, it seems probable that ecclesiastical interference was only attempted when there was every chance of success. The most effective form of reconciliation between two feuding clans would be when, the score being equal, an intermediary might be called in. This itself was a face-saving device, since honour would not then be compromised. Such a peace was frequently cemented by one or more marriages being arranged between members of the two clans to act as an earnest of future good relations.

Occasionally, however, the central political authority would enforce a termination of blood-feuds, generally during wartime. This was done by decreeing a *besë* (truce), with or without the payment of blood-money. Both the Turkish government before Albanian independence, and the Austro-Hungarian occupying forces during the First World War had resort to the *besë*. This was never entirely effective, however, as the various occupying forces or military missions in Albania discovered during the Second World War. Although a national *besë* was called on several occasions, in no case was it ever entirely effective or permanent, although several times the truce was tolerably complete. A *besë* was declared at the time the Young Turk constitution was accepted, but the Turkish authorities were (wisely) not satisfied with this precaution against bloodshed, and stipulated that if any individual joined an outlaw band, his whole family should be exiled and their goods confiscated. In this way a whole *bajrak* might be punished.

Another general truce was declared in December 1918 to cover the first period of national reconstruction, and again after the first National Congress at Lushnjë in January 1920 – thus indicating the only temporary effectiveness of the truce. Again the chiefs of Mirditë met in 1927 to compound all blood-feuds within the clan, thereby strengthening clan solidarity at a politically critical moment. The *besë* must be viewed, therefore, as a temporary device of dubious durability.[18]

The blood-feud was thus clearly a public mechanism of control by which the ancient but accepted code of law was enforced, by which clan solidarity was expressed, and the social structure maintained. The Bishop of Pultit (Pulati?) summarized this very well in conversation with Rose Wilder Lane (1923, pp. 29-31) in 1921:

'The blood feud is not a lawless thing, as strangers sometimes think. Nor has it anything to do with personal strife or hate. It is a form of capital punishment such as all nations have, and it is governed by most strict laws. . . . This Law of Lec is based on personal honor, which is also the honor of the tribe . . . the Law of Lec holds them, and it is, after all, their only civil law.'

The extent of the blood-feud, and its only gradual elimination by the centralized political authority, are significant. Despite rigorous attempts by successive administrations, by the Turks in 1857,[19] by occupying armies, and later by the government of King Zog, the pursuit of the blood-feud, with Lekë Dukagjini cast in the role of the Marquess of Queensberry, continued right up to the last war. The earliest full estimate of the toll of a feud, is that of the Albanian-born Bishop of Pulati, whose estimate of deaths in the feud for each *bajrak* in his parish during the two-year period 1854-1856 is worth giving in full (Hecquard, 1858, p 378):

	Houses	Men killed
Giovanni (?)	115	9
Kiri	93	7
Pulati	180	17
Dushman	145	17
Toplana	53	3
Shalë	275	25
Shoshi	170	4
Nikaj and Merturi	387	51
	1,418	133

Thirty-five years later there appears to have been some decline, as Baron Nopcsa's (1910, p. 61) figure of 7 murders out of 73 deaths of grown males dying in Vukle between 1891 and 1906 shows. Elsewhere in the north, however, the blood-feuds continued unabated. Degrand (1901, p. 159n.) states that there were 42 murders in one month in a single village in Mirditë, and Don Ernesto Cozzi (1910, p. 660) writing in 1910, estimated that the percentage of males dying in the feud ranged from 42 per cent (of the total male deaths?) in Toplana to 5 per cent in Reçi. That same year one of the Franciscan priests of Shoshi told Edlinger (1910, p. 84) that as many as 80 per cent of male deaths there were from the feud. The government of King Zog was perhaps a little more successful: the prefect of Mati told Newman (1936, p. 244) that, whereas in 1925 there were two deaths in the feud every week, by 1935 the toll had declined to one a month. Mati however was the king's own tribe, and the authority of his administration might be expected to be strong there. Another estimate (Matthews, 1937, p. 106) for the same period (1934) records that only 30 per cent of the inhabitants of the high valleys ever died in their beds; and in a forty-year period in Malësia e Vogël 40 per cent of male deaths were attributed to homicide (Sestini, 1943, p. 274). The priest of Zejë told Amery (1948, pp. 292-293) that in five years' residence there he had never been able to reconcile a single feuding

273

party; and even in the midst of guerilla actions in the last war in 1944 the blood-feud was being given priority by the participants.

These figures refute Peacock's suggestion (1914, pp. 125-128) that the blood-feud was perpetuated by the corruption of the Turkish courts, since the carnage continued after the attainment of independence. The feud was even pursued into the national capital, Tiranë, where one man was murdered in a feud in 1924. In Shkodër, the edict against carrying arms in the city was responsible for the virtual elimination of the blood-feud there somewhat earlier. The time that elapsed between a crime and its being avenged might be considerable: in 1909 the Shalë clan avenged themselves by killing a man from Shkreli for a crime committed 65 years before. Outside the towns the feud and the Canon survived, to bedevil governments and to provide anthropologists with a glimpse of the tribal vendetta in a European setting.

The religious factor

One final aspect of Gheg society must be mentioned: the question of religious adherence. To an Albanian, religious affiliation is a matter to be decided in the light of personal advantage and family honour. It becomes an issue to be decided collectively, sometimes at the level of the village. One village in Kiri valley allegedly embraced Islam because their priest slept in on the day of a church festival (Edlinger, 1910, p. 85). The village of Ana-Malit near Shkodër similarly went over to Islam after a slight by the Catholic priest (Hecquard, 1858, pp. 25-26). It was argued that many of the Catholic priests did not in fact have the energy to fight the non-Christian habits of the people. This evaluation is however less than fair, as is also the remark by Miss Durham (1910, p. 455): 'You cannot live long with the up-country tribesman without finding that the religion he professes is the merest surface veneer.'

It is more correct to see religion as a less fundamental value than honour. The action of the priests mentioned was in each case interpreted as an insult to honour. Expediency might however also play a part. Ten families in Rapscia in Hoti were reported to have been converted to the Muslim faith to obtain the favour of the local (Turkish) pasha (Hecquard, 1858, p.

161). These families had complete equality with the Catholic majority thereafter, taking part in the blood-feud as before. In fact, Muslim converts among the Shkreli clan continued to pay their Catholic tithes.

One of the more acceptable reasons for an individual's abjuring Christianity was to enable him to enter the Turkish army – although in this case it was usually a Tosk (from Southern Albania) who made the change. Since the recruit would thus leave his home-village, any tensions over the conversion would easily be avoided. Such changes may seem curious to us, but it must be remembered that John Kastrioti, the father of the great Albanian Christian culture-hero, Skënderbeg, was a Catholic in 1407, Greek Orthodox from 1419 to 1426, Muslim from 1430 to 1438, and died a Catholic in 1443 (Noli, 1947, p. 21). We might well echo Julian Amery's (1948, pp. 11, 112) comment that these three religions 'represented traditional loyalties rather than living creeds to the Albanians'.

There were even some parts of the country where Catholics and Muslims would invariably intermarry. The Captains of Mirditë themselves used to take Muslim women for their wives,[20] while Mgr Kaciori, a former Bishop of Durrës (Durazzo), who died in 1918, had Muslim relatives. Apart from their ruling family it seems that the Mirditans were strict in such matters, allowing neither apostasy nor the immigration of Muslims. To quote Amery (1948, p. 314) again: 'For the Mirdites, Christianity is, above all, an expression of nationalism.'

In Lurë, where Christians and Muslims often intermarried, the children were allowed to choose their own religion, apparently free from patrilineal pressures. In families where one brother was of one faith and another of a different one, there seems to have been full familial harmony. In Merturi and Nikaj men adopted two sets of names, the one Christian and the other Muslim, the latter being used when they travelled. Although, therefore, one cannot endorse the absurd characterization by Vokopola and Coblenz (1954, p. 153), in a United States Senate report, of '. . . the inherently religious nature of the Albanian people . . .', it is clear that religious adherence was an issue that had to be subservient to other structural pressures. As we shall see, this utilitarian approach was later repeated in the world of modern politics.

TOSK SOCIAL STRUCTURE

Our knowledge of Tosk social organization during this same period is much more fragmentary. Its greater geographical accessibility led to the region coming much more firmly under Turkish rule. The principal feature of this was the break-up of the large *zadruga*-type units of peasant extended families farming cooperatively, and their replacement by latifundia owned by powerful landowners – the *beys* of Albanian history – each with their own estate, or *çiflik*, to use the conventional Turkish term.[21] The *beys* were usually converts to Islam, and their allegiance to the Sultan was secured by the granting of administrative positions elsewhere in the Ottoman Empire, from which they derived much of their wealth.[22] These latifundia were usually confined to the plains, but the process of their consolidation was a continuing one. Landowners would get peasants into their debt, often by assisting them during a famine, as for instance occurred at Zverneci, north-west of Vlorë in 1921-1922, and thus establish themselves as the feudal patrons of formerly independent villagers.

In this way a largely Muslim endogamous aristocracy developed, whose life-style was in marked variance to that of the peasantry,[23] many of whom retained their Orthodox faith, and who gradually assumed the characteristics of an oppressed social class. Exceptionally for the Balkans, the break-up of the collective families did not lead to a proletarianization, but rather to the creation of a feudal society (Busch-Zantner, 1936, p. 88). The political power of the *beys* varied, but their economic control remained. The agronomist Lorenzoni (1930, p. 14) estimated that in 1930 two-thirds of the land belonged to large landowners, 165 families controlling 213,000 hectares.[24] In this way the old strategy of *divide et impera* strengthened the Turkish hold over the Tosks, while the aristocracy achieved the highest positions the Sublime Porte could offer, even to the establishment in Egypt of a native Albanian khedival dynasty.

Any consideration of Albanian political history must, however, take account of the sharp contrast between the independent familistic mountaineers, the Ghegs, and the passive, oppressed Tosk peasantry, living on the latifundist *çifliks*[25] and often represented (albeit unwillingly) in the political field by the *beys* themselves. This feudal society survived so long largely because of the lack of any bourgeoisie (Busch-Zantner, 1939, p. 28).

Finally, attention must be drawn to the existence of a small buffer region, separating the Tosk and Gheg areas. Around the capital, Tiranë, there was an area having a freehold system of land tenure, with only the feudal estates of the Toptani and Vrioni families breaking the pattern, and adjacent to it the mountainous district of Mati, which has been described as:

'. . . the region where the tribal system of the mountains mingled with the feudalism of the coastal plain. The lands and flocks were still owned in common by the different clans; but the chiefs were already known as *Beys*; and the wealthier among them employed hired labour and rented out some of their fields to poorer families' (Amery, 1948, p. 105).

It was out of this region that the later King Zog emerged.

MODERN NATIONALISM AND TRADITIONAL SOCIETY

Albanian nationalism first became an effective movement in 1878, when the Tosk-inspired League of Prizren[26] was started, although it did not effect any basic political changes. The Young Turk constitution of 1908, which was accepted by a conference of Gheg chieftains meeting in *kuvënd*, in practice made little difference to the Albanians. Indeed, after an initial period of euphoria there was a serious revolt which was put down by a Turkish general with great cruelty.[27] At this period the main impetus for change was external: coming both from Tosks who had emigrated to the United States and who were directing a nationalist campaign at a distance, and also from the neighbouring northern principality of Montenegro,[28] ever eager to extend its boundaries at the expense of Albanians. The Montenegrins incited the Catholic tribesmen of the north to revolt against the Turks in March 1911, and repeated the procedure in the first Balkan War of 1912. In this conflict the figure of Esad pashë Toptani emerged, since he was responsible for the surrender of the important port of Shkodër (Scutari)[29] to the Montenegrins, hoping at the time that he might himself obtain the Albanian crown. Such an advancement could hardly have been accepted by the Gheg tribesmen, however, since apart from the disreputable fact of the surrender itself, he was disgraced by not having avenged the murder of his guest, Hassan Riza bey, who indeed many thought had been killed with Esad's own connivance.[30] The Balkan Wars led directly to the declaration of Albanian independence by the (Tosk) Ismail Qemal bey Vlora[31] on 28 November 1912 at his home town of Vlorë. This was subsequently confirmed at the Conference of London, which terminated the Balkan War in 1913, and in turn determined the boundaries of the new Albanian state (although thereby opening up an endless source of disagreement), and called for the selection of a Sovereign Prince by the Great Powers. There was, however, clearly no general knowledge of conditions in the new state to guide their choice.

The Great Powers eventually agreed upon the candidature of Prince Wilhelm zu Wied for the Albanian throne and he arrived in his new domain early in 1914. At this time power was to a large extent in the hands of three men: Ismail Qemal bey Vlora from the south, Esad pashë Toptani from Durrës in central Albania, and Prenk Bib Doda, hereditary Captain of Mirditë in the north.[32] The Prince zu Wied first made the supreme error of choosing Esad's centre of influence, Durrës, as his capital, where in the subsequent conflict he was immobilized. He rapidly fell foul of Esad himself. And after his forces, under the command of a foreigner, had broken a traditional truce (*besë*) by opening fire at Shjak,[33] with the First World War starting and the support of the Great Powers accordingly withdrawn, the Prince was obliged to retire from Albania after a reign of only six months.[34] The task which he essayed would doubtless have defeated a stronger man with a greater comprehension of the intricacies of clan politics. As Ismail Qemal bey (Vlora, 1920, p. 382) himself observed:

'William of Wied's[35] short reign, which was richer in grotesque episodes than in incidents tending to the reorganization of a renascent State, displayed the little care that the Powers had taken in the choice of this Sovereign for a country whose happiness depended on a fortunate selection.'

278

The cardinal point is that the brief period of unification was insufficient to instil any real unity or common action: centuries of isolation and enforced division naturally militated against the Albanians immediately grasping the benefits of a centralized administration (Swire, 1929, pp. 59-60).

Indeed, with the beginning of the general European war, with invading foreign armies competing for possession of her soil, Albania became more decentralized, with five or more spheres of power in the form of confederacies emerging only to be drawn back into conditions verging on anarchy, and with no attempt being made to set up a central government. These conditions continued even after the Peace of Versailles, until a National Assembly met at Lushnjë in January 1920, which in turn called for the election of a parliament (Godart, 1922, pp. 123-134; Lamouche, 1920, p. 248). When the electoral air had cleared there were two groups, the first, known as Popularists, comprising social reformers, some of whom like their leader, Bishop Fan Noli, were straight home from the States filled with the ardour of the convert to democracy.[36] The other party, the Progressives, largely consisted of bureaucratic *beys* who had experience of administration under the Ottoman Empire, and who advocated feudal tenure and opposed agrarian reform.[37]

At this point emerges the figure of Ahmet bey Zogolli or Zogu, the chief of the significantly located Mati in Central Albania, 'the wildest and least educated of the tribes', as they have been described (Durham, 1928, p. 31). Educated in Constantinople, he led 2,000 clansmen in the first Balkan War when barely 17 years old. He took part in the short-lived Albanian political movements during the First World War, commanded the Albanian volunteer corps under the Austro-Hungarian High Command at the age of 21, and in 1921 lent the support of his clansmen to Fan Noli's Popularist party, thus adding a Gheg element to a government that was primarily Tosk.

At this time the hereditary Captain of Mirditë, Gjon Marka-gjoni, who had succeeded his childless cousin Prenk Bib Doda in a somewhat equivocal manner, led a revolt seeking to establish a Republic of Mirditë, aided by the willing forces of Yugoslavia. The revolt was put down by Ahmet bey Zogu himself. The precise causes are too complex to dispose of summarily; one may, however, say that they represented in some measure a Gheg protest against the development of a centralized state, and also an attempt to assert the supremacy of the Captains of Mirditë. At this stage Ahmet bey Zogu himself changed sides; quarrelling with Fan Noli, whose programme of agrarian reform had assumed a decidedly socialistic flavour, he ousted him from power, and sent him into exile, ultimately back to the United States, where he resumed his pastoral functions and led an Albanian literary revival. Bishop Fan Noli had encountered a characteristic difficulty in applying advanced Western political theories to tribal or feudal communities where the Ottoman tradition of government still prevailed. In his own words (Swire, 1929, p. 444):

'By insisting on agrarian reforms I aroused the wrath of the landed aristocracy; by failing to carry them out I lost the support of the peasant masses.'

More than anything, however, the departure of Fan Noli was the end of a period of Tosk supremacy, and from that time onwards the Ghegs controlled Albania until the development of a Communist-inspired Partisan guerilla movement in the Second World War.[38]

Until then, Ahmet bey Zogu remained in control of Albania, with one brief interlude when his fiancée's father took over. He cemented his power in the north by governing through a quadrumvirate of four strong clan chiefs, whom, in due course he later felt able to remove, transferring them to positions of power without influence.[39] To secure the loyalty of the clansmen he called 240 *bajraktars* to Tiranë in March 1927, invested them with military rank of officers of the reserve, placed them on half-pay, and sent them home equipped with uniforms and a regular pay cheque. At the same time he skilfully played one faction in a clan dispute against another, by giving the pliant party's relations government posts or scholarships to study abroad. All the officials in the north were Tosks, and in Catholic regions the gendarmerie were Muslim. In August 1928 he was 'elected' King of the Albanians, and took the name of Zog I. As King, his rule was entirely personal; political parties were eliminated: 'Zog played minister against minister, commander against commander, tribe against tribe, interest against interest'

(Skendi, 1956, p. 95). Clearly, he had been educated thoroughly in Constantinople.

Here we return to the question of the apparent vacillation of Albanians between various political and religious affiliations. Kin groups lent their support to political causes only after considering the alignments of their traditional rivals.[40] This trend became particularly noticeable after the Zogist regime had collapsed on the Italian invasion in April 1939, and the subsequent involvement of Albania in the Second World War, first as an Italian base in operations against the Greeks, and later as a country occupied by the Germans after the Italians had capitulated. Zog's[41] departure was brought about by purely external events, but with him went the concept (albeit still embryonic) of a central government, and the country fell into the same tribal anarchy as had occurred during the First World War. Slowly, however, there developed three different resistance or guerilla movements, of which the Zogist 'Legality' movement, led by Abaz Kupi, a clan chieftain of Krujë, and the Partisans, led by the Moscow-trained teacher Enver Hoxha,[42] a Tosk, were the most prominent. A third, Balli Kombëtar, was essentially led by Tosk *beys* and was more concerned with checking the growth of the communists than with eliminating the Germans or Italians.

In this situation the fact that his traditional rivals were Partisans would be the prime motive in inducing a Gheg to join the Zogists, irrespective of the ideologies of the two groups. The only exception might be when a clan or *bajrak*, as a measure of insurance against miscalculation, divided its own members among the different factions.[43] As one example of this process I might mention Çen Elezi, whose family, formerly Republican, competed somewhat unsuccessfully during the monarchy with the monarchist Kaloshi tribe for the supremacy of Dibër; in the conflict he came to some accommodation with the Italians and lived in Tiranë with his eldest son; his brother, however, was a communist Partisan of North Dibër, his nephew led the Partisan First Division, while two of his other sons were with the Zogists.

'The ideologies of Liberalism, Fascism, or Communism could not be deeply felt among the Albanian tribes; for Albania was still a country where a man took sides in politics less to express a preference than to place a bet' (Amery, 1948, p. 221).

However, the Partisans were led most ably by a group of people with a determined political ideology, and, having skilfully gained the support even of the British Military Mission, they were eventually able to eliminate the other movements[44] by discrediting them as collaborationists, whose supply of arms from the Allies was withdrawn. It was the children of Tosk officials and merchants, who received a European education either abroad or at one of the foreign schools within Albania, who lacked roots either in property or clan allegiance, who were particularly susceptible to the influence of revolutionary ideas, and who thus became the backbone of the communist organization. This group achieved power in 1945, and has since directed the People's Republic of Albania, initiating a programme of agrarian reform designed to eliminate the power of the *beys* in the south and of the clan hierarchies in the north (Skendi, 1956, pp. 26-27, 128).

This survey has, of necessity, been greatly curtailed. I hope, however, that it will have shown that it is possible to understand Albanian history in terms of the conflict of social attachments and systems, rather than by resort to those explanations based upon personal charisma which have so monopolized Albanian historiography in the past.

APPENDIX

Sources for the Reconstruction of Traditional Albanian Society

A brief methodological note on sources will, perhaps, indicate the cumulative richness of the material on Albanian social structure, although almost all the individual items in this bibliography would be inadequate for citation by themselves. I should perhaps state as a point of autobiographical detail that my attention was first drawn to these people when, after trying to piece together the surviving fragments of data relating to clan feuds in Scotland in the sixteenth to eighteenth centuries, I came to the conclusion that those fragments could not be interpreted without some comparative data on blood-feuds from other European groups. I accordingly embarked upon an ambitious comparative analysis of the blood-feud in Albania and Montenegro, with the hope that this might be extended by an analysis of the material from Sicily, Sardinia, and perhaps the Ozark communities of the Appalachians. The political situation prevented me from entering Albania, but I did some fieldwork among Albanophone communities in both Monte-negro and Yugoslav Macedonia, and subsequently I have extended my research by discussions with Albanian refugees elsewhere. Nevertheless, the main focus of this study has been documentary, since the corpus of material was not too large to be encompassed by one person, granted the superbly generous lending facilities of the Library of Congress in Washington, D.C.

As will have been clear, I was assisted by the fact that several earlier studies were done in this area by anthropologists, although none of them had a modern functionalist orientation. Among these one must single out Mary Edith Durham (1863-1944) who travelled widely in the Balkans at the turn of the century, and who also became prominent in England for her work for an independent Albanian state. Her approach was ethnological; but the richness of her data overcomes the draw-backs of her theoretical orientation. Another Englishwoman who wrote less prolifically, Mrs Margaret Hasluck (1885-1948), lived in Elbasan in the south between 1926 and 1939. Her compilation of the traditional law, if not so thorough as that of Father Gjeçov, is nevertheless most useful (see Kastrati, 1955). Father Shtjefën Gjeçov (1874-1929) collated the tradi-tional Canon of Lekë Dukagjini, as has already been mentioned. Finally one should single out the Hungarian Baron Franz Nopcsa (1929, pp. 15-16; 1918), whose prolific writings suggest a deeper acquaintance with Albania than is actually the case. In all he only seems to have spent some 360 days in the country, scattered over many years.[45]

I believe, however, that by piecing together the scattered comments of innumerable travellers and historians, inter-preting them firstly in the light of the writings of the four anthropologically oriented writers I have mentioned, and supplementing these sources with personal data obtained from persons who took part in these events and are for the most part now refugees, one can build up a fairly coherent picture of the interrelationship of tribal structure and national politics in Albania between the years 1910 and 1950.

NOTES

1. Miss Durham found only one case of descent being calculated through a woman in all Northern Albania, among the Nikaj clan (Durham, 1909, pp. 195-196).

2. The Catholic Church prohibited marriage within the sixth degree in either male or female lines; the Muslims did not recognize cousinhood through females as any impediment (Durham, 1909, p. 22; 1910, p. 458).

3. The role and functions of the elder are discussed in Hasluck (1954, pp. 130-147). The social role of the *bajraktar* is discussed in ibid. (pp. 115-129).

4. The *kuvënd* is fully discussed in Hasluck (1954, pp. 148-162).

5. Hecquard says (1858, p. 229) only the people of Mirditë had not amended the Canon.

6. Hecquard is somewhat unclear on this point, according the primacy to both Mirditë and Hoti (1858, pp. 162, 368). Two other sources confirm the primacy of Hoti (Gopčević, 1881, p. 290; Peacock, 1914, p. 221).

7. The chiefs and elders of the clans of Reçi and Loko (?) which together form one *bajrak* were frequently consulted by other tribes to adjudicate in such small local issues (Hecquard, 1858, p. 148).

8. The Captain was often miscalled 'Prince' through a misinterpretation of the name Prenk (= Peter) – (Hecquard, 1858, p. 219; e.g. Bourcart, 1921). The descent of the Gjomarkaj family is discussed by Gopčević (1881, pp. 565-568) and Degrand (1901, p. 319). The first known chief was really Gjon Marko (*floreat* 1750). There was, however, an internal vendetta in the ruling family from about 1825 to 1835 (Hecquard, 1858, pp. 238-242).

9. Conflict occurred between Bib Doda, Captain of Mirditë, and his clansmen in 1855 over their relations with the Turks, who had disarmed some of the Mirditans contrary to their ancient rights. This internal conflict was resolved by a truce (*besë*), but Hecquard, writing in 1858, said that at that time the Captains had very restricted powers (Hecquard, 1858, pp. 227, 243-246).

10. Such a realignment of the clans would account for the detailed differences in the consitutution of the various clans between the description of Miss Durham (1928) and that of Professor Coon (1950) – cf. Coon (1950, pp. 31-32).

11. Patetta (1941, p. 10); the Dukagjini genealogy is discussed in this connexion by Degrand (1901, p. 315) and Nopcsa (1910, pp. 35-38).

12. Father Gjeçov, who is said to have been murdered by the Yugoslavs, is discussed by Kastrati (1955, pp. 124-125) and Mann (1955, p. 106). There is a photograph of him in Libardi (1935, Vol. I, facing p. 48).

13. The supremacy of family honour to the neglect of personal safety is well illustrated in a description of a killing in a blood-feud witnessed by Degrand. The offender, who was captured by the authorities, displayed a complete disinterest in his personal future (Degrand, 1901, pp. 161-164).

14. Cozzi (1912, pp. 318-321). Degrand describes (1901, p. 155n.) one such sworn virgin whom he encountered, while Miss Durham in her extensive travels met no less than seven who wore men's clothing (Durham, 1928, pp. 194-195). Some twenty years later, in 1929-1930, Coon only encountered two, and only one wore masculine dress (Coon, 1950, Fig. 10*d*). The other was busy philandering with one of his horse-drivers! Newman met another (or the same) in 1935 (Newman, 1936, pp. 260-261 and plate facing p. 260). It is probable that there is some confusion here between sworn virgins who have taken the place of a male for the purposes of the blood-feud, and those who have sworn virginity to avoid marriage with somebody to whom they were betrothed in their infancy (a practice that was still common among the Dukagjini in 1928, if Miss Durham's information (1928, p. 194) was up to date at that time). This latter category would probably not assume male dress. The principle of family honour is present in both categories, however. The girl who rejected her betrothed did so at the risk of insulting his family honour; indeed vengeance might be taken on a girl's kinsmen unless she swore publicly that she did so of her own accord (Hasluck, 1933, p. 192). This insult was offset if she guaranteed to avoid an alliance with some other family.

15. Miss Durham is quite emphatic that by the time she arrived in Malësia e Madhe in the first decade of this century only the man who had actually taken blood might be shot, and not his relatives (1928, p. 164).

16. The laws of hospitality are codified in Gjeçov (1941, pp. 184-195); see also the discussion of Mirditan hospitality (Frasheri, 1930, pp. 25-27).

17. See the instance quoted in the account of a *hoxha*'s journey from Jakovë to Shkodër (Steinmetz, 1905, pp. 36-37); cf. Markgraf (1930, p. 58).

18. One must discount the somewhat exaggerated remarks by Godart (1922, p. 75): 'La Bessa, c'est la religion albanaise, c'est la religion du peuple'.

19. Mustafa pasha, Vali of Shkodër in 1857, passed a law ordering exile to all those who gave asylum to murderers, and close relatives of the guilty party might be arrested and imprisoned (Hecquard, 1858, pp. 371-372).

20. Bib Doda pashë, the father of Prenk, married a Muslim woman from Lurë as his second wife; she is illustrated in Degrand (1901, p. 172). She was baptized not long before the wedding; cf. Mousset (1930, pp. 112-113).

21. The *çiflik* system seems to have emerged in the eighteenth century, although there was a temporary recession in the power of the *beys* during the early nineteenth century, perhaps on account of the centralized rule of Ali, pasha of Tepeleni (Skendi, 1956, pp. 6-7).

22. The Muslim religion spread after two insurrections in 1740 (Chekrezi, 1919, p. 40).

23. There were several different types of land-tenure in operation (cf. Urban, 1938, p. 81; Zavalani, 1938, pp. 44-47; Chekrezi 1919, p. 174). For a good description of the gilded youth of the young *beys*, see Vlora (1920, pp. 13-15).

24. Matthews (1937, p. 7) estimated that one-third of all land was owned by 200 proprietors who let out their land on a crop-sharing basis. This must be the basis of Redlich's observation (1936, p. 67) that 95 per cent of the inhabitants in 1924 were landowners, and hence they were reluctant to engage in the radical experiments of Fan Noli. Busch-Zantner estimated (1936, pp.

92-94) that the Vlora family (whose life is described in Patsch, 1904, columns 18-19) owned 60,000 hectares, as did also the Vrioni family; the Toptani had 50,000 and the Zogolli less; cf. Rosati (1915, pp. 154-160).

25. There is good study by Lorenzoni of 60 *çifliks* (1930, pp. 141-200) and a much more recent one of the Rëmbec *çiflik* by Gjergj (1962, pp. 194-198).

26. The Albanian League for the Defence of the Rights of the Albanian Nation met at Prizren in Kosovë in 1878, but was abolished by the Turks three years later (Skendi, 1956, pp. 8, 72).

27. The issue of opposition to the Young Turks was their attempt at imposing taxation and conscription, from which the Ghegs had previously been exempt (Seton-Watson, 1917, p. 138); for a personal account of the Young Turk regime see (Basri-Bey, 1920). Vlora, with hindsight, states (1911, p. 8) that the Albanians distrusted the Young Turks from the start.

28. The Montenegrin frontier, drawn in 1878, 'a purely political and in no way ethnographic line' (Durham, 1909, p. 20) had divided clans that traditionally intermarried (Robinson, 1941, p. 16).

29. For eye-witness accounts of the siege of Shkodër see Egli (1913); Giesl (1927, pp. 230-244); Zambaur (1914).

30. Berri (1913, pp. 159-171); assessments of Esad vary greatly according to the politics of the writer (cf. Louis-Jaray, 1914, pp. 59-60; Laffert, 1916, p. 17; Wallisch, 1931, pp. 14-17; Durham, 1920b; Busch-Zantner, 1939, p. 44; Wilhelm, n.d., p. 9; Swire, 1929, p. 154; Konitza, 1918, p. 55; Helmreich, 1938, pp. 419-421).

31. For a discussion of the role of the Vlora family in the creation of an independent Albanian state see Godin (1914, pp. 35-49, 57-61); as with Esad, assessments of Ismail Qemal bey vary widely (cf. Bachrich, 1913; Godin, 1914, pp. 49-57; Deli, 1914, pp. 139-141; Rappaport, 1927, p. 99). Prince Wilhelm himself wrote of him (n.d., p. 10): '... der von dem eines Schwindlers nicht weit entfernt war'.

32. For comments on Prenk Bib Doda see Durham (1920a, pp. 107-109, 189-190; Edlinger, 1910, p. 76; Gopčević, 1881, pp. 118-119, 312). Prince Wilhelm in his memoirs (n.d., p. 9) mentions four people who held the main power of the country in their hands: Ismail Qemal bey, Esad pashë, Xhemal Zogolli (the father of Ahmet, later King Zog) in Mati, and Omer pashë in Orosh (cf. Federal Writers' Project, 1939, pp. 19-20).

33. Durham (1920a, p. 265); Chekrezi (1919, pp. 147-150); Thopia (1916, pp. 264-265). The account of one of the Dutch officers involved, Fabius (1918, pp. 212-214), gives no indication that the Dutch officers did not understand the rules of the *besë*, however; see also Bourcart (1921, p. 138); Swire (1929, p. 212).

34. Ismail Qemal bey's comments on Prince Wilhelm provide a good riposte to the Prince's view of Ismail quoted above: 'Like a speculator whose business has failed, William of Wied realised there was nothing to do but to depart' (Vlora, 1920, p. 386).

35. Estimates of Prince Wilhelm differ, but most are negative: cf. the remarks of Brailsford (1919, p. 252), usually an acute observer of the Balkan scene: '... a German princeling, who lacked not merely sympathy and good sense, but even common animal courage'. The Kaiser was equally reserved in his comments (Wilhelm II, 1922, pp. 165-166). The Prince's own memoirs are a superficial chronicle of events (Wilhelm, n.d.).

36. For contrasting appraisals of Fan Noli, see Baerlein (1922, pp. 74-77, 131); Busch-Zantner (1939, pp. 85-86). A curtailed autobiographical account of his career is in Noli (1960, pp. 116-127).

37. There were a few more enlightened landowners in this group, such as Mehdi Frashëri (about whom see Amery, 1948, p. 15).

38. The Zog-Noli conflict was perhaps partly one of geography, i.e. Tosk versus Gheg (cf. Amery, 1948, p. 18; Lane, 1923, pp. 299-300), but was also one of theories of social transformation (cf. Grant, 1963, pp. 13-14).

39. The quadrumvirate consisted of Muharrem Bajraktar, Lord of Lumë (see Amery, 1948, pp. 37, 142-144, 307-308); Fikri Dine, one of the more influential chiefs of Dibër (ibid., pp. 13, 162, 296, 321); Xhemal Herri, whose patrimony was Zali i Herrit (ibid., pp. 191-192, 244-245); and Prenk Previsi of Kurbenesh (ibid., pp. 296, 303-306).

40. 'The persistence of the blood feuds presented Abas Kupi with a serious problem, for every time a clan was won to his cause their blood enemies would side automatically with his rivals' (Amery, 1948, p. 112).

41. For assessments of King Zog see in particular Matthews (1937, pp. 88-95); Ryan (1951, pp. 316-317, 340); Ronart (1933, pp. 57-72); Tocci (1938); Szinyei-Merse (1940, *passim*); Dako, 1937.

42. For the development of the Partisan movement seen from a Yugoslav viewpoint see Dedijer (1949); see also Hoxha (1957; Dedi *et al.*, 1959). On Abaz Kupi see Amery (1948, *passim*; Davies, 1952, pp. 83-84, 171).

43. Archer (1944, p. 97); the complexities of the situation baffled alike the British Military Mission (cf. Kemp, 1958, pp. 217-218, 240-241, 253; Tilman, 1946, pp. 146, 152), the Germans (cf. Frank, 1957, *passim*), and the Italians (cf. Bonasera, 1953); Umiltà, 1947, p. 116.

44. Other movements not discussed above include that led by Gani Kryeziu of Jakovë in the north, whose brother Cena bey had been a brother-in-law of Zog, at whose behest he was murdered. This family history precluded Kryeziu joining the monarchists, a fact strengthened by their hereditary relations with Mirditë.

45. Nopcsa (1929, pp. 15-16); note his useful bibliography (Nopcsa, 1918) and fuller study (Nopcsa, 1925).

ACKNOWLEDGEMENTS

Thanks are due to the author for permission to reproduce excerpts from *Sons of the Eagle: A Study in Guerilla War* by Julian Amery (London: Macmillan & Company; New York: The Macmillan Company), and to Methuen & Company and Harcourt, Brace & World, Inc. in respect of passages from *Land without Justice* by Milovan Djilas.

The author also wishes to thank the Trustees for nominating him for the Wygard Award for 1962 for an earlier draft of this article, thereby affording him considerable encouragement and practical support.

REFERENCES

AMERY, J. 1948. *Sons of the Eagle: A Study in Guerilla War*. London: Macmillan.

ARCHER, L. 1944. *Balkan Journal*. New York: Norton.

BACHRICH, H. 1913. An der Küste Albaniens. *Wochenschrift des niederösterreichischen Gewerbevereins* **74** (4): 61-64. Wien(?).

BAERLEIN, H. 1922. *Under the Acroceraunian Mountains*. London: Parsons.

BASRI-BEY, D. Z. 1920. Le Monde Oriental et l'Avenir de la Paix (3rd revised edition). Paris: Perrin.

BERRI, G. 1913. *L'Assedio di Scutari Sei Mesi dentro la Città Accerchiata*. Milano: Treves.

BONASERA, F. 1953. *Albania 1943-1944*. Ancona: [Spoltere.]

BOURCART, J. 1921. *L'Albanie et les Albanais*. Paris: Bossard.

BRAILSFORD, H. N. 1919. The Peace in the Balkans. *The Adriatic Review* **1** (7): 249-255. Boston.

BUSCH-ZANTNER, R. 1936. Ländernachrichten – Albanien: Agrarreform und Agrarverfassung in Albanien. In *Berichte über Landwirtschaft*, New Series, **20**: 87-109. Berlin.

—— 1939. *Albanien: Neues Land im Imperium*. Leipzig: Goldmann.

CHEKREZI, CONSTANTINE, A. 1919. *Albania past and present*. New York: Macmillan.

COON, CARLETON S. 1950. *The mountains of giants: a racial and cultural study of the North Albanian Mountain Ghegs* (Papers of the Peabody Museum of American Archaeology and Ethnology, Harvard University vol. 23, No. 3). Cambridge, Mass.

COZZI, D. ERNESTO. 1910. La vendetta del sangue nelle montagne dell'Alta Albania. *Anthropos* **5**: 654-687. St. Gabriel-Mödling.

—— 1912. La donna albanese. *Anthropos* **7**: 309-335, 617-626. St. Gabriel-Mödling.

DAKO, CHRISTO A. 1919. *Albania: the master key to the Near East*. Boston: Grimes.

—— 1937. *Zogu the First, King of the Albanians*. Tirana: Luarasi.

DAVIES, BRIGADIER 'TROTSKY'. 1952. *Illyrian Venture*. London: Bodley Head.

DEDI, VELI et al. (eds.). 1959. *Dokumenta e materiale historike nga Lufta e Popullit Shqiptar per Liri e Demokraci 1917-1941*. Tiranë: Arkivave Shtetërore.

DEDIJER, VLADIMIR. 1949. *Il sangue tradito: relazioni jugoslavo-albanesi 1938-1949*. Varese: Periodici Italiani.

DEGRAND, A. 1901. *Souvenirs de la Haute-Albanie*. Paris: Welter.

DELI, IRTA (= L. VON THALLÓCZY). 1914. *Tudákos levelek 1914.* Budapest: Hornyánszky.

DJILAS, MILOVAN. 1958. *Land without justice.* New York: Harcourt, Brace.

DURHAM, MARY EDITH. 1909. *High Albania.* London: Arnold.

—— 1910. High Albania and its customs in 1908. *Journal of the Royal Anthropological Institute* 40: 453-472. London.

—— 1914. *The struggle for Scutari (Turk, Slav, and Albanian).* London: Arnold.

—— 1920a. *Twenty years of Balkan tangle.* London: Allen & Unwin.

—— 1920b. The story of Essad Pasha. *The Contemporary Review* 118 (August 1920): 207-215. London.

—— 1928. *Some tribal origins, laws and customs of the Balkans.* London: Allen & Unwin.

—— 1931. Preservation of pedigrees and commemoration of ancestors in Montenegro. *Man* 31 (no. 163): 154-155. London.

EDLINGER, LUDWIG. 1910. Wanderungen durch das östliche Bosnien, Montenegro und Albanien. *Mitteilungen des Vereins für Erdkunde zu Leipzig* (1909), pp. 63-88. Leipzig.

EGLI, KARL. 1913. *Drei Monate vor Skutari.* Bern: Gemminger.

FABIUS, J. 1918. *Zes maanden in Albanië.* Haarlem: Willink.

FEDERAL WRITERS' PROJECT OF THE WORKS PROGRESS ADMINISTRATION OF MASSACHUSETTS, members of the. 1939. *The Albanian struggle in the Old World and New.* Boston: The Writer.

FRANK, HERMANN. 1957. *Landser/Karst und Skipetaren* (Landser am Feind 1). Heidelberg: Vowinckel.

FRASHERI, STAVRE TH. 1930. *Permes Mirdites ne dimer.* Korçe: Peppo-Marko.

GIESL, BARON WLADIMIR. 1927. *Zwei Jahrzehnte im nahen Orient* (ed. *Generalmajor Ritter* v. Steinitz). Berlin: Kulturpolitik.

GJEÇOV, P. STEFANO COST. 1941. *Codice di Lek Dukagjini ossia Diritto consuetudinario delle montagne d'Albania* (Reale Accademia d'Italia: Centro Studi per l'Albania 2), Trans. *P. Paolo Dodaj,* ed. P. Giorgio Fishta & Giuseppe Schirò. Roma.

GJERGJ, ANDROMAQI. 1962. Provë për një studim etnografik në fshatin Rëmbec (Korçë). *Etnografia shqiptare* 1: 193-246. Tiranë.

GODART, JUSTIN. 1922. *L'Albanie en 1921.* Paris: Presses Universitaires de France.

GODIN, MARIA AMELIA FREIIN VON 1914. *Aus dem neuen Albanien.* Wien: Roller.

GOPČEVIĆ, SPIRIDION. 1881. *Oberalbanien und seine Liga.* Leipzig: Von Duncker & Humblot.

GRANT, HUGH G. 1963. Minister Hugh Grant addresses Commemorative Assembly. In *Shield and Diamond* **72** (3): 12-16. Little Rock.

HASLUCK, MARGARET. 1933. Bride-price in Albania: a Homeric parallel. *Man* **33** (no. 203): 191-195. London.

—— 1954. *The unwritten law in Albania* (ed. J. H. Hutton). Cambridge: University Press.

HECQUARD, HYACINTHE. [1858]. *Histoire et Description de la Haute Albanie ou Guégarie*. Paris: Bertrand.

HELMREICH, ERNST CHRISTIAN. 1938. *The Diplomacy of the Balkan Wars 1912-1913* (Harvard Historical Studies Vol. 42). Cambridge: Harvard University Press.

HOXHA, ENVER. 1957. *Vlijanie velikoj Oktjabr'skoj revoljutsii na Albaniju* (Oktjabr'skaja Revolutsija v Rossii i Mirovoe osvoboditel'noe dviženie). Moskva: Političeskoj literaturij.

IPPEN, THEODOR A. 1907. *Skutari und die nordalbanische Küstenebene* (Zur Kunde der Balkanhalbinsel: Reisen und Beobachten Vol. **5**). Sarajevo.

KASTRATI, QAZIM. 1955. Some sources on the unwritten law in Albania. *Man* **55** (no. 134): 124-127. London.

KEMP, PETER. 1958. *No colours or crest*. London: Cassell.

KONITZA, MEHMED BEY. 1918. Memorandum on Albania. *The Adriatic Review* **1** (2): 52-58. Boston.

LAFFERT, GERTRUD V. 1916. *Vier monate in Albanien*. Berlin: Stilke.

LAMOUCHE, COLONEL L. 1920. La legislation en vigueur en Albanie. *Bulletin mensuel de la société de législation comparée* **49** (July-December 1920): 244-249. Paris.

LANE, ROSE WILDER. 1923. *Peaks of Shala*. New York: Harper.

LIBARDI, CAV. CAMILLO P. 1935. *I primi moti patriottici albanesi nel 1910-1911-1912 specie nei Dukagini*. 2 vols. Trento: Ardesi.

LORENZONI, GIOVANNI. 1930. *La questione agraria albanese* (2nd edn.). Bari: Laterza.

LOUIS-JARAY, GABRIEL. 1914. *Au jeune royaume d'Albanie*. Paris: Hachette.

MANN, STUART E. 1955. *Albanian literature: an outline of prose, poetry, and drama*. London: Quaritch.

MARKGRAF, FRIEDRICH. 1930. *In Albaniens Bergen*. Stuttgart: Strecker & Schröder.

MATTHEWS, RONALD. 1937. *Sons of the Eagle*. London: Methuen.

MOUSSET, ALBERT. 1930. *L'Albanie devant l'Europe (1912-1929)* (Bibliotheque d'Histoire et de Politique). Paris: Delagrave.

NEWMAN, BERNARD. 1936. *Albanian backdoor*. London: Jenkins.

NOLI, BISHOP/METROPOLITAN FAN STYLIAN. [1947]. *George Castrioti Scanderbeg (1405-1468)*. New York: International Universities Press.

—— 1960. *Fiftieth Anniversary Book of the Albanian Orthodox Church in America 1908-1958*. Boston: Albanian Orthodox Church in America.

NOPCSA, BARON/BARÓ FRANZ/FERENCZ. 1910. *Aus Šala und Klementi* (Zur Kunde der Balkanhalbinsel: Reisen und Beobachten Vol. 11). Sarajevo.

—— 1912. Beiträge zum Vorgeschichte und Ethnologie Nordalbaniens. *Wissenschaftliche Mitteilungen aus Bosnien und der Herzegowina* 12: 168-253. Wien.

—— 1918. *Az Albániárál szólól jegúabb irodalom*. Budapest: Hornyánszky.

—— 1925. *Albanien: Bauten, Trachten und Geräte Nordalbaniens*. Berlin: De Gruyter.

—— 1929. *Geographie und Geologie Nordalbaniens* (Geological Hungarica series, Geologica Vol. 3). Budapestini.

PATETTA, FEDERICO. 1941. Introduzione to Gjeçov, 1941, pp. 7-47.

PATSCH, CARL. 1904. *Das Sandschak Berat in Albanien* (Kaiserliche Akademie der Wissenschaften – Schriften der Balkankommission – Antiquarische Abteilung vol. 3). Wien.

PEACOCK, WADHAM. 1914. *Albania: the foundling state of Europe*. London: Chapman & Hall.

RAPPAPORT, ALFRED. 1927. Der Tirana-Vertrag. *Europäische Gespräche* 5 (Feb. 1927): 96-109. Hamburg.

REDLICH, BARON MARCELLUS D. A. R. VON. 1936. *Albania yesterday and today*. Worcester, Mass.: The Albanian Messenger.

ROBINSON, VANDELEUR. 1941. *Albnaia's road to freedom*. London: Allen & Unwin.

RONART, STEPHAN. 1933. *Albanien von heute*. Wien: Pays et peuples.

ROSATI, UMBERTO. 1915. Condizioni economico-agrarie dell'- Albania. Part IV of Umberto Rosati & Gaetano Baudin, *Studi agrologici* (*Relazione della Commissione per lo Studio dell'Albania*. Part II) [pp. 127-195] (Atti della Società Italiana per il progresso delle scienze). Roma.

RYAN, SIR ANDREW. 1951. *The last of the dragomans*. London: Bles.

SCHIRÒ, GIUSEPPE. 1941. Appendice al Kanun di Lek Dukjagjini: esempi di applicazione del Kanun. In Gjeçov, 1941, pp. 283-319.

SESTINI, ALDO. 1943. Le regioni dell'Albania. In Reale Società Geografica Italiana (comp.): *L'Albania*, pp. 253-412. Bologna: Zanichelli.

SETON-WATSON, R. W. 1917. *The rise of nationality in the Balkans*. London: Constable.

SKENDI, STAVRO. 1953. Beginnings of Albanian nationalist and autonomous trends: the Albanian League, 1878-1881. *American Slavic and East European Review* 12 (2): 219-232. Philadelphia.

— 1954. *Albanian and South Slavic oral epic poetry* (Memoirs of the American Folklore Society vol. 44). Philadelphia.

— 1956. *Albania* (East-Central Europe under the Communists – Praeger Publications in Russian History and World Communism vol. 46). New York: Praeger.

STEINMETZ, INGENIEUR KARL. 1904. *Eine Reise durch die Hochländergaue Oberalbaniens* (Zur Kunde der Balkanhalbinsel: Reisen und Beobachten vol. 1). Wien.

— 1905. *Ein Vorstoss in die nordalbanischen Alpen* (ibid. vol. 3). Wien.

SWIRE, J. 1929. *Albania: the rise of a kingdom*. London: Williams & Norgate.

— 1937. *King Zog's Albania*. London: Hale.

SZINYEI-MERSE, ANTOINETTE DE. 1940. *Ten years ten months ten days* (trans. Paul Tabori). London: Hutchinson.

THOPIA, KARL. 1916. Das Fürstentum Albanien. In Ludwig von Thalloczy (ed.), *Illyrisch-albanische Forschungen* vol. 2, pp. 219-289. München: Duncker & Humblot.

TILMAN, H. W. 1946. *When men and mountains meet*. Cambridge: University Press.

TOCCI, TERENZIO. 1938. *Il re degli Albanesi* (Collezione tempo nostro vol. 13). Milano: Mondadori.

UMILTÀ, CARLO. 1947. *Jugoslavia e Albania* (Vita vissuta, 2nd series). Cernusco sul Naviglio: Garzanti.

URBAN, MARTIN. 1938. *Die siedlungen Südalbaniens* (Tübinger geographische und geologische Abhandlungen 2nd Series vol. 4). Öhringen: Rau.

VILLARI, SALVATORE. 1940. *Le consuetudini giuridiche dell'Albania*. Roma: Società editrice del libro Italiano.

[VLORA, EKREM BEY] E. B. V. 1911. *Die Wahrheit über das Vorgehen der Jungtürken in Albanien*. Wien: Fromme.

[VLORA,] ISMAIL KEMAL BEY. 1917. Albania and the Albanians. *The Quarterly Review* 228 (452) (July 1917), 140-168. London.

— 1920. *The memoirs of Ismail Kemal Bey* (ed. Somerville Story). London: Constable.

[VOKOPOLA, KEMAL & COBLENZ, WILLIAM A.] LEGISLATIVE REFERENCE SERVICE OF THE LIBRARY OF CONGRESS. 1954. *Tensions within the Soviet captive countries: Part 6: Albania* (83rd Congress 1st Session Senate Document No. **70** Part 6). Washington: U.S. Government Printing Office.

WALLISCH, FRIEDRICH. 1931. *Neuland Albanien.* Stuttgart: Franck'sche.

WILHELM, FÜRST VON ALBANIEN, PRINZ ZU WIED. n.d. *Denkschrift über Albanien.* [Glogau-Berlin.]

WILHELM II, EMPEROR OF GERMANY 1888-1918. 1922. *The Kaiser's Memoirs.* (Trans. Thomas R. Ybarra) New York: Harper.

ZAMBAUR, HORTENSE VON. 1914. *Die Belagerung von Skutari (10 Oktober 1912 bis 22 April 1913).* Berlin: Stilke.

ZAVALANI, DALIB. 1938. Die landwirtschaftlichen Verhältnisse Albaniens (*Berichte über Landwirtschaft* New Series Part 140). Berlin.

NOTES ON CONTRIBUTORS

ARDENER, EDWIN. Born 1927, England; educated at London University, B.A. 1949.

Treasury Studentship, 1949-1952; Research Fellow, later Senior Research Fellow WAISER/NISER, University College Ibadan, Nigeria, 1952-1962; Oppenheimer Student, Oxford, 1961-1962; Treasury Fellowship, 1963; Lecturer in Social Anthropology, Oxford, 1963.

Author of *Coastal Bantu of the Cameroons*, 1956; *Divorce and Fertility*, 1962.

Joint author of *Plantation and Village in the Cameroons*, 1960.

BRADBURY, ROBERT ELWYN. Born 1929, England; studied at London University, B.A., Ph.D.

Research Fellow, International African Institute, 1952; Research Assistant, University College London, 1954; Research Fellow, University College, Ibadan, 1956; Lecturer, University College London, 1961; Lecturer in Anthropology, University of Birmingham, 1964.

Author of *The Benin Kingdom and the Edo-speaking Peoples*, 1957.

CREGEEN, ERIC R. Born 1921, England, of Manx parentage; educated at Cambridge University, B.A., M.A.

Assistant-Director, Manx National Museum, 1948-1950; Schoolmaster, 1950-1954; Resident-tutor in Argyll, Glasgow University Extra-Mural Department, 1954-1964; Carnegie Fellowship, 1962-1963; Nuffield sociological award to study social history and social anthropology at Cambridge, 1964-1965; Lecturer in the School of Scottish Studies, University of Edinburgh, 1966.

Editor of *List of Inhabitants on the Argyll Estate in 1779*, 1963; *Instructions of the 5th Duke of Argyll to His Chamberlains, 1771-1805*, 1964.

HOPKINS, KEITH. Born 1934; educated at King's College Cambridge, B.A. 1958.

Assistant Lecturer in Sociology, University of Leicester, 1961-1963; Lecturer in Sociology, L.S.E., and Fellow of King's College, Cambridge, 1963-1967; Professor of Sociology, Hong Kong University, 1967.

Articles in *Population Studies, Classical Quarterly, Comparative Studies in Society and History*, etc.

LEWIS, IOAN MYRDDIN. Born 1930, Scotland; studied at Glasgow University, B.Sc., and Oxford, B.Litt., D.Phil.

Research Assistant, Chatham House, 1954-1955; Colonial Social Science Research Council Fellow, 1955-1957; Lecturer in African Studies, University College of Rhodesia and Nyasaland, 1957-1960; Lecturer in Anthropology, Glasgow University, 1960-1963; Lecturer and from 1966 Reader and Tutor in Anthropology, University College London, 1963-.

Author of *A Pastoral Democracy*, 1961; *Marriage and the Family in Northern Somaliland*, 1962; (with B. W. Andrzejewski) *Somali Poetry*, 1964; *The Modern History of Somaliland*, 1965.

Editor of *Islam in Tropical Africa*, 1966.

LLOYD, PETER C. Born 1927, Bournemouth, England; studied at Oxford University, B.A., M.A., B.Sc., D.Phil.

Research Fellow, West African Institute of Social and Economic Research, Ibadan, Nigeria, 1950-1956; Land Research Officer, Ministry of Lands and Labour, Ibadan, 1956-1959; Lecturer in Sociology, University of Ibadan, 1959-1962; Senior Lecturer, 1962-1964; Senior Lecturer in Sociology, University of Birmingham, 1964-1966; Reader, 1966-1967; Reader in Social Anthropology, University of Sussex, 1967.

Author of *Yoruba Land Law*, 1962; *Africa in Social Change*, 1967.

Editor of *The New Elites of Tropical Africa*, 1966; co-editor of *The City of Ibadan*, 1967.

MORTON-WILLIAMS, PETER. Born 1922; educated at University College London, B.Sc. 1949, Ph.D. 1967.

Horniman Studentship,1949-1951; Research Fellow WAISER, University College Ibadan, 1951-1956; Yoruba Historical Research Scheme, 1956-1958; Research Assistant, University College London, 1959-1961; Lecturer and Research Fellow, University of Ghana, 1962-1964; Lecturer, University College London, 1964-.

Author of *Cinema in Rural Nigeria*, 1956; and many papers on the Yoruba and other West African peoples.

SOUTHWOLD, MARTIN. Born 1929, England; studied at Cambridge University, B.A., M.A., Ph.D.

Research Assistant in Social Anthropology, Manchester University, 1957-1959; Assistant Lecturer in Social Anthropology, Cambridge University, 1960-1962; Lecturer in Social Anthropology, Manchester University, 1962.

WHITAKER, IAN. Born 1928, United Kingdom; studied at University of St Andrews; Cambridge, M.A.; University of Oslo, Dr.Philos.

Research Fellow, School of Scottish Studies, University of Edinburgh, 1952-1959; Associate Professor of Sociology and Anthropology, Memorial University of Newfoundland, 1959; Professor, 1962; Director of Sociological Research, Institute of Social and Economic Research (St John's Newfoundland), 1961-1964; Visiting Professor of Sociology, University College of South Wales and Monmouthshire, Cardiff, 1964; Senior Lecturer in Sociology, University of York, 1965; Reader, 1966.

Author of *Social Relations in a Nomadic Lappish Community*, 1955.

Editor of *Small-scale Agriculture in Selected Newfoundland Communities*, 1963.

Author Index

Adams, M. I., 190
Ajayi, J. F. A., 21, 35, 59
Alfonse, J., 88
Allardyce, 190
Allen, W., 21
Amery, J., 263, 265, 273, 275, 277, 279-82, 287, 288
Anderson, H. O., 110, 122
Anderson, J., 190
Archer, L., 281, 287, 288
Ardener, E., 81, 95, 97, 100, 102, 111, 114, 116, 118, 122, 295
Ardener, S., 118, 122
Argyle, J., xvii, xxvi
Argyll, Duke of, 190
Arnett, E. J., 21
Asmis, Dr, 122

Bachrich, H., 278, 287, 288
Baerlein, H., 279, 286, 288
Baikie, W. B., 15, 21
Bailey, F. G., xiv, xxvi
Bankes, T., 109, 122
Barbot, J., 81, 93, 97, 100, 102, 108, 109, 116, 118, 122
Barlow, R., 88, 122
Barnes, J., xiv, xx, xxvi
Barros, J. de, 83, 114, 122
Barth, H., 7, 21
Bascom, W. R., 25, 59
Basri-Bey, D. Z., 277, 288
Basto, R. E. de Azevedo, 83, 85, 122
Bath, B. H. Slicher van, 156, 188, 190
Beattie, J. H. M., 141, 151
Becroft, J., 22
Berri, G., 278, 288
Blake, E. W., 122
Blake, J. W., 115, 122
Blok, D. P., 114, 122
Blommaert, S., 101, 111
Bohannan, L., xviii, xxvi
Bonasera, F., 281, 287, 288
Bosman, W., 202, 252
Boswell, J., 190
Bottomore, T. B., 251, 252
Bouchaud, J., 81, 83, 104, 114-17, 123
Bourcart, J., 262, 278, 284, 286, 288
Bowen, T. J., 19, 22
Bradbury, R. E., xxi, xxiii, xxiv, 193, 194, 196, 197, 202, 208, 229, 252, 295
Brailsford, H. N., 278, 286, 288
Braimah, J. A., xxvi

Brown, P., xxvi
Brown, R., 123
Brun, S., 93, 103, 104, 108, 111, 115, 116, 118, 123
Brutsch, J. R., 112, 123
Bry, J. I. de, 123
Bry, J. T., 123
Burdon, J. A., 22
Burns, A. C., 216, 252
Burt, E., 162, 190
Burton, R. F., 93, 116, 123
Busch-Zantner, R., 276, 277, 279, 286, 288

Campbell, R., 19, 22
Carr, E. H., x, xvi, xxv, xxvi, 3
Carreira, A., 112, 115, 125
Carter, G. T., 22
Chekrezi, C. A., 276, 278, 286, 288
Chilver, E. M., 118, 123
Churchill (Messrs), 96, 123
Cinatti, R., 113, 115
Clapperton, H., 18, 22
Clarke, J., 22
Coblenz, W. A., 275, 293
Cohen, A., xix, xxvi
Coles, D. T., 123
Confino, M., 185, 191
Cook, A., 122
Coon, C. S., 255, 260, 263, 267, 284, 288
Cordeiro, L., 117, 123
Coser, L., 60
Cozzi, D. E., 267, 273, 288
Crabb, D. W., 121, 123
Cregeen E. R., 153, 181, 183, 191, 295
Crowther, S. A., 12, 15, 19, 22, 23
Cunnison, I., xviii, xxvi

Dahrendorf, R., 29, 60
Dako, C. A., 264, 287, 288
Dalzel, A., 22
Dapper, O., 81, 93, 95, 97, 100, 101, 107, 108, 110, 111, 116, 123
Darling, F. F., 191
Davies, Trotsky, 281, 287, 288
Dedi, V., 281, 287, 288
Dedijer, V., 281, 287, 288
Degrand, A., 262, 264, 265, 273, 275, 284, 288
Deli, I., 278, 289
Delp, 123
Dias, A. E. da Silva, 83, 84, 123
Dinkelacker, E., 123

297

General Index

General Index

social change
  conflict and, xx-xxv, 53-6
  processes, 27
social control, blood-feud and, 264, 265-
  270
social relationships, conflict in, 31
Sokoto, 8
Solagberu, 18
soldiers, recruitment, 64
songs, Albanian epic, 265
Ssekamaanya, 142, 143
Ssemakookiro, 141, 145, 146, 148, 149
Ssingo, 141
Ssuuna I, 142
Ssuuna II, 141
Stewarts of Appin, 159
Stuart dynasty, 158
succession conflict in Benin, 201-2
supernumeraries, 182

tack-holders, 160
tack lands, 160
tacksmen, 161, 163
Talbot, P. Amaury, 227, 230
taxation, direct, 217, 236
Taxpayers Association, Benin Community, 240
Tebandeke, 140, 144
tenancies
  condition of, 175-6
  instability of, 173, 174
tenant farmers, private enterprise scheme,
  169
tenurial system, new, 169-74
Thaba Flamore, 104
Tiranë, 277
Tiree, 173
  case-study in resistance to improving
    movement, 178-83
  economic development in, 180
  hostility to House of Argyll, end of,
    183
  leases, 181
  overcrowding, 179
  rents, 181
  resistance to change in farms, 182
Toptani, Esad pashë, 277, 278
Tosks, 253
  end of supremacy, 280
  social structure, 276-7
Town Fulani, 6
trade, European, 108
trading associations, Benin, 198
trading-point, 109
tribal structure and national politics,
  Albania (1910-1950), 253-93
Tsafo, 16

Urhobo immigrants, 210
Urhonigbe, 212-14
Uselu, 201
'Uthmān, Shaykh, 8
Uwaifo, H. O., 235
Uzama, 195, 197

Vërlaci, Shefqet bey, 269
Vlora, Ismail Qemal bey, 278
vocabulary, Coastal Bantu, 101, 119-22

Walusimbi, 143
Water Rate Agitation, Great, 239
Watt, James, 216
West Highlands, economy, 166
Whigs, 158
Womboko, 99
Women
  position of, in blood-feud, xxiii, 267
  Roman, role of, 70

Yaji, Sarkin Kano, 12
Yoruba, 9-15
  conflict in kingdoms, 25-60
  contest for throne of, 45-7
  Fulani penetration, 1-24
  growth of power, 15
  Kings of, 45-7
    power of, 44
  missionaries to, 9
Yoruba Muslims, 12
Yoruba town, 34-6
  government, 33
  homicide in, 40
  individual rights in, 40-1
  land interests in, 38-9
  marriages in, 40
  political power in, 39-40
  resolution of conflict in, 41-5
  role of women in, 35
  settlement structure, 33
  structure of descent groups in, 36-8
Young Turk constitution, 277

zadruga, 256
Zaki, Usman, 17, 18, 19
Zambus, 91
Zaria, 26
Zazzau, Fulani conquest of, 5
Zazzau, Sarkin, 8
Zog, King, 262, 263, 277, 280
Zogist regime, collapse of, 281
Zogolli, Ahmet bey, 279
Zogu, Ahmet bey, 279, 280
Zuguma, 16
zu Wied, Prince Wilhelm, 278